DOMINATION AND RESISTANCE

TITLES OF RELATED INTEREST

Animals into art
H. Morphy (ed.)

Archaeological approaches to cultural identity
S.J. Shennan (ed.)

Archaeological heritage management in the modern world
H.F. Cleere (ed.)

Centre and periphery: comparative studies in archaeology
T. C. Champion (ed.)

Chalcolithic, Bronze and Iron Age cultures in South Asia
M. Lal (ed.)

Conflict in the archaeology of living traditions
R. Layton (ed.)

The excluded past: archaeology in education
P. Stone & R. MacKenzie (eds)

Food, metals and towns in African history: African adaptations in subsistence and technology
T. Shaw *et al.* (eds)

Foraging and farming: the evolution of plant exploitation
D. Harris & G. Hillman (eds)

From the Baltic to the Black Sea: studies in medieval archaeology
L. Alcock & D. Austin (eds)

Global record: semi-arid regions
C. Gamble & O. Soffer (eds)

Global record: temperate latitudes
O. Soffer & C. Gamble (eds)

Hominid evolution, behaviour and dispersal
M. H. Day *et al.* (eds)

Hunters of the recent past
L. Davis & B. Reeves (eds)

The meanings of things: material culture and symbolic expression
I. Hodder (ed.)

Pleistocene perspective: innovation, adaptation and human survival
A. M. ApSimon & S. Joyce (eds)

The politics of the past
P. Gathercole & D. Lowenthal (eds)

Signifying animals: human meaning in the natural world
R. Willis (ed.)

State and society: the emergence and development of social hierarchy and political centralization
J. Gledhill *et al.* (eds)

The walking larder: patterns of domestication, pastoralism, and predation
J. Clutton-Brock (ed.)

What is an animal?
T. Ingold (ed.)

What's new? A closer look at the process of innovation
S. Van der Leeuw & R. Torrence (eds)

Who needs the past? Indigenous values and archaeology
R. Layton (ed.)

DOMINATION AND RESISTANCE

Edited by
Daniel Miller, Michael Rowlands
Christopher Tilley
Department of Anthropology, University College London

London
UNWIN HYMAN
Boston Sydney Wellington

Published by the Academic Division of
Unwin Hyman Ltd
15/17 Broadwick Street, London W1V 1FP, UK

Unwin Hyman Inc.,
8 Winchester Place, Winchester, Mass. 01890, USA

Allen & Unwin (Australia) Ltd,
8 Napier Street, North Sydney, NSW 2060, Australia

Allen & Unwin (New Zealand) Ltd in association with the
Port Nicholson Press Ltd,
Compusales Building, 75 Ghuznee Street, Wellington 1, New Zealand

First published in 1989

British Library Cataloguing in Publication Data

Domination and resistance.— (One world archaeology).
1. Cultural domination. Archaeological sources
I. Miller, Daniel, *1954 –* II. Rowlands, Michael III. Tilley, Christopher
IV. Series
303.3

ISBN 0–04–445022–2

Library of Congress Cataloging in Publication Data

Domination and resistance/[edited by] D. Miller, M. Rowlands, and C. Tilley.
p. cm. — (One world archaeology)
Papers from the World Archaeological Congress held in Southampton, England, in September 1986.
Includes bibliographies and index.
ISBN 0–04–445022–2 (alk. paper)
1. Social archaeology—Congresses. 2. Dominance (Psychology)—Congresses. 3. Social evolution—Congresses. I. Miller, Daniel, 1954– . II. Rowlands, M.J. III. Tilley, Christopher Y.
IV. World Archaeological Congress (1986: Southampton, Hampshire)
V. Series.
CC72.4D66 1988
930.1—dc 19

88–14440
CIP

Typeset in 10 on 11 point Bembo by Columns of Reading and printed in Great Britain at the University Printing House, Oxford.

List of contributors

Senake Bandaranayake, Postgraduate Institute of Archaeology, University of Kelaniya, Sri Lanka.
Barbara Bender, Department of Anthropology, University College London, UK.
Elizabeth M. Brumfiel, Albion College, Michigan, USA.
Jonathan Friedman, University of Copenhagen, Denmark.
John Gledhill, Department of Anthropology, University College London, UK.
R. A. L. H. Gunawardana, Department of History, University of Peradeniya, Sri Lanka.
J. A. Hall, Department of Sociology, University of Southampton, UK.
B. K. Jahangir, Director, Centre for Social Studies, Dhaka University, Bangladesh.
Philip L. Kohl, Department of Anthropology, Wellesley College, Massachusetts, USA.
Kristian Kristiansen, Centre for Research in the Humanities, University of Copenhagen, Denmark.
Susan Kus, Rhodes College, Memphis, Tennessee, USA.
Mogens Trolle Larsen, Centre for Research in the Humanities, University of Copenhagen, Denmark.
Simon Mays, Ancient Monuments Laboratory, English Heritage, London, UK.
Daniel Miller, Department of Anthropology, University College London, UK.
Pedro Portugal, Chitakolla, Centro do Formación e Investigación sobre las Culturas Indias, La Paz, Bolivia.
P. L. Prematilleke, Department of Archaeology, University of Peradeniya, Sri Lanka.
Michael Rowlands, Department of Anthropology, University College London, UK.
Owen B. Sichone, African Development Studies Department, University of Zambia, Lusaka, Zambia.
Gloria Thomas-Emeagwali, Department of History, Ahmadu Bello University, Zaria, Nigeria.
Christopher Tilley, Department of Anthropology, University College London.

Foreword

This book is one of a major series of more than 20 volumes resulting from the World Archaeological Congress held in Southampton, England, in September 1986. The series reflects the enormous academic impact of the Congress, which was attended by 850 people from more than 70 countries, and attracted many additional contributions from others who were unable to attend in person.

The *One World Archaeology* series is the result of a determined and highly successful attempt to bring together for the first time not only archaeologists and anthropologists from many different parts of the world, as well as academics from a host of contingent disciplines, but also non-academics from a wide range of cultural backgrounds, who could lend their own expertise to the discussions at the Congress. Many of the latter, accustomed to being treated as the 'subjects' of archaeological and anthropological observation, had never before been admitted as equal participants in the discussion of their own (cultural) past or present, with their own particularly vital contribution to make towards global, cross-cultural understanding.

The Congress therefore really addressed world archaeology in its widest sense. Central to a world archaeological approach is the investigation not only of how people lived in the past but also of how, and why, changes took place resulting in the forms of society and culture which exist today. Contrary to popular belief, and the archaeology of some 20 years ago, world archaeology is much more than the mere recording of specific historical events, embracing as it does the study of social and cultural change in its entirety. All the books in the *One World Archaeology* series are the result of meetings and discussions which took place within a context that encouraged a feeling of self-criticism and humility in the participants about their own interpretations and concepts of the past. Many participants experienced a new self-awareness, as well as a degree of awe about past and present human endeavours, all of which is reflected in this unique series.

The Congress was organized around major themes. Several of these themes were based on the discussion of full-length papers which had been circulated some months previously to all who had indicated a special interest in them. Other sessions, including some dealing with areas of specialization defined by period or geographical region, were based on oral addresses, or a combination of precirculated papers and lectures. In all cases, the entire sessions were recorded on cassette, and all contributors were presented with the recordings of the discussion of their papers. A major part of the thinking behind the Congress was that a meeting of many hundreds of participants that did not leave behind a published record of its academic discussions would be little more than an exercise in tourism.

Thus, from the very beginning of the detailed planning for the World Archaeological Congress, in 1982, the intention was to produce post-Congress books containing a selection only of the contributions, revised in the light of discussions during the sessions themselves as well as during subsequent consultations with the academic editors appointed for each book. From the outset, contributors to the Congress knew that if their papers were selected for publication, they would have only a few months to revise them according to editorial specifications, and that they would become authors in an important academic volume scheduled to appear within a reasonable period following the Southampton meeting.

The publication of the series reflects the intense planning which took place before the Congress. Not only were all contributors aware of the subsequent production schedules, but also session organizers were already planning their books before and during the Congress. The editors were entitled to commission additional chapters for their books when they felt that there were significant gaps in the coverage of a topic during the Congress, or where discussion at the Congress indicated a need for additional contributions.

One of the main themes of the Congress was devoted to 'Comparative Studies in the Development of Complex Societies'. The theme was based on discussion of precirculated full-length papers, covering three and a half days, and was under the overall control of Dr Tim Champion, Senior Lecturer in the Department of Archaeology, University of Southampton, and Dr Michael Rowlands, Reader in the Department of Anthropology, University College London. The choice of this topic for a major theme arose from a desire to explore, from a worldwide and interdisciplinary perspective, the assumptions that are embodied in the common use by archaeologists and others of concepts such as 'complex societies', a supposed stage in social development often also assumed to be marked by the invention and wide usage of literacy.

This awareness of the dangers of assuming that archaeological terminology is a precise language consisting of terms which have a single accepted meaning, with well-authenticated qualitative connotations, derived, at least in part, from lessons learnt from the last major interdisciplinary consideration of urbanization in 1970 (Ucko *et al.* 1972) At that time discussion led Stuart Piggott (1972, pp. 948–9) to stress

> that we must avoid semantic confusion when we use certain words and names for things. We use the word 'town' or 'city', and in the classical world this was *polis* or *urbs*, and what we have to consider is whether we are falling into that well-known trap of confusing names with actual things, and while using the name embodying modern concepts, we forget that these concepts were not those of literate antiquity, and therefore by reasonable assumption not of non-literate antiquity. Consider for instance the Latin use of *urbs* in relation to the Celtic population of barbarian Europe. What did a Latin writer really mean when he called a hill-fort, *urbs*, as indeed on occasion they did? It did not mean it was like Rome, although he used the same word

> for the city, the Imperial City, as he would for this barbarian earthwork enclosure, the functions of which, or the functions of any hill-fort, we very imperfectly understand. Let us avoid the ancient belief in the magic power of words, which can make us turn names into real things, and so fulfil a primitive conviction that when you have given a thing a name you have a command over it, like knowing someone's secret name. It is possible to persuade oneself that having named a concept, therefore, it actually exists and can be dealt with accordingly.

The overall theme therefore took as its starting point the assumption that the concept of social complexity needed to be re-examined and probably refined. A narrow parochial approach to the past, which simply assumes a European development to urbanization and literacy as the valid criterion for defining a complex society, totally ignores the complexity of non-literate civilizations and cultures such as the Inca of Peru or that of Benin in Nigeria. However, a world archaeological approach to a concept such as that of social complexity focuses attention on precisely those features which archaeologists all too often take for granted.

Discussions during the Congress were grouped around five main headings and have led to the publication of three books. The first subtheme, organized by Barbara Bender, Department of Anthropology, University College London, was concerned with 'The Development of Complexity'; the second, under the control of Daniel Miller and Christopher Tilley, also of the Department of Anthropology, University College London, was on 'Modes of Domination', and the third, organized by Michael Rowlands, was on 'European Expansion and the Archaeology of Capitalism'. The contributions from these three subthemes which were discussed on two different days, form this book. The fourth subtheme on 'Centre–Periphery Relations', which was discussed for one day, is edited by its organizer, Timothy Champion, under the title *Centre and periphery*. More than a day was devoted to the fifth subtheme, 'State and Society; the Emergence, Development and Transformation of Forms of Social Hierarchy, Class Relations and Political Centralization', which has been edited by its organizers, John Gledhill of the Department of Anthropology, University College London, and Mogens Larsen of the Centre for Research in the Humanities, Copenhagen, Denmark, with Barbara Bender, under the title *State and society*.

The approach adopted within the overall theme of 'Comparative Studies in the Development of Complex Societies' was based on a consideration of the *processes* involved in the creation and establishment of the elements of social organization, and social activities, which archaeologists and others commonly claim to be the visible end results of the activities of complex societies. In a comparative context, attention is focused on the reasons why, and mechanisms by which, the non-literate civilizations of, for example the Inca of Peru, built and maintained some 23 000 km of 'roads' and what their function was within the sociopolitical state system of some 6–12 million peoples with diverse backgrounds and identities who lived in environmental conditions as different as the desert and the High Andes. Within the non-literate Inca state, political control of heterogeneous social groups was achieved by an hierarchical system of regional administrative centres with an inevitable complexity of relations existing between centres and the hinterland. Given this complexity, which exists in the absence of literacy in the Inca state, the traditional focus of the study of complex societies on the better-known literate 'civilizations' of the Old World appears odd and misguided.

If the traditional assumptions about 'complexity' can thus be discarded, so too can the equally traditional, and virtually exclusive, emphasis on development and evolution. The conventional concern with determining where and when 'state' and 'class' originated, gives way to more fundamental questions about the processes of long-term social change and the very complex relationships which exist between social and cultural identity and perception, order, and development.

Key concepts in such an approach, essential to our understanding of the relevant social processes, are those of 'authority' and 'power'. Contributors to the theme on 'Comparative Studies of the Development of Complex Societies' examined both concepts in an attempt to disentangle any Eurocentric assumptions embedded in the terms themselves, and also to describe precisely the forms which power and authority may take in other societies, both today and in the past.

Inherent in all of the contributions is the assumption that social relations have never been any more equal and symmetrical in societies in the past than they are in contemporary societies. Many of the perspectives adopted in these books explore the details of these asymmetrical relations, considering not only the variety of forms that have been adopted over different times and in different parts of the world, but also the different mechanisms which have been employed to bolster and reinforce such inequalities. With such inequalities in the distribution of power, and in access to knowledge, come equally varied forms of control over symbolism, ritual, religious cults, and even literacy.

A particular focus of interest therefore lies in the detailed exploration of the different forms and functions of literacy in different societies, an exploration that clearly reveals that these were in no way uniform and that literacy, in itself, cannot be used as a clear marker of social qualitative development (see *Who needs the past?* edited by R. Layton) – to be able to read and write is not, in itself, to be a member of a qualitatively complex society.

Another form of inherent asymmetry in human societies derives from centre–periphery relations. The presence at the Congress of so many participants from the so-called Third and Fourth Worlds made it possible to examine in detail these relations in a very wide variety of forms, in particular those frequently glossed over in the archaeological literature under rubrics such as 'civilized'/'barbarian', 'urban'/'non-urban', sedentary/nomadic, and agriculturalist/pastoralist.

In focusing on the nature of the varying relationships that can develop between centre and periphery, one is led inevitably to detailed questions about imperialism, colonialism and acculturation. In part these forms of relationships are a matter of ideology (of 'empire', of 'nation' and of ethnic groups), but it is the mechanisms of expansion, incorporation and maintenance which are clearly vital to our understanding of the past and present, and which are examined by several contributors.

In this book Daniel Miller, Michael Rowlands, Christopher Tilley and their contributors analyse, from an impressive variety of contexts – including China, Mexico and Madagascar – what would colloquially be referred to as 'power bases'. As in several of the other books in the *One World Archaeology* series, the approach adopted is interdisciplinary. It also incorporates many of the principles and data derived from the study of societies and cultures of the modern world. *Domination and resistance* goes far beyond the concerns of the so-called 'New Archaeology' which emphasized cross-cultural generalization and the behavioural correlates of unitary processes underlying the formation of the archaeological record. The concern is both with sociocultural specificity and with a comparative framework for understanding. As the title of this book suggests, the social processes under discussion are as relevant today, and to the understanding of contemporary societies, as they must have been throughout the past.

As with *State and society*, edited by J. Gledhill, B. Bender and M. T. Larsen, the contributions in this book reveal, with striking clarity, the way that many of the preconceptions in the archaeological and anthropological use of terminology such as 'complex societies' are not only subjectively based and the product of a particular European historical experience, but have also shaped what we view as desirable 'pasts', as well as our attitudes towards peoples and cultures 'without histories'. The book demonstrates the Eurocentrism of ideas about 'civilized identity' with, in some cases, a smattering of Near Eastern Orientalism thrown in. Domination, as we all know, may take many subtle forms – operating through conceptual imperialism – not only by means of physical force. *Domination and resistance* challenges its readers to examine the nature of their preconceptions about development, and questions the legitimacy of many of our most cherished assumptions and views about 'other cultures' and about the place of European cultures on any scale of social and political development.

Some of the subtle manifestations of past systems of domination may come as a surprise, as may also the realization of how central a concept 'style' remains in archaeological enquiry and analysis (and see *The meanings of things*, edited by Ian Hodder, and *Animals into art*, edited by Howard Morphy). A secure identification and understanding of the processes leading to stylistic differentiation, and the subsequent correct interpretation of their use and consequences, may make the difference between seeing Palaeolithic social groups as essentially localized and isolated, versus essentially ritual-sharing and periodically conglomerate, or perceiving the Aztec period as having *continued* a prior situation of factionalism versus the Aztec period having *developed its own* unique form of competitive interactions.

A particular form of insidious conceptual domination applies to the kind, and nature, of archaeological conceptualization, both as it has been applied to, and in, non-European areas and countries. Conceptualizing the past (and see *Conflict in the archaeology of living traditions* and *Who needs the past?*, both edited by Robert Layton) in a particular form, both with regard to the nature of the past and its potential application in current conditions, spheres and problems, has led to a peculiarly slanted approach to what archaeological evidence is, and what is not, of research interest and potential. In this way whole areas of a people's or nation's past may be relegated to a level of supposed total unimportance, with no realization of the dispossession and domination that this may cause to the identities and aspirations of a group, society, or even country.

In a strangely powerful way, therefore, the discipline of archaeology can have a special responsibility in the creation and dispossession of identity (and see *Archaeological approaches to cultural identity,* edited by Stephen Shennan) – whether it be through the ascription of well-worn concepts such as tribalism or the new (almost as imprecise) one of ethnicity. Of course, all of this raises, in acute form, another of the consequences of developments since the 'New Archaeology', namely the fact that archaeologists must now first recognize, and then investigate, the problems which are relevant to the wider community. In doing so archaeologists now accept that the nature of archaeological data leads to subjective interpretation, and that all such interpretation is bound to be value-loaded. The point at issue is to recognize what these values are, not simply to suspect subjectivity and therefore to shy away from interpretation.

Domination and resistance deals with some of the most important of the social and political processes which exist, and it forces into the open a consideration of the values that are commonly, and often unconsciously or semi-consciously, ascribed to them. The kind of archaeology presented here is a challenging one – and one which cannot help but cause us to stop in our stride, and to reflect.

P. J. Ucko
Southampton

References

Piggott, S. 1972. Conclusion. In *Man, settlement and urbanism*, P.J. Ucko, R. Tringham & G.W. Dimbleby (eds), 947–53. London: Duckworth.

Ucko, P.J., R. Tringham & G.W. Dimbleby (eds) 1972. *Man, settlement and urbanism*. London: Duckworth.

Contents

POLITICAL ECONOMY AND IDEOLOGY: HISTORICAL TRANSFORMATIONS

Preface

This book is one of three which have emerged from five days of discussion held at the World Archaeological Congress in Southampton in 1986. As already mentioned in the Foreword, the original concern of the session was with comparative studies in the development of complex societies. It may therefore appear surprising that the term 'complexity' does not arise in this or any of the other titles of the subsequent volumes. This is because one of the conclusions of our discussions was to agree to deconstruct this overgeneralized category which has all too often been assumed as unproblematic, providing a 'common-sense' basis for comparing social forms.

The aim of the discussion at the Congress was to consider how to return attention to the more specific problems raised by the concept of complexity for studies of historical transformation and social reproduction, while evading some of the unfortunate legacies of its ancestry within unilinear evolutionary theory. One of these has been the tendency to assume a direct association between complexity and inequality, often using concepts such as stratification or social control as if they were of general and universal importance rather than the product of a given set of historical circumstances. This book focuses on forms of domination and resistance as more flexible concepts, although it must still be recognized that, like any others, the terms suffer from the dangers of reification and abstraction unless systematically explored, modified and developed through comparative understanding of cultural variation and difference. The main concern was with archaeological investigations and contributions to this area. However, it is increasingly being realized that archaeology can only contribute to such an issue if it does so within the framework of interdisciplinary analysis and conceptualization. Artificially maintained academic boundaries create a very real constraint on understanding, and it is increasingly important that they be undermined. One of the most positive features of the World Archaeological Congress was precisely its emphasis on interdisciplinary collaboration of global scope.

In this book we have included a broad collection of chapters from archaeology, anthropology, ethnohistory, social theory and historical sociological analysis to consider general questions of the relationship of dominance and resistance to complexity. There is no *a priori* reason why the specificity of disciplinary allegiances should not be enhanced by a more general concern with major issues in understanding the nature of social forms. All of the chapters were presented for discussion at our sessions, except that by Tilley, which replaces his contribution in the volume of precirculated papers. The chapters by Friedman, Hall and Kohl were precirculated, although the authors were not present for the discussions. The book was scheduled to appear in the summer of 1988, but because of a series of delays that were beyond our control, including the loss of proofs in the post, it has not been possible to publish it until the spring of 1989.

We gratefully acknowledge the assistance provided by a number of people, both in the organization of the original sessions held at the World Archaeological Congress at Southampton and in the subsequent preparation of this book. In particular, we would like to thank Phil Kohl for helping to organize the session on European expansion and the archaeology of capitalism, and John Gledhill, Mogens Larsen and Thomas Patterson for chairing sessions. Of course, we have had to select from a wide range of stimulating and substantial papers, in order to construct a thematic volume. We would like to thank all those contributors who are not represented in this book for their support. We are much indebted to Caroline Jones and Paul Crake for their tremendous help in organizing both the sessions and the subsequent editorial labours. Finally, none of this could, of course, have been possible without the indefatigable and enthusiastic support of Peter Ucko.

Daniel Miller
Michael Rowlands
Christopher Tilley
London

Introduction

DANIEL MILLER, MICHAEL ROWLANDS
and CHRISTOPHER TILLEY

The issue of 'complexity' has been in the forefront of archaeological investigation since the inception of the discipline. It is clearly premised in innumerable discussions concerned with the origin of the state, civilization, literacy or urbanization. Consideration of these problems of origin have almost always, at least implicitly, been bound up with conceptions of general evolution which remain one of the most powerful legacies of 19th-century thought pervading contemporary archaeology.

We suggest that there have been two main trajectories in the attempt to deal with the issues raised within such a broad interdisciplinary framework. The one that dominates contemporary archaeological theory and practice has been an attempt to tackle the notion of complexity head-on by the construction of a large series of abstract modelling procedures which produce a 'logic' of complexity against which actual historical developments may be compared. In a number of recent volumes (e.g. Renfrew & Cooke 1979, van der Leeuw 1981) which have as their ultimate justification the use of archaeological materials to investigate issues of social complexity, the direct focus of attention has been mathematical modelling and the construction of formal abstract models. Often terms such as 'managers', 'hierarchies' or 'peer-polity' interaction are used, but in a sense which has very little to do with their social connotations. Similarly, the use of information theory or catastrophe theory has tended very strongly to obscure rather than aid a consideration of the irreducibly social dimensions of complexity. The mathematical sophistication of the models used is not matched by an equal sophistication in their 'translation' into social terms. Indeed, it has become quite apparent that mathematical logic cannot replace sociological understanding, and contributes little towards this goal. When attempts are made to effect such a translation it is often through devices evoking concepts of 'simple' and 'complex' societies which repeat the worst excesses of the discourse of primitivism and general evolution.

An alternative trajectory, taken up in this book, is based on the presumption that all concepts such as complexity, when used properly within the social sciences, are about the forms taken by social relations. The goal of such academic study is the concrete comparative study of social relations (Rowlands 1982). By this we refer to detailed studies that emphasize understanding the nature of societal differences and the conditions that promote societal change and continuity while eschewing objectivist tendencies to work solely towards the production of high-level cross-cultural generalizations. The utility of the concepts we use and the manner in which we employ them have to be constantly subjected to these criteria. Any attempt to produce reified abstract categories as ends in themselves has to be resisted. This is to assert that the meaning and value of the conceptual frameworks we actually do employ is relative to the kinds of knowledge entailed in the analysis of different kinds of historical conjuncture. Such a way of working would, we hope, be capable of providing a general arena within which archaeological studies and those of other disciplines within the social sciences may be interchanged in as much as these other disciplines concur with the primacy of this object of enquiry.

In Chapter 1 Rowlands argues that the definition of complexity in Western thought is irreducible to the construction of difference through forms of social exclusion. He argues that this is because social complexity in the West has consistently been associated with a historically unique experience of modernity. Other cultural definitions of social exclusion and difference will generate different developments of social complexity. Such an understanding introduces a break with the ethnocentric connotations of much contemporary writing concerned with the issue of complexity. For example, this means at least a critical reappraisal of that view of complexity which equates it with increasing differentiation and specialization of social institutions and their functions (Weber 1947).

Even since the inception of the social sciences in the writings of the Enlightenment it has been evident that one of the major issues in comprehending the complexity of the internal dynamics of society has been that of inequality (see Bender, Ch.4). This is hardly surprising, since the term complexity presupposes the emergence of heterogeneity. When considered in terms of social relations, heterogeneity appears almost inevitably to emerge as inequality. However, the opposition between 'simple' and 'complex' societies was framed by Enlightenment philosophy largely in moral terms so as to explain the nature of current social ills and express nostalgia for lost forms and wished-for utopias. A contradiction has underlain these aspirations ever since. On the one hand, they have impelled human action to achieve the elimination of difference, e.g. class, gender, race etc., if constituted as forms of oppression. And on the other, to have promoted fierce loyalties based on difference, for example, ethnic, nationalist and tribal; if serving to maintain identity (in modern settings at least). A clash between perceptions of objective conditions of exploitation and subjective feelings of identity and being has been one result. Inequality therefore, if perceived superficially as the conditions of rank or status ordering, or as the relative distribution of power in society, is too unsubtle a concept to encompass this diversity of heterogeneity in social forms that might need to be addressed as being 'complex'. For this reason the more specific concepts of domination and resistence were selected as a focus to elaborate a comparative study of all forms of societal complexity. By addressing ourselves to the vocabularies that define the nature of difference, the processes of subordination, the creation of social categories of the ineligible, the inferior and the outsider in different social and historical settings, we get closer to those forms of social closure, exclusion and differentiation common to all social systems.

In the other two books deriving from this Congress theme, *State and society* and *Centre and periphery*, the issue of complexity is re-examined in terms of the development of the state, forms of social and political transitions, and the large-scale interregional links which need to be taken into account in considerations of social reproduction or transformation. Societies do not exist in splendid isolation and, moreover, a very real problem is how to determine their 'edges'. As is made clear by Gledhill in the Introduction to *State and society*, there is a need to de-reify concepts such as the 'state' or 'class', and to use them productively in the study of concrete social practices using the kinds of more-flexible and sensitive forms of characterization which are discussed in this book.

If the articulation between archaeology and other social sciences is considered with respect to this issue, then it develops as an exchange about the forms taken by social inequalities in definite social practices. A considerable amount of theory and research has been devoted, especially in the past two decades, to increasing our sophistication in the conceptualization of power relations and their role in social reproduction. The two terms used in the title of this book – domination and resistance – are essentially evocations of this new work.

Approaches to the study of domination and resistance

In this section we introduce a few general comparative theoretical perspectives on forms of social domination and resistance that have already been influential in archaeological and historical analyses. These sketches should be regarded as a series of alternative approaches that have been developed to grapple with these questions within the limits of Western social theory. Our account indicates that they may have radically different implications for interpreting the same set of materials. They also provide a background to some of the more detailed discussions which follow. A comparative perspective on forms of domination and resistance in different social formations is absolutely essential in order to avoid the twin pitfalls of ethnocentrism and reductionism, and this is emphasized throughout the structure and organization of this book.

It might be argued that many of the limits imposed on the conceptualization of domination and resistance which face us today are based on the Western experience of 'modernization'. It is increasingly being recognized that the classic sociological traditions of the 19th century, stemming from Marx, Freud, Comte, Weber and Nietzsche, have specific preoccupations that cannot be universalized. There is a need for a more radical recontextualization of social theory than has hitherto been the case. Part of this recontextualization will involve a requirement that the conceptual structures we employ be made shifting rather than rigidly fixed. In other words, concepts such as domination and resistance will be invested with new contents depending on the situation being investigated. Any attempt to search for and provide absolute and unchanging definitions of these concepts that will be applicable to all societies is never likely to be very successful. All these concepts, like the notion of complexity, are radically contestable and will very probably take on rather different meanings according to the specific analysis in hand. Such concepts are convenient shorthand terms, but they only acquire real utility in substantive analyses. Such a view of these concepts as having no single or irreducible definition or meaning should be regarded as something productive rather than an unfortunate flaw in social analysis.

Domination: exploitation and coercion

Marx and Weber, along with many other 19th-century theorists, inherited the Enlightenment concern with freedom and truth to provide a basis for humanitarian anthropology along with a series of all-pervasive dualisms in Western thought, for example, rationality–irrationality; subject–object; reason–passion; nature–culture.

Marx, in the *Grundrisse* (pp. 831–2), argued against Enlightenment wisdom that freedom could be defined negatively as freedom from domination. When Adam Smith defined freedom in *The wealth of nations* as the 'absence of toil' (i.e. justifying social acts which increase leisure or tranquillity) or Hobbes defined it in *Leviathan* as the absence of external impediment to one's will, Marx claimed that they left no positive content for freedom itself. It meant that individual self-consciousness would *not* be the product of pursuing a positive freedom to act to achieve something, but simply that which is left as a private, individual domain after the removal of externally derived constraints. When Marx states that 'the overcoming of obstacles is itself a liberating activity' (*Grundrisse*, p. 611), his purpose is to claim that freedom is an activity and not just a state of being. Marx is not original in this view, but follows in the tradition of Kant and Hegel by adhering to the notion that self-creation is a product of a continuous realization of what is external to oneself. To make nature good or useful by transforming it according to one's conscious wishes or acting to overcome obstacles to one's conscious aims are, Marx argued, the necessary means 'of actualising a potentiality'. Yet, whereas for Hegel the dialectic of freedom is an historical process in which the activities of individual subjects are ultimately part of a larger process of realizing an Idea of human freedom, Marx asserted that self-determination arose as an achievement in itself, from one's interactions with others within shared empirical material conditions of existence. Marx posited that freedom was not a matter of claiming a choice between options, but participating in the creation of new options for oneself.

For Marx, human objectification takes place through definite forms of social relations that could be grouped into historical stages. Each has its own particular form of domination which he broadly defined as the control by one group over the production and reproduction of another. In capitalism, he argued, this takes a specific form of exploitation or alienation through the appropriation of surplus value from a formally free but propertyless labouring class by capital, and the belief by labour that the products of their own work should belong to the owners of capital. Capitalist domination thus has the potential of convincing both dominators and dominated alike of the fairness of their social relationship. In the various types of precapitalist societies that Marx describes, relations of domination take instead the form of *personal* relations between individuals. Subordinated individuals, serfs to lords or slaves to masters, are bound by force or coercion or by weight of tradition which makes their servility appear to be part of nature. The subordinated do not recognize themselves as agents or persons, but to be part of the natural, inorganic conditions of production. It is the unique feature of labour in modern societies that it should acquire autonomy from the objective conditions of production, and therefore the capacity to recognize its own conditions of exploitation. Marx also sees these relations of domination occurring within specific forms of property. In communal modes of production – for instance, where individuals hold their property by virtue of their being members of a community – domination is exercised over non-members by possessing them as things and over women and children through their dependence on often male communal ownership of property.

In some variants of Marxism, domination has been conceptualized as involving either the direct use of force or sanctions, the threat of such force or sanctions, or both. It may also be effected through systems of symbolic signification concerning the legitimacy of the social order, and therefore not directly dependent on violence or its threat. The most obvious and 'visible' form of social domination is effected through physical force directly restricting the freedom of agents. Physical violence and incarceration provide some of the most direct examples and effects of social domination (see Jahangir, Ch.21). Such direct violence is almost always coupled with sanctions and coercion involving the threat of the use of force in order to effect outcomes complying with the interests of those in positions of authority. In contemporary capitalist societies of the West the nation-state exercises a virtual monopoly over the means of violence, which may be directed internally (as, for example, in Northern Ireland or the recent British miners' strike), but more usually externally. The significance of military power and warfare between states in shaping the contemporary world scarcely needs emphasizing: the threat of nuclear annihilation now hangs like a shadow over the entirety of humanity. Military power or its threat remains pervasive and has never been more generalized (Mann 1987, Giddens 1986). The effectiveness of systems of social dominance based directly on forms of violence depends upon agents being convinced of both the capacity and the willingness of those in positions of authority to use force. Actual use of violence may be comparatively rare and periodically repeated to work as exemplars and deterrents. Violence is a very effective medium for enforcing the unequal distribution of life-chances (e.g. as in contemporary South Africa) in the short term, but is costly to maintain and often in contradiction to the 'modern' institutions of legitimation (Habermas 1976).

Domination and authority

One of the fundamental tenets of Weber's conceptualization of the social order is closely linked to Marx's view of class domination. Domination is for Weber a special type of power. Power he defines as a peršn's ability to impose his will upon others *despite* resistance (Weber 1947, p .152). Weber distinguished two types of domination: that based on influencing indirectly people's perceptions of their interests through such mechanisms as market forces, and another that rests on authority – that is, the power to command and the duty to obey. A fundamental feature of authority 'is a certain minimum of voluntary submission', i.e. without the requirement of persuasion or the threat of force. Since authority entails voluntary submission to a superior, it obviates the need for coercive force to enforce obedience. Hence, Weber did not explictly deal with coercive power in his analysis of domination, although it has been noted that he frequently uses the term *Herrschaft* to imply a more general form of domination involving the symbolic or ritual use of violence (Gilsenan 1985).

What occupies much of Weber's work is his analysis of different types of legitimacy, since this is fundamental to the right to command and the duty to obey. Weber's three types of authority are therefore defined by their modes of legitimation, viz. traditional authority based on the holder's responsibility to ensure the continuation of the social order as a natural or a sacred order; charismatic authority based on the qualities of a leader to mobilize collective support and belief; legal authority based on a belief in the rationality of law and bureaucratic procedure. His discussion of each of these types deals extensively with the various subtypes of dependence and submission. It is at this more specific level that the contrast with Marx's analysis of different social forms becomes quite explicit. In feudalism, where Marx stressed the relation of exploitation between lord and serf based on the ownership of land by the former, Weber would stress the relation between lord and vassal as a species of contract freely entered into for the mutual support of both. The contrast between Marc Bloch's and Maurice Dobb's analysis of French and English feudalism, respectively, are well-known examples of the difference of interpretation possible (Holton 1984). Finley's (1973) account of the Ancient Economy is equally a Weberian reading which opposes the classic Marxian slave mode of production by denying the significance of master–slave relations in contrast with the politics of belonging to a body of free citizens (to be contrasted with St Croix 1980).

One consequence is that Marx, guided by a philosophy of freedom founded in labour, provides us with a theory of exploitation, whereas Weber, concerned more with the conditions that promote obedience, provides a theory of authority. However, there is a less well-known aspect of Weber's work on domination, which promises a closer reconciliation with Marxian notions of exploitation. This is his principle of exclusionary closure, which is the attempt by one group to secure privileges for itself through tactics which give rise to a social category of social ineligibles or outsiders (Rowlands 1985). In the sense that this may be resisted by the ineligibles, Parkin (1979, p. 45) has argued that social closure involves two forms of social action: exclusion and usurpation. Traditional caste systems, ethnic stratification and gender subordination are all the results of exclusionary practices closing off access to rewards and privileges to those defined as inferior by those monopolizing the definition of values. To conceive of power as a built-in attribute of closure means that it is not something distributed or allocated in society, but is constituted by forms of social action that define eligibility and ineligibility to it. Weber emphasized the positive aspect of social closure as essential to the formation of collective life for 'the satisfaction of material and spiritual interests' (Weber 1968; I, p. 43). Yet the exclusion by the dominant group may be so powerful as to prevent a subjugated group any possibility of creating its own closure and therefore of combating its underprivileged status. Hence, to take the capitalist–worker class division as an example, this may be defined both in terms of their place in the productive process, and this can in turn be seen as one consequence of a larger process of closure, exclusion and usurpation, including education and lifestyle, which effectively validates a universal bourgeois culture as against the hedonism and disorder of working-class culture. In particular, it justifies Marx's own perception that property as capital is the most important, though not the only, cause of social closure in industrial societies (for example, Weber emphasized educational qualifications as replacing property in importance and Bourdieu argues that consumption and lifestyle now justifies exclusionary practices; Bourdieu 1984). This can be developed further by asking whether certain kinds of closure facilitate domination (e.g. property, education or capital) whereas others are more frequently selected as a means of resistance in the absence of such resources (e.g. race, ethnicity and religion). Yet the problem of the characterization of such strategies is, in the end, less important than the crucial questions which remain unexplained, although a great deal more illuminated, as to why property here and religion there can be the object of social closure.

Marxism and structural-Marxism: domination, power and ideology

Analyses of domination have been considerably extended through the influence of Althusser's linkage of Marxism with structuralist thought (Althusser 1969, 1970, 1984). This was developed against two targets: one being those crude forms of orthodox Marxism that assumed that economic organization directly determined the nature of the rest of society; the other is the view that human beings are naturally free agents (voluntarism) who by evading constraints and 'seeing through' the conditions of domination, can determine what happens in history.

This work is particularly significant because it represents an increasingly sophisticated aspect in Marxist thought of the role of political and ideological strategies in reproducing systems of social domination. While Althusser held the 'economic to be determinant in the last instance', the relative autonomy granted to each level or structure within a social formation entailed that each be studied within its own specificity. His concept of structural causality also required that defining which of these structures dominated the others would be a matter of empirical investigation.

Whereas Althusser agreed with Marx that only in capitalist societies did the economy both dominate and determine all other aspects of the social formation, he maintained that in all precapitalist social formations political and ideological relations necessarily dominated the functioning of the economy. By this he meant that the appropriation of surplus, which in a capitalist society was organized economically through the relation of worker to capital, would instead be structured politically and ideologically in personal relations in precapitalist societies. For example, in feudalism where the peasant did not own but could effectively *control* the land he worked, the extraction of surplus would have to depend on the ability of a lord to exercise political power over his vassals or, in the ancient economy, the ideological definition of freedom governing the master–slave relation would determine the rate of surplus extraction possible from coerced labour versus that of 'free citizens'.

For anthropologists anxious to escape simple culturalist versus materialist models of society, such an approach held out an alternative means of theorizing precapitalist social formations (see Kahn & Llobera 1981, for a summary). It appeared to allow the recognition and comparison of distinct modes of production, relations of production, exploitation and social classes. For example if domination in lineage societies was exercised by elders over junior males through the former's control of the provision of wives and access of the latter to social knowledge gained at initiation, then kinship formed the dominant social relations in these types of society (Rey 1979). Different variants of lineage society could then be distinguished depending on whether power and exploitation was defined materially, (e.g. control over prestige goods) or ideologically, (e.g. revealing sacred knowledge), but still within a kinship idiom. Resistance would necessarily be expressed in the same idioms and forms as that governing exploitative power relations.

A similar debate based on a revision of the concept of Asiatic mode of production was influential in reorganizing perceptions of how religion and cosmology could be linked to material and political practices (Bailey & Llobera 1981, Friedman 1975, Auge 1978). Clastres (1977) initiated a novel debate on the 'primitive state' in which he contrasted chiefly power based on ritual to modern state power based on coercion (to compare with Poulantzas 1980 on the modern state) which has been developed further by Sahlins (1985) and others. Wallerstein and others generated a more straightforward reinterpretation of Marx's explanation of the origins of capitalism in which exploitation was to be located within the larger regional system (cf. Wallerstein 1974, for influence in archaeology, cf. Kohl 1978, Rowlands *et al.* 1987). These re-readings of Marx encouraged a rethinking in anthropology of such basic questions as the relations of power and exploitation in lineage societies and the nature and definition of premodern states, by establishing a system for interpreting the articulation of different structures or levels in the reproduction and cumulative development of different types of social formation. In so doing 'it has substituted analysis of the effects of domination for that of functional relations, and the notions of transition and disjunction for that of evolution' (Auge 1982, p. 67).

It was particularly the interest that this work aroused in the relationship between anthropology and history that probably accounts for the ease with which some of these debates have been taken up in archaeology. Friedman's particular version of structural-Marxism was perhaps the most strongly historically based since he recognized that explaining the articulation of structures would have to be seen as a product of cumulative development, otherwise explanation would inevitably be synchronic and functionalist (Friedman 1974, Friedman & Rowlands 1977). Without history and in the absence of the traditional economic determination of class struggle, he argued, there could no longer be any clear idea where political conflicts and hence social change comes from. The lineage mode of production model has been used in European prehistory (Kristiansen 1979, Frankenstein & Rowlands 1978, Bradley 1984); for the transition to agriculture (Bender 1978); and similar arguments have been used to describe parts of the American South-west and Midwest as prestige good systems peripheral to phases in Mesoamerican civilization (Gledhill 1978, McGuire 1986, Bender 1985). The strengths of this approach therefore lie in its vigorous support of a comparative approach and a belief in the existence of historical processes operating in the long term that cannot be reduced to the unintended consequences of human action.

The second major concern of Althusserian Marxism was to expose the notion of agency as itself ideologically constructed. The claim is that the experience we have of being the authors of our own actions is in some sense mistaken or deluded and that, although we have no choice but to believe this, what really happens is that pre-existing social conditions determine our actions. How this is achieved will vary from one social formation to another and in different historical epochs.

The argument involves, above all, the elevation of the importance of the concept of ideology (Althusser 1984, Poulantzas 1973, 1980). Althusser claims that the imaginary sense of being a subject comes from ideological apparatuses that exist before we are born which map out the roles that we all play in social reproduction, viz. how family background, wealth, education and relative deprivation define our relative life chances. For instance, the ideological dominance of the ruling class is effected through institutional forms and practices – ideological state apparatuses (religious, educational, family, legal, political, trade union, communications and cultural) diffusely linked to a much more unified repressive state apparatus (police, law courts, prisons, army, civil service). The influence of Lacan is particularly apparent in the Althusserian assertion that what appears to be our independent selfhood is actually constructed by the way in which we become inserted into the symbolic order of culture (Lacan 1977, p. 53).

Ideology creates the type of subjects suitable to be 'supports' of social relations and inserts people into places predefined by the structures of the social formation. According to Poulantzas the ideological region within capitalist societies is autonomous from the political region hence the dominant ideology has an apolitical or 'scientific' appearance or both, distinguishing it from the directly political role of ideology in pre-capitalist social formations (Poulantzas 1973, p. 140). It is this very separation of the ideological from the political that allows it to perform a role in securing social domination. Opposed to the dominant ideology the 'spontaneous' ideology of the dominated class lives its revolt against the bourgeoisie within concepts, categories and values drawn from the dominant ideology. Carried to this conclusion, all human actions are depressingly ideological, functioning only to reproduce the conditions of domination regardless of the overt intentions and aspirations of the actors. It is the pessimism of such a conclusion, found most deeply formulated in Foucault, that has drawn most criticism (cf. Hirst 1979, also Miller & Tilley 1984 for the implications of other approaches for archaeological interpretation).

Despite these criticisms, the work of the Althusserians has served to emphasize ideological legitimation as playing a key role in the maintenance of relations of dominance. Another legacy arising from Althusserian structural-Marxism is the concept of totality emphasizing the multiplicity of economic, political and ideological structures, their relative autonomy and the non-reduction of their complex interaction to a single element or essence. The emphasis in all this work is on the practical relevance of the concept of the mode of production and its relation to ideology, and empirically this has been its most creative result. The most widespread complaint of their work has been the rigidity of separating human action from the overarching structures of the social formation, resulting in a sense of the determined and passive subject that can neither 'see through' its ideological conditions of existence or change them (the extended critique of Althusser here is by the historian Thompson 1978). The question this leaves, and that has concerned subsequent writers such as Bourdieu, has been how to reassert subjectivity as active. Even if the subject is caught at an interesection of discourses and practices, how can people 'see through' those conditions, in order to change them. Yet, what is so fruitful in the Lacan–Althusser formulation is the theme of personhood as constituted by social relations. 'Agency' is therefore itself constituted, is historically relative and is mutable.

Resistance and repression

A tension between studies that see the analysis of structures, institutions and roles as determinant in social life and those that emphasize the subjective capacities of human beings to gain insight into, and to master, their objective conditions, is not peculiar to Marxism in Western thought. The writings on praxis of the young Marx versus the analysis of the laws of capitalist development of the older Marx evoke a clash of values redolent of Western culture. Enduring conflicts between humanist and positivist–'scientific' approaches to social life are an indelible part of the changing forms of domination and the actions of libertarian movements in Western historical experience.

Charles Taylor has lucidly demonstrated the dualism in Western culture which equates science with objectivism, and the humanities with subjectivism (Taylor 1986, pp. 80–3). He would argue that it has been the inclination for Enlightenment reason to legitimize the domination of nature and society that has been resisted by those that would stress the arbitrary and the irrational in human nature. It is unfortunate that the consequences of such a bizarre clash of values between science and humanism are with us still in increasingly dangerous forms. However, a loosely articulated tradition that shares in common a consistent faith in the capacity of a humanistic ideology to resist dominatory thought and expand the limits of collective social action includes Lukacs, Gramsci, the Frankfurt school of critical theory, Arendt and Habermas. This diverse group cannot easily be subsumed by a few generalizing statements, yet their mutual concern with humanism as the essence of resistance to inevitable tendencies that promote an increasingly totalitarian world forms a common thread.

Lukacs is most well known for rescuing the concept of reification from Marxist reductionism and arguing that since the proletariat has the most immediate and total experience of capitalist alienation, it also has the greatest interest and propensity to develop a 'self consciousness' of it. It is their class situation that drives workers towards consciousness of their conditions of existence while the partiality of self-interest will necessarily lock bourgeois thought into 'false consciousness'. Essential to his argument is the contention that thought or knowledge is not abstract, but is a collective product and necessarily bound up with the genesis and structure of definite social groups. He is one of a long series of Western thinkers who emphasize consciousness of society as a coherent totality or what he termed 'grasping society from the centre as a coherent whole' (Jay 1984).

Another approach to resistance which complements a concern with consciousness with a political awareness of the mechanisms of organization and mobilization has centred around the concept of hegemony, which has become the central terminological question in the interpretation of the work of Gramsci (Gramsci 1971, Mouffe 1979). His concern with hegemony was not, as with Althusser and other writers, a means of understanding dominance, but precisely the opposite. It was significant as the central concept in theorizing and then enacting the complex forms of resistance that could lead to the actual overthrow of a dominant group. What was necessary was the gradual build-up of a complex of associations by which other groups who saw a common interest in their resistance to the ruling formation were bound together as an emergent force. From here the subaltern groups engaged in 'a war of positions' which Gramsci compared explicitly with a military campaign, in which they gradually build up their influence and then take over a wide variety of elements within society prior to any formal overthrow of the state.

This meant that the concept of hegemony was essentially anti-reductionist. It did not represent solely a particular set of interests or a particular class; it also meant that hegemony was irreducible to economistic forces. Although it incorporated the emergent proletariat defined in terms of their relation to production, it could not be solely identified with them. This critique of more-economistic approaches by Gramsci went hand-in-hand with an appreciation of the importance of various cultural elements, which had in some versions of Marxism been dismissed as superstructural. Gramsci was a major source of ideas as to the pivotal position of the party and also the importance of those intellectuals who struggled out of their normal position as passive reproducers of dominant ideologies to become the purveyors of the new oppositional hegemony. As with the Church in previous periods, he saw this as an arena in which ideas were developed and expressed by which people could think through the alternative society and the concomitant world-views they were creating.

Gramsci's work represents an ability to theorize historical change which is not reducible to instrumental analysis based on a narrow view of either economistic or class interests. Rather it provides a guide as to the manner by which a wide variety of groups may ally themselves at moments of key historical transitions in order to effect a major societal change. It also shows the crucial importance of institutions such as religious orders, and small-scale but populist cultural formations to counterbalance histories which have focused largely on the state and a much narrower definition of the domain of politics. It indicates a stage in which people develop world-views and experience new forms of order prior to control of a state. Gramsci's ideas on the war of positions carried on through a variety of domains is capable of encompassing some of the complexities of historical change encountered by archaeologists, anthropologists and historians in the field. He thereby provides for an understanding of the structural dimensions to historical change, but balanced with a concern for contingency and the role of individual and, in particular, of group consciousness in social life.

A similar attempt to resolve structure and practice, but with very different results, characterizes the development by the Frankfurt school of critical theory. It was a school which emphasized the active role of cognition; theory was not simply a reflection of the social conditions within which one lived, but the product of a critical examination of them. This privileging of the work of the free-floating critic was combined with a difficult synthesis of the insights of Marx, Weber and the work of Freud on repression (cf. Held 1980). The work of Marcuse, Adorno and Horkheimer was heavily coloured by their living in a period of an unprecedented extension of the productive forces and the increasing importance of the mass media and entertainment industries. Theirs was an experience of late-capitalist society taking on a fundamentally different form to that initially analysed by Marx. The continued extension of the division of labour and state intervention in the market render class-based exploitative domination increasingly less obvious and enable the effects of positivistic thought, and to develop it instead as a type of critical reflection capable of furthering human emancipation (cf. Habermas 1971, in particular). His defence of Western rationality as capable of still fulfilling its Enlightenment promise stands against the nihilism of poststructuralism and postmodernism (Habermas, in Dews 1986), and reveals a desire still to believe in the possibilities of 'the unmasking of illusions' and to redeem the promise of a future utopian state of freedom.

Culture and symbolic violence

Two figures have been instrumental in developing contemporary conceptions of the mechanisms of repression and forms of symbolic violence: Foucault with respect to historical studies, and Bourdieu to studies of contemporary culture.

Foucault's work follows at least some of the Frankfurt school's concerns with the domination of the inner nature of humanity through external controls developed as disciplinary technologies. In his study of penal history he brilliantly contrasts forms of domination in the absolutist and capitalist Western state. The contrast Foucault draws is that between premodern and modern modalities of the exercise of power and social domination. In the emerging industrial societies of the capitalist West, disciplinary procedures and surveillance of the population provide the primary modes of social subjection. Discipline is located and exercised in a wide variety of institutional forms: factories, schools, hospitals, prisons and military organizations, to name a few. This discipline creates subjects of a certain sort providing procedures for the training or coercing of people through hierarchical observation, the normalizing judgement (of, for example, the teacher or the social worker), and the examination involving the compilation of documents and the constitution of case histories. Surveillance takes place in the work place, increasingly separated from the home, and through the systematic collection and organization of information that can be stored and used to monitor populations. The factory-based labour process renders bodily behaviour routine, repetitive, subject to codifiable rules and accessible to surveillance and calculation. The factory's logic is thus political rather than purely economic. It is simply more efficient in terms of an economy of power, as is incarceration as opposed to the public spectacle of torture.

For Foucault the humanitarianism of the Enlightenment merely results in new forms of domination linked to innovations and refinements in surveillance technologies. Truth, reason and science are mere slogans of a new, more systematic and totalizing technology of power and Marxism is itself embroiled in such a conception. Foucault's analysis forgoes any faith in remnants of authentic human nature waiting to be liberated and leaves little room for the optimism built into all those analyses of ideologies that envisage the possibility of working towards a future of state of greater freedom.

His own historical work on topics such as madness and sexuality as discourses structured in the realms of power, yet divorced from any class conflict to be quite successfully managed. The relations of production, as for Marx, are still regarded as demarcating relations of domination, but class experience constituting a point of possible or actual resistance becomes less significant with increasing specialization of skills and tasks, and as the unity of knowledge fragments. The consequence is that domination becomes even more depersonalized than in liberal or *laissez-faire* capitalism. People become mere functionaries within an international capitalist order appearing to have a life and needs of its own, increasingly bureaucratized, and beyond human purpose. In *The dialectic of enlightenment* Horkheimer and Adorno set out to discover why humankind 'instead of entering into a truly human condition is sinking into a new kind of barbarism' (1979, p. xi).

If social freedom is inseparable from enlightened thought, why has the progressive thought of the Enlightenment led to relations of unfreedom? According to Horkheimer and Adorno one of the fundamental features of Enlightenment thought is its conception of nature as pure matter, governed by laws, capable of being captured and known through instrumental science. Nature becomes something to be dominated, the relationship between people and nature becomes one of pure utility. Such a relation between people and the domination of the natural world embraces people, themselves embodiments of the natural. The domination of nature and social domination are thus integrally linked, part of the same general process, working itself out most fully in the developing scientism or instrumental reason of the Enlightenment but pre-dating it. Relations of unfreedom are intimately linked with and sustained by that same reason permitting the instrumental domination and exploitation of nature.

In the work of Marcuse the theme that the domination of external nature and that of social life are part of the same process is extended to include self-domination. He draws on Freud's metapsychology (Freud 1930) in which the history of human society becomes the history of the repression of desire (Marcuse 1955). In the past, he argues, it had been necessary for the reality principle to subjugate the pleasure principle to serve humanity's need to establish mastery over nature in a struggle against scarcity. In advanced capitalist societies, such repression becomes surplus repression as a result of the enormous expansion of the productive forces, and is used by the state to extend its power into all aspects of personal life, and to shape personal ideas of worth and success consistent with instrumental rationality.

With perhaps the exception of Gramsci, we can recognize that, for all the authors discussed in this section, resistance is a metaphor for the enlarging and clarification of human consciousness. Freedom is a matter of being able to 'see through' and to challenge the conditions that divert living subjects from a real understanding of their interests and their conditions of existence. The turning away of critical theory from pursuing critical social science threatened the fulfilment of this promise. Returning to 'the problem of modernity' has been the inspiration of the work of Habermas (1971, 1976). His concern has been to enlarge the domain of reason from a narrow view of science and the preoccupations of concern with agency, class or institution, has been the centre of debate and influence amongst historians for some years now (for example, Weekes 1981, Dews 1984). His refusal to admit to any position from which a moral perspective might be generated has been a feature of a range of post-structuralist writings and the principal reason for the widespread rejection of its principal tenets (e.g. criticisms by Anderson 1983, Dews 1984, Habermas 1986, Taylor 1986).

Within anthropological and archaeological studies equivalent refinements in the analysis of power and the mechanisms establishing the pervasive nature of dominance have, in many instances, been derived from the work of Bourdieu on symbolic violence. For Bourdieu (1977), domination is conceived as a more diffuse but also more penetrating condition in which subtle normative orders permeate vast areas of day-to-day social encounters, and in which the very language and forms through which people express themselves provide instruments for their own oppression. There is an almost obsessive linkage in his writings between cultural forms, in the widest and most anthropological sense, and forms of domination and violence. For him, some account of culture in a given society or period is a necessity to answer the old questions of when and why people obey, why they appear to collude in or positively accept their own inferior social position, oppression or exploitation and even, in some sense, be oblivious to what appears to the analyst to be their subordination.

Bourdieu (1977, pp. 183–97) is therefore concerned with social and cultural production within what he calls *fields* of such production and their roles in the reproduction of class relations (*rapports de forces*). His own original ethnographic work was devoted to non-state small-scale societies in Algeria, in which relations of domination can only be set up and maintained at the cost of repeated social practices. This involves the endless articulation of the same elements, because the institutional conditions required for a lasting appropriation of the goods and services of dominated agents simply do not exist. Those who benefit from an asymmetrical distribution of power must work directly and personally to maintain the conditions of existence for their daily domination. The dominant cannot appropriate labour, services, goods or the honour and respect of others without establishing and maintaining an interpersonal bond. In such a social situation strategies of symbolic violence are more economical in terms of power than pure violence. By symbolic violence, Bourdieu means the processes by which wealth becomes social and symbolic capital and the forms of speech, gesture, taste and appearance by which patterns of domination are acted out *as if* the content of the rule defined the right to command. For example, in Kabyle society if a master wants to persuade his *khammes* (a *métayer* who receives only a small share of the crop) to devote himself over a long period to his master's interests, he has to try and associate him entirely with those interests misrepresenting the asymmetrical nature of the relationship by symbolically denying it in his day-to-day behaviour and through gifts and debts. Bourdieu (1977, p. 191) notes that:

> The reason for the pre-capitalist economy's great need for symbolic violence is that the only way in which relations of domination can be set up, maintained, or restored, is through strategies which, being expressly oriented towards the establishment of relations of personal dependence, must be disguised and transfigured lest they destroy themselves by revealing their true nature; in a word, they must be *euphemized*.

On the whole, analyses of domination have tended to centre very much on macro-forms of social analysis and structural constraint. By contrast, discussion of resistance to domination tends to emphasize agency, and operates within a more limited overall field of analysis. Bourdieu claims to find a way between this paradox of 'objectivism' (for example, of structuralism) and 'subjectivism' (for example, of phenomenology and semiology) and instead reveals an attempt to combine a Marxist strain in the critical sociologist who reveals a hidden interest behind every apparently 'disinterested' act or 'taste' for certain kinds of cultural products, and a Weberian strain in the concern with legitimacy and how people are led to obey regardless of whether it is objectively in their interests so to do. This is the Weber of the last pages of *The Protestant ethic and the spirit of capitalism* (1930) where, in a secularized world stripped of magic and religion, people's lives must be filled with new forms of social enchantment. Here again is the already-encountered theme of closure and the definition of inferiority, but extended more pungently into cultural studies.

However, there are crucial differences between Foucault on discipline and Bourdieu on symbolic violence. Bourdieu's concept of strategy (1977, pp. 38–58) insists that the reproduction of dominant relations is always reconstructed within an explicit consideration of social agency (for example, class). The field is continually contested, and the struggles over the hierarchization of hierarchies and the continual redrawing of the boundaries of social closure and exclusion as new 'fronts' are opened up provides for a re-entry of the problematics of resistance.

Bourdieu thereby attempts to provide an articulation of the two major strands of theoretical development which have been outlined here. His excavation of the minutiae of symbolic homologies in material culture and the rituals of everyday life exemplifies the considerable advances which have been made in the analysis of power relations. These, he shows, are grounded in the most intimate experiences of cultural forms but articulated within the overarching arena of structural relations. In his recent work on the sociology of modern cultural products, Bourdieu (1984) evokes the constant work involved in producing the body, foods, play and opinions appropriate to a particular social fraction within contemporary French society. These are constructed within a systematic opposition between a range of 'higher' cultural practices and distinctions, disdainful and disinterested in representations and content, in response to which the culture of the dominated class presents an aesthetic, valuing immediate sensual gratification based in a culture of necessity.

Conversely, even at the synchronic level of structural oppositions, Bourdieu alludes to more than the atmosphere of normative order portrayed by Foucault. In his appraisal of the dynamics of these fields, and in the profusion of contested 'bodies' and 'foods', he recalls Gramsci's 'war of positions' and Weber's notion of struggle around competing strategies of exclusion. Yet, in his tendency to reify 'class' or 'tradition' he lacks the sense of how conventions and pre-existing orders are internalized in such practices which we see in the Althusserians and Foucault.

We have outlined several different and yet often overlapping approaches to the study of domination and resistance, which have been developed in Western social thought since the 18th century. Whereas this has been selective, it is still possible to detect certain underlying themes that have structured this discourse. The difference between Marx and Weber has generated a long-standing polarity that still structures much of contemporary debate. Marx's emphasis on a philosophy of freedom achieved through the praxis of labour produced a theory of exploitation on the one hand, and the analysis of ideology as 'false consciousness' on the other. Weber's concern with legitimacy and forms of social exclusion posed the more subjective questions of why people obey and what leads them to act in ways apparently contrary to their objective self-interests. Various combinations or extensions of these arguments characterize all subsequent authors whose work has been examined here.

However, there remains a real sense in which the trajectories and developments outlined here present a genuine advance on the 'classic' texts from which they drew their inspiration. The reformulation by Althusser of the role of politics and ideology in defining social relations of production, the brilliance and detail by which Foucault reconstructs the development and pervasive nature of a particular normative discourse, the portrayal by Gramsci of the particular and contingent political alliances leading to the overthrow of an historically dominant order, and Bourdieu's excavations of the power of apparently trivial material taxonomies, provide powerful amplifications of the analytical possibilities for the social sciences concerned with these problems. In the chapters that follow the perceptivity of particular historical analysis, the parameters within which forms of explanation are constructed, and the central emphases which are abstracted from the mass of prehistoric and historical materials to account for social change, are derived in the end from the possibilities established by these debates.

Structure of the book

This book is organized into three sections. The first of these consists of chapters which directly elaborate on arguments touched upon within this Introduction. The second section examines a wide range of historical and prehistoric studies which, however, all refer to essentially pre- or non-capitalist contexts. In the final section the transformations under analysis are all effected under conditions that saw the emergence of capitalist systems, although several are on the periphery of the major centres of capitalist development. It is precisely this articulation between the development of indigenous trajectories and their resistance to much larger world systems which is increasingly at issue.

Domination and resistance

The Introduction began with an explanation of why a session originally oriented towards the question of the development of complexity has been re-ordered in terms of the themes of domination and resistance. In Chapter 1 Rowlands enlarges upon this shift, indicating the centrality of underlying issues to a wide range of apparently separate disciplines and debates. As such, assumptions about the development of complexity have become a kind of 'master discourse' running through European social theory, which Rowlands attempts to address directly in order to release the subsequent discussion from some of the constraints and 'closures' which these assumptions have tended to impose upon the analysis of long-term social transformations. Rowlands argues that the themes explored in this book may provide an alternative comparative framework focused upon the formation and dissolution of forms of social exclusion.

Following on from this re-orientation of discussion, Tilley (Ch. 2) and Miller (Ch. 3) highlight two relatively specific instances within this field, in order to explore them further. Tilley enlarges upon the contribution of Foucault to the analysis of discourse, and exemplifies his argument with an archaeological case-study taken from contemporary rather than prehistoric practices, using the inaugural lectures given for the Disney Professorship of Archaeology at the University of Cambridge. The normative patterns and self-referential and reverential structures that have emerged provide insights into the origins of other institutional structures of dominance, of which Foucault has been an indefatigable excavator.

Miller isolates one element of the introductory debates – the nature of resistance as a contribution to the dynamics of social transformations. The discussion of Gramsci's work has already touched upon this theme, but Miller attempts a more general classification of arenas within which resistance may arise, using largely historical and ethnographic examples. Starting from the intrinsically contradictory nature of power, Miller explores the potential for cosmological inversion, competition between different claimants to authority, and the struggle for legitimation of such claims, as well as questioning the pervasive nature of dominant ideologies. In all cases he focuses upon the contribution these factors have made to effective transformations in political and moral orders.

Political economy and ideology: historical transformations

If the contributions to this book may be characterized in summary form, it is that they provide a wide range of specific case-studies that largely concentrate on the importance of social inequalities to long-term social development and change. This is central to the concerns of archaeology, and highlights one of the most evident, if not unique, contributions of that discipline to the social sciences. It is important that the subsequent insights are not exhausted within the confines of the discipline, but develop as the foundation for a genuine dialogue with the social sciences. This depends upon more than just bracketing references to this dialogue which, as it were, start and close a particular investigation with token references to more general concerns. In this book either the presentation is throughly permeated by interpretive insights based on precisely these broader issues, or the juxtaposition of more specifically focused chapters contributes to particular points of articulation which indicate how archaeological findings and methods, or ethnographic and historical observations may be compared and related.

Bender (Ch. 4) begins appropriately by simultaneously addressing the central point of the book, that is the transformation of a question about the origins of complexity into one about the nature of inequalities in social relations, and positing this question in terms of the earliest materials available for the study of that social form within which the human species first developed. Bender is thereby able to confront the common claims which are made concerning some natural inequality contained within the biological development of gender relations, and insist upon the essentially cultural nature of human inequalities.

Her contribution then exemplifies the general concern of the subsequent chapters which ground many of the themes already discussed in terms of particular historical transformations. Although the insights provided by Marx as to the nature of social inequalities have become so pervasively influential as to be largely implicit in these studies, this book reflects a trend in recent studies in the social sciences which focuses explicitly upon questions of authority and legitimation for which Weber provides the substantive theoretical foundation, although writings on ideology (for example, by Althusser) also appear influential. The chapters by Hall (Ch. 5) and Gledhill (Ch. 6) are primarily concerned with the macro-structural factors that have determined the parameters for long-term social change. They provide a more specific evocation of Weber which emerges as a study of the conditions arising over the long term, and which were eventually to either predispose, or act as a barrier, to the later emergence of capitalism and different forms of the state. As with Weber, they use a broad comparative methodology and defend the implications of such a method; for example, contrasting archaeological discoveries in Meso-America with historical sources on the Chinese state. Gledhill notes that in competition between small states there may be a premium upon innovations in cosmologies within such struggles. This theme is developed further by Brumfiel (Ch. 7) although the emphasis is shifted in two directions; first, towards the factional quarrels within a given state, and secondly, to examine ideology in terms of the points of articulation between an aristocracy and the mass population.

In broad terms the order of the chapters correlates with certain contrasts which have been developed in this Introduction. Tensions have been noted between a concern with structural and macro-factors in the development of dominatory patterns and theorists who were increasingly concerned with the formation of human consciousness and its possibilities, or non-possibilities, of emancipation in terms of the specific development of particular fields, taxonomies or discourses. Lukacs (1971) and Gramsci (1971) provide the point of articulation, where the macro-conditions of political and economic change provide the possibilities of perspicacity amongst the alienated mass population. The later writers provide a wide variety of insights based on more-specific conjunctures and developments. Such concerns include the parallels forged in modernism between the domination of nature and that of humanity, the particular practical taxonomies which construct Bourdieu's habitus, or the trajectory of normative and oppressive institutions as traced by Foucault (1977, 1980).

In similar terms, Chapter 8 by Kus acts in a manner parallel to that of Lukacs and Gramsci in its specific examination of the linkages between the long-term emergence of a state in the interior of Madagascar with the demands this process makes upon the consciousness of its citizens. Kus stresses the active involvement of the mass population in historical change and, echoing those previous contributions which have looked at the relationship between state and citizen, she examines the precise mechanisms by which consent is generated and sustained. Her argument is sometimes closely reminiscent of questions raised by the Frankfurt school. She locates similar parallels between the principles of an order that controls nature and that of the royal authority over the populace. For example, in the case where she notes that the king makes claim that his real enemies are natural disasters, the process by which domination is made to appear to be necessary collusion appears to be as a germane to this case as to the development of European positivism.

In a sense the three chapters on Sri Lankan history and archaeology provide a case-study in the grounding of these themes within terms of a particular material field – that of architecture as urban form and ritual structure. Gunawardana's chapter (Ch. 9) makes this linkage with particular clarity, but sets it within a broader context which exemplifies the manner by which these general theoretical issues may be grounded in detailed historical analysis. He addresses the contribution of the classic theorists such as Weber and Marx on the Asian city directly, but provides additional materials from, for example, Sombart on consumption and later writers on religious and spatial order (for example, Wheatley 1971). Gunawardana's exemplification indicates how different domains of royal power, such as the forms of control over irrigation systems and the extraction of surplus, and other activities which asserted dominance over ritual order, may best be understood within a larger framework within which they are directly related. The material correlates of ideas on the reproduction of dominant orders are traced through details of spatial form such as the construction of an inner and outer city and the positioning of monasteries or 'unclean' social fractions. This chapter also complements

Chapter 3, in providing clear evidence of diverse historical instances of resistance to particular regimes emerging from rival factions within the aristocracy, competition within religious groupings and between them and secular powers, occasionally with the active intervention by the urban populace itself. All of this, often turbulent, history is considered in terms of one of the most stable long-term urban sites in world history.

With the complementary Chapters 10 and 11 by Bandaranayake and Prematilleke, respectively, the discussion moves closer to the concerns of Althusser, Foucault and especially Bourdieu, with the precise orders involved in the cultural form of symbolic violence. Bandaranayake abstracts from a sequence of architectural development lasting some two millennia the key principles of spatial order in monastic structures which link them directly with the principles of and fluctuations in political control (cf. Panofsky 1957). This chapter focuses on centrifugal and centripetal tendencies in political control, with their varied expression in architectural order. Much of this work is based on continuing archaeological investigations, and the importance of this mode of research is brought out by Prematilleke, who relates these general concerns with competing forms of authority (e.g. urban and forest-based Buddhism), to the specific excavations of a monastic complex of the 12th century AD. This chapter indicates the potential of archaeological excavation and the careful recording of architectural remains for elucidating further the highly complex relationships that these three chapters describe. (A similar synthesis of archaeological and architectural analysis may be found in recent studies at Vijayanagara by Fritz *et al.* 1984).

Bourdieu's anthropological studies of homologies in taxonomic and classificatory orders found in spatial and other domains have been highly influential with archaeologists concerned with the translation of patterning in archaeological materials into ideas about the development of social relations, and in the material nature of ideology (for example, Hodder 1982, Miller & Tilley 1984). This theme is taken up in several of the chapters in this section. Here the archaeological work on Sri Lanka described by Bandaranayake and Prematilleke is complemented by the final section of Chapter 7 by Brumfiel, which focuses on the implications of her ideas on factional conflict for changes in the Aztec ceramic sequence, the linkage between the two being constructed in terms of the study of what has been called household consumption rituals. It is also illustrated by an aspect of Bender's Chapter 4, not previously referred to, which is her original analysis of palaeolithic art, not just as a symbol, but as an important instrument in the construction of fundamental cultural inequalities.

The chapters by Brumfiel and Bender (as also, in a different way, that by Gunawardana) provide a further instance of the resolution of the theoretical tensions considered in this Introduction through specific historical analysis, in a form which is an explicit theme in Chapters 12 and 13 by Kristiansen and Mays, respectively. These deal with the relationship between studies of archaeological patterning as ideology and the macro-issues of the long-term development of social relations which has been a central concern in Marxist and structural-Marxist writings. Kristiansen's study provides a very specific example of how an equation may be drawn, in this case, linking shifts in the deposition of bronze artefacts in the European Bronze Age between hoards and burials with changes in social and ideological order – for example, gender relations and the balance between communal ritual and personal prestige goods. Finally, Mays, by applying techniques of analysis to specific archaeological materials such as grave goods and skeletal variation, attempts to investigate the suitability of models drawn from Marxist theories about the forms of exploitation in lineage-based societies.

European expansion, colonialism and resistance

This section addresses some aspects of the role archaeology has played in understanding the consequences of European precolonial contact, colonial expansion and settlement in the making of the modern world. In this regard archaeology, like its neighbouring disciplines anthropology and history, has played an ambiguous role. In part it has the undistinguished record of assuring the dominated of their right to rule, and convincing the dominated of their duty to obey. However, it has also been shaped by such roles, with the consequence that significant shifts have occurred in the perception of why certain kinds of archaeological investigation should be more important than others.

A recent but growing critical perception of their practices has meant that archaeologists are now aware of such histories (for example, Trigger 1984, Miller 1980). This has led the subject to play a more important role in revealing the history and prehistory of European contact and expansion, and indigenous resistance to colonial settlement, and to understanding better its own involvement and bias in the reconstruction of these processes. By far the greatest amount of research has been conducted in regions of intense white-settler occupation, where most attention so far has been directed to the study of colonial settlement and the historical archaeology and material culture of colonial society (for example, FitzHugh 1985, Reece 1975). An historical archaeology was created that defined the study of contemporary indigenous populations as unchanging 'primitives' and of little importance. Evaluating the effects of 'primitivist' definitions of 'native populations' on archaeological practices in North America, Australia and Southern Africa has produced an extensive recent literature (for example, Trigger 1980, Mulvaney 1981, Garlake 1982, Ucko 1983, Hall 1984).

The chapters by Larsen, Kohl, Portugal, and Rowlands (Chs 14, 15, 17, 18) are concerned with only one aspect of this theme, which is the creation in European consciousness of 'the other' as the opposite to its own particular 'civilized' identity. Larsen and Kohl are both concerned with the construction of 'Orientalism' and how this has shaped both an ideology of the uniqueness of Western civilization and defined those scholarly goals in Near-Eastern history as being significant for archaeological investigation.

The 'Orientalist thesis', as they discover it operating in Near Eastern archaeology, involves the transfer of basic cultural, social, technical and religious inventions, distinctive of 'Western civilization' from the Ancient Orient to Europe and from there, in modern times, to the rest of the world. Identifying the transfer of civilization over time has organized scholarly research to the extent, as Kohl shows, that the archaeology of later periods and particularly of more recent times, has been relatively neglected or wilfully ignored. If 'Orientalism' represents 'high civilization', then Africa in European discourse is its opposite. Rowlands discusses the subordination of Africa as a European idea, and the way this became internalized by both colonizers and colonized. In the case he details, this led to the fulfilment of the 'primitivist prophecy' and the emergence of a devolved peasantry from a more developed precolonial political structure. Here archaeology plays a vital role in providing an alternative empirical base to written history and oral tradition in evaluating these competing versions of the past.

In fact, Cameroon, like many other African countries with small white-settler populations, was able to resist early colonial rule quite effectively. Portugal's chapter by contrast, demonstrates the outcome of a history of extensive conquest and colonization by Europeans – in a diverse and internally fractured population that seeks unity in 'culture' to combat its own discontinuous past. 'Western' ideals and prescriptions are to be rejected to pursue what he and others call 'ethnodevelopment', which also means to privilege the community over the nation-state. Finally, in Chapter 16 Friedman locates such shifts in Western identity and the construction of that of others within a much broader-ranging discussion of modernity and post-modernity as responses to the expansion and reorganization of global culture.

The theme of inventing tradition is continued in Chapter 19 by Sichone, where it is argued that 'tribalism' is essentially a creation of European colonialism on the Rhodesian Copperbelt. The argument seems to be the familiar one that 'tribal populations' were encouraged by colonial authorities to form in the townships and the countryside as a means of maintaining a partially self-sustaining labour force. In fact, he claims urban tribalism to be neither modern nor traditional, but the creation of a separate African identity based on a new construction of ethnicity. Chapters 20 and 21 by Thomas-Emeagwali and Jahangir respectively, argue for the relevance of class analysis in the precolonial Middle Belt of Nigeria and in Bangladesh. Thomas-Emeagwali claims that it is a Marxist definition of exploitation and class formation which most adequately interprets the precolonial and colonial historical periods. The essential question is how a universal model of class can be applied, a point that leads Jahangir to modify the Marxist framework by emphasizing the militarism of the state and its control of relations of force in Bangladesh, and to use Weber in stressing that an ideology of sharing underlies the responsibility to obey.

It is perhaps ironic that whereas Western archaeologists from the metropoles often discuss their materials in ambiguous and diffident terms, sometimes conveying the impression that coming up with generalizations, explanations and clearly defined positions is unlikely or undesirable, it is Third World practitioners, espousing Marx or Weber or a combination of theoretical insights, who confidently apply them to their material. The explanation for this that could be derived from Friedman's Chapter 16 would be that such shifting conceptions are structured by significant movements and crises in legitimacy within the reality of the global system of relations of dominance and resistance. Although we may doubt whether such complex realities are so easily captured, it is a sufficiently important point on which to complete this Introduction.

References

Althusser, L. 1969. *Reading Capital*. London: New Left Books.

Althusser, L. 1970. *For Marx*. London: Penguin.

Althusser, L. 1984. *Essays on ideology*. London: Verso.

Anderson, P. 1983. *In the tracks of historical materialism*. London: Verso.

Auge, M. 1978, *Pouvoirs de vie, pouvoirs de mort. Introduction à une anthropologie de la répression*. Paris.

Auge, M. 1982. *The anthropological circle*. Cambridge: Cambridge University Press.

Bailey, A. & Llobera, J. 1981. *The Asiatic mode of production*. London: Routledge and Kegan Paul.

Barthes, R. 1973. *Mythologies*. London: Paladin.

Bender, B. 1978. Gatherer-hunter to farmer: a social perspective. *World Archaeology* **10**, 204–22.

Bender, B. 1985. Emergent tribal formations in the American midcontinent. *American Antiquity* **50**, 52–62.

Bourdieu, P. 1977. *Outline of a theory of practice*. Cambridge: Cambridge University Press.

Bourdieu, P. 1984. *Distinction*. London: Routledge & Kegan Paul.

Bradley, R. 1984. *The social foundations of prehistoric Britain*. London: Longman.

Clastres, P. 1977. *Society against the state*. Oxford: Blackwell.

Dews, P. 1984. Foucault's theory of subjectivity. *New Left Review*, **144**, 72–95.

Finley, M. 1973. *The ancient economy*. London: Chatto & Windus.

Fitzhugh, W. W. 1985. *Cultures in conflict*. Washington: Smithsonian Institution.

Foucault, M. 1977. *Discipline and punish*. New York: Vintage Books.

Foucault, M. 1980. *Power/knowledge*. Hassocks: Harvester.

Frankenstein, S. & M. Rowlands 1978. The internal organisation and regional structure of the Early Iron Age in South West Germany. *Bulletin of the Institute of Archaeology, London* **15**, 73–112.

Freud, S. 1930. *Civilization and its discontents*. London: Hogarth Press.

Friedman, J. 1974. Marxism, structuralism and vulgar materialism. *Man* **3**, 444–69.

Friedman, J. 1975. Tribes, states and transformations. In *Marxist analyses in anthropology*, M. Bloch (ed.) London: Tavistock.

Friedman, J. & M. Rowlands 1977. *The evolution of social systems*. London: Duckworth.

Fritz, J., G. Mitchell & M. Nagaraja Rao 1984. *Where kings and gods meet*. University of Arizona Press.

Garlake, P. 1982. Prehistory and ideology in Zimbabwe. *Africa* **52**(3), 1–19.

Giddens, A. 1986. *Nation state and violence*. Oxford: Polity Press.
Gilsenan, M. 1985. Patrimonialism in North Lebanon. *Critique of Anthropology* **5**, 1–15.
Gledhill, J. 1978. Formative development in the North American South West. *British Archaeological Reports* **47**, 241–84.
Gramsci, A. 1971. *Selections from the prison notebooks*. London: Lawrence & Wishart.
Habermas, J. 1971. *Knowledge and human interests*. London: Heinemann.
Habermas, J. 1976. *Legitimation crisis*. New York: Beacon Press.
Habermas, J. 1986. Life forms, morality and the task of the philosopher. In *Habermas: autonomy and solidarity*, P. Dews (ed.).
Hall, M. 1984. The burden of tribalism: the social context of Southern African Iron Age studies. *American Antiquity* **49**(3), 455–67.
Held, D. 1980. *Introduction to critical theory*. London: Hutchinson.
Hirst, P. 1979. *On law and ideology*. London: Macmillan.
Hobbes, T. 1958. *Leviathan*. New York: Liberal Arts Press.
Hodder, I. (ed.) 1982. *Structural and symbolic archaeology*. Cambridge: Cambridge University Press.
Holton, R. J. 1985. *From feudalism to capitalism*. London: Macmillan.
Horkheimer, M. & T. Adorno. 1979. *Dialectic of Enlightenment*. London: Verso.
Jay, M. 1984. *Marxism and totality*. Oxford: Polity Press.
Kahn, J. & J. Llobera. 1981. *The anthropology of precapitalist societies*. London: Macmillan.
Kohl, P. 1978. The balance of trade in Southwest Asia in the mid 3rd millenium BC. *Current Anthropology*. **19**(3), 463–92.
Kohl, P. 1981. Materialist approaches in prehistory. *Annual Review of Anthropology*, **10**, 89–118.
Kristiansen, K. 1979. The consumption of wealth in Bronze Age Denmark. In *New Directions in Scandinavian Archaeology*, K. Kristiansen & Paluden-Muller (eds).
Lacan, J. 1977. *Ecrits. A selection*. London: Tavistock.
Lukacs, G. 1971. *History and class consciousness*. London: Merlin Press.
Mann, M. 1987. Militarism and the state. *New Left Review* **162**.
Marcuse, H. 1955. *Eros and civilisation*. New York: Beacon Press.
Marx, K. 1973. *Grundrisse*. London: Penguin.
McGuire, R. 1986. Economics and modes of production in the prehistoric Southwestern periphery. In *Ripples in the Chichimec Sea*. F. Mathien & R. McGuire (eds). Carbondale: Illinois University Press.
Miller, D. 1980. Archaeology and development. *Current Anthropology* **21**(6), 209–26.
Miller, D. & C. Tilley 1984. *Ideology, power and prehistory*. Cambridge: Cambridge University Press.
Mouffe, C. (ed) 1979. *Gramsci and Marxist theory*. London: Routledge & Kegan Paul.
Mulvaney, D. J. 1981. Gum leaves on the golden bough: Australia's Palaeolithic survivals discovered. In *Antiquity and Man*, J. D. Evans, B. Cunliffe & C. Renfrew (eds). London: Thames & Hudson.
Panofsky, E. 1957. *Gothic architecture and scholasticism*. Ohio: Meridian.
Parkin, F. 1979. *Marxism and a bourgeois critique*. London: Methuen.
Poulantzas, N. 1973. *Classes in contemporary capitalism*. London: NLB.
Poulantzas, N. 1980. *State, power, socialism*. London: Verso.
Reece, R. H. 1975. *Aborigines and Australian society*. Sydney: University of Sydney Press.

Renfrew, C. & K. Cooke (eds). 1979. *Transformations*. London: Academic Press.
Rey, P. P. 1979. Class contradictions in lineage societies. *Critique of Anthropology* **13/14**, 41–61.
Rowlands, M. 1982. Processual archaeology as historical social science. In *Theory and explanation in archaeology*, C. Renfrew, M. Rowlands & B. Segraves, (eds). New York: Academic Press.
Rowlands, M. 1985. Exclusionary tactics in the logic of collective dynamics. *Critique of Anthropology* **5**, 60–71.
Rowlands, M., M. Larsen, K. Kristiansen 1989. *Centre and periphery relations in the ancient world*. Cambridge: Cambridge University Press.
Sahlins, M. 1985. *Islands without history*. Chicago: Chicago University Press.
St Croix, G. de 1980. *Class in Ancient Greece*. Oxford: Oxford University Press.
Smith, A. 1896. In *Lectures on justice, police, revenue and arts*, E. Cannan (ed.). Oxford: Oxford University Press.
Taylor, C. 1986. Foucault on freedom and truth. In *Foucault: a critical reader*. D. Couzens Hoy (ed). Oxford: Blackwell.
Thompson, E. P. 1978. *The poverty of theory*. London: Macmillan.
Trigger, B. 1980. Archaeology and the image of the American Indian. *American Antiquity* **45**(4), 662–76.
Trigger, B. 1984. Alternative archaeologies: nationalist, colonialist, imperialist. *Man* **19**(3), 1–15.
Ucko, P. J. 1983. Australian academic archaeology: Aboriginal transformation of its aims and practices. *Australian Archaeology* **16**, 11–26.
Van de Leeuw, S. (ed). 1981. *Archaeological approaches to the study of complexity*. Amsterdam: University of Amsterdam Press.
Wallerstein, I. 1974. *The modern world-system*. New York: Academic Press.
Weber, M. 1947. *The theory of economic and social organization*. New York: Free Press.
Weber, M. 1968. *Economy and society*. Vol. 3. New York: Bedminster Press.
Weekes, J. 1981. *Sex, politics and society*. London: Longman.
Wheatley, P. 1971. *The pivot of the four quarters*. Edinburgh: Edinburgh University Press.

DOMINATION AND RESISTANCE

1 *A question of complexity*

MICHAEL ROWLANDS

The aim of this chapter is to examine the epistemological status of the concept of complexity. The discussion will be limited to the dominant archaeological understanding of the term, derived as it is from the social Darwinist philosophy of the late 19th century. It is argued that it has an origin in the Judaeo-Christian tradition (especially the Paulinian writings) on the origin of evil. By revealing the ontological basis through which the idea gained a potency and meaning in Western thought, I claim that it is possible not only to describe the Eurocentric limits of the concept, but also to redefine it in such a way that more useful questions may be posed concerning the nature and causes of cultural difference.

One of the key assumptions in archaeology is that the development of human societies can be studied in terms of the transition from earlier simple forms, in which one set of social relations may perform many functions (homogeneity), to later complex forms where 'institutions' carry out specialized functions (heterogeneity). Discontinuity characterizes the transformation from one social form to the other. Whether the latter be characterized by social inequality, state formation, urbanism, regional specialization and exchange, or bureaucracy and levels of territorial administration, what fascinates is the idea that the unintended consequences of historically remote events are still relevant to the way we live today. 'Complex societies' describe us in contrast to 'simple societies', which is more about what we are supposed to have lost. Perhaps the best example is the characterization by Sahlins of hunter-gatherer economies as the 'Zen road to affluence', by which he meant the satisfaction of finite needs with infinite resources in contrast with capitalist preoccupations with infinite needs that have to be satisfied with finite resources (Sahlins 1972).

The purpose of this chapter is not to query the empirical basis for the distinction. That, in some sense, human societies have evolved forms of social closure and exclusion of strikingly rigid forms is undeniable. What is at issue is that, in Western discourse, complexity defined in terms of differentiation has been accepted as a metaphor for social inequality. The result is that simple societies are believed to demonstrate their egalitarian nature simply by displaying evidence of a lack of differentiation, and complex societies the inverse. However, it is by no means so obvious that this is or ever has been the case (see Bender, Ch. 4, this volume.) After all, the fact that a very particular notion of 'complexity' is used to describe 'egalitarian' and 'stratified' societies in general is consistent with the implication of its 19th-century derivation, that Western societies are its most advanced and superior exemplar. The 'primitive societies' of an imperialistic epoch in European affairs were 'simple' in the sense that they were quite literally inferior to the superior technology and administration of their dominators. Being inferior was defined by an evolutionary scale of values that was experienced and believed in by both dominators and dominated. Social inequality is, therefore, redolent with the definitions of inferiority characteristic of a historically specific scale of values. This is why stratification, urbanism, etc., must stand as its defining characteristics.

Weber argued that whoever is in a position to define the scale of values forms 'positively privileged status groups'. The language of closure and the language of power are thus closely intertwined and promise a more flexible approach to studying 'complexity'. To Weber, exclusion was the major form of social closure, and broadly referred to any device, stratagem or indicator that was used by one group to define another as *inferior* in a scale of values of its own making (Parkin 1979, Rowlands 1985). In modern capitalist societies, for example, he claimed that the two main criteria that the bourgeoisie uses to construct and maintain itself as a class are property and privileged access to professional qualifications and credentials. Each is defined by a set of legal arrangements to restrict access to rewards and privileges, and to monitor entry to key positions within the division of labour. Weber's concern was to show how this could answer the old questions of why and when people obey. Why do people appear to collude in or positively accept their own inferior social position, oppression or exploitation? Why are the conditions that promote this consciousness not easily 'seen through' by those objectified as categories of outsiders and inferiors? Why will both dominators and dominated share equally in the practices that convince each of their own relative superiority and inferiority?

Such issues have constantly preoccupied social theorists, most recently Althusser (1971) on ideological state apparatuses, Bourdieu (1977) on symbolic violence, Foucault (1977, 1980) on technologies of surveillance and discrimination, and Lacan (1977) on the formation of subjectivity through the construction of difference. In their view it is the ways in which categories of difference (e.g. age, occupation, race, ethnicity, gender and sexuality) constitute the ineligible, the inferior and the outsider, and how these are internalized in the formation of subjectivity, that entwines the language of closure and the language of power.

It is of course true that these indicators of difference are peculiar to modern societies, in the sense that it is only here that persons confront themselves as objects or as attributes of objects, i.e. as potential commodities. In such cases, social categories are elaborated that emphasize either possession of, or a denial of, the significance of such attributes. The idea that this was never the case in pre-modern societies is highly doubtful and certainly was not what Marx originally meant by the contrast of use value and exchange value (Marx 1971, p. 48). Hence, recent discussions that have stressed the inalienability of the gift versus commodity exchange as a traditional–modern contrast are empirically refutable. However, when gods or kings are given the credit for the existence of the social order, and closeness to them defines your relative superiority based on sacred power, it is demonstrably the case that a different scale of values is in operation.

The cosmological origins of complexity

A longer historical perspective moderates this 'modern' perception of complexity even further. Even within Western discourses it can be shown to be not a recent product of capitalism, but part of the basic ontology of Western existence and constituted as a part of its movement from a divine to a secular rational ordering in history. Current understanding of the opposition between simple and complex societies in archaeology is a very good example of such structuring. It opposes an original state of homogeneous social relations that may be differentiated in unity (as in most cosmological notions of ritual power), to others distinguished by increasing heterogeneity or pluralism of social identities in which differentiation is a matter of absolute values.

In his structural analysis of the myth of Genesis, Leach (1969), for example, shows that, in the Judaeo-Christian tradition, it is only after having sinned that human beings began to think in terms of difference: good and evil, life and death, man and woman. Moreover, Adam's sin is not only due to a transgression of divine law, but also to the accomplishment of the sexual act; after having eaten the forbidden fruit, Adam 'knew' Eve, *his wife*. Death as the punishment of sin condemns sexuality to be an evil which men cannot escape. Death, both real and symbolic, is the necessary atonement of evil (Morin 1972). It was this aspect of evil that was stressed in medieval asceticism. Introspection, the suffering of the body and sacrifice are all justified by the desire to punish the human interior evil, i.e sexuality (Turner 1986). McFarlane suggests, contra Leach, that Genesis, rather than containing the knowledge to discriminate between good and evil, contains the deadly knowledge that it is now impossible to distinguish with certainty between the two (McFarlane 1985, p. 87). In the Christian tradition evil is thus the transgression of difference, the causes of which are uncertain and a threat to a reality which is continually vulnerable to dissolution. Evil has to be scourged (e.g., the fight against 'the flesh'); John, speaking of the victory of Jesus against death and sin, stressed that it had to be so that he could make judgement on this world and expel Satan as the personification of evil (John 12:31).

The Christian tradition is therefore part of a more universal discourse that defines evil as a threatening power which dissolves difference and thus undermines the unity of the cosmos. As Kapferer (1984, p. 10) argues, in the case of Buddhism, demons introduce disorder through the subversion of hierarchy and order based on the recognition of established difference. Oppositions between undifferentiated, unstructured, timeless, primeval chaos and historical narratives of the heroic events and symbolic acts by which worlds were made different and hierarchies rebuilt, are cosmological universals. After all, so is the tendency for purification to depend on the annihilation of unacceptable forms of difference and a belief in the existence of some category of human being deemed to be the agents of corruption and the incarnation of evil.

Complexity as historical narrative

Although it runs the risk of unduly homogenizing a diversity of interpretations, it will be convenient to summarize the forms that simple–complex dualism has taken in archaeology in the following manner.

(a) Those studies (the majority probably) of diverse theoretical persuasion that view change from simple to complex social forms as an advance through a sequence of successive differentiations. This is derived from Herbert Spencer's notion that life as a whole develops from a stage of incoherent homogeneity to cohorent heterogeneity (Spencer 1876, p. 291). By differentiation, Spencer meant specialization and hence greater efficiency. The dynamic is adaptationist in the sense that specialization, as for example an increase in the division of labour, is evaluated in terms of whether this results in the more efficient use of matter.

(b) The contrast between simple and complex social forms has been used to describe cumulative development as well as the discontinuities of social change. In the former, increasing differentiation is seen as a smooth, unfolding process in which earlier forms are present in later developed forms (according to, but not reducible to, the organic analogy from which it is derived; cf. Friedman & Rowlands 1977). In the latter, a savage–barbarist social form is seen as the inversion and negation of its civilized counterpart. An example is found in different versions of the opposition between state and stateless societies. The first variant argues for a difference in social type in terms of concentration of increasing amounts of power due to various forms of control, ranging from means of production to sacred knowledge (e.g. Cohen & Service 1978). The second argues for the inversion of the state–stateless categories, as in the approach of Pierre Clastres, who claims that 'primitive societies' practise a kind of anti-power (in contrast to the coercive power of the modern state) that takes the form of socially castrated chiefs who, while occupying the locus of social power are, in their practical relation to society, a negation of that power. The chief is thus reduced to a symbol to be manipulated by society, a practical negation of that which he represents (Clastres 1977). In a more ethnohistorical vein this approach has been developed further by Sahlins in his study of diarchy in Hawaii (Sahlins 1985).

(c) Although differentiation is observed at all stages, the term 'complex society' is most strongly associated with a stage of evolution in which notions such as the state, cities, writing, social stratification, bureaucratic administration, craft specialization and long-distance trade figure prominently. The significance of these categories for the development of social life owes its origin to European deliberations on the important innovations marking the beginnings of modernity.

This has several consequences. Earlier periods may be invested with meanings that are effectively anti-modernist in content. Pasts are searched for those elements that can be contrasted, usually favourably, with modernity. Historical sequences that lack all or most of the features that define complexity become 'problematic' in the sense that they cannot be placed on any sort of evolutionary continuum. In a more enlightened global culture it has been deemed urgent to discover an independent version of Western complexity (food production, the state, literacy, etc.) for each non-Western centre of 'civilization'. A universal monologue on the nature of social complexity has thus been successfully disseminated from its original European power base. In the process the modernist assumptions are made clearer of much Western theorizing on the 'origins of civilization', 'the state' and 'social complexity' in general.

For example, Renfrew's (1972, p. 11) definition of civilization has a definite modernist ring to it:

> And whereas the savage hunter lives in an environment not so different in many ways from that of other animals, although enlarged already by the use of language and of a whole range of other artefacts in the culture, civilised man lives in an environment very much of his own creation. Civilisation, in this sense, is the self made environment of man, which he had fashioned to insulate himself from the primaeval environment of nature alone.

A modern Western disposition to associate the domination of nature with social domination is refashioned to characterize not only the origins of Western civilization, but apparently all others as well.

However, most other 'civilizations' do not appear to agree with this at all. For example, take this quotation about the Aztecs which can be replicated in many other cultural settings:

> The Mexica saw the relationship between their city (Tenochtitlan) and its environment as an integrated cosmological structure – an ordered universe within which the natural phenomena were regarded as intrinsically sacred, alive, and intimately relatable to the activities of man (Chang 1984).

Chang goes on to argue that none of the elements used to define civilization by Gordon Childe, Renfrew and others apply in the cases of either Ancient China or Mesoamerica. Instead, in what he calls the Maya–China continuum, politics is inseparable from ritual; religion 'encompasses' politics, violence, warfare and destruction; writing serves the purpose of divination and ritual, rather than administration, and ancestors are venerated as extensions of kinship.

In contrast with 'this vast cultural continuum' that goes back, he claims, to long before the Maya or Shang China, he reiterates the familiar theme that Western civilization represents a significant, if peculiar, historical 'break out' in which technological progress, territorial administration, bureaucracy, the separation of religion from politics, and the principle that freedom and justice should be based on the triumph of reason, came to dominate the inner logic of the structure of Western civilization either in the 4th or the 1st millennium BC, or the 16th century AD or, as some might now argue, only after World War II (Chang 1984, p. 21, Anderson 1984). The strength of the Western ideal of complexity in archaeology can be gauged in the responses to Chang's Orientalist thesis made by Lamberg-Karlovsky and by Willey who take for granted that such a 'break out' took place, and debate whether it is the idea of political freedom or the ability to contain yet sustain commerce that characterizes the uniqueness of Ancient Mesopotamian 'city-states', and hence the legacy of the Ancient Near East for the development of Western civilization and its pursuit of reason, technical progress and individual liberty (Lamberg-Karlovsky 1985, Willey 1985).

Of course, the question is, how has or how does archaeology render service to this faith in a unique historical destiny for Western civilization? Moreover, to what extent is the creation of this non-Western ideal 'culture', one free of alienation, simply a product of the paradoxical creation of Western identity? On the one hand it represents the profound sense of loss that Western civilizational standards have to bear and, on the other hand, it glories in emphasizing the 'uniqueness of the West' and its capacity for dynamic growth and social change (Rowlands 1984, and in press). Such a paradox is by no means a novel theme (see Larsen, Ch. 14 this volume). When Layard first brought the Assyrian sculptures from Nimrud to the British Museum, a storm of protest was unleashed that such monstrous figures could have anything to do with Western identity, the heirs of classical Greece and Rome. Bernal has shown brilliantly how Europe's foundation in Ancient Greece had to be shorn of its 'borrowings' from Ancient Egypt (Bernal 1987). The monstrosity of an Afro-Asian origin of classical civilization was effectively banished by scholarship. The 19th-century quarrel, born in the Romantic movement, over the interpretation of the Etruscans as a stately and integrated archaic civilization that was brutally conquered and destroyed by the rather loathsome, rational and pragmatic Romans is still with us today. Pallottino (1986, p. 14) refers to the paradox of those who have wished to interpret the Etruscans as somewhere between the Greek experience and the Roman, and quite discernible within 'the panorama of ancient Italy' in contrast to the wishes of more modern 'savage writers' who will have none of scholarship and evoke the mysterious and inpenetrable nature of a lost civilization, to emit a sense of loss which is in fact a suppression of outrage against the conditions of their own contemporary existence. Moreover, when D. H. Lawrence espouses the Etruscan cause it is not to lament a lost Utopia, but rather to reclaim it and assert that it will live again:

> But who wants object-lessons about vanished races? What one wants is a contact. The Etruscans are not a theory or a thesis. If they are anything, they are an *experience*. (Lawrence 1986, p. 24.)

It is not surprising that, in this tradition of writing, the Etruscans have been catalogued with Buddhism and other forms of Eastern mystical religions in opposition to loathsome Western rationalism. The German historical tradition versus Enlightenment rationalism is, after all, a scholarly reflection on a basic view of what it is to be human. The opposition between inhabiting an authentic, totalizing and unified life world opposes itself to the fragmentation and alienation of modernity.

Complexity as a master discourse

By going outside the discipline we can perceive that the dissemination of complexity as a meta-narrative of world prehistory is not, itself, a product of the success of archaeology. This is because simple–complex and traditional–modern dualisms are not actually a product of archaeological empirical investigation. Instead, the dualism of simple and complex has been, until recently, a common understanding of the nature and experience of modern development. It is worth pointing out the number of disciplines that share the same master discourse with archaeology.

Sociology. Most current sociology still works with a language derived from 19th-century debates on the nature of modern versus traditional society, e.g. Durkheim's mechanical to organic solidarity; Tonnies' *Gemeinschaft* and *Gesellschaft*; Weber's habitual action to goal-oriented action (traditional versus legal rational authority); Marx's ontologies of primitive communism and capitalism; Talcott Parsons' model of structural differentiation; the phenomenological separation of the I and the Me.

Social and Economic History. The transition from embedded to disembedded social forms. Polanyi's substantivist argument that social evolution has been basically a process of increasing autonomy of market economies from political and moral prescription is predicated by an original unity that has been dissolved and would be regained at a higher 'socialist' form of unified existence when redistribution of resources would be fairly allocated.

Psychology and Psychoanalysis. Freud's distinction of the unconscious as the product of repression. The separation of conscious and unconscious worlds. Piaget's and Lacan's opposing notions of the infant as an undifferentiated mass of conflicting instincts and drives (*l'homelette*) that is differentiated through socialization (the mirror and the symbol stages).

Linguistics. Saussure's (1924) separation of language structure (synchronic) from language process (diachronic); the separation of language structure from speech utterance.

By no means are these necessarily the major influence in all disciplines at present. The fact is that they either have been, or still are, in a disguised textualized form – Lacan's (1977) re-reading of Freud is one recent and creative instance.

The ideological construction of the simple : homogeneous : complex : heterogenous narrative is disguised by the ability it has shown to sink into different academic discourses and become enveloped in distinct empirical clothings and reified within particular methodological expertise. The archaeological version is little different in this respect. Few authors would be willing to pronounce overtly on the nature of complex societies, except perhaps in first-year undergraduate lectures, and perhaps even then with some trepidation. Firmer ground is struck with the concrete categories that are the residue of the discourse. Long-distance trade is eminently empirical and observable (supposedly); large tomes on the definition and nature of urbanism exist. The inadmissible parts of the narrative assume an unproblematic, taken for granted, if not common-sense understanding of the subject, precisely because its origins are not archaeological.

Simple and complex in creative contradiction

It is the form of narrative we use to grasp this experience that requires the temporal separation of simple from complex societies. A past undifferentiated social world where needs were limited and resources limitless has been replaced historically, as we perceive it, by desires and wants, by inequality in the pursuit of scarce resources, by the breaching of self-contained social worlds and by the external demands of trade, diplomacy and violence, (i.e., power). It is probably true that earlier visions of the temporal succession from noble savage to rational man would be regarded sceptically by contemporary Western archaeologists. The ideological nature of the sequence would be easily recognized. What is less certain is whether this radically affects the underlying dominance of the narrative; i.e., the sequence from incoherent homogeneity to coherent heterogeneity or differentiation and specialization as a meta-sign of progress.

In the sense that the narratives are constructed by excluding into an homogeous and undifferentiated world all elements which are considered by us 'moderns' as inimical to or the antithesis of dynamism, action and progress, we create historical periods and culture areas that exemplify the former characteristics. For Childe (1930, pp. 8–9) the European Neolithic was one such closed, communal world that only exceptionally imported raw materials from beyond its boundaries. Given that these are periods and culture areas where archaeology represents the major source of evidence for historical reconstruction, such entities are condemned to an inferior history and to be a romanticized myth as the embodiment of the simple, the homogeneous and the traditional for the West. Of course, this would not deny each culture area its own historical sequence and cultural content, only that it ensures that the score and the arrangement of parts will have been already preselected and orchestrated from a particular point of view.

The meta-narrative of simple to complex is a dominant ideology that organizes the writing of contemporary world prehistory in favour of a modernizing ethos and the primacy of the West. Its historical context is that of the politics of colonialism and imperialism, and the construction of a civilized identity for all classes within the metropolitan centres. For these reasons, such constructions of history have formed dominant ideologies, although with changes in culture content corresponding to changes in geopolitical centre, e.g., from British linear evolutionism to American neo-evolutionary, multilinear trajectories. Moreover, responses to claims for cultural autonomy and historical independence by a former colonized world have largely taken a form of cognitive apartheid. Each region discovers its own unique form of urbanism, statehood, writing, etc, but the master discourse is still Western-dominated. A universal dialogue about the nature of universal humanity has therefore been sustained, but now with a radical emphasis on variation. There are signs that this universalism is no longer desired in either European or North American archaeologies, and a collapse into an entirely pluralistic universe of incomparable difference is a likely result. What is at issue is not only whether comparison, dialogue, the elucidation and respect for difference will still be possible, but also whether such tendencies are not part of a more general political dissolution and antagonism in global culture (see Friedman, Ch. 16, this volume). If so, what constitutes an adequate response?

The simplest answer follows from what has been said and claims resistance through the 'reactivation of local knowledge', or what Foucault calls 'minor knowledges', as opposed to the hierarchization of knowledge and the effects intrinsic to its power. The problem with this response is that the form that resistance can take cannot be separated from, and may already be defined historically as, an inversion to the dominant mode of discourse. It may have become little more than the oppositional 'Other' of such prevailing forms. Whether it can be a source for pluralizing difference is problematic when knowledge is defined as an inversion of that which prevails. The only escape from the dilemma is to posit that local knowledge can be gained of a real past, the excavation of which forms *the only* authentic path to cultural identity. It does so at a cost which is to claim that authenticity derives from access to a life world that is organic and limited to those encompassed by it. In other words, legitimacy rests on the claim that it is closed to understanding except for those born within it. Of course, in the process, such vitalism mystifies local bases of power and the origins of local domination itself becomes a mystery. In a world economy where identity is, to say the least, problematic, the capacity for such naturalizing of local pasts to serve the needs of local and global domination is already very much in evidence.

A second response, although scabrous of all teleological and totalizing visions of the past, would be equally scathing of claims to 'folk culture' or local knowledge as an authentic, i.e. true, source of creating a sense of difference. This is because such subordinated forms of knowledge come out of, and are therefore internal to, the prevailing dominant mode of conceiving the nature of identity through difference. That all cosmologies may have dominant and subordinate canons and interpretations which may change in relative effect and influence, often in quite regular cycles or in predictable situations, suggests that the interpretations of the dominant and dominated serve together to reproduce the whole. To be truly opposed to any form of dominant knowledge, and try to bypass this relativist notion of resistance, requires a radical disordering of belief in all structures of thought and action on the premise that anarchy is the only defence against a natural tendency towards social closure and exclusion. In this post-structural culture all that remains is to proliferate the lines of resistance to the existing form of domination on an 'anything goes' principle. This strategy runs the risk that it collapses the whole enterprise of writing into the nihilistic enterprise that prehistory can be whatever 'we' take it to be. A local cultural *avant-garde* can form itself around the ethos of resistance to the status quo through the construction of as many accounts of localized pasts as there are people, or social groupings, willing to produce and act towards them. This not only frees the participants from engaging in any genuinely collective project, but the idea that all pasts are essentially incomparable and unique serves to deny any verification process or assertions concerning the capacity for such different versions to account for a reality as externally constituted to them. An unintended consequence of such politics is to reinforce hierarchy, since although the subordinated and the powerless may have identity, the powerful will lay claim to science as the only means of ensuring an independent access to truth and knowledge.

A third response has worked within the recognition that the results of science must be justified by serving political purposes. If the simple to complex meta-narrative served a dominant world order that was intent on modernizing itself, it did so within discrete historical conditions. If it no longer does so, then it is because these conditions have changed. This view argues that there is no longer a simple developed–underdeveloped world. Notions like the Third World are no longer relevant. One consequence of the industrialization of the Third World, it is argued, will be to create a no-doubt fractured, yet for the first time genuinely international, working class. For such a class not to realize itself, it must surely be in the interests of the dominant order to pursue the ideology of local difference and localized culture history, so that an ideology of localized identity and nationalist difference may continue to obscure the realities of internal class contradictions. A simple to complex ideology may thus already be part of a passing global order when it was essential that a cultural hegemony of the core would organize a colonial or neo-colonial periphery. It is by no means certain that this is the case any longer, and that a stress on radical heterogeneity and cultural difference would, in fact, be more compatible with the aims of dominant élites in an industrializing Third World seeking autonomy and identity in order to obscure and mystify the sources of their own power. Moreover, it should be in the interests of their Western counterparts to share in this ideology of radical cultural difference. One of the unintended consequences of examining the notion of complexity in archaeology is, therefore, the irony of creating the very conditions for one mode of domination to replace another without specifying any of the intervening conditions by which prehistory may serve the cause of resistance.

Conclusion

It is the last point that would support the argument that some version of a belief in a scientific basis for world prehistory needs to be safeguarded, at least in terms of a return to a confidence in the Enlightenment project of human liberation being achieved through the rational understanding of our worlds. If the temporal sequencing of simple and complex implies a teleological act of closure, it does so by separating out in time what is experienced as aspects of contemporary reality. It suggests that a creative tension exists between the seeking of wholeness and unity through difference, and a perception that this is defined by its opposite produced by the forces of alienation in modern life. That such an ideal of wholeness and totality has been projected into the past should not obscure the real and genuine desire that exists in modern life for such a sense of identity. Moreover, that both life worlds exist in modern times does not, itself, deny the possibility that similar dualisms existed in the past. To investigate the characterization of difference and the ordering principles of past social totalities by avoiding the conditions which constitute them as characteristic only of the present, defines archaeological study of premodern 'complex societies'.

Acknowledgement

My thanks to Barbara Bender for her comments on this chapter.

References

Anderson, P. 1984. Modernity and revolution. *New Left Review*, **144**, 96–113.
Bender, B. 1989. The roots of inequality. In *Domination and resistance*, D. Miller *et al.* (eds), 83–95. London: Unwin Hyman.
Berrnal, M. 1987. *Black Athena*. London: Free Association Books.
Chang, K. C. 1984. Ancient China and its anthropological significance. *Symbols*, spring/fall issue. Cambridge, Massachusetts: Peabody Museum.
Childe, V. G. 1930. *The Bronze Age*. Cambridge: Cambridge University Press.
Clastres, P. 1977. *Society against the state*. Oxford: Blackwell.
Cohen, R. & E. Service 1978. *Origins of the state*. Philadelphia.
Friedman, J. 1989. Culture, identity and world process. In *Domination and resistance*, D. Miller *et al.* (eds), 246–60. London: Unwin Hyman.
Friedman, J. & M. Rowlands 1977. *The evolution of social systems*. London: Duckworth.
Kapferer, B. 1984. *A celebration of demons*. Bloomington: Indiana University Press.
Lacan, J. 1977. *Ecrits. A selection*. London: Tavistock.
Lamberg-Karlovsky, C. C. 1985. The Near Eastern 'breakout' and the Mesopotamian social contract. *Symbols*, Spring issue. Cambridge, Massachusetts: Peabody Museum.
Larsen, M. T. 1989. Orientalism and Near-Eastern archaeology. In *Domination and resistance*, D. Miller *et al.* (eds), 229–39. London: Unwin Hyman.

Lawrence, D. H. 1986 (1932). *Etruscan places* London: Olive Press.
Leach, E. R. 1969. *Genesis as myth and other essays*. London: Cape.
MacFarlane, A. 1985. The Root of all Evil. In *The anthropology of evil*, D. Parkin (ed.). London: Tavistock.
Morin, E. 1972. *L'homme et la mort*. Paris: L'Harmattan.
Pallottino, M. 1986. Foreword to D. H. Lawrence, *Etruscan places*. London: Olive Press.
Parkin, F. 1979. *Marxism and class theory: a bourgeois critique*. London: Macmillan.
Renfrew, C. 1972. *The emergence of civilisation*. London: Methuen.
Rowlands, M. 1984. Conceptualising the European Bronze and Early Iron Ages. In *European social evolution*, J. Bintliff (ed.). Bradford: Bradford University Press.
Rowlands, M. 1985. Exclusionary tactics in the logic of collective dynamics. *Critique of Anthropology*, **5**(2) 47–69.
Rowlands, M. (in press) European barbarism and the search for authenticity. In *The humanities between art and science*, M. Harbsmeir & M. Larsen (eds). Copenhagen: Verlag Press.
Sahlins, M. 1985. *Islands of history*. Chicago: Chicago University Press.
Saussure, F. de. 1924. *Elements for a course on linguistics* London: Routledge & Kegan Paul.
Spencer, H. 1876. *First principles of sociology* 4th edn. London.
Turner, B. 1986. *The body and society*. Cambridge: Cambridge University Press.
Willey, G. 1985. Ancient Chinese–New World and Near Eastern ideological traditions: some observations. *Symbols*, Spring issue. Cambridge, Massachusetts: Peabody Museum.

2 *Discourse and power: the genre of the Cambridge inaugural lecture*

CHRISTOPHER TILLEY

This chapter is an initial and preliminary attempt to develop a wider programme for relating archaeological work produced in academia to its institutional and social setting. The first section outlines some themes in the analysis of discourse, drawing especially on the work of Foucault. In the second section an analysis is made of the genre of the Cambridge inaugural lecture in archaeology. Especial attention is given to the delimitation of principles underlying these texts. The concern is not so much with the content of what is being said, but why some things are said rather than others. Constitutive of discourse is a complex relationship between desire and power. The texts analysed do not just consist of words and sentences strung together in relation to discursive object (the past), they have power effects in the present. These texts are not being analysed for what they may or may not tell us about the past or the study of the past, but for what they reveal about the sociopolitical context of the production of archaeological knowledge in the present.

Discourse

The analysis of discourse may be considered to be, in the most general sense, the consideration of speech, conversation and texts in terms of their internal dynamics and the 'external' principles structuring what utterance may or may not be made or combined with others in any particular social context. In an obvious way the discourse taking place in a public house will differ markedly from that of the lecture theatre or the seminar room. In considering discourse we are partly concerned with the establishment of argumentative subject positions from the vantage point of a linguistic medium. However, discourse is not simply reducible to the 'ideas' which may or may not be successfully relayed to an audience. To produce a discursive analysis of verbal utterances or graphic traces on the page is to underline the fact that all communication is social. The social contextuality of discourse both permits its construction and simultaneously constrains its forms of appearance. The statements made and the meanings of the words employed depend on the context (where) and in relation to what (other discourses, individuals or institutions) they are to relate. Discourses are always historically and socially positioned and constituted. Any discipline or institution sets up, acts upon and maintains a mode of distribution of discourses and a hierarchy of these discourses. These distributions and hierarchies account for the positions and viewpoints from which a subject speaks and writes. The textual form of discourse permits the storage and physical dissemination of what would otherwise be lost in speech or only retained in tradition or folk memory. Discourses take on their effects and retain their powers either directly or indirectly in relation to other discourses. In other words, discourse is 'intertextual'. There is no pure, unmediated or unsullied text.

Discourses embrace certain objects of concern or knowledge. Learning archaeology is a learning discourse about reality. It is not learning about reality itself, which is something that is always bracketed off. In all discourses some concepts and objects of speech and thought are given priority at the expense of others. Discourse has no end, but individual discourses do. Discourses are not the creation of free individuals, but remain situated and positioned groups of statements. A corollary of this is that the meanings of the words employed are not stable or fixed, but alter according to the discourse in which the words are used. In this sense discourses actively set up their own discursive meanings, meanings which are internal to the discourse and cannot be assimilated to a pure and originary linguistic medium standing outside the discourse and merely used to describe objects or enunciate concepts. So discourse is not simply a subject's way of inhabiting a language, a necessary medium for self-expression. Consequently, discursive relations do not just consist of: (a) a set of ideas; (b) categories of logic; (c) rhetorical tropes; and (d) sentences or propositions. These form important features of discourse, but discursive relations also provide objects about which it is possible or impossible to speak, write and reason. The crucial question that must be addressed is: what are the social conditions of possibility structuring discourse and allowing it to take place?

Discourse and power

These conditions of possibility have been cogently investigated by Foucault in 'The order of discourse' (1981), and will be used here to provide a framework for the discursive analysis which follows in the second section below. Foucault's thesis is that in every society discourses are controlled, selected, organized and distributed in specific ways. He links discourse – the rules, systems and procedures constituted by a 'will to knowledge' – with desire on the one hand and institutional constraint on the other. Discourse forms both an object and manifestation of desire. It is linked to power and social domination, but discourse is not simply negative, 'that which translates struggles or systems of domination, but is the thing for which and by which there is struggle, discourse is the power which is to be seized' (Foucault 1981, pp. 52–3). The effects of discourse depend on its usage and manipulation. Desire wants discourse to be unrestricted, infinitely open, something in which the subject is carried along, with others fitting in with his or her expectations, and truths emerging one by one. Conversely, institutions insist that discourse only comes into being through restraint, control and formalization. It is only in this manner that discourse possesses power. Subjective desire and institutional restraint are aspects of the same material process, constituting each other like the ego and the id.

Foucault analyses discourse in terms of these institutional constraints opposed to subjective desires identifying social controls on the production of discourse and the conditions of its application. The social controls acting on discourse may fall outside it, act internally, or be neither exactly outside nor inside discourse. The external controls are characterized as being principles of exclusion involving (a) prohibitions; (b) divisions; and (c) oppositions.

Prohibitions on the production of discourse are the most obvious. Certain types of speech or writing are forbidden. We all know that we do not have the right to say anything and cannot just speak about anything in any particular circumstances. Discourses become divided into those which are acceptable and socially sanctioned, those worth listening to and those banished from serious consideration, e.g. the division between 'reason' and 'madness'. Perhaps more important is the structuring of discourses around principles of opposition, the most prevalent of which is that between truth and falsity. The search for knowledge is a 'will to truth', and so it is part of a system of exclusion. Empiricism constitutes such a desire for knowledge, a desire which anticipates its own contents and formulates its objects in advance in terms of a scheme of possibilities: observable, measurable, classifiable objects. The will to know these objects is imposed on the knowing subject (the subject who *will* know.) Such a position requires that the subject must see rather than read signs, verify rather than produce commentaries and interpretations. Such a will to truth rests on definite institutional supports and practices which control the permitted discourse in terms of forms of pedagogy, books, libraries and learned societies. It simultaneously produces and constrains discursive practices.

Internal controls on discourse are those constraints whereby discourses operate their own control in terms of principles of classification, ordering and distribution. These are: (a) the commentary; (b) the author; and (c) the discipline. Commentary is a vital component of discourse. Texts generate other texts, and the generation of texts depends on a hierarchy of primary and secondary works. A primary work can endlessly generate secondary works, but it also serves to limit them. Secondary texts go 'beyond' the primary texts and yet can never escape them. Commentary allows us to go beyond the primary text merely to complete it, to fill in the gaps: 'the new thing here lies not in what is said but in the event of its return' (Foucault 1981, p. 58).

The author principle allows the grouping of what may otherwise be a group of disparate texts into a supposed unity. It links discourse by removing elements of chance and randomness, as does the commentary. A group of texts are to be related to a named subject – a self. However, such a principle is also inherently unstable. Are only finished works to be included, or the sum total of an author's writings? Where are the lines to be drawn? Do we include notes, jottings, sketches, shopping lists and partial drafts? The author principle is an attempt to forge coherence on discourse – naming unifies. It also has the effect of creating a subject who will 'cut out, from everything he could say and from all that he does say every day at any moment, the still trembling outline of his oeuvre' (Foucault 1981, p. 59).

Principles of disciplinary unitary stand opposed to the principles of commentary and the author function insofar as disciplines depend primarily on a domain of objects, methods and propositions held to be true at any one time. Disciplines (the very term reveals constraint on desire) consist of rules, definitions, tactics and instruments formalizing their own will to truth. The discipline is constituted essentially as an anonymous system at the disposal of anyone who is willing to work within it and on its own terms. Disciplines fix limits to permitted discourse, sift between potentially true or false statements, proper and improper knowledges: 'any system of education is a political way of maintaining or modifying the appropriation of discourses, along with the knowledges and powers which they carry' (Foucault 1981, p. 64).

A third set of constraints on discourse are neither external nor external to it, but consist of principles of discursive application: the imposition and stipulation of roles on speaking and writing subjects. Not just anyone is permitted to occupy these roles. The educational and institutional system divides and gives some individuals the right to speak, to make themselves heard, excluding others. An archaeological or a medical statement to be accepted as an archaeological or medical statement cannot be made by just anyone. Learned societies serve to preserve certain statements and speaking roles as opposed to others. Journals, presses and editors both create and restrain discursive possibilities, acting both positively and negatively as part of a system of power and social control. Doctrinal practices link subjects to specific types of enunciation rather than to others. 'Doctrine brings about a double subjection: of the speaking subjects to discourses, and of discourses to the (at least virtual) group of speaking individuals' (Foucault 1981, p. 64).

Foucault links these three sets of constraints on discourse with a number of dominant intellectual traditions. Philosophy has traditionally been a form of discourse lending itself perfectly to limitations and exclusions in proposing the notion of some kind of asocial truth as a law for the formation of discourses and a notion of immanent rationality as a principle for the unfolding of this truth. This has led to a denial of the specificity of discursive relations in particular historical and social settings. Western thought has always tended to 'squeeze' discourse and compress it into the smallest possible space between thought and speech. Discourse is conceived as merely a bridge between speaking and thinking, denying discourse its autonomy. Of course, to ascribe an autonomy to discourse is not to deny that it has real and material social conditions of existence.

Foucault argues that we should problematize our will to truth and restore to discourse its character as an event, throwing off the notion of a sovereignty of the signifier and its relation to the sign. In other words, we should examine the social constraints on discourse, considering discourse as structured event rather than creative process and avoid reducing discourse simply to the text. In order to do this, Foucault suggests we should understand discourse in terms of four principles: reversion, discontinuity, specificity and exteriority.

The principle of reversion moves us away from the notion that discourse has its sources solely in the author, discipline or 'will to truth'. These ideas cut up or are a rarefaction of discourse. We oppose the idea of the *creation* of discourse with that of the *event* of discourse. The principle of discontinuity is one that views discourses as constituting a discontinuous series variously interacting, juxtaposed to, and excluding, each other. This opposes the strongly held notions of there being an essential unity to a work, a theme, an epoch or a discipline. The principle of specificity suggests that we cannot think of discourse in terms of a play of pre-existing signification, a connection of language to the world. Instead, there is a radical gap between language and the world. Discourse is a violence we do to things, a practice we impose. The principle of exteriority is one which requires that we do not analyse discourse in terms of some inner core of meaning inherent within it. We move from an analysis of the inside of a text to its external conditions of possibility – the external conditions that make it possible for a discourse to be a discourse and which give rise to the specific forms of the appearances of discourses. We analyse the manner in which discourses are fixed in relation to each other, and post limits on social practices and the construction of alternative discourses. Foucault thus proposes to replace four traditional notions in the history of ideas (creativity, unity, originality and signification) with an alternative set of concepts: the event, the series, regularity and conditions of possibility:

event–creation
series–unity
regularity–originality
conditions of possibility–signification

The fundamental concepts in analysing discourse are no longer consciousness and continuity, with their correlates, freedom and causality, nor sign and structure, but the event and the series. Discourse in such a conception is a series of discursive events having definite conditions of possibility and arranged in a series, a discontinuous series. This moves us away from the idea of discourses simply building on each other in a mechanical way, as in traditional representations of the histories of disciplines, and reinstates the importance of the social and political conditions surrounding the production of discourse – discourse as a contingent production. Discourse is to be studied in relation to power, as a form of power and as a way of creating and maintaining social divisions. Discourse is also a power which may be seized to subvert these divisions. So discourses are neither necessarily subservient to dominant power structures nor are they automatically raised up against them. Rather, they are indelibly situated in relation to power. They can form a point of resistance to power, and the starting point for a strategy resisting repression.

Discourse, discursive formations, discursive modalities

The term discourse, as already mentioned, generally refers to any individual or series of discursive acts (speaking or writing). We can identify 'discursive formations' if: (a) statements refer to one particular object; (b) there is a regular 'style' in which the statements are situated, a common way in which the statements are made; (c) there is a regularity in the manner in which concepts are employed; (d) the statements support a common theme or a recognizable pattern. To identify a discursive formation (which may or may not coincide with a 'paradigm', to use a more familiar term) we need to reveal the systems of rules and relations underlying the discourses in question. These rules and relations will make possible and sustain the object(s) of the discourse, i.e. what it is about. Such discursive formations are not fixed, but are constituted by a system involving the dispersion of statements:

> Whenever one can describe, between a number of statements, such a system of dispersion, whenever between objects, types of statement, concepts, or thematic choices, one can define a regularity . . . we are dealing with a *discursive formation*. (Foucault 1972, p. 38.)

A discursive formation consists of a set of statements defined not by the identity of these statements (as repetitions, propositions or sentences) but by their systematic dispersal in the texts, their relations to objects of discourse, concepts and thematic choices. By a *discursive modality* will be meant here a subset of a discursive formation, a particular genre that inhabits any particular discursive formation. It is to the analysis of such a genre, the genre of the Cambridge inaugural lecture in archaeology, that the discussion now turns.

The Cambridge inaugural lecture

The Cambridge Chair of Archaeology was founded by John Disney in 1851, and since then the Chair has been occupied by ten incumbents:

John Disney (founder of the chair in 1851)
The Reverend John Marsden (1851–1865)
Churchill Babington (1865–1879)
Percy Gardener (1879–1887)
The Reverend George Browne (1887–1892)
Sir William Ridgeway (1892–1926)
Sir Ellis Minns (1926–1938)
Dorothy Garrod (1938–1952)
Grahame Clark (1952–1974)

Glyn Daniel (1974–1981)
Colin Renfrew (1981–)

In this section the inaugural lectures of the last four Disney Professors will be analysed (Garrod 1946, Clark 1954, Daniel 1976, Renfrew 1982). The Disney Chair was only made a full Chair of Archaeology in 1927, and it is from that date that the Cambridge inaugural lecture in archaeology (hereafter IL) has taken on its recognizably modern form. Previous Disney Professors sometimes gave 'introductory lectures' in archaeology, but these were substantially different from the ILs since World War II.

The IL is particularly interesting to analyse because it may be held to be a manifestation of the sociopolitical micropractices of power in the academy in a particularly visible form. The four texts analysed must be understood as texts, and therefore as divorced and somewhat transformed relics of the particular social events from which they are derived. In other words, the printed IL is the sifted and subsequently embalmed speech of the Disney Professor, preserved for posterity. Speech in public is immediately theatrical, a collection of cultural and oratorical codes which are largely lost in the texts. This is not to suggest that speech has an inbuilt spontaneity and that the text is lacking in some way, but it is necessary to point out that speech and text constitute different forms of mediation between the subject and the world. The body of the text ceases to coincide with the person who formulated it. It lacks the speaker's image repertoire, but gains another power in that it can be read and re-read, permitting time to uncover aspects of structure and meaning which may not be readily apparent within the discursive time–space of the event of its delivery.

Rhetoric and genre

The IL performs work in the world. It has a persuasive and rhetorical end. Rhetoric, classical or modern – the term meaning here quite simply something written without any derogatory connotations – can be divided into five moments: *inventio*, the search for argumentative matter; *dispositio*, the arrangement of arguments; *elocutio*, the verbal adornment of matter; *memoria*, the memorizing of the adorned text; and *actio* and *pronuntiatio*, the visual and auditory delivery (see Pleet 1985). These five moments account for and constitute part of the content of the IL, the rhetorical style differing markedly between the speakers. In concerning ourselves with rhetorical style we are emphasizing differences between the lectures. The employment of rhetorical devices partly construct the speaker or authors making him or her more 'visible'.

By contrast, a consideration of genre requires that we search for similarities, underlying discursive rules and relations which reside beneath the rhetorical surface and connect the lectures together as a discursive modality operating within a wider discursive formation. Here we are analysing something rather different from the discursive tropes and strategies employed. We are not primarily concerned with the names (Garrod, Clark, Daniel and Renfrew) stamped on the lectures, although they will have to be employed. For the purposes of most of this analysis these names are largely interchangeable, and we will be concerned with the rules of formation for the lectures going substantially beyond their rhetorical surfaces of difference. The argument is that the discursive genre of the IL determines in part what position can be occupied and what statements can be made by an individual speaker. The Disney Professor is not a free agent. The content of what may be said in the IL and the way in which it may be said is restricted by the genre of the IL itself. In analysing the IL's genre we are not very interested in argumentative content. These lectures are not being read or interpreted to relay or criticize the detailed content of any arguments made. We are more interested in what has been said in relation to what is left unsaid, and the manner in which words or statements are made and their relations of dispersion in the texts. We are not attempting to recover the intentions of the speakers, but the principles underlying the genre in which they find themselves positioned and situated.

The inaugural lecture as a rite of passage

The IL represents a personal rite of passage. First, and in an obvious sense, it is a formal university public lecture in which the newly elected professor presents himself or herself and establishes a position in the university. It marks the inhabitation of power by a new dominant tongue. The Disney Professor speaks from a specific institutional site, which partly determines what can and cannot be said. He or she is sanctioned by tradition and precedent to speak to a university and not just to an archaeological audience. The impact of the speech derives more from the institution than from the individual giving it.

Secondly, and like virtually all rites of passage, the inaugural lecture may be held to have a basic tripartite structure. It moves from (a) the secure ground of tracing ancestral links with previous Disney Professors (see below) to (b) moving out into a 'liminal' discursive space in which the speaker puts forward his or her particular theme – the relationship between environment, tools and human groups for Garrod, the nature of prehistoric studies for Clark, the history of Cambridge archaeology for Daniel, and cognitive archaeology for Renfrew – defining an actual or possible object for archaeology as a discursive practice, and finally returning to (c) basic justifications for the study of archaeology or the role of Cambridge archaeology, or both, in the world. The 'liminal' period is longest for Garrod and shortest for Daniel. It is particularly marked in Renfrew's lecture. This is partly because, unlike his predecessors, whose lectures consist basically of rehearsing ideas already well worked out elsewhere in their work, Renfrew consciously uses the occasion to suggest a new dimension to archaeological theory and practice.

The final phase of the lectures involving the justification for the study of archaeology *in general* is absolutely essential to legitimate the position of the Disney Professor. The 'liminal' phase may or may not be widely accepted as important by the audience, but basic justifications for archaeology, irrespective of the particular characteristics or points of view put forward, are much more crucial and likely to be acknowledged. The justifications given are, for Garrod, archaeology as a humanistic pursuit of change and development throughout the human past connecting with our present. The past is 'like a skein with a mass of broken ends, yet . . . somewhere within that skein . . . is the thread which leads clear back from us here on earth to-day to the lowly forbears' (Garrod 1946, p .29). Renfrew (1982, p. 28) asserts the importance of the 'universality of the study of the early past of humankind' and that archaeology is 'one of the few humane disciplines which is relevant to anyone, whatever their land of origin' (1982, p. 29). Daniel ends with a quote from Worsaae suggesting that it is inconceivable for a nation which cares about itself and its identity not to study the past. He also reminds the audience that the past is something to be appreciated and 'enjoyed as our common heritage . . . Through archaeology we own the pleasures of past time, as well as its historical witness' (Daniel 1976, p. 30). Clark (1954, p. 35) asserts 'the veneration of antiquity is surely an emotion worthy of cultivation. . . Reverence for a common past is the sheet-anchor of patriotic feeling'.

These justifications situate the 'value' of archaeology in a field of exteriority. Part of the unity of archaeology is its appeal to claimed natural aspirations of humankind: nationalism, patriotism, liberalism, a need to trace ancestry, pleasure, and the cultivation and pursuit of knowledge in general. Archaeology is relevant because it upholds and nurtures these 'natural' and 'universal' human needs.

Principles of the genre

As the IL is directed towards a university rather than a purely archaeological audience, this contrains the discourse to be a particular kind of address – general rather than specific. The IL provides, first, a commentary about archaeological objects and events in a general way: a definitional principle mapping out relevant archaeological objects of past or future discursive practice. This is the most obvious aspect of the substantive argumentative content of the IL, and the least interesting from the point of view of this analysis. Secondly, the IL operates on a genealogical principle involving the requirement to trace ancestry. Thirdly, it involves a principle of institutional and disciplinary division and comparison. Archaeology is defined in its difference, its irreducibility and even its heterogeneity. Fourthly, it establishes a principle of internationalism (or imperialism). Fifthly, it aims to create and sustain social relations, a principle of interpersonality. Sixthly, it establishes a personal role and function for the speaker. Each of these principles of the genre will be considered below, with attention also being paid to the rhetorical strategies involved in their presentation.

Defining objects of archaeological discourse All of the speakers from Garrod to Renfrew (prehistorians) are self-conscious of the Chair having been held previously by six classical archaeologists or 'men of letters', and that

Marsden, in his introductory lecture, attempted to define the Chair as one of classical rather than 'general' archaeology. Babington, the second professor, took a broader view of the subject. In all the ILs Babington is used either directly or indirectly to define the proper discursive object of the Disney Chair as prehistory. This may be accompanied by playing off Babington's views against those of the unenlightened Marsden.

Daniel briefly traces the surfaces of emergence of archaeology as a contemporary social practice in relation to antiquarianism. For Garrod the discursive space of archaeology is marked out as the relationship between the physical environment and the functional use of tools. Ethnography can flesh out such a discursive space more fully:

> The proper method is to compare the whole economy of a modern primitive people with the economy . . . of a prehistoric people at approximately the same stage of social development, and living under similar conditions. Thus Sollas' comparison of the Mousterian, the Aurignacian and the Mousterian cultures with those of the Australian, the Bushmen and the Eskimo respectively is, in the main, legitimate. (Garrod 1946, p. 16.)

Similarly, for Clark, archaeology is defined as dealing with artefacts, the interrelationship of people and nature, and especially the reconstruction of economic practices. As well as being supposedly empirically predicated with regard to the nature of archaeological data, this is also a matter of disciplinary honour:

> Indeed as a matter of principle . . . let us each stick to his own last: for those whose interests lie in the field of social structure, there are still plenty of societies functioning without having to resurrect dead ones. (Clark 1954, pp. 28–9.)

Renfrew, by contrast, attempts to set out a new domain of discursive objects for archaeology involving a middle-range theory approach to prehistoric cognitive processes. Now there is nothing particularly remarkable about this specification, extension, modification and diversification of grids of possible archaeological discursive objects delimiting what archaeological discourse is supposed to be about: realistic goals for archaeological practice. Nor is it surprising that empiricist canons of evidence should be adhered to. What is more interesting is the manner in which these (and other) archaeological discourses internally limit themselves, tie themselves down to narrow confines and restrict possibilities for discursive practice. The ILs do not open out the past to human agency in the present, but impose a will to truth strictly confining possibilities for knowledge. Little ventured – little gained.

Establishing genealogies An important component of the genre of the Cambridge inaugural lecture is a process of establishing power and authority in the present – in this case the *right* to speak as a new Disney

Professor – by means of reference to the past. One form such legitimation characteristically takes is the insertion of the speaker into an already established ancestral genealogy. It amounts to the production of fictive kinship links with non-blood 'relatives', variously referred to as 'predecessors', 'successors', 'Chair holders' or 'Disneys'. The newly elected Disney Professor situates and positions himself or herself within an historical line of succession in a manner analogous to royalty. All four inaugural lectures begin by establishing ancestry.

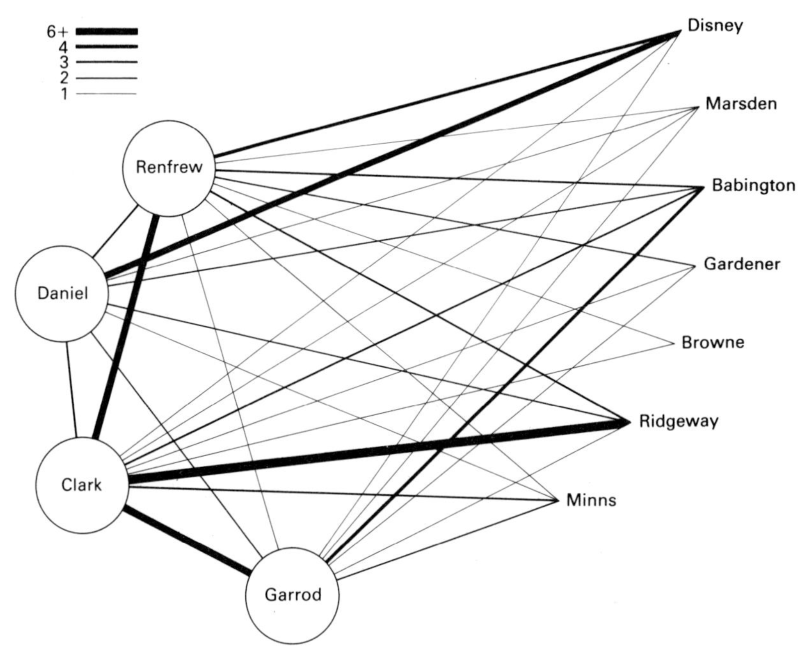

Figure 2.1 The frequency with which previous Disney professors are named in the texts of the inaugural lectures of Garrod, Clark, Daniel and Renfrew.

The simplest form consists of a list of names and dates, sometimes accompanied by the stipulation of specific subject areas. This is part of the strategy adopted, in particular, by Garrod and Clark:

> Percy Gardener (1879–87) was a classical archaeologist . . . the next Professor, the Rev. G. F. Browne (1887–92), later to be Bishop of Bristol, was a student of the later Anglo-Saxon period. (Clark 1954, p. 3.)

There may be varying degrees of completeness and incorporation. Renfrew and Clark assiduously name all their predecessors, whereas Garrod and Daniel leave one or two out of the account. In terms of the specifics of the genealogies, varying degrees of emphasis my be placed *vis-à-vis* specific ancestors, which may be assessed in terms of the number of times they are specifically named in the course of the lecture (Fig. 2.1). The importance of genealogical links is clearly greatest for Clark and Renfrew. Gardener and Browne, in all cases, constitute a genealogical weak point.

Creating ancestral links by mere naming of predecessors is clearly insufficient, and another essential feature is to quote the words of at least some of your ancestors. Renfrew employs nine separate quotations from the works of the first five Disney Professors, and also includes the founder of the Chair. Garrod quotes twice from Babington, whereas Clark cites Babington once and Marsden three times. A clear trend is evident here (Fig. 2.2): the more ancient the predecessor is, the greater the likelihood they will be specifically cited. In this respect it is particularly appropriate to cite the first Disney Professor. Although Daniel does not quote directly from any of his predecessors, he more than makes up for this by either mentioning or discussing the founder of the chair, John Disney, no less than seven times. It is significant that immediate ancestors are never directly quoted. When such a 'presence' of a previous Professor is required in the course of the lecture, the strategy adopted is to assert fidelity with distant rather than more recent ancestors. The Chair founder or the first Professor, Marsden, take on added significance precisely because they constitute a point of origin, the initiation of archaeology as an institutionally sanctioned discursive practice at Cambridge. Their resurrection or 'rediscovery' ritualizes authority, providing an avenue of return to the present.

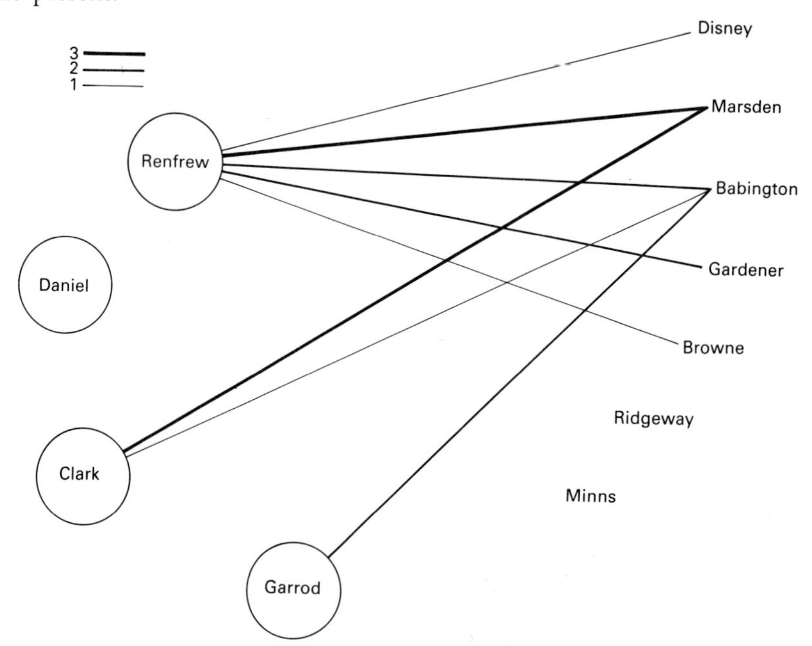

Figure 2.2 The frequency of quotations from previous Disney Professors in the inaugural lectures.

Quotation is frequently accompanied by the direct naming of books or articles by previous Professors. Here it is more appropriate to refer to the work of immediate predecessors. Renfrew is most thorough in this regard, diligently referring either in the course of his lecture or in the endnotes, or in both, to one or more of the works of his predecessors, including the inaugural lectures of Garrod, Clark and Daniel. Daniel mentions Clark's books three times, and Clark refers to Garrod's IL.

Of course, intertextuality is a prominent feature of the IL. Reference to the work of other Disney Professors has already been mentioned. The speakers are also aware, either at a level of practical or discursive consciousness, of the particular tropology required in the discursive form of the lecture. Furthermore, the footnotes and some passages make it clear that in order to write an IL it is necessary to have read one first and, ideally, go one stage further. Renfrew's lecture, the last, is absolutely exemplary in this respect. He not only covers some of the basic ground dealt with in previous lectures (e.g., reference to the early Disney Professors, justifications for archaeology, the importance of Cambridge in the world), but goes much further in terms of introducing a new discursive object for archaeology (see above). Intertextuality is manifest at a specific as well as a general level. For example, at one point in his lecture Daniel complains about the 'gobbledygook' jargon of the 'new' archaeology (Daniel 1976, p. 28). Renfrew covertly replies to this, citing a quote from Evans (1897) and another from Tollius drawn from one of Daniel's own books, demonstrating that jargon is hardly absent even in the writings of antiquaries.

Detailed personal biographical details of previous Disney Professors are surprisingly rare, their subjectivity is largely deemed irrelevant. Clark, Renfrew, and especially Daniel, discuss the Chair founder's aspirations and background. Mention of others remain purely side issues. For example, Clark refers to Ridgeway's apparent 'horror of cross-cousin marriage' (Clark 1954, p. 4) and 'fascination with barbarians' (1954, p. 5).

In the context of the IL the speaker walks on a tightrope. On the one hand the importance of their own distinctive approach to archaeology needs to be made clear. On the other hand the importance of precedent and genealogical ties must be maintained. A complex and subtle strategy of self-definition by both establishing bonds of solidarity and contrasts in relation to previous Professors is required: incorporation and opposition. When referring to one's ancestors, 'learned', 'distinguished', 'eminent' and 'erudite' are appropriate epithets. To indulge in much explicit criticism of their work on this very public occasion would inevitably weaken and detract from the status of the speaker, for part of their power and significance resides in the past. A studied deference is required. What is important is not what they may have done, said or written, but the event of their return in the IL. So Daniel refers to the introductory lectures of Marsden and Babington as 'full of good sense and interest' (Daniel 1976, p. 11), and Clark draws comfort from:

> the fact that the Disney Chair has been too long established and that

> it has been held by too many distinguished archaeologists for its standing to be seriously impaired by any single occupant. There is indeed a majesty in antiquity, and a professor of archaeology may be excused for glorying in it. (Clark 1954, p. 1.)

The naming and quotation of previous Disney Professors, particularly the first four occupants of the post, is quite obviously a tactical ploy, and part of the trope of giving an IL at Cambridge. Although not claiming to have read all the work of the last four Disney Professors, if these early Disney Professors were really so auspicious the absence of previous references or quotations from them in the major works of Garrod, Clark, Daniel or Renfrew is really rather surprising.

The importance of Cambridge: institutional division and comparison All archaeological institutions and archaeologists are equal, but some are more equal than others. An evaluative hierarchical structure of universities in Britain, with Cambridge and Oxford residing together as uneasy bedfellows at the zenith, is well known. A certain degree of personal and academic prestige may perhaps be gained by relating, associating or playing-off one university against the other. Naturally, in the lectures Cambridge University or Cambridge colleges are referred to with some frequency. Clark makes 20 separate references, Renfrew 19 and Daniel 36. The only other university in the world mentioned by Garrod or Renfrew is Oxford. Clark mentions five other universities, one of which is Oxford, whereas Daniel mentions 12 other universities, including eight separate references to Oxford. Daniel and Clark are particularly self-conscious of the 'need' to situate Oxford in a comparative perspective. Daniel (1976, pp. 1,18) notes that:

> Oxford can claim without doubt priority over us in one necessary aspect of archaeology, namely the provision of a museum. . . Oxford has no C14 laboratory.

and (1976, pp. 11,19–20)

> In the early eighties there were rumours that Oxford was awakening to the fact that it ought to have an archaeological Chair . . . If we ever have a Chair of American Archaeology here . . . it ought to be called the Maudslay Chair. He was a Trinity Hall man . . . and had honorary Doctorates of Science from both ourselves and Oxford.

The third Disney Professor, Gardener, was no doubt somewhat a black sheep. Both Clark and Renfrew note his defection to Oxford! Clark (1954, p. 10) contrasts the views of prehistory of Hawkes, at Oxford, and those of Sir Mortimer Wheeler with his own:

> It is natural to Cambridge men to take a more detached, scientific view of the past.

Solidarity is thus forged with the Cambridge audience. The IL operates indirectly as a discursive struggle with other institutions and academics.

The IL goes substantially beyond mere ethnocentricism to establish a remarkably hermetic 'Cambridgeocentric' world viewpoint. This can be readily assessed from those named individuals referred to in the lectures. The only foreign archaeologists Renfrew refers to in the text of his lecture are Binford (twice) and the Abbé Breuil, and British non-Cambridge archaeologists are similarly few. This pattern of lack of reference to non-British and non-Cambridge archaeologists is repeated in the lectures of Clark and Daniel. Garrod hardly bothers to mention anyone at all.

Internationalism The importance of the Disney Professorship is presented as not only being of regional or national, but of international significance. Again, the importance of precedent and antiquity loom large here. Daniel introduces his lecture by stating that the Disney Chair is the oldest in the British Isles. He goes on to admit that it is not the oldest chair of archaeology in Europe (i.e the world), that distinction belonging to Sweden. Nevertheless, something can be salvaged by virtue of the claim (incorrect) that 'we [Cambridge University] have been professionally in this business longer than any other university in western Europe' (Daniel 1976, p. 4). Clark consciously broadens out such an approach, noting in the introduction to his inaugural lecture that the Cambridge Chair is 'by a substantial margin the senior one devoted to archaeology in the British Commonwealth' (Clark 1954, p. 1).

The global scope of Cambridge research is much emphasized. No part of the Earth's surface should remain unprobed by Cambridge scholars. The tentacle-like arms of the Cambridge Archaeology Department should ideally encompass and incorporate within its own interpretative framework the distant past of the entirety of humankind, brooking no regard for national, international, ethnic, linguistic or geographical boundaries. Renfrew (1982, p. 6) praises the 'global scope' of Clark's *World prehistory* and Daniel's *First civilisations*, and notes that at Cambridge University the archaeology of the Near East, India, Africa, the Pacific, the Far East as well Europe can be taught (1982, p. 28). An area of evident concern both for him and for Daniel (1976, p. 19) is that with the death of Bushnell the archaeology of the Americas escapes the ambit of the Cambridge department (a problem which has now been solved). Renfrew (1982, p. 28) also notes that Cambridge graduates fill senior positions in universities over the entire world. Clark (1954, p. 14) states with pride that:

> we can count ourselves fortunate that while scholars nodded in sundry studies, men and women of a more scientific temper went out into the field, it might be to the Torres Straits, Greece, the Fayum, Mount Carmel, Greenland . . . to apply the techniques of scientific research in the vast laboratory which is the world of all ages.

Clearly Cambridge's global incorporation of world prehistory and expansionist tendencies lend increasing importance to the role of the Disney Professorship. They also fit perfectly Trigger's (1984) category of imperialist archaeology.

Establishing social relations Attaining the position of Disney Professor at Cambridge can in many ways be taken to represent the pinnacle of archaeological achievement in Britain: one can go no higher. Thereafter advancement depends on extra-disciplinary factors, such as being appointed Master of a Cambridge college, Vice-Chancellor of the University or, perhaps, obtaining a knighthood or being made a member of the House of Lords. All four speakers acknowledge what a great honour has been bestowed on them, but remain only partially conscious of the power effects of their discourse. One feature of the IL, utilized by Clark, Daniel and Renfrew, is the forging or maintenance of connections with other disciplines or powerful individuals in those disciplines. Other professors at Cambridge are referred to using formal titles, e.g, 'My colleague, the William Wyse Professor of Social Anthropology . . .' (Clark 1954, p. 14, cf. Renfrew 1982, pp. 7, 26). Chair names of non-Cambridge professors (irrespective of whether they possess them) are not used. Lesser colleagues in the archaeology department may also be mentioned, and in this connection it is interesting to note that Garrod and Daniel more or less point to potential successors (Garrod 1946, p. 11, Daniel 1976, p. 28).

In some respects the Disney Professor operates in a similar way to Malinowski's description of the chief as a 'tribal banker'. He or she is no longer in a situation involving competition for prestige and power with immediate peers (although competition may still operate on a global scale – perhaps somewhat stultified by the absence of a Nobel Prize – at an interdisciplinary level or with renowned archaeologists of the past), hence the redistribution of largesse and honours on others, painting either with very broad strokes (Clark 1954, pp. 25,33):

> Let us not forget . . . the contributions made and still being made by Cambridge men and women to quaternary research in far-off lands . . . I would particularly like to recall the distinguished part played by Cambridge men in the prehistory of the New World.

or a finer-grained perspective (Daniel 1976, pp. 20–1, cf. Renfrew 1982, pp. 27–8):

> We are fortunate at the moment in having the archaeology of Oceania and Australia taught by Peter Gathercole . . . and of having African archaeology taught not only by John Alexander and Pat Carter . . .

is entirely appropriate within the context of the IL.

Contemporary academic hierarchies involving competition, achievement, power and authority find strong support in the IL of Clark. He claims that the driving force of cultural change throughout history is dependent upon emulation processes and increased 'opportunities for social competition' associated with cultural diversification and subdivisions of labour (Clark 1954, p. 30), a theme that he has subsequently widened to suggest that capitalist society is too egalitarian (Clark 1979, 1983).

In the IL there is space and time for the incorporation of a fair number of quotations and the naming of individuals other than previous Disney Professors. Daniel excels in the discursive arena of naming and quoting. In his text individuals are named on no less than 179 occasions. In all he manages to refer to no less than 111 different individuals. Almost everyone is there from sisters of Babylonian kings to Shakespeare and Napoleon. In a relation of monotony, name is piled upon name upon name. The majority are quite transparently irrelevant to his chosen theme of the history of archaeological studies at Cambridge, for example (Daniel 1976, p. 4):

> Eugene O'Curry was made Professor of Irish Antiquities in the Catholic University in Dublin in 1854: his first two courses of lectures were attended by a young man who subsequently became Cardinal Newman.

Almost all Daniel's IL is an immense, rambling, name-dropping exercise, including both Cambridge antiquaries and his contemporaries. At one point (1976, pp. 12–13) he actually goes so far as to 'explain' this practice:

> I have learnt, as many of us have over the years, that not only in national politics but in the minor politics of city and university life, it is tactically and strategically not declared policies and principles that really matter but people and practice and personalities and the goodwill that can be engendered.

'The goodwill that can be engendered' – Daniel's IL is quite nakedly to do with his own personal power and prestige – something which the other Disney Professors at least have the modesty partially to conceal. This leads us to the role of the IL in establishing an institutional position for the individual speaker.

Prestige: mastery and incorporation A Disney Professor must demonstrate in the IL knowledge and erudition not only in his or her particular field or subfield, but of the general pursuit of human knowledge. The connotations of power are to be clothed in the elegant form of art and learning. Such academic mastery may be shown in a variety of ways – in quotations, the naming of books, individuals or disciplines, in footnotes or perhaps the use of foreign languages. Of course, there is a limit to how much may be accomplished in about an hour or in the space of only around 30 pages – the average length of the IL. Emphasis may be placed on various dimensions (Fig. 2.3). All except Renfrew avoid heavy referencing. Use of a foreign language is surprisingly confined to a few French words or phrases in common English parlance, although the odd sentence is occasionally clearly acceptable (Renfrew 1982, p. 22, Daniel 1976, p. 3). Daniel also manages to insert Dutch, Latin and one Danish word. Renfrew demonstrates knowledge of sociobiology, rotating neutron stars, social theory, anthropology and philosophy, either in quotations or in the process of his discourse, mentions Hamlet and Thucydides, and ends with a lengthy citation from Sophocles' *Antigone*.

One feature that might be analysed further is the actual quotation pattern. The relative absence of named non-British and non-Cambridge archaeologists has already been mentioned. Apart from former Disney Professors, those archaeologists who are actually quoted are generally prehistorians working outside Cambridge. Garrod quotes from two

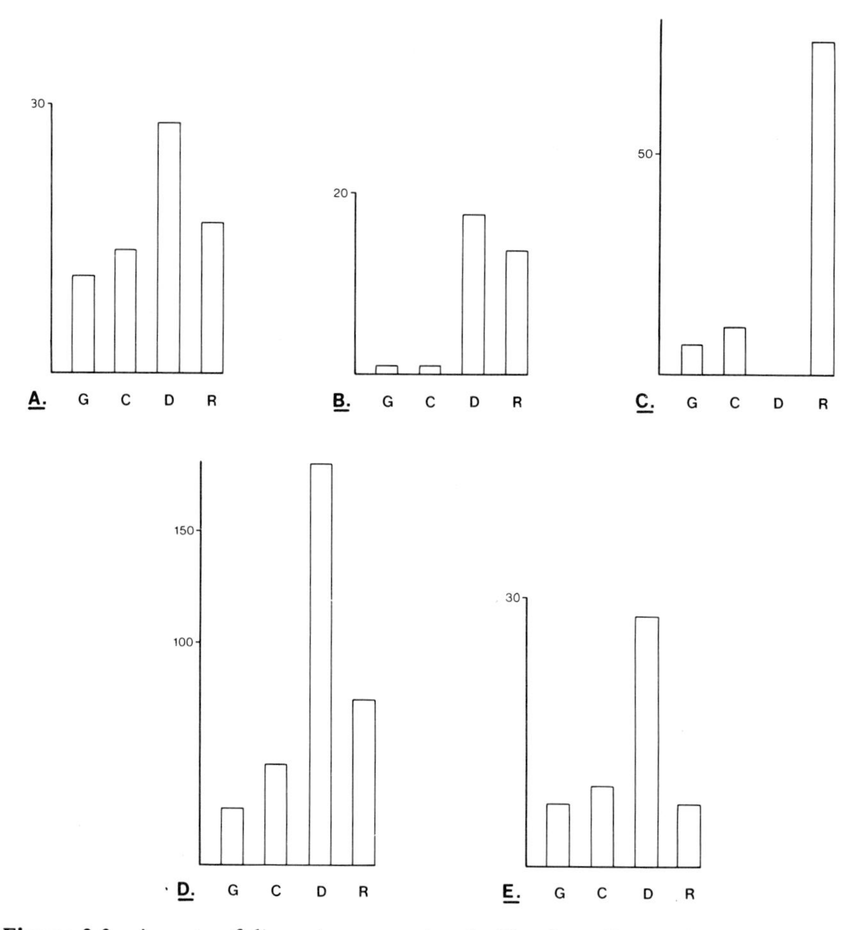

Figure 2.3 Aspects of discursive strategies: A. Number of quotations. B. Number of books or articles referred to by title in the text. C. Number of footnotes. D. Number of times individuals named in the text. E. Number of quotations, excluding those from Disney Professors. G = Garrod, C = Clark, D = Daniel, R = Renfrew.

non-Cambridge archaeologists and two historians. Clark similarly quotes from two non-Cambridge archaeologists, three anthropologists, and Toynbee, Linton, Marx and Stern. Renfrew again quotes from two non-Cambridge archaeologists, two antiquaries, and from Walpole, Cassirer, Feibleman and Sophocles. Daniel is altogether more liberal, citing a wide range of fairly obscure antiquaries and a galaxy of literary writers including Shakespeare, Siegfried Sassoon and Shackerley Marmon, while paraphrasing Aubrey and A. E Housman. The general picture to emerge is that of a fine balance between non-Cambridge archaeologists and non-archaeological writers. Obviously, from exactly *whom* a Disney Professor should cite, apart from other Disney Professors, is a delicate matter.

What is particularly interesting is the use of writers who have nothing whatsoever to do with the discipline of archaeology to define what archaeology is or should be. Renfrew (1982, p. 1) uses Horace Walpole to define the nature of archaeological data (1982, p. 1) and Sophocles to define archaeology as the complex study of both the thoughts and actions of humanity. For Daniel and Clark Dr Johnson performs a similar role, and he is referred to negatively in order to assert the positive value of the study of prehistoric material culture. Clark uses Toynbee to suggest the dynamism of prehistoric social groups, whereas Garrod refers to Carlyle and Trevelyan to suggest that a scientific understanding of humanity will always prove to be inadequate. All of this is rather surprising: has no archaeologist defined archaeological data in a satisfactory manner, or the aims and goals of the discipline? Such quotation obviously has the rhetorical purpose of broadening out and enlivening the scope of the lecture. None of the quotations is taken up or analysed in any detail, thereby pointing to their purpose as embroidery. They also help to enhance considerably the distinction, status and prestige of the speaker – his or her cultural capital.

The use of non-archaeological writers can be a productive exercise in breaking down the academic disciplinary space that restrains discourse, but this is not the use to which they are put in the IL. Their purpose is precisely the opposite: to re-establish a supposed identity of archaeology, maintaining its distance and autonomy from other disciplines. The quotations in the IL remain marginal devices (often physically), lacking integration into the text. Their meaning and use is often to imply that 'we are all the same, share the same aspirations, and always have done so for as long as matters'. They mask divisions, different aspirations and struggles.

At one stage in his IL Daniel even refers to himself as an 'emperor' engaged in 'empire building' (somewhat jokingly) (Daniel 1976, p. 22), but such an allegorical reference to his own position and newly found authority is not so far from the truth. He both quotes from and refers to his own books. He also quotes from a previous inaugural lecture as Professor of the History of Art at the University of Hull, and mentions his Donald Dudley Memorial lecture at Birmingham. He obviously draws some satisfaction from noting that the first two Disney Professors came from his own Cambridge college, St John's, mentioning in addition the St

John's antiquaries Purchas and Henneage. He also puts in a plug for Anglia Television (of which he was a director), makes reference to influential friends such as the Vice–Chancellor at Oxford, and mentions that he is the chairman of various committees. Daniel's IL demonstrates perfectly the truth of that old adage: 'It's not what you know but who you know that counts'. In the context of Daniel's self–glorification, that he refers to ordinary men and women (i.e non–academics) as 'that great non-scholarly mob' (Daniel 1976, p. 29) comes as little surprise.

What really is being said, and why? Who is the IL addressed to? The speaker? The audience? Sub-sections of the audience? For important individuals? Or for all? The speakers may place different degrees of emphasis on themselves as speakers, relating to an audience. At a fine level this can be seen in the use of first-, second- or third-person singulars or plurals. The use of 'I', 'myself', 'my' and 'me' obviously emphasizes themselves as speakers, whereas 'we', 'our', 'us', 'you', 'your' and 'one' may suggest more of a feeling of solidarity and communality with the

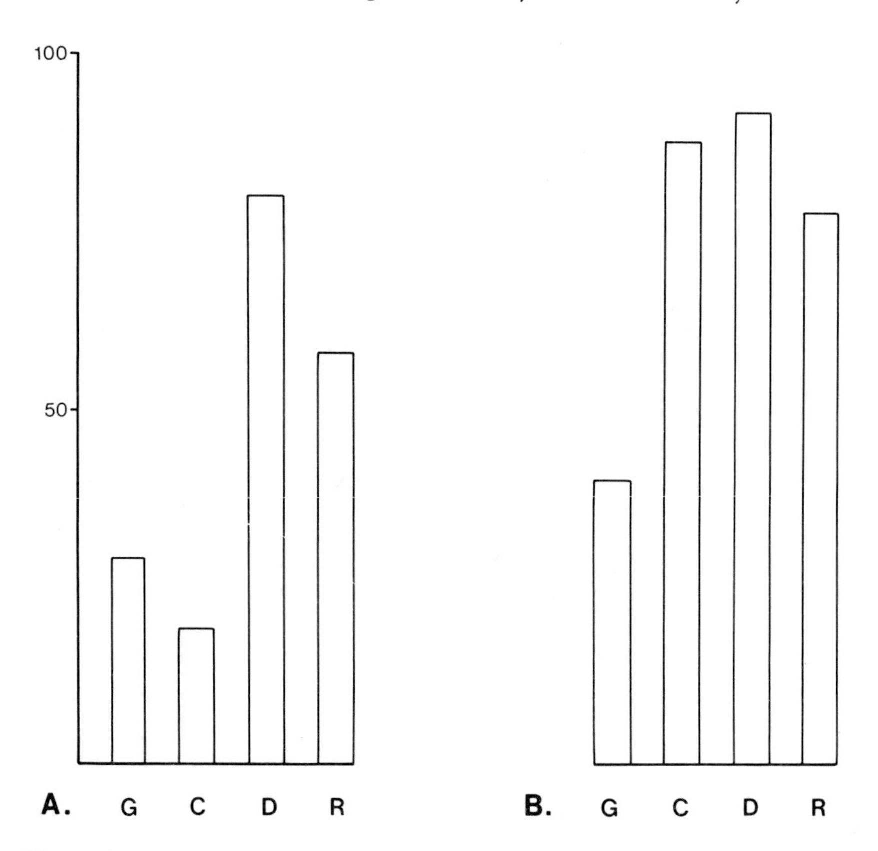

Figure 2.4 A. Frequency of the use of first-person narrative, e.g., 'I' 'myself' 'me'. B. Frequency of use of first- or second-person plural narrative, e.g., 'we' 'our' 'your' 'you'. G = Garrod, C = Clark, D = Daniel, R = Renfrew.

audience, a sharing of basic problems and perspectives. An appeal to a 'we' in the IL is an attempt to establish consensus: shared traditions and value systems, a common framework for thought and conditions in terms of which it can be validated. Use of the third-person singular,'he', 'she' or 'it', suggests a discourse distanced from both the speaker and the audience, a more 'neutral' and abstracted form of discourse. Third-person narrative, or use of the first-person plural, 'we', dominates in the lectures of Garrod and Clark . For large sections of their lectures both they and the audience virtually disappear into the narrative in a relation of decentred personal and social distanciation. Renfrew, and especially Daniel, by contrast maintain a high first-person singular presence (Fig. 2.4) throughout their lectures. Pronoun switches are of interest in highlighting relations of power and authority:

> *I* think *we* should agree that what *I* have termed primary prehistory is of *universal* relevance. (Clark 1954, p. 11, emphasis added.)

Here one almost has the feeling of the audience being intimidated so as to agree with Clark. All archaeologists ought to share the same goals and values – unless aberrant or deliberately deviant. Archaeology clearly requires submission to a norm. The more you submit to this norm, the greater your own individual 'freedom' in the discipline will be increased.

Conclusion

The status of the Disney Professor involves criteria of competence and knowledge within an institutional framework, defining a person who has the right to make archaeological statements and expect them to be accepted as serious speech acts. What defines the importance of the statements actually made is not their propositional content, but the fact that their conditions of enunciation involve the status of the Disney Professor and his or her institutional site. The ILs have been treated as discursive events within a series displaying principles of regularity underlying their propositional content, and relating to their social conditions of exercise within a specific institutional framework. What have been highlighted in this chapter are features of archaeological writing which have generally remained little considered. A 'normal' reading of these ILs would, no doubt, attempt to recover and comment on their argumentative content. In concentrating on these issues the underlying regularities and their relationship to institutional power and control would be likely to be lost. The IL is a privileged discourse that is both internally constrained by its genre and externally limited by its institutional setting, and it has definite power effects.

Of course, there is a danger in overvalorizing the significance of the IL. Few people outside Cambridge go to the IL and, generally, ILs are not widely referred to and constitute a relatively minor aspect of contemporary archaeological discourse. However, ILs as a discursive modality form part of larger discursive formations in archaeology which require systematic analysis in the future. Such analyses are productive and useful, in that they aid a deeper understanding of the social production of archaeological knowledge and the power structures in which this knowledge is embedded. An analysis of discourse increases the possibilities for self-reflexivity and the generation of alternative discourses. Power cannot be detached from discourse, but we may perhaps legitimately distinguish (on political grounds) between repressive and enabling discourses. Such work leads to a realization that the primary event of archaeology is not the event of the past, but the event of discursive production without which there would be no past.

Acknowledgement

I would like to thank Michael Sharib for drawing the diagrams.

References

Clark, J. G. D. 1954. *The study of prehistory, an inaugural lecture.* Cambridge: Cambridge University Press.

Clark, J. G. D. 1979. Archaeology and human diversity. *Annual Review of Anthropology* **8**.

Clark, J. G. D. 1983. *The identity of man.* London: Methuen.

Daniel, G. 1976. *Cambridge and the back-looking curiosity, an inaugural lecture.* Cambridge: Cambridge University Press.

Evans, J. 1897. *The ancient stone implements, weapons and ornaments of Great Britain.* London: Longmans Green.

Foucault, M. 1972. *The archaeology of knowledge.* London: Tavistock.

Foucault, M. 1981. The order of discourse. In *Untying the text.* R. Young (ed.). London: Routledge & Kegan Paul.

Garrod, D. 1946. *Environment, tools and man, an inaugural lecture.* Cambridge: Cambridge University Press.

Pleet, H. 1985. Rhetoric. In *Discourse and literature.* T. van Dijk (ed.). Amsterdam: John Benjamins.

Renfrew, C. 1982. *Towards an archaeology of mind, an inaugural lecture.* Cambridge: Cambridge University Press.

Trigger, B. 1984. Alternative archaeologies: nationalist, colonialist, imperialist. *Man* **19**, 355–70.

3 *The limits of dominance*

DANIEL MILLER

Introduction

This chapter is intended to be complementary to several others in this book which take as their central concern the various conditions and mechanisms which favour the construction, reproduction and maintenance of dominance. By dominance I refer to the condition in which a set of ideas or practices, usually favourable to a particular minority within a society, appear to hold sway over the whole of that society and act to reproduce this same condition. Dominance may be exercised through sufficient coercive force as to be independent of the acquiescence of the dominated population, but more commonly it relates to principles of ideology and underlying discourses which structure both the construction of the subject and the subsequent acknowledgement by that subject of at least some of the legitimation claims made by the dominant group. Dominance therefore tends to be hegemonic, pervasive, exclusionary and conservative. Despite the dynamic and diachronic emphases of the foundational social theory developed by Marx, academic works which attempt to characterize dominance in a particular instance may have a tendency to deny change, especially when constructed in the absence of any consideration of the limitations of dominance. This is often the result of a simple process through which the naturalization of authority passes quite easily from the analysed to the analysis.

Archaeology is part of the larger study of human history and, as such, its most dramatic contribution is in terms of its perspective on long-term social change, complementing the shorter perspective of most historical studies. Given the centrality of this issue to archaeology, it follows that those cultural practices which are particularly conducive to change and development are of special interest to the discipline. Inasmuch as dominance tends to be associated with stasis, all of those factors that contribute to its limits may come to hold a particular significance for the discipline.

The problem with attempting to discuss the limits of dominance is that this involves generalizing over vast periods and areas to uncover certain characteristic features of social resistance or other modes by which authority is transformed. However, this may tend to the positivistic assertion of cross-cultural social processes, or merely the uncovering of patterns in such processes (for example, Kroeber 1948). To avoid this there needs to be an awareness that the particular forms taken by non-dominant ideologies are only understandable in terms of the specific historical conditions which have created the forces of dominance against which these limits are posed.

In this chapter the problem of the limits to dominance has been, somewhat arbitrarily, divided into five key areas, for convenience of presentation. These are:

(a) Recent changes in social theory which make agency and resistance integral to the definition of power and dominance;

(b) the nature of dominance as a cosmological or structural principle which inevitably incorporates inversion within itself, providing a possible foundation for its own overthrow;

(c) the multifactorial nature of dominance which tends not to consist of a single linear hierarchy leading upwards from dominated to dominant, but usually several different and often competing hierarchical classifications whose tensions may contribute to the limitation of any one of them in maintaining hegemonic conditions;

(d) the tension between coercion and legitimacy as a more specific instance of this problem of structural differentiation;

(e) the often limited and non-pervasive nature of dominance, evident when consideration is given to the mass population.

Theories of dominance

Traditional accounts of power have tended to identify it almost entirely with coercive and negative instruments of control, against which could then be arrayed some equally discrete forces of resistance. However, most recent studies have preferred to see power as a force establishing a domain of possibilities incorporating within itself the generation of both dominance and the modes of its resistance. The most ambitious development in this direction by Foucault (1979, see also Dews 1984) may have over-reached itself as an approach by removing power from any consideration of agency, but this dynamic force within the conception of power itself is found in a number of other contemporary approaches (Miller & Tilley 1984a). Perhaps still the most powerful account of the dialectical nature of power comes in Hegel's Master–Slave relation (Arthur 1983), where the perspective of the Slave as worker is the instrument by which alone the Master can obtain consciousness of himself as such. Hegel is here asserting that the social relation in which dominance operates is always based upon some cultural form as a practice, and that this form is inherently contradictory. If the very concept of power asserts the mutuality of the relationship between dominant and dominated, then power is always a dynamic relationship rather than merely an instrument of an active agent set against a passive subject. The reflexive definitions and perspectives of both sides of the relationship must be ascertained and understood always in relation to each other.

When examined in the context of observable relations of control, the inherently problematic and contradictory nature of power implied in Hegel becomes clearer. First, the cultural form taken by relations of dominance often lies in an ambiguous relation with the specific interests or benefits that are expected to accrue to the dominant. The idea that culture as objectification may tend to autonomy from human interest is exemplified by the way in which roles and legitimations adopted in the routinization and sedimentation of authority may become elaborated and eventually submerge the actual interests of the holders of office, whose ability to act is constrained by the forms of their own authority. For example, Geertz (1980, pp. 121–36) noted a certain atrophy in the positions of power held in 19th-century Bali, where the person who acts as the embodiment of power become constrained by this symbolic function from any active engagement with or utilization of that which they had come to represent.

Giddens (1979) and Bourdieu (1977) have, in different ways, focused upon the relationship between structure and agency in the practice of dominance. Giddens, arguing the logic of functionalism which imputes teleology to the social order itself, asserts the necessity for an approach to structure incorporating agency, whereas Bourdieu, castigating structuralism for its rule-based normative orders, asserts the importance of strategy as integral to any consideration of the mechanisms of social reproduction. Both positions take agency and strategy as parts of a larger cycle that incorporates the subject's being constructed within symbolic structures, which are in turn generative of their degree of autonomy. This suggests that dominance is not a practice whose internal structural contradictions may be resolved, but rather it is a lived condition which works through an often precarious balance between various forces of coercive–legitimatory, collectivist–individualist, structural–calculative, practical–representational natures, which may always threaten to break down into the relative autonomy of their constituent parts unless agents act in furtherance of the maintenance of the present actual or apparent cohesion.

This shift in theoretical characterizations is also matched by a resurgence of interest in empirical studies, in mass ideologies which also bring to the fore the coexistence of competing, alternative and multivalent ideas within what has been described as a given society. This includes what Kahn (1985, p. 49) has described as the 'rediscovery' of peasant ideology in the Third World, the importance of populist alternatives to authoritative control or instruction found, for example, in mass agrarian practices (Richards 1985), and the history of popular and mass culture in Europe. All of these have come to supplement the more traditional literature on peasant uprisings and revolution as forces in social change (for example, Wolf 1969).

Attempts to relate the evidence for the existence of such mass ideologies to their place in the mechanisms of social change have been most fully developed in Marxist theories which have the revolutionary event at their centre of concern. The work of Gramsci, who was particularly interested in the revolutionary implications of those limits to dominant ideologies that he could observe from his own experience amongst peasants and workers in Italy, has been especially influential in this regard (see Introduction).

Dominance and inversion

All societies exist only through cultural practices which are integral to their formation. Cultural forms are always ambiguous in that, on the one hand, they structure actual human social relations and practices but, on the other hand, they tend to autonomy and reification which order them according to their own structural logic irrespective of the social interests through which they operate. This contradiction will be a central element of all the situations considered in this chapter and, indeed, when considered in relation to human agency, will be taken as the foundation for most social change.

The principles by which a society attempts to assert legitimacy and abstract its cultural logic are often considered as forming a cosmology, which usually consists of a series of assertions as to the nature of the world, and criteria about what is necessary for truthful and moral propositions. For such constructions to be meaningful, they must incorporate notions and models of the opposite forces in the mirror of which they are contained. These may be used to define areas that place humanity in its larger universe, as in ideas about hell, witchcraft, negation and evil. Such inversions are often objectified as other peoples beyond one's own boundaries, as in the Occident's construction of Orientalism and Primitivism. As social practices are constructed in accordance with dominant cosmologies, these may often include the specific objectification of such forms which may include extremes, alternatives or actual structural inversions. Structural anthropology and the ethnographies influenced by it suggest the common occurrence of such objectifications.

Cosmological inversion may be characterized as practices which, being antithetical to the dominant cosmology, can be understood as emerging from these same ideas and not from some alternative source. Although, as illustrated in the work of Lévi-Strauss (1982), inversion may occur as a spatial phenomena operating between two adjacent peoples, the instances of concern here occur within the same locale. For example, Kapferer has recently illustrated how the principles of evil in Sinhalese Buddhism, which are throughly encompassed as a generative force within the overall cosmology and defined in relation of opposition to the constitutive principle of order, may have been projected onto the minority community of Tamils with disastrous consequences (Kapferer 1987). In other cases a minority group itself attempts to objectify in its practices the principles of inversion. Most of the writings about such inversion has divided into two schools: that which regards them as a vicarious and cathartic force contributing to the maintenance of dominance, and that which sees them as a force with revolutionary potential. Many ethnographies have noted inversion at a relatively particular pole within the social practices of that society. For example, Parry's recent work (1982) on the funerary priests of the sacred city of Varanasi in India, where certain priests who eat the left-overs of dogs from human skulls attempt to embody an extreme and systematic opposition to principles of ordinary Hindu life. Other studies have concentrated on particular cults that appear to embody often equally extreme and inverted forms of the dominant cosmology as a strategy for obtaining mystical power.

One of the most interesting cases of such inversion, since it involves the mass of the population in its practice, although within strict temporal bounds, is that of Carnival. There are numerous studies of this phenomena, both in its medieval European form, but also in contemporary South American, West Indian and European variants. The most influential single analysis, that by Bakhtin (1968), based on a literary analysis of the work of Rabelais, places considerable stress on the practice of inversion. The major characteristics of Carnival, wherever it is practised, is that it occurs at a specific time of year sanctioned by religion, as in Lent, or by secular authorities as, for example, an Independence Day celebration. The main revellers are from the lower classes. There are competitions with a totemic element, music, dance, feasting, processions through the streets, the use of masks and anonymity, explicit social critique and a general tension between order and disorder.

Bakhtin's analysis of the phenomena provides the best source for understanding its very existence. Analysing its religious base, he demonstrates the centrality of inversion and laughter in the medieval mass population's conception of the mystical terror of God, and balance between the consecrated and the forbidden. In Carnival it is forms normally excluded which are here pronounced, such as excreta, disorder, vomit and the excoriation of priests. For Bakhtin parodies of the Church are an integral part of its entrenched position in consciousness. Thus, however Carnival is judged in terms of political efficacy, its existence as a phenomenon must first be understood structurally – that is, inversion as a phenomenon is resultant from structural logic, not political potential.

What has been strongly contested is the conclusion Bakhtin draws from this analysis, which is that Carnival's polysemic voice is always radical and directly expressive of oppressed classes. On this issue there are two quite opposed positions. Some, including Eco (1984) and De Matta (1977), imply in their analyses or state directly that Carnival as inversion is a force which affirms the dominant ideology, and acts as vicarious action or cathartic release which will then lead to a restoration of the true normative order. Others, such as Le Roy Ladurie (1981), Gilmore (1975) and Bakhtin himself, seem to argue that Carnival is a more direct expression of popular social critique, that rites which include cries such as 'flesh of Christians at four dernier a pound' (Le Roy Ladurie 1981, pp. 69–215) are always potentially calls for the overthrow of the dominant group. A third approach analyses Carnival's specific forms in relation to attempts to assimilate social change itself, and to create new fusions within this dynamic (for example, Manning 1977; compare also Worsley 1970 on inversion in Cargo Cults as a response to social and economic change in Melanesia).

One of the most satisfactory mediations between these positions is found in Cohen's (1982) analysis of the Notting Hill Carnival in which he argues that it is precisely the tension between political and aesthetic forms which gives Carnival its force, and that attempts either to remove any overt political commentary or to turn it into solely a political gesture tend to repress its efficacy. This suggests that we have a phenomenon of inversion which can be understood on structural grounds as essential, but that its political implications are always contingent; in one social and economic context it may be supportive of dominance, in another it may prove the catalyst for revolution, generally operating through this same ambiguity.

That structural inversion may at times erupt as a potent force in the destruction of an old order, and the creation of a new political regime with its own ideology, is clear from the history of South Asia. Tambiah (1976, p. 19) has shown how Buddhism appears to develop as a studied and ironic inversion of certain basic tenets of Hinduism, which it replaced for over a millennium as the dominant force in the region. Using archaeological evidence for the Harappan civilization, I have tentatively suggested that the early Vedic Hinduism itself may have arisen in part in a contrastive mode to the ideas which had been dominant and generated the state which preceded it (Miller 1985, pp. 62–3). Thus, symbolic inversion may have been one of the most potent forces in social change over several millennia.

The multifactorial nature of dominance

Approaches to dominance centred around the nature of structure and cosmology sometimes tend to over-homogenize the forms of power generated by such cultural constructions. However, the more profound analyses have always asserted that, although cosmological orders tend at the most abstract level to present a goal of coherence and totality, when considered in relation to the societies that they orchestrate they may generate often contradictory and heterodox formations. Leach's (1954) classic analysis of political systems in Highland Burma illusrated the dynamic interplay between different emphases within an overarching set of principles when encountered under different conditions and expressed in different political formations. Gilsenan (1982) has recently shown how the abstract notions of Islam are made compatible with a wide variety of often feuding and contradictory societies today. In more general terms Weber (e.g. 1968) developed an approach to social theory that was centred upon the dynamic interaction between what he nevertheless recognized as separate and competing sources of authority.

Although most cultural structures have generated forms of social distinction and differential access to power, even the smallest-scale community rarely accords with the single linear hierarchies sometimes assumed in archaeological interpretations. The multitude of different polarities glossed as coercive power, legitimation, class, status and wealth appear in many ethnographies to be undergoing a constant struggle for what Bourdieu (1979, p. 80) has termed the hierarchy of the principles of hierarchization. These classificatory dimensions are usually in an ambiguous relation; in part, mutually translatable, but not entirely reducible one to another. For example, wealth may be used to gain reputation, but does not amount to it. Coercion may require legitimation, but is often in conflict with it as an ideal. Commonly, again, even in relatively small-scale communities, these orders are objectified in different individuals or lineages, and it is this structural heterogeneity of power which is one of the major sources for those elements that seek to counter or limit dominance. Each such hierarchy commonly tends towards an autonomy reifying the particular element of social order it enshrines, and seeking to subordinate all others to itself.

Here a single instance of this problematic will be focused upon, one which has already proved a major resource for attempts to interpret the evidence for change in prehistory; that is, the potential conflict between economy and society. The ethnography of exchange tends to divide between various versions of the dichotomy between gift and commodity, for example the distinction between substantivist and formalist approaches. This is based upon the tendency for flexible economic exchange, as found in market conditions, to create a bifurcation through which the social position of the exchanger becomes irrelevant to the value of the objects exchanged. This antisocial aspect provides a constant model for possible antagonism between economy and society, with the former acting as the foundation for some principle of freedom from the latter. Similarly, expanding trade and merchant power has long been seen as the foundation for threats to conservative interests within the state.

The importance of this with respect to the present argument is that this 'economic' practice may have a tendency towards autonomy and reification, through which it provides a particular mode of power and dominance, but one which is always partial in relation to society as a whole, and thus always a potential source of subversion or alternative order. In the case of South Asia the heterogeneity of power was established forcibly through the work of Dumont (1972) in his analysis of the caste system. Hindu society provides a fascinating example of the constant tension between an independence asserted by the market and attempts to reincorporate it.

The evidence for market economic practices tending towards autonomy from other social values is clear, stemming in part from the need for the transactors to free themselves of the social obligations and responsibilities which could limit their freedom to demand payments for goods, though these claims to autonomy are commonly circumscribed (Douglas 1967). In his pioneering study Bailey (1957) showed that as what he called the 'economic' frontier reached an isolated section of rural Orissa, those members of the community who became most involved with trade started to distance themselves from the main community and to appeal more to outside forces in cases of dispute. In the urban areas of the classic states, the community of merchants exemplify elements of the 'Stranger' status analysed by Simmel (1971, pp. 143–9). Such communities, as studied by Fox (1969), Mines (1977) and others, have shown the antipathy of the merchant to the values both of traditional socially integrative networks and to modern alternative sources of value such as education. The merchant communities tend to show extreme reliance on monetary-based values in themselves as the source for both their power and their own internal criteria of worth.

In relation to this tendency towards economic autonomy, Hindu society has constructed a wide variety of structurally integrative classifications and orders. One of the most ancient, encompassing the legitimation of the caste system, is the concept of *vaishya* as one of the four classic *varna*, into which classical sources divide Hindu society. This, although recognizing the minimalist nature of merchants with respect to social transactions, as shown by Marriot (1976), nevertheless places them within systems of categories and, to that degree, attempts to assert control over them with respect to larger hierarchies. In contemporary rural South Asia the most elaborate attempt to place market transaction within a larger framework which turns its antisocial potential into a bulwark for the continuance of embedded social orders is found in the symbiotic relationship between market exchange and the *Jajmani* system, by which the flexibility and autonomy of market exchange provides the response to practical *ad hoc* demand which in turn permits the more structured *Jajmani* exchange to be protected from the vagaries of everyday life (Miller 1986).

Although the *Jajmani* system effectively subordinates market economics to social principles for some rural areas, the situation is more difficult in urban contexts, where independent merchant communities have arisen as described above. Historically there has been a fluctuating relationship between merchants as independent interests and the major source of political power, as in Kingship. At certain periods, for example during the elaborate guild systems of the Mauryan Empire, the merchants were strongly integrated within the state through these guilds (Saletore 1975), but political regimes were often, in turn, reliant upon merchants both to provide the specific component of their sumptuary expression as prestige goods, and to conduct and control areas from which they, as political figures, were barred owing to the perceived unsuitability of such operations. Indeed, it is clear that, however powerful the merchant community, the potentially antisocial nature of the economy is expressed by the low regard in which mercantilism in general is held by Hindus in South Asia (although not for Muslims, amongst whom other strategies prevail).

At times when the state control has been weak, the tendency for economic power to exert its independence has been pronounced. In South India warrior merchant communities have proved powerful enough to become the dominant force in regional politics in certain periods (Mines 1984). Under contemporary democratic and bureaucratic regimes merchants may still find ways to exert considerable, though subtle, control over political authorities, as in the Indian state of Tamil Nadu (Harriss 1984). However, it is also in the South that one of the most elaborate systems for integrating merchants within larger holistic orders is found, as merchants are organized as the leading actors in what are termed left-hand castes (Mines 1984), a grouping which may be allocated specific places of residence and specific ritual activities commensurate with this classification. However, what the left-handedness of the merchant community also indicates is that, insofar as merchants were regarded as an independent potential source of power as against, for example, land-holding or brahminical authority, they had accrued to themselves the support of a number of other castes who utilized this division within the dominant castes to attempt to assert their own position.

Although it is a particularly clear example of the tendency towards autonomy, the economic interest of the merchant is only one of a whole series of potential sources for divisions within the forces that might construct such dominance. Control over proto-industrial production, various forms of land-tenure systems, martial prowess and professional bureaucrats are just some of the niches through which other groups have attempted to exert a similar influence. It is these divisions which account for the major contradiction in South Asian history, at one level so stable and conservative with the continuance of the caste system despite invasion and change, but actually within that overarching classificatory system constantly changing in both cyclical and linear fashion.

Dominance and legitimacy

Of all those divisions within systems of dominance that allow for the emergence of alternative forces that result in the overthrow of that which had considered itself immortal, it is the conflict between legitimacy and coercion that appears most often. There have been extensive studies of the manner by which coercion and morality collude and collide, a field in which Weber is again the key pioneer. Recent studies of ideology have developed increasingly sophisticated methods for uncovering the manner by which partial interests manifest themselves under the guise of more general social practices. Some emphasize ideology as mediating in the relation between the representation of hierarchy and its practice as a disconnection between power and rank which nevertheless secures the continuance of dominant interests (for example, Bloch 1977), whereas others have analysed systems of legitimacy as more constraining of simple coercion by the wielders of secular power (Dumont 1972). The structural possibilities presented by the various forms of amalgamation and separation between social groupings associated with legitimacy and coercion has recently been illustrated with particular clarity by Rowlands (1986) in a study of a series of chiefdoms within a small region of West Africa.

In terms of European history this structural cleavage is most clearly evident as the struggle between the Church and the state. Although it might appear that direct control over coercive power should tend towards the general dominance of the latter at times of conflict, as, for example, in the power of Henry VIII of England, or the various attacks on the papacy by European monarchs, it is noticeable how often the forces which seem most potent in dictating social change have come from the struggle over the interpretation of cosmic order, for example the struggle between Reformation and Counter-Reformation. As Hill (1972) has shown with respect to the English Civil War, what has traditionally been presented in terms of relatively clear struggle over authority between parliament and kingship has masked powerful and heterogeneous struggles within the mass population, in which a large range of independent utopian, millenarian libertarian and other forces have waged war. In his book *Montaillou*, Le Roy Ladurie (1980) illustrated clearly the continuance of forms of heterodoxy, which, as it were, lie fallow, but then may become available for use by forces wishing to challenge the particular form of religious authority that appears supportive of the present state regime. The struggles between Empire and the claims of world religion are equally entwined in the histories of Islam, Buddhism and the politics of pre-Columbian American states.

As a form of resistance to dominance, there are two particularly common strategies taken by an appeal to legitimacy: one facing outwards to mass participation, the other inwards to personal salvation. The first tends to take the form of an appeal to the original texts, an attempt to clean them of what are seen as the accretions by which dominant forces have attempted to manipulate them into support for their particular regime. In Chinese history this is regarded as a virtually cyclical and always moral process, by which dynasties are overthrown and replaced (Meskill 1965). Today its most obvious manifestation is in that fundamentalism which seeks to overthrow a relatively secular state authority. As religion is in some areas no longer the dominant force behind claims to legitimation, so the same strategy invades other domains. For example, Bourdieu (1980) notes a tendency in academic change to emerge first as the attack on some orthodoxy, spearheaded by an appeal to a new, more basic interpretation of some classic text such as Marx or Durkheim.

Legitimatory concepts such as democracy may also be used in this way as the 1986 election in the Philippines was the catalyst for a popular uprising against the Marcos regime. Often the very principles which have been used to maintain dominance become turned against themselves. The clearest example of this in recent history is nationalism, which once appeared to be the central force by which individual nation-states could not only also use this ideal of control over smaller groups with no such claim, but could also use this ideal of nationalism as a force maintaining order within their boundaries. However, in recent years the pluralism expressed in the new ethnicity, which has led ever-smaller and less-cohesive groups to assert claims to statehood as a means of resisting the larger instruments of control, has made nationalistic sentiment not only one of the major threats to established states, but also an actual instrument in the creation of an ever increasing number of small states around the world. Nationalism as ideology has thus been extremely powerful in both maintaining and overthrowing state dominance (for example, Anderson 1983, Smith 1981). Although based on mass movements, the inspiration behind such change is often millenarian in focus and individual, charismatic, in leadership.

The other common strategy is a retreat into the self, an individualist assertion of personal spirituality, ranging from Indian *sannyasi* renouncers, to the hippies of the 1960s. This might be thought a candidate for the series of alternative ideologies that seem to coexist with, rather than threaten, dominance as in the next class to be discussed, but for the fact that these are often highly collectivist in their organization and seem to use the development of inner spirituality as the generator of a moral force which historically is often potent as a form by which orthodoxy may be overthrown. This is found in monastic and sainthood systems, as related to both Christian and Buddhist traditions (for example, Tambiah 1984), certain forms of Puritanism, and perhaps also sections of the New Left.

How pervasive is hegemony?

The next series of forces which must be considered in relation to the assumption of total domination is a whole range of ideologies that appear to coexist alongside apparent dominance, but which may not provide a basis for the actual overthrow of dominant ideologies, but only limits as to their assumed pervasive nature. An example of this is children's culture. Although it is clear in studies of folklore and other sources that children, in their games, fantasies and play, often construct a long-lasting cultural form filled with ideals which are quite an anathema to all those principles and values asserted by the dominant adult society. Clearly this does not, of itself, pose any threat to the continuation of that dominance (for example, James 1979).

More problematic is the assertion that in societies where males have taken a dominant role in the control and order of society, both with respect to public and legitimatory practices and with coercive sanctions, there may exist another, often 'silent' but equally ordered and principled, discourse which is specific to the women of that society. This idea was developed by Ardener (1975), and was most clearly exemplified in the analysis of women's exchanges in the Trobriands by Wiener (1976), which had been ignored by the earlier ethnographic accounts. Again it is unclear how far these are forces generative of change to the dominant ideology, at least until the advent of modern feminism, whose efficacy is now well-established with respect to most spheres of social action.

In more general terms Abercrombie *et al.* (1980) have argued that the assumption that dominant ideologies are generally pervasive through the mass of the population is itself questionable, and using historical evidence they suggest that classic examples such as feudalism were in fact surprisingly limited in their actual effect at the relevant historical epoch. This idea has been explored in more detail by the various approaches to popular culture in historical researches, ranging from studies of the emergent working class in relation to its own particular ideals, pioneered by Thompson (1968), to studies that continue the theme of medieval Carnival into more class-specific sets of forms defined against the dominant class during the emergence of modern Europe (Burke 1978, Mukerji 1983). Contemporary studies include emphases on 'resistance through rituals' amongst youth subcultures (Hall *et al.* 1976) and the existence of 'traditional' ideologies in the face of a dominant modernity of both right and left in studies of the peasantry (Kahn 1985, pp. 62–5).

Other studies have concentrated upon what might be seen as the periphery of ordered societies, noting the common occurrence of groups such as bandits (Hobsbawm 1969), or the dacoits of the Chambal valleys of Central India who developed a Robin Hood image, representing the oppressed as a form of resistance to dominant forces but rarely exerting more than a troublesome impact. A similar romanticism of the periphery is found in some of the popular culture studies of youth and the mass media. More potent as a potential revolutionary force have been various populisms that suggest the continuance of an often cynical if fatalist attitude to dominant ideologies amongst the mass population, but which may give rise, through the democratic process, to quite major political shifts, as in the granting of very extensive political power to populist film stars in South India.

An interesting case-study has been made from the untouchable community within Hindu-dominated South Asian society. Here is a community which is an eloquent example of structural oppression, and one which is never likely to obtain power of the kind necessary to be instrumental in the overthrow of that system of dominance which is causative of their oppression. Many of the strategies that the untouchables have followed in attempting to ameliorate their situation have proved of little consequence; however, others have been effective, at least in maintaining an independent ethos that limits the pervasive nature, though rarely the coercive pressure, of dominance. For example, strategies of mass conversion to Islam, Buddhism and Christianity, which have had virtually no effect where the dominant Hindu culture still regards as equally derisory those converted. Strategies of emulation are also found in which untouchables reproduce the fine levels of discrimination and caste differentiation from which they have been excluded (Moffatt 1979). On the other hand, there is evidence that some untouchables, where possible, simply utilize their peripheral position to advantage as cynical exploiters of those that oppress them (Freeman 1980). As a communal rejection, untouchables may use inversion and difference to establish themselves. For example, the Benares sweepers studied by Searle-Chatterjee (1981) tend to a gender equality as inverted rejection of the dominant culture which enshrines extreme inequality and purdah systems.

What was most interesting about this last case is evidence that, when various changes limited the coercive powers of their exploiters, the sweepers were able to use their very untouchability to their advantage (Searle-Chatterjee 1981). In terms of modern industrial relations, sweepers form an extreme example of a closed shop, since there are no others willing to undertake their work. In a time of increasing trade unionism, and with limits on the traditional violent forms by which the aspirations of such groups could be suppressed, the sweepers suddenly found themselves in a potentially very strong position. As sweeper women threaten by their mere touch to pollute the bureaucrats they are challenging, through the weapon of strikes they have been able to increase their wages to a level comparable with highly respected professions in Benares, such as university lecturing (Searle-Chatterjee 1979). As in other instances already cited, cultural change is not to be seen here as merely the result of 'underlying' economic development, but rather there exists a constant dynamic tension between different areas of practice and representation in which the structural possibilities of one may act as either constraint or catalyst for the other.

The maintenance of this existent alternative ideology, amongst often the majority of the given population, is essential for understanding actual revolutionary action. Most theorists differentiate the kind of peasant rebellion that was a characteristic failure in European history, from revolutions which incorporate an alliance between mass discontent and some claim to wider and longer-lasting legitimacy, today usually some version of Marxism. The importance of revolutionary consciousness was stressed by both Lukacs and Gramsci, and has been taken up by many modern writers on peasant ideologies (for example, Arnold 1984, Kahn 1985). Within Marxist theory this may be generalized to the necessity for actual structural contradiction manifesting itself in terms of class conflict, although this particular phenomenon has been relatively neglected in terms of this chapter since it is already so well established as an issue in academic analysis. When the implied teleology of classic Marxist approaches to social change is countered, this approach may reduce to the more general and contingent relations between agency and structure that characterize most current attempts to provide a diachronic edge to structuralist analyses.

Conclusion: archaeology and limits of dominance

The consideration of the implications of the limits of dominance for archaeologists is part of the more general question about the importance of contradiction in culture as a force in social change (Miller & Tilley 1984b). If such contradictions are not to be postulated within some functionalist model as inherently causative of change, then they must be understood as manifesting themselves as practical tensions in the way agents perceive and act within their historical context though, as Freud and Marx amongst others have shown, resistance may be symptomatic rather than conscious or intentional. In the survey presented above, contradictions are understood as tendencies towards reification in elements of a structure. Social fractions identify with such particular forces; for example, mercantile interest, an oppressed group perceived as inversion from the norm, the holders of millenerian utopian ideals, and so forth. Such groups encourage this tendency to increasing autonomy, and thereby threaten the current dominance that is always itself based on often precarious balancing activities, since, however coherent its legitimatory claims, they always include their structural opposites, their contradictions and the tendencies towards autonomy of their internal components.

Archaeology has both a major disadvantage and advantage in uncovering evidence for these tensions. On the one hand, material culture often hides its own polysemic nature, since specific configurations of objects may be differentially incorporated within competing systems of ideas, without necessarily changing themselves, and often a dominated group is better able to retain the appearance of conformity while maintaining its alternative perspective on the world. On the other hand, archaeology always has the advantage of *déjà vu*. It is able to uncover what happened at the next stage of societal development, and to look back to see the seeds of what was to come within the previous social formation. A further advantage of archaeology, best seen when it is used alongside history, is that it contributes a detailed picture of the objective conditions and cultural forms inhabited by mass populations, while historical records may tend towards the official records of dominant groups. Archaeology itself therefore becomes an instrument of the limits of dominance by recovering that history which time itself was expected to repress in favour of the state chronicler.

Recent work on the concept of ideology in the interpretation of archaeological remains (for example, Miller & Tilley 1984) is important in this regard, because it indicates the end of the traditional archaeological expectation that the various forms of evidence in the archaeological record must be expected to be coherent with respect to their supposed signification. It is becoming increasingly clear that in a given society where the burials appear to evoke an ideal of hierarchy, the housing may illustrate an actual equality, or vice versa.

Most of the kinds of tension and resistance which have been discussed here have also been used in specific archaeological reconstructions of social change. Most developed have been studies of the conflict between social sections based on coercive power, mercantile interest and legitimacy such as priesthoods in studies of the early states (for example, Gledhill & Larsen 1982, Rowlands 1980). For some approaches such resistance only manifests itself at periods when structural contradiction has reached sufficient tension for fragmentation to occur (for example, Friedman & Rowlands 1977). Depending upon the emphasis, this may be a tension between class interest and the productive base of society, or some more general legitimation crises (for example, Tilley 1984). However, on the basis of the ethnographic and historical evidence presented in this chapter, it may be suggested that archaeologists might well investigate as a more general phenomenon the manner by which alternative, competing and inverted ideologies emerge, reproduce themselves and remain latent even within periods of apparently stable political dominance.

References

Abercrombie, N., S. Hill, & B. Turner 1980. *The dominant ideology thesis*, London: Allen & Unwin.
Anderson, B. 1983. *Imagined Communities*. London: Verso.
Ardener, S. (ed.) 1975. *Perceiving women*. London: Malaby Press.
Arnold, D. 1984. Gramsci and peasant subalternity in India. *Journal of Peasant Studies* **11**, 155–77.
Arthur, C. 1983. The master–slave relationship. *New Left Review* **142**, 67–75.
Bailey, F. 1957. *Caste and the economic frontier*. Manchester: Manchester University Press.
Bakhtin, M. 1968. *Rabelais and his world*. Cambridge, Massachusetts: MIT Press.
Bloch, M. 1977. The disconnection between rank and power as a process. In *The evolution of social systems*, J. Friedman & Rowlands (eds), 303–40. London: Duckworth.
Bourdieu, P. 1977. *Outline of a theory of practice*. Cambridge: Cambridge University Press.
Bourdieu, P. 1979. Symbolic power. *Critique of Anthropology* **13–14**, 77–85.
Bourdieu, P. 1980. The production of belief. *Media, Culture and Society* **2**, 261–93.
Burke, P. 1978. *Popular culture in early modern Europe*. London: Temple Smith.
Cohen, A. 1982. A polyethnic London carnival as a contested cultural performance. *Ethnic and Racial Studies* **5**, 23–42.
De Matta, R. 1977. Constraint and license: a preliminary study of two Brazilian national rituals. In *Secular rituals*, S. Moore & B. Myerhoff (eds), 244–64. Assen: Van Gorcum.
Dews, P. 1984. Foucault's theory of subjectivity. *New Left Review* **144**, 72–95.
Douglas, M. 1967. Primitive rationing. In *Themes in economic anthropology*, R. Firth (ed.) 119–46. London: Tavistock.
Dumont, L. 1972. *Homo hierarchicus*. London: Paladin.
Eco, U. 1984. The frames of comic freedom. In *Carnival*, U. Eco, V. Ivanov & M. Rector (eds), 1–9. Berlin: Mouton.
Foucault, M. 1979. *The history of sexuality*. Harmondsworth: Penguin.
Fox, R. 1969. *From zamindar to ballot box*. Ithaca: Cornell University Press.
Freeman, J. 1979. *Untouchable: an Indian life history*. London: Allen & Unwin.
Friedman, J. & M. Rowlands. 1977. Notes towards an epigenetic model of the evolution of civilisation. In *The evolution of social systems*, J. Friedman & M. Rowlands (eds), 201–76. London: Duckworth.
Geertz, C. 1980. *Negara*. Princeton, New Jersey: Princeton University Press.
Giddens, A. 1979. *Central problems in social theory*. London: Macmillan.
Gilmore, D. 1975. Carnival in Fuenmayor. *Journal of Anthropological Research* **31**, 331–49.
Gilsenan, M. 1982. *Recognising Islam*. London: Croom Helm.
Gledhill, J. and M. Larsen. 1982. The Polanyi paradigm. In *Theory and explanation in archaeology*, C. Renfrew, M. Rowlands & A. Segraves (eds), 197–229. London: Academic Press.
Hall, S., J. Clarke, T. Jefferson & B. Roberts (eds) 1976. *Resistance through rituals*. London: Hutchinson.
Harriss, B. 1984. Agrarian change and the merchant state in Tamil Nadu. In *Understanding green revolutions*, T. Bayliss-Smith & S. Wanmali (eds), 53–83. Cambridge: Cambridge University Press.
Hill, C. 1972. *The world turned upside down*. London: Maurice Temple Smith.
Hobsbawm, E. 1969. *Bandits*. London: Weidenfeld & Nicolson.

James, A. 1979. Confections, concoctions and conceptions. *Anthropological Society of Oxford* **10**, 3–95.
Kahn, J. 1985. Peasant ideologies in the Third World. *Annual Review of Anthropology* **14**, 49–75.
Kapferer, B. 1987. *Legends of people, myths of state.* Washington, DC: Smithsonian Institution Press.
Kroeber, A. 1948. *Anthropology.* New York: Harcourt Brace & Jovanovich.
Leach, E. 1954. *Political systems of highland Burma.* London: Athlone Press.
Le Roy Ladurie, E. 1980. *Montaillou.* Harmondsworth: Penguin.
Le Roy Ladurie, E. 1981. *Carnival in Romans.* Harmondsworth: Penguin.
Lévi-Strauss, C. 1982. *The way of the masks.* Seattle: University of Washington Press.
Manning, F. 1977. Cup match and carnival. In *Secular rituals*, S. Moore & B. Myerhoff (eds), 265–81. Assen: Van Gorcum.
Marriot, M. 1976. Hindu transactions: diversity without dualism. In *Transactions and meaning: directions in the anthropology of exchange and symbolic behaviour*, B. Kapferer (ed.), 109–42, Philadelphia: IHSI.
Meskill, J. (ed.) 1965. *The pattern of Chinese history.* Boston: D. C. Heath.
Miller, D. 1985. Ideology and the Harappan civilisation. *Journal of Anthropological Archaeology*, **4**, 34–71.
Miller, D. 1986. Exchange and alienation in the Jajmani system. *Journal of Anthropological Archaeology* **42**, 535–56.
Miller, D. & C. Tilley. 1984a. Introduction. In *Ideology, power and prehistory*, D. Miller & C. Tilley (eds), 1–15. Cambridge: Cambridge University Press.
Miller, D. & C. Tilley 1984b. Conclusions. In *Ideology, power and prehistory*, D. Miller & C. Tilley (eds), 147–52. Cambridge: Cambridge University Press.
Mines, M. 1977. *Muslim merchants.* New Delhi: Shri Ram Centre for Industrial Relations and Human Resources.
Mines, M. 1984. *Warrior merchants.* Cambridge: Cambridge University Press.
Moffatt, M. 1979. *An untouchable community in South Asia.* Princeton, New Jersey: Princeton University Press.
Mukerji, C. 1983. *From graven images.* New York: Columbia University Press.
Parry, J. 1982. Sacrificial death and the necrophagous ascetic. In *Death and the regeneration of life*, M. Bloch & J. Parry (eds), 74–110. Cambridge: Cambridge University Press.
Richards, P. 1985. *Indigenous agricultural revolution.* London: Hutchinson.
Rowlands, M. 1980. Kinship, alliance and exchange in the European Bronze Age. In *Settlement and society in the British later Bronze Age*, J. Barrett & R. Bradley (eds), 15–56. Oxford: British Archaeological Reports.
Rowlands, M. 1986. Power and moral order in pre-colonial west-central Africa. In *Specialisation and exchange in complex societies*, E. Brumfiel & T. Earle (eds). Cambridge: Cambridge University Press.
Saletore, R. 1975. *Early Indian economic history.* London: Curzon Press.
Searle-Chatterjee, M. 1979. The polluted identity of work. In *The anthropology of work*, S. Wallman (ed.), 269–86. London: Academic Press.
Searle-Chatterjee, M. 1981. *Reversible sex roles: the special case of the Benares sweepers.* London: Pergamon Press.
Simmel, G. 1971. The stranger. In *George Simmel on individuality and social forms*, D. Levine (ed.), 143–9. Chicago: University of Chicago Press.
Smith, A. 1981. *The ethnic revival.* Cambridge: Cambridge University Press.
Tambiah, S. 1976. *World conqueror and world renouncer.* Cambridge: Cambridge University Press.

Tambiah, S. 1984. *The Buddhist saints of the forest and the cult of the amulets.* Cambridge: Cambridge University Press.

Tilley, C. 1984. Ideology and the legitimation of power in the Middle Neolithic of Southern Sweden. In *Ideology, power and prehistory*, D. Miller & C. Tilley (eds), 111–46, Cambridge: Cambridge University Press.

Thompson, E. P. 1968. *The making of the English working class.* London: Penguin.

Weber, M. 1968. *Economy and society*, Vol. 2. New York: Bedminster Press.

Wiener, A. 1976. *Women of value, men of renown.* Austin: University of Texas Press.

Wolf, E. 1969. *Peasant wars of the twentieth century.* New York: Harper & Row.

Worsley, P. 1970. *The trumpet shall sound.* London: Paladin.

POLITICAL ECONOMY AND IDEOLOGY: HISTORICAL TRANSFORMATIONS

4 *The roots of inequality*

BARBARA BENDER

A major concern of this book is to elucidate the different ways in which the term 'complexity' has been constructed, and how these relate to specific historically and socially defined perceptions and preoccupations.

Other chapters discuss the intricacies of the lineal, 'progressive' notion of complexity that has been in vogue in Europe and America since at least the late 19th century. I want to focus on something that indirectly relates to this, which is the almost universally held and taken for granted assumption that the starting point for 'complexity' (however defined) was the development of farming. If gatherer-hunters are mentioned it is as a foil, a counterpoint, to the discussion. This way of dichotomizing things means that somehow the discussion and definition of 'complexity' make little reference to 2 or 3 million years of hominid evolution.

I want to analyse why it is that farming is construed as a necessary condition for the development of 'complexity', which, for my purposes here, I simply define as involving a degree of institutionalized social inequality – and why divisions in gatherer-hunter societies are desocialized and therefore ignored. I shall use an example taken from the south-west European Upper Palaeolithic to show how social inequality might be inaugurated and institutionalized within a gatherer-hunter milieu.

Farming as a precondition

What is it about farming that makes it appear to be both a precondition and an attribute of 'complexity'? Food production *per se* is a technological innovation that lies at one end of a spectrum of plant and animal manipulation (Higgs 1972). It can be, and often has been, simply a minor element in an otherwise wild procurement existence. When, and if, it becomes a more significant subsistence strategy, it makes certain demands on social practice. It often requires a degree of sedentism; it requires labour inputs on which there are delayed returns; land clearance and agricultural practices mean that one generation quite literally feeds off the labour of an earlier generation, and this tends to reinforce generational bonds (Meillassoux 1972, Bender 1985). This generational debt becomes a potential source of inequality – junior service, senior authority. The fact that land takes on value and therefore becomes something material, something that can be possessed, something to which access can be restricted and the products of which can be controlled, again creates conditions for inequality. Moreover, farming permits a control over nature which, at the cost of high labour inputs, yields greater returns, and these are also open to manipulation. Thus, the assumption is that technology (farming) is the tail that wags the social dog (complexity). Such assumptions have been present across a wide spectrum of social theorizing for a long time. Engels (1972, p. 117) wrote: 'the dominance of animals . . . developed a hitherto unsuspected source of wealth and created entirely new social relations', and Morgan (1963, p. 19) pronounced: 'It is accordingly probable that the great epochs of human progress have been identified more or less directly with the enlargement of the sources of subsistence'. In this century Childe continued to stress the significance of changes in the forces of production. The Neolithic Revolution permitted 'the escape from the impasse of savagery' (Childe 1942, p. 48), and the more ecologically minded 'schools' have been content to accept these readings. In recent years a slightly different version emerges. Woodburn (1980) contrasts the immediate return system of most gatherer-hunters, which is associated with egalitarian social relations, with the delayed returns of some gatherer-hunter groups that technically mimic farming practices and thus have similar social configurations.

This very widespread acceptance of a technological prime-mover or, at least, a technological precondition, must in some part relate to our own embeddedness within heavily industrialized societies in which the very process of industrialization seems to act as a significant force for change, and in which technological change and increased complexity become almost interchangeable concepts. This recourse to farming as prime-mover seems also to legitimate and naturalize concepts of property and control by relating them to the exigencies of subsistence practices. Social phenomena are brought into line with nature, creating a form of environmental legitimation of 'the scheme of things'.

'Natural' divisions in gatherer-hunter societies

This 'naturalization' of social complexity created by tying it to subsistence requirements is echoed in the explanations offered for the development of gatherer-hunter societies. The lack of complexity, the supposedly egalitarian nature of gatherer-hunters, is linked to the inability to control resources, the inability to prevent access, etc. Social differentiation – as opposed to inequality – is acknowledged and linked to age and gender, both of which are then linked to the mode of subsistence. Elders have power because they have experience and are the repositories of knowledge on how to do things. To that extent they have some control over juniors. In many accounts this is adjudged to be only a temporary 'inequality', for juniors will eventually become seniors. As O'Laughlin (1977) pointed out, a wonderful myopia creeps in, for the seniors tend to be male, and the juniors on their way to becoming seniors are also male, so only one half of the population is involved in this inoffensive social progression.

This Eurocentric (indeed more widespread) bias which only discusses 'power', or lack of it, in terms of male activities, also permeates the discussion on gender division. It has become much clearer in recent years how, unconsciously, the reconstruction of early hominid societies has been used to naturalize gender divisions within our own societies (Conkey & Spector 1983). For example, it is assumed that a characteristic of early hominids, something that set them apart from other primates, was a division of labour. A division in which the male, endowed with greater strength and unencumbered with infants, was the hunter, taking on the dangerous 'outside' world, and woman was the child-rearer and localized plant gatherer, centred on the domestic sphere. A 'macho' version of this scenario in which the men got credit for inventing tools and weapons, and for promoting the complex sharing strategies that put a premium on intellectual development, was set out by Washburn & Lancaster (1968); a more *gentle*-manly version by Isaac (1978) still maintained the division of labour, but gave full credit to the women for being the more reliable foragers and for being the probable inventors of carrying equipment. Feminist protestations notwithstanding, this insistence on the naturalness of the division of labour was iterated in a recent article which was presumably meant to be taken seriously (Quiatt & Kelso 1985). The authors insisted that the early hominid division of labour was the most 'natural' way of going about things, since the women would be 'house-bound' (3 million years ago, in the middle of the African savannah!). There would be pair-bonding because it made food-sharing easier, the family would be nuclear – 'child serving and child centred' – and the juveniles would baby-sit and run errands and, in the process, would learn 'the complex routines of bulk food collecting, transporting and processing' (clearly such juveniles would do as well, if not better, in the jungles of New York or London).

Interestingly, the feminist critiques written in the 1970s by Slocum (1975), Tanner (1971) and Zihlman (1981) did little more than reverse the scenario – 'Man the Hunter' (the title of the 1968 symposium) is replaced by 'Woman the Gatherer' (Dahlberg's symposium, 1981). They stress that gathering is more important than hunting in the early time ranges and, while both males and females gathered, it was the females that began the process of sharing, for they would have shared food with their increasingly dependent offspring. Moreover, sharing required collecting as opposed to gathering, and this too, with its associated technology, would have been inaugurated by women. In this scenario the division of labour remains intact and, moreover, current notions of child-rearing are accepted as the norm – that women succour, carry, and provide for their own infants. Indeed, it reads like a legitimation of the one-parent family.

In reality none of these divisions or obligations is written into nature. There are plenty of societies where women succour babies that are not their own, or where child-rearing is communal. There is recent evidence from the Philippines of Agta women who hunt large game on a regular basis, who stop hunting for a couple of weeks prior to giving birth, and take it up again a month later, leaving their infants to be suckled by other women at the camp (Estioko-Griffen & Griffen 1981). It may be that males do have some advantages over females as hunters, in terms of size and body weight and because of their more extensive foraging range, but these are not sufficient advantages to enforce a sexual division of labour; that division, when it occurs, has much more to do with social distinctions and social taboos. On quite pragmatic grounds it seems most likely that early hominids – small and highly vulnerable, in no position to hold onto game in the face of determined opposition from carnivores – would have been opportunistic scavengers, and the sharing would have been equally opportunistic. Shipman (1986) notes that the African savannah of 3 million years ago would have had more game – both prey and predator – than today, and that the form of cut- and gnaw-marks on animal bones found in the early deposits suggests a 'cut-and-run' strategy, possibly linked with a retreat to the treetops, rather than a hunting–home base existence. Hamilton (1984) points out that the strong sexual dimorphism found in early hominid populations may not only indicate the polygynous nature of the males, but a female adaptation which permitted a reduced calory intake and thus a reduced foraging range. The need for such a physiological adaptation would suggest that females were not significantly dependent upon the males for food. It seems probable that, rather than divisions of labour, flexibility would have been the key to survival. The increase in types of foods consumed, the volatility and complexity of relationships among these ranging, foraging, scavenging, vulnerable groupings, with dependent offspring, with rudimentary technological skills to be passed on, would from the outset accentuate the need for social interaction and communication.

There have been some moves towards the scavenging model for early hominids (Leakey 1981), but this has simply meant that the introduction of a 'natural' division of labour and of ensuing changes in social organization are pushed forward in time. The Mark II version of Man the Hunter moves on to the Middle Palaeolithic, around 200 000 years ago, and the emergence of *Homo sapiens*, or even the Upper Palaeolithic (c. 35 000 years ago) and *sapiens sapiens*. In this version it is suggested that groups adapting to the rigours of the European climate under extreme glacial conditions had to depend upon big-game hunting. This required skill and co-operative action by unencumbered males. Increased co-operation required a more systematic network of contacts which ran counter to an earlier pattern of open breeding networks and forced a degree of social closure. A precondition for such closure was a reasonable density of population, which was not attainable until the Middle to Upper Palaeolithic. Social closure created tensions, since those on the periphery of the network were at a disadvantage compared with those at the centre, and these would be relieved by increased ritual, emphasizing social solidarity between and within groups (Wobst 1976). Social closure and ritual are the hallmarks of culture, so, once again, men, because they are the big-game hunters, set the evolutionary process in motion.

The resilience of the Man the Hunter–Woman the Home-maker model is really quite remarkable, yet, again on pragmatic grounds, it has little to recommend it. Europe, during parts of the Upper Palaeolithic, undoubtedly suffered severe climatic conditions, but big-game hunting was by no means the only response. For example, in Cantabria in the earlier Upper Palaeolithic, base-camps in the upland areas exploited a range of animals including red deer, roe deer, ibex, chamois and horse. In the later Upper Palaeolithic a dispersed pattern of small sites is associated with a greater reliance on red deer and on a wider range of resources, including shellfish and small game (Freeman 1973). As Gilman (1984) points out, Upper Palaeolithic techniques were so advanced that groups could and would either exploit a wider range of species or specialize in a single species 'as conditions rendered either strategy more cost effective'. Many of these strategies would not have required co-operative tactics. Undermining the big-game hunting hypothesis still further are the findings that in other parts of the Old World, unaffected by the glacial advances, and with varied subsistence strategies, there is again evidence of social closure and ritual in the Middle and Upper Palaeolithic.

The purpose of this long exegesis is to demonstrate how the explanation of social phenomena, be it the division of labour, age-sets or potential inequalities in both gatherer-hunter and early farming societies, have tended to be naturalized and made law-like by stressing the dominance of techno-environmental/alias subsistence forces. We legitimize the divisions and inequalities in our own societies by making them the inevitable outcome of inevitable forces. This use of history is part of our dominant ideology, just as alternative 'histories' are often part of an attempt to undermine or demote aspects of contemporary social relations. If we want to understand the roots of social differentiation and social inequality, we will have to look at quite specific prehistoric and historic social configurations and see how it is that in some societies ideology and practice – including, no doubt, past history – was used to create, maintain or subvert sets of social relations that are by no means written into nature or subsistence. I am not suggesting that the level of technology does not impose constraints upon forms of social relations, but it does not explain change or variability. Farming of itself does not create the necessary surplus to underwrite more hierarchized positions; surplus is relative and is initiated by society: 'There are always and everywhere potential surpluses available. What counts is the institutionalised means of bringing them to life' (Parker-Pearson 1984). I want to consider the way in which such 'institutionalization' might occur and social differences and inequalities might be promoted in the context of certain prehistoric gatherer-hunter societies living in south-west Europe towards the end of the Ice Age. It is, at most, a partial analysis concentrating only on a limited aspect of social relations.

An example from the Upper Palaeolithic of south-west France

The cave and mobile art of north-west Spain and south-west France have been extensively analysed and explained. Leaving to one side the structural analyses of Leroi-Gourhan and Laming, much recent theorizing emphasizes that this art must be seen as an aspect of social action. Both Conkey (1978) and Gamble (1982) equate art with 'style', and 'style' with the signalling of social identity. Conkey recognizes that style is not simply a 'reflection' of social action and ritual, but rather 'it IS ritual communication' (Rowntree & Conkey 1980). Nevertheless she views it as reflexive in an adaptive sense. It is 'an information regulator', a 'parsimonious response to stress' (Conkey 1978). Conkey has undertaken an interesting analysis of stylistic variation in the portable art at the great cave of Altamira in northern Spain, and has quite convincingly demonstrated that a number of local groups must have come together at the site and that it was the locus of regional interaction. She suggests, following Johnson (1982), that such aggregation creates scalar stress which has to be met with shifts in social organization towards a sequential hierarchy, shifts which are formalized and negotiated through ritual. The explanation for both aggregation and ritual remains, again, techno-environmental. In earlier writings Conkey tended to view aggregation as a response either to the need to congregate in order to pool information about the environment, or as a response to demographic circumscription. More recently she seems to see it as a response to subsistence needs – the salmon are running, the deer congregating (Conkey 1985). The resultant stress is dealt with by a temporary shift in social strategy, mediated by ritual. When the groups disaggregate, the ritual goes away. Whereas Conkey's recent writings shade off towards less adaptive modelling, Gamble continues to provide a more straightforwardly environmental-demographic explanation (Gamble 1982, Champion *et al.* 1984, pp. 84–7). He ties 'style' to alliance networks, and alliance networks to problems of resource predictability. Jochim, too, proposes a stress model. He suggests that extreme glacial conditions between 25 000 and 17 000 years ago led to the abandonment of northern and much of central Europe, and the consequent retreat into south-west Europe created population pressure (Jochim 1982). These 'stress' scenarios sit uneasily with the empirical evidence. The major period of cave art was from 18 000 to 8000 years ago. It coincides at most with the end of the glacial advance. From 17 000 BP climatic conditions were ameliorating, and large tracts of northern central and northern Europe were being colonized (Champion *et al.* 1984, pp. 54–7). It is difficult to get a realistic notion of population densities, but one estimate suggests that in Cantabria site densities were around 0.2 per millennium in the Mousterian (Middle Palaeolithic), 1.2 in the Aurignacian–Perigordian (Early Upper Palaeolithic), 11.00 in the Solutrean, 11.7 in the early Magdalenian and 12 in the Late Magdalenian (Straus 1977). White (1982) believes that population increases in Périgord were of the same magnitude, but stresses that the figures for the later periods may well be 'inflated' by better site preservation. He suggests that there was a very gradual population increase, and this would accord more readily with Bordes' famous description of south-west France as 'a human desert swarming with game', than with Jochim's more extreme scenario (Bordes, cited in Leakey 1981).

An alternative reading requires that we re-socialize art, and in the process re-socialize gatherer-hunters. Art, then, is part of what Wolf (1984) has called 'insistent signification', part of the ideological imprinting. It is 'the coercion of a fan of potential connotations into a few licensed meanings'; part of a process of institutionalization, not only of what is to be said and thought, but how it is to be said and who is to say it – part, therefore, of an on-going process of negotiation and renegotiation of social relations.

With art, ideology takes material form. In kin-based societies, as Munn (1970) and Weiner (1985) have so elegantly shown, objects are not 'property' in our sense of the word, they are 'inalienable'. Among the Walbiri or the Maori – and surely among late prehistoric gatherer-hunters – objects 'belonged to particular ancestors, were passed down particular descent lines, held their own stories and were exchanged on various memorable occasions' (Weiner 1985, cited in Rowlands 1987). They are 'inalienable' and related to specific sets of relations, to particular groupings in particular contexts. They 'anchor' and celebrate a 'socio-moral' order in which authority runs from the ancestor to the senior to the junior in an unending process (Munn 1970). The generational ebb and flow may or may not be gender-specific. Among the Walbiri ritual objects anchor an authority that runs from father to son. Women are acknowledged – in myth and ritual – as 'begetters', but their fecundity is socially appropriated by the males (Miller 1987).[1] It is the process of such appropriation that can dimly be perceived among certain societies in the later Upper Palaeolithic of south-west Europe.

While I shall continue to use the term 'art', and to concentrate upon Upper Palaeolithic cave and mobile art, it must be acknowledged that this reflects the reification of 'art' in our own societies, and sets up a false division within the gamut of material culture. Upper Palaeolithic art must be seen as a facet, no more, of ideological and ritual expressiveness. It reiterates and elaborates concepts that permeate every material and non-material aspect of life. At El Juyo in northern Spain we almost catch the ephemeral action: the creation and recreation of mud 'rosettes', the construction of small pits and hummocks, the precise placement of needles and bone points, the location of a rough stone carving placed so that from one position the human face is visible, from another the feline face (Freeman & Echegeray 1981). Further afield, at Mezhirich on the Central Russian Plain, we see very clearly how house form is another expressive medium: the tents were encased in layer upon layer of mammoth mandible and long bone, carefully arranged in patterned and often mirrored formations (Sofer 1985). At Gönnersdorf, near Cologne, hut floors were covered with schist plaques with rough female engravings on the undersides. In the Ukraine six different musical instruments made of mammoth bone have been found, and two six-hole flutes from Russia and France again extend the range of expressive media. We only have the durable remains. The faint traces of paint found on some of the figurines hint at other, non-durable, forms (Marshack 1987).

Not only is there material reiteration, but also social action is confirmed, given depth and continuity by re-use and invocation. Material objects show signs of long usage, of touch and wear; the sculptures, engravings and paintings of objects and on cave walls are touched and retouched over and over again, the animal representations are splattered with markings (Marshack 1977, 1987). Within the caves earlier representations are re-incorporated and, no doubt, re-interpreted (cf. Lewis-Williams & Loubser 1986). The actual durable, immoveable fabric of cave and rock-shelter again creates a sense of continuity and makes them part of the process by which the landscape is socialized and 'claimed' (Layton 1986, Miller 1987). We can be fairly sure that artefact, cave and landscape demarcate a ritual rather than an economic homeland. As Munn (1970) puts it: 'the importance of these sacred countries is not economic in the sense that it does not define the limits over which those who reside may forage . . . Rather [it is] a symbol of stability'. Yet this sense of stability and continuity remains an ideological construct, and it masks the process by which social relations are subtly re-evaluated and re-aligned. For example, when an earlier painting is re-incorporated, it both cross-references the past, and takes on new meaning (Layton 1986).

To get a sense of this process of re-evaluation and alignment – and thus of change – we need also to keep in mind the immense timespan within which this cave and mobile art occurs (Conkey 1985, Marshack 1987). Within a 20 000-year span (35 000 to 10 000 BP) the 'domains of discourse' must vary very greatly. For long millennia social relations may have been such that the 'signfication' of these material expressions was open to all members of the group, forming part of the process of socialization from birth to death. Objects made of imported shell or fine stones, small sculpted or engraved animals and female figurines, annotated objects, are found in habitation sites right across Europe. Form, distribution and significance changed at different times and places. For example, Marshack (1987) noted that it is only towards the end of the Palaeolithic that there are engravings that have quite specific seasonal connotations. Nevertheless, however varied, this repertoire has in common that it is visible and found in domestic contexts. It is accessible (Hahn, cited in Conkey 1985, Marshack 1987). Personal adornments were often placed in burials, and the lavish endowment of some children's graves (for example, at Sungir in Russia) would also be an expression of communal ritual, since the children can have attained little in their own right. However, there are times, and places, when part of the art and ritual becomes circumscribed, when there is a degree of social closure – by gender, age or status. Access to social knowledge is curtailed and thereby inequalities, however minor, are institutionalized and legitimized.

In the earlier part of the Upper Palaeolithic, entrances to the caves of south-west France and northern Spain were often used as habitations, and entrances, accessible passages and chambers were painted and engraved. Socialization and ritual seem wide open. At some time after 17 000 BP the pattern changes.[2] Certain caves, such as Altamira, Castillo, Lascaux and Pech-Merle, become the foci of regional aggregation and ceremonial activity. In Périgord four of the 86 known Magdalenian sites (Laugerie-Basse, La Madeleine, Limeuil and Rochereil) have 80 per cent of the embellished artefacts (White 1980, cited in Conkey 1985). In Cantabria two of the eight Early Magdalenian have 60 per cent, and in the Late Magdalenian one has 30 per cent. In the Pyrénées, Isturitz and Mas d'Azil stand out. As the arena of ritual and ceremony, such sites would have been associated with intense activity. Things would have to be collected together, made and exchanged. There had to be provisioning for feasting as well as for everyday subsistence. In this later Upper Palaeolithic, the number of paintings in the big caves increases enormously, but part of the ritual now moves inwards. The large, accessible chambers, at Lascaux or

Altamira, with their great tableaux, may have remained 'open', but small side chambers and passages show a much more intensive retouching of animals and innumerable 'annotations' (Marshack 1987). At Tuc d'Audoubert in the Pyrénées the ceiling of a small chamber has an engraved horse's head, surrounded by 84 P signs, made in various styles with various tools, and sometimes renewed. An almost identical configuration is found in the neighbouring cave of Trois Frères (Marshack 1987). Often the paintings and engravings are placed far from the cave entrance (Rouffignac 2 km from the entrance; Niaux between 500 m and 2 km; Tuc d'Audoubert and Trois Frères about the same), access is difficult, and the space cramped. Exclusivity can take other forms – at El Juyo in Spain the roughly sculpted stone placed near the entrance reads from the outside as a man's head, but from inside the cave it becomes a feline (Freeman & Echegaray 1981).

Who, then, is being excluded? A strong possibility is that these secret places were an arena for the initiation of young males, and the 'capturing' of the animals in the painting was part of the capture of hunting as a male preserve. They become part of the process by which the 'female controlled biological power of reproduction is subsumed by male cultural control over social reproduction' (Miller 1987). There is – as was noted earlier – no reason in nature for the sharp gender divisions found in many gatherer-hunter societies, they have to be created by proscription and taboo, they have to be 'naturalized' through ideology and ritual.

Other aspects of the later Upper Palaeolithic art of this region, both cave and mobile, may substantiate this notion of increased exclusiveness. Although the animal representations have received most of the attention, there are, in reality, many more geometric signs in the caves. These signs are less frequently found on mobile art, they fall into fairly well-defined classes and have tight regional groupings – there is none of the widespread dissemination associated with mobile art (Leroi-Gourhan 1977–8). They increase in number and variety and become more abstract in the later Upper Palaeolithic. They are often used to 'annotate' animal representations (Marshack 1977). Increased abstraction permits increased ambiguity, creates a code that is harder to crack – an individual sign may carry different meanings depending upon the context of use and specific juxtapositions (Munn 1973). There can be a multiplicity of codes that are differentially available to groups within groups. Layton (1986) notes how a North Arnhem Land artist explained that if he were representing the subject matter in an exclusive male context rather than an open camp, he would use 'geometrics'.

Another interesting feature is that not only are there very high concentrations of decorated pieces at the large sites in Périgord, the Pyrénées and Cantabria, but certain artefacts – spear-thrower, shaft-straightener, harpoon and rod – begin to be highly embellished (Bahn 1982). We seem to be witnessing part of the process by which symbolic representation extends and engulfs the surface of other media, to which access is again limited. Munn (1973, p. 213) noticed such a development in the male iconography of the Walbiri. Such artefacts have tight distributions; they move in constrained spheres of exchange, available only to socially designated partners.

Social differentiation hinges, in the first instance, on differential access to social knowledge. However, this can be 'converted' into more material control. There is the possibility of exclusive exchange, there are the demands made on people's labour as part of the whole process of ritual, of material creations, of display and feasting. The labour of elder or shaman, young initiate or uninitiated male or female appears, both to us and to the people involved, as a form of communal appropriation. This 'ideology' of communality disguises the way in which the labour is called into being and used by only a limited number of people within the society.

It would seem that the social configuration of areas of south-west France and northern Spain during parts of the Upper Palaeolithic was different from that of contemporary groups, and that the art was part of a process of social negotiation, part of a symbolic 'naturalization' of increased social differentiation. No doubt the seasonal aggregations at the great sites in Périgord, Cantabria and the Pyrénées were made possible by their optimal locations for culling herds or catching salmon, but their ecological setting does not explain the size of aggregation or the intensity of ritual. People came together to celebrate, and they chose locations and seasons that permitted such congregations. No doubt they intensified their subsistence strategies to meet their temporary needs – just as Australian aborigines dug artificial eel runs to permit large ceremonial gatherings (Lourandos 1980). It may even be that the emphasis on reindeer hunting was as much a response to a demand for antler to make into fine artefacts as a demand for meat (White 1982). No doubt such seasonal aggregations permitted the pooling of much practical information, but it also permitted the control rather than dissemination of social knowledge. The ceremony and ritual of the great caves was part of a process of social reproduction which need not have been to the advantage of each and every member of the society.

It is obvious that the developments charted above are still immensely crude. With tighter control of the evidence it may be possible to chart cyclical developments within the different regions. There were perhaps times when the demands made on labour and resources became too great, and a more egalitarian configuration re-emerged.

Conclusions

Marx once exclaimed: 'Man's innate casuistry'! To change things by changing their names. And to find loopholes for violating tradition while maintaining tradition, when direct interest supplie[s] sufficient impulse' (cited in Engels 1972, p. 120). I have tried to suggest that to understand the emergence of social divisions and inequalities we need to examine the way in which ideological constructions, material and immaterial, promote change. I have not, in this chapter, taken up the question of how such constructions mesh with other aspects of evolving social relations, particularly those of alliance and exchange (but see Bender 1978, 1985). Binford (1982) has said:

> one of the greatest confusions to have plagued the social sciences is the

> confusion between regularities in the internal dynamics of cultural systems (synchronic and internal–functional) and the nature of the dynamics which conditioned changes in the organization of systems themselves and in their evolutionary diversification and change (diachronic and external-ecological).

One purpose of this chapter is to stress that no such internal : functional adaptive/external : ecological causative dichotomy is permissible. Societies attempt to reproduce themselves – as societies, not as biological units. The strategies employed may seem adaptive to the participants, they may even be adaptive in the short term, but they are frequently less viable in the longer term. Thus, they hold the seeds of their own destruction, or rather, since human societies are immensely flexible, of change.

Ideological representations are integral to relations of power and control. In some instances these relations make demands on labour and on production, and these demands may, in turn, promote technological developments. The beginnings of inequality do not start with the onset of farming, or with any other ecological input, they lie far back in the varied social configurations and ideologies of gatherer-hunter societies.

Notes

1 Munn (1970) describes a Walbiri myth which gives a sense of the social appropriation of female fecundity. At the behest of the son, the father snake emits a design-marked board which changes into women with digging sticks. The women move from place to place creating water-holes with their digging sticks, into which their progeny go. They are followed by men who pick up the women's faeces and turn them into sacred boards which they make into head-dresses. Then they dance. When they go into the women's camp they leave the boards outside so that the women cannot see them. In this myth the women are portrayed as life-givers and providers (digging sticks–water-holes–progeny), but this natural fecundity is 'socialized' and pre-empted by the male. In the first instance the ancestral male (snake father) is transformed into a cultural artefact (decorated board) which 'creates' the female. The female then creates in nature, but her (natural) products, her faeces, are taken by the male and re-socialized (into boards and head-dresses) which are then used in ritual. Artefacts and ritual are then kept outside the female domain. The myth also shadows the process whereby the young male is removed from the female 'hearth' and joins the domain of the male initiates.

2 Layton (1986) contrasts the 'open', communal and person-orientated art of some Australian aboriginal groups and the southern African San, and the 'closed', hieratic art of other, totemic, societies in Australia and Upper Palaeolithic groups of south-west Europe.

References

Bahn, P. 1982. Inter-site and inter-regional links during the Upper Palaeolithic: the Pyrenean evidence. *Oxford Journal of Archaeology* **1** (3), 247–68.

Bender, B. 1978. Gatherer-hunter to farmer: a social perspective. *World Archaeology* **10**, 204–22.
Bender, B. 1985. Emergent tribal formations in the American midcontinent. *American Antiquity* **50**, 52–62.
Binford, L. 1982. Comment on R. White's paper: Rethinking the Middle/Upper Palaeolithic transition. *Current Anthropology* **23** (2), 177–81.
Champion, T., C. Gamble, S. Shennan & A. Whittle 1984. *Prehistoric Europe.* London: Academic Press.
Childe, G. 1942. *What happened in history*. London: Penguin.
Conkey, M. 1978. Style and information in cultural evolution: towards a predictive model for the Palaeolithic. In *Social archaeology. Beyond subsistence and dating,* C. Redman, M. Berman, E. Curtin, W. Langhorne, N. Versaggi & J. Wanser (eds), 61–85. New York: Academic Press.
Conkey, M. 1985. Ritual communication, social elaboration, and the variable trajectories of Paleolithic material culture. In *Prehistoric hunters and gatherers: the emergence of cultural complexity,* T. Price & J. Brown (eds). New York: Academic Press.
Conkey, M. & J. Spector 1984. Archaeology and the study of gender. In *Archaeological method and theory*, Vol. 7, M. Schiffer (ed.), 1–38. New York: Academic Press.
Dahlberg, F. (ed.) 1981. *Woman the gatherer.* New Haven: Yale University Press.
Engels, F. 1972. *The origin of the family, private property and the state.* London: Lawrence & Wishart.
Estioko-Griffin, A. & P. Griffin 1981. Woman the hunter: the Agta. In *Woman the gatherer*, F. Dahlberg (ed.), 121–51. New Haven: Yale University Press.
Freeman, L. 1973. The significance of mammalian faunas from palaeolithic occupations in Cantabrian Spain. *American Antiquity* **38**, 3–44.
Freeman, L. & J. Echegaray 1981. El Juyo: a 14,000-year-old sanctuary in northern Spain. *History of Religion* **21**, 1–19.
Gamble, C. 1982. Interaction and alliance in Palaeolithic society. *Man* **17**, 92–107.
Gilman, A. 1984. Rethinking the Upper Palaeolithic revolution. In *Marxist approaches to archaeology*, M. Spriggs (ed.), 115–26. Cambridge: Cambridge University Press.
Hamilton, M. 1984. Revising evolutionary narratives: a consideration of alternative assumptions about sexual selection and competition for mates. *American Anthropologist* **86**.
Higgs, E. (ed.) 1972. *Papers in economic prehistory*. Cambridge: Cambridge University Press.
Isaac, G. 1978. The food-sharing behavior of protohuman hominids. *Scientific American* **238** (4), 90–108.
Jochim, M. 1982. Palaeolithic art in an ecological perspective. In *Hunter–gatherer economy in prehistory*, G. Bailey (ed.), 212–19. Cambridge: Cambridge University Press.
Johnson, G. 1982. Organizational structure and scalar stress. In *Theory and explanation in archaeology*, C. Renfrew, M. Rowlands & B. Segraves (eds), 389–421. New York: Academic Press.
Layton, R. 1986. Political and territorial structures among hunter-gatherers. *Man* **21**, 18–33.
Leakey, R. 1981. *The making of mankind.* London: Book Club Associates.
Leroi-Gourhan, A. 1977–8. Résumé des cours et travaux de l'année scolaire 1977–78. *L'Annuaire du Collége de France*, 523–34.
Lewis-Williams, J. & J. Loubser 1986. Deceptive appearances: a critique of Southern

African rock art. In *Advances in world archaeology*, F. Wendorf & A. Close (eds), 253–89. New York: Academic Press.
Lourandos, H. 1980. Change or stability? Hydraulics, hunter-gatherers and population in temperate Australia. *World Archaeology* **11**, (3), 245–64.
Marshack, A. 1977. The meander as a system. In *Form in indigenous art*, P. Ucko (ed.), 286–317. London: Duckworth.
Marshack, A 1987. The archaeological evidence for the emergence of human conceptualisation. Paper delivered at Santa Fé, April 1987.
Meillassoux, C. 1972. From reproduction to production. *Economy and Society* **1** (1), 93–105.
Miller, D. 1987. *Material culture and mass consumption*. Oxford: Blackwell.
Morgan, L. 1963. *Ancient society*. Cleveland: World Publishing Company.
Munn, N. 1970. The transformation of subjects into objects in Walbiri and Pitjantjatjara myth. In *Australian Aboriginal anthropology*, R. Berndt (ed.), 141–63. Canberra: Australian Institute of Aboriginal Studies.
Munn, N. 1973. *Walbiri iconography*. Ithaca: Cornell University Press.
O'Laughlin, B. 1977. Critique of Meillassoux's Femmes, Greniers et Capitaux. *Critique of Anthropology* **8** (2), 3–32.
Parker-Pearson, M. 1984. Economic and ideological change; cyclical growth in the pre-state societies of Jutland. In *Ideology, power and prehistory*, D. Miller & C. Tilley (eds), 69–92. Cambridge: Cambridge University Press.
Quiatt, D. & J. Kelso 1985. Household economies and hominid origins. *Current Anthropology* **26** (2), 207–22.
Rowlands, M. 1987. Centre and Periphery: a review of a concept. In *Centre and periphery in the Ancient World*, M. Rowlands, M. Larsen & K. Kristiansen (eds), 1–11. Cambridge: Cambridge University Press.
Rowntree, L. & M. Conkey 1980. Symbolism and the cultural landscape. *Annals of the Association of American Geographers* **70** (4), 459–74.
Shipman, D. 1986. Scavenging and hunting in early hominids: theoretical framework and tests. *American Anthropologist* **88** (1), 27–43.
Slocum, S. 1975. Woman the gatherer: male bias in anthropology. In *Towards an anthropology of women*, R. Reiter (ed.), 36–50. New York: Monthly Review Press.
Soffer, O. 1985. In *Prehistoric hunter-gatherers: the emergence of cultural complexity*, T. Price & J. Brown (eds). New York: Academic Press.
Straus, G. 1977. Of deer-slayers and mountain men: Paleolithic faunal exploitation in Cantabrian Spain. In *For theory building in archaeology*, L. Binford (ed.), 41–76. New York: Academic Press.
Tanner, N. 1971. *On becoming human*. Cambridge: Cambridge University Press.
Washburn, S. & C. Lancaster 1968. The evolution of hunting. In *Man the hunter*, R. Lee & I. Devore (eds), 293–303. Chicago: Aldine.
Weiner, A. 1985. Inalienable wealth. *American Ethnologist* **12**, 210–27.
White, R. 1982. Rethinking the Middle/Upper Paleolithic transition. *Current Anthropology* **23** (2), 169–92.
Wobst, M. 1976. Locational relationships in Palaeolithic society. In *The demographic evolution of human populations*, R. Ward & K. Weiss (eds), 49–58. New York: Academic Press.
Wolf, E. 1984. Culture: panacea or problem? *American Antiquity* **49** (2), 393–400.
Woodburn, J. 1980. Hunters and gatherers today and the reconstruction of the past. In *Soviet and Western anthropology*, E. Gellner (ed.), 95–117. New York: Columbia University Press.
Zihlman, A. 1981. Women as shapers of the human adaptation. In *Woman the gatherer*, F. Dahlberg (ed.), 75–102. New Haven: Yale University Press.

5 *Towards a theory of social evolution: on state systems and ideological shells*

J. A. HALL

Introduction

In this chapter I offer an account of the role of political and ideological factors in the rise of capitalism. The argument is based on a comparison between Rome and China, or, more specifically, between the 'blocking' of capitalism in Imperial China and its triumph in Europe after the fall of Rome. However, I believe that this case-study points to a more general theory of social evolution, and this accounts for my title.

I need one piece of theoretical scaffolding to get my argument under way. When thinking about state power we need to distinguish between the despotic and infrastructural faces of power. Mann (1986) has combined these factors to produce this four-fold table:

		DESPOTISM	
		High	Low
INFRASTRUCTURE	High		
	Low		

I have left this table blank, but I can highlight my argument immediately with reference to the categories involved. I argue that Imperial China (and Imperial Rome) have states high in despotism, but weak in the ability actually to penetrate social relationships and largely incapable of providing infrastructural services for their societies. This type of state blocked the emergence of capitalism; it was, in this specific sense, an evolutionary dead end. In contrast, the feudal state of north-west Europe, weak in both despotism and infrastructure, *became* an organic state, weak in despotism but strong in infrastructure; this political form favoured the triumph of capitalism.

'Bureaucracy [in pre-industrial conditions] kills capitalism' (Weber 1978)

The Chinese empire was bounded to the north by the Great Wall, manned by troops whose supplies were sent up the Grand Canal from the fertile, double-cropping rice lands of the south. What is implied by this simple statement? The extensive area of the empire was created by and held together by military might, just as the legions had created and maintained the *Pax Romana*. In contrast it seems likely that culture was passive, secondary and certainly *not* larger than the state. The examination system, which encouraged intellectuals to serve this civilization as bureaucrats rather than as priests, was created by the state, first under the Han and much more decisively by the Tang. Does the presence of an imperial state manned by bureaucrats schooled in Caesaropapist creed give evidence of a strong state? Was the mandarinate a bureaucracy of great efficiency? There were never enough mandarins to form an efficient governing class. The first Ming Emperor in 1371 sought to have as few as 5488 mandarins in government service and, by the 16th century there were still only about 20 400 in the empire as a whole, plus another 50 000 minor officials (Huang 1981; Ch. 2). A local official might well have managed 500 to 1000 square miles with the aid of only three assistants. So, the Chinese state did not have the means of total control envisaged in Wittfogel's fantasy of *Oriental despotism* (1957). Of course, it sought, as did other imperial states, to gain such autonomy, but arbitrary action against individuals was counterbalanced by an inability of the state to fundamentally go against the gentry class as a whole. The state sought to improve the economy, but had very limited means with which to push through any plan of its own. Reformer after reformer tried to establish a decent land registry as the basis for a proper taxation system, but all were defeated by landlord refusal to co-operate. The empire as a whole witnessed a power stand-off between state and society which led to the inability to generate a large total sum of societal energy.

This stalemate can be seen at work in the dynastic cyclical pattern. A newly established dynasty sought to create a healthy peasant base, both for its tax and for its military potential. Yet even without internal or external pressures, the state tended to lose control of society. The power of the gentry locally enabled them to increase their estates and to avoid taxation. Other pressures on the empire were usually present as well. Internally, an expansion of population, by no means discouraged by the gentry, eventually caused land hunger and peasant rebellions. Externally, the nomads on the borders found the empire increasingly attractive as its prosperity waxed in front of their eyes. Such nomads were often employed as mercenaries by empires in their later days; as a result they learnt military techniques which, when allied with their inherent military resource of great mobility, made them a formidable force. The imperial state was, of course, forced to increase taxation rates. It was at this moment that the power stand-off between state and society proved to be important, for many landlords chose to shelter peasants who refused to pay such increased taxation, and thereby increased their own local power. The combination of feudal-type disintegration and overpopulation led to a constant decrease in the number of taxpaying peasant smallholders. Rodinski cites the census of 754, which showed that there were only 7.6 million taxpayers out of a total population of 52.8 million (Rodinski 1983, p. 78). In such circumstances the state was forced to tax even more heavily where it could, and this in turn fuelled peasant unrest. Breakdown ensued. However, a new dynasty was established in the long term, either by nomads or by leaders of peasant revolts, forced eventually to co-operate with the gentry.

Nevertheless, the Chinese empire was restored several times. The mandarins, unlike the Latin Christian Church at the Fall of Rome, held together and remained true to the imperial ideal. On a number of occasions barbarians tried to rule without them, partly because the mandarins were wont to stay away from a dynasty that did not respect the fundamentals of Confucianism. Any consideration of the rather small numbers of the élite shows that an enormous confidence trick was played on the gentry. They remained loyal to the state, but the paucity of their numbers is evidence that they did not do at all well from it. Furthermore, there was great insecurity attached to office-holding. This is not, it must be stressed, to resurrect the notion of a totalitarian strength on the part of the state. This did not exist and, in most matters and for most of the time, the scholar-gentry class could block imperial initiatives, albeit *individuals* amongst its number did suffer in one way or another. The argument being made is that there was a definite autonomy of the state, of the political, in Chinese history, because the state *was* strong enough to force class relations into a particular pattern. This makes us consider the key question: in what ways, if any, did the imperial form effect the Chinese economy?

Medieval China witnessed considerable economic advance of a broadly capitalist type. Interestingly, the greatest expansion took place during a period of disunity. The Northern Sung did rule China from 960 to 1127, but even they were faced with the militant nomadic Jurchen. Disunity encouraged the Southern Sung to build a navy in order to man all waterways which stood between them and their Northern competitors. More generally, the market and cities gained autonomy during the period of disunity in Chinese history. The quality of coinage provided by states tended to improve during disunity, because traders would not themselves return to or trust governments which manipulated the coinage (Elvin 1973, Ch. 14).

How did the empire, when it was reunited, react to capitalist forces that had flourished previously? The state controlled the autonomy of cities. Little is known about the collapse of the iron and steel industries of Sung China. However, we can explain the collapse of the Sung naval strength. The foundation of a native dynasty which improved the Grand Canal (so no longer necessitating ocean-going transport from north to south) undermined the navy; most obviously, between 1371 and 1567, all foreign trade was banned. *The* most spectacular way in which politics could affect the economy concerned the fate of the explorations undertaken by the eunuch admiral Cheng-Ho in the 1430s. The mandarins were always extremely jealous of the emergence of sources of power alternative to their own. They were naturally opposed to Cheng-Ho, precisely because he was a eunuch, whose cause was promoted by the eunuchs at court. The centralization of political life mattered. Although the bureaucracy was not able to penetrate far into society, it could and did prevent other forces from gaining much autonomy. A classic instance of this was that of the suppression of Buddhist monasteries.

Chinese imperial government deserves the appellation *capstone*. The Chinese élite shared a culture, and sat atop a series of separate 'societies' which it did not wish to penetrate or mobilize; it feared that horizontal linkages it could not see would get out of control. This capstone government blocked the fully-fledged emergence of intensive capitalist relationships. The concern of the mandarinate was less with intensifying social relationships than in seeking to prevent any linkages which might diminish its power. This can be seen particularly clearly in an analysis of Ming taxation (Huang 1974, p. 290):

> As the Ming administrators saw it, to promote these advanced sectors of the economy would only widen the economic imbalance which in turn would threaten the empire's political unity. It was far more desirable to keep all provinces on the same footing, albeit at the level of the backward sectors of the economy.

This is *not* say that the impact of the state upon capitalism must always be negative. A different type of state, the European organic state, once capitalist relationships were established, provided crucial services for capitalism. The Chinese state was incapable of doing so (Huang 1974, pp. 318–19):

> It must be pointed out that in the late Ming most of the service facilities indispensable to the development of capitalism were wholly lacking. There was no legal protection for the businessman, money was scarce, interest rates high and banking undeveloped. At the same time merchants and entrepreneurs were hindered by the frequent roadblocks on the trade routes, government purchase orders and forced contributions, the government's near monopoly of the Grand Canal and active involvement in manufacturing. On the other hand, the security and status of land ownership, the tax-exemption enjoyed by those who purchased official rank, and the non-progressive nature of the land tax increased the attraction of farming to the detriment of business involvement.

Politics and culture in China tended to have the same extensive reach, and this pattern was crucial to China's fate. The fact of centralized power allowed for the blocking of capitalism, while the absence of any real competitors made this sort of low-intensity rule a viable proposition.

Trahison des clercs

In the context of the origins of Christianity, it is worth emphasizing that the Roman state felt nervous about it precisely because it represented an unofficial, horizontal communication channel. It is necessary to describe briefly the concordat reached between Church and state between the conversion of Constantine and the fall of the Empire. How well did both sides do from this new relationship?

The Church gained enormously from détente. It became extremely rich. More importantly, its very form of organization, the hierarchy of bishop, deacon and presbyter, was modelled on that of the secular state. The Church also called upon the state to help it in its battles. Throughout the 4th century the Church pushed the state towards a position increasingly hostile to traditional paganism, even though such paganism was especially strong amongst the traditional landed and Roman aristocracy. Augustine had no compunction whatever in using the secular arm to hunt out those he considered to be heretics; Christian persecution to establish a single Church organization rapidly took the place of earlier persecution of Christians.

But what of the state? How well did it do from the bargain? The immensely interesting answer to this is that it did very poorly indeed out of the deal; it is proper to talk only of an attempted takeover of the Church since that attempt, in fact, failed.

One imagines that Constantine himself might have had some disquiet by the end of his reign. In the course of the two decades after the adoption of Christianity he found himself in a hornets' nest of controversy. Donatism in North Africa asserted that those who had apostasized during the persecutions should not be accepted as leaders of the Church. This might seem a trivial point, but a very great deal was involved in it. The Donatists wished to emphasize the purity of the Church community – that is, they wished to remain a sect opposed to a world which would sully their purity; perhaps in this Donatism was a rallying cry for disaffected provincials who were tired of Rome's overlordship. Constantine also found himself deeply involved in the long-running squabble between Arius and Athanasius over whether Christianity was to be rigidly monotheist. Constantine attempted to compromise at the Council of Nicaea between those who believed God had made Jesus (and was thus the *only* true God himself) and the trinitarians, by saying that Jesus, God and the Holy Spirit were 'essentially of the same substance'. This did not resolve the conflict, which continued in the Middle Eastern provinces, in the form of monophysitism, until the Islamic conquests.

Are these matters not theological in another sense entirely, that is, trivial and unimportant to most Christians? Even more important, was not the empire beginning to gain loyalty from the Church? Certainly Eusebius of Caesarea positively welcomed his role as advisor in a sort of Caesaropapist doctrine centred on Constantine, and it seems that some Western bishops were also rallying to the empire. Augustine, after all, fiercely attacked the Donatists, and did so with some success (Brown 1967). Yet we must note the arguments he used against the Donatists. He accused them of lacking imagination in wishing to be a sect, anti-society. He was quite as puritanical as they were, but insisted that a much greater historical opportunity lay in front of them: the Church could *become* society rather than merely constituting an opposition to it. So if the Church integrated people into society, it is vital to insist that society was Christian rather than Roman. There is a distinctive difference here between East and West, caused perhaps by the fact that the emperor spent so much more time in the Eastern provinces, and finally, of course, cemented by the fact that the emperor *did* save the Eastern empire. Augustine was one of the socially mobile provincials who came first to Rome and then to Milan, where he was elevated to a Professorship of Rhetoric. The influence of St Ambrose upon him in Milan led him to abandon the service of the empire and retreat to private study at Cassiacum and then in North Africa, before becoming a servant of the Church. Of course, his *City of God*, perhaps the single most important theological work in medieval Christendom, famously argued that God's kingdom could not be associated with the destiny of Rome. God's timetable was his own, and should not be conflated with the destiny of Rome. This was a remarkable, indeed foolhardy, judgement given that, at the time, the basic infrastructure of the Church – that is literacy – was not yet provided by the Church but was the general product of Roman civilization.

In the West the Church moved from ingratitude to, and scorn of, the state to a realization that it could, in fact, do without it. It was the Church that negotiated with the barbarians at the walls of most cities, and arranged for them to be saved rather than destroyed. Where Chinese intellectuals refused to serve barbarians until they accepted the imperial form, and thus put themselves on the road to assimilation, in Western Christendom, exactly the opposite was the case. The élite broke ranks. The intellectuals went out to the barbarians and provided services for them as well as the promise of universal salvation. For the chiefs of tribes, the Church, as the bearer of literacy, proved invaluable in allowing legal codification. Thus Gregory the Great's mission to England landed in 597, and by 616 more than 90 laws had been written down. Much the same story could be told of the codification provided for the Lombards and the Franks, but perhaps underlying all this is something much simpler. The Church, as Anderson (1974, pp. 128–44) stresses, wore the mantle of Rome, it *was* civilization and the hope of a better life.

So the City of God came to be dissociated from the imperial structure, and it is a story pregnant with consequences. In China and Rome a large geographical space was chained together by political and military means. However, in Christian Europe, as in Islam and in the land of the Brahmans, cultural identity was more extensive than the political order. Latin Christendom held together an extensive space until approximately 1100 but, lacking its own political theory, it then provided the shell within which organic states could develop. The manner in which this took place concerns us below. One contention necessary to the rest of the argument must first be made. It is now something of a commonplace amongst medieval historians to note that great technological breakthroughs occurred in European history in the years between 800 and 1000 (Duby 1974, Postan 1975, Cipolla 1976), that is, precisely in those years in which Europe was held together culturally but not, in the fullest sense of the word, governmentally. The extensive area of Latin Christendom created a market, and helped the restoration of trade. Furthermore, the egalitarian nature of Christian belief, so much in contrast to classical Hinduism, perhaps proved to be an energizing force. Crucially, the fact that the Christian Church was not a full-blooded government meant that property relations could gel and set without state interference. This is extremely important. Where Chinese mandarins could look to the state for money, it became quite clear from early on that medieval landlords – and peasants, particularly of the kulak variety – had to look to their estates for increased income. The exact causes of the intensive and capitalist turn of the European economy do not concern us here (Hall 1985, Ch. 5). What is important is to see the relationship between a pre-existing civil society – for this is what the prior establishment of property relationships, cities and churchly power, that is, the emergence of strong and autonomous social groups, amounted to – and a particular type of state.

The organic state in the state system

The intensive nature of the early medieval economy is not unique; similar bursts of development took place in other civilizations. What concerns us is the relation between commercial capitalism and state organization in Europe. The earliest economic advance had been made, by and large, without the real presence of states, for monarchies and chiefdoms were short-lived and feeble. However, from about 1100, and slightly earlier in the case of England, it became clear that a number of states were likely to remain part of the political scene. How did this multipolar system affect capitalism?

The first and most obvious argument takes the form of a counterfactual. Imagine what European history might have been like had the Roman Empire somehow been reconstituted, or had any empire taken its place! Pre-industrial empires are too centralized for their logistical capacity, and thus have produced capstone government based on their sensible appreciation that secondary organizations are dangerous. Such empires sought to encourage the economy, but this form of government never ultimately allowed sufficient leeway to the economy for it to gather self-sustaining momentum. Why should an imperial Europe have been any different?

This can be put in a rather different manner. A decentralized market system came into place during those years in which there was no government which could interfere with its workings, but an organization which nevertheless made medieval men realize that they belonged to a single civilization. An imperial form would probably have sought to control such 'natural' processes. Consider the European city. All historians agree that Max Weber *was* correct in the more materialist part of his theory concerning the rise of the West, namely in his contention that only in Europe did the city gain full autonomy. This autonomy provided a space in which the merchant was king, and in which bourgeois values could gel and solidify. We live in the world created by this civilization. With a matter of such import, it is essential to ask how this autonomy occurred. The most satisfying answer is that the North Italian cities were themselves the creation of the absence of a single centre of power in Europe. Specifically, they gained their autonomy as the result of a power vacuum between pope and emperor, such that they were able, as is often the case in the Third World countries today, to get the best for themselves by opportunistically chopping and changing their allegiance (Burke 1986). How much they owed to their freedom from interference and freedom to experiment is simply seen: once they became part of the Spanish mini-empire they contributed virtually nothing new to European civilization. Much the same point could be made by indulging in a 'thought-experiment': had Philip II created a long-lasting empire based on his new Spanish possessions, what would have happened to the social experiments taking place in Holland and Great Britain? Had an empire been established at any time, it seems likely that social experiments at the peripheries would have been ruled out.

This first point amounts to reiterating that political fragmentation was a necessary condition for the autonomy of the market. The Islamic case has demonstrated that such fragmentation is not sufficient by itself to encourage economic dynamism. What else was involved? It might at first sight seem contradictory to say that the organic state helped economic development after the largely negative comments made to this point about state 'interference', but there are *different* types of state in different historical and social circumstances. Two general principles about the relations of government to the economy can be maintained. First, the absence of all government is disastrous, since it encourages disorder and localism, and thus prevents trade, and the insistence that Christianity held medieval Europe together shows that no anarchistic vision is encouraged here. Secondly, bureaucratic and predatory governments *were* hostile to economic development. As noted, it is mistaken to consider such government strong, since it was based on weak infrastructural penetration of the society; indeed, arbitrariness partly results from weakness. This gives the clue to the distinctiveness of the European state: a limit to arbitrariness combined with, and in part caused by, considerable and ever-increasing infrastructural penetration. Two such limits are important.

The first limit is straightforward. The European state evolved slowly and doggedly in the midst of pre-existing social relationships. One uniqueness of the West is the role that parliaments played in its history: indeed, so unique has this role been that German historians have considered the *Standestaat*, the representation of the three functional estates, Church, Noble and Burgher, a distinctive stage in world history (Myers 1975). It is quite clear that the prominence of such assemblies owes a great deal to the Church, which owned so much land that it was as jealous as any noble of the powers of the crown to tax. Hence it generalized two tags of canon law – 'no taxation without representation' and 'what touches all must be approved by all', and these became crucial to these estates. However, 'liberties' were widely diffused throughout society, and churchmen had allies amongst nobles, burghers and yeomen. European pluralism, in other words, has an extremely long history. In these circumstances there was a movement, in terms of Mann's argument, between a feudal state, weak despotically *and* infrastructurally, to a more *organic* state, still low in despotism, but with ever-increasing infrastructural penetration. The monarch's only way of gaining money was to co-operate with this pre-existing civil society.

The paradox of this situation is that restraint on government eventually generated a larger sum of power in society. Perhaps the most important mechanism in this process was the making of money via the provision of a certain infrastructure to the society. This is most clearly seen in the provision of justice. Fees were charged for every legal transaction, and these came to provide an important part of the revenue of most monarchs after about 1200. This is not to say that the law was equally open for all to use; but it was available. European states provided other sorts of infrastructural help. They became good at managing disasters of various sorts; by the 18th century, for example, considerable help was available to the victims of earthquakes, while disease was quite rigidly controlled by quarantine laws (Jones 1981). Furthermore, the internal colonialism whereby Scots, Irish and Welsh were integrated into a single community – a similar process repeated elsewhere in Europe – created a single market. In the more advanced European states (i.e. not France until after 1789) this process went hand-in-hand with the removal of internal tariff barriers, and this was an incentive to trade. These policies were not designed with the improvement of the economy in view, but rulers *had* consciously encouraged trade for a long time. They did so because a disproportionate bulk of their revenues came from customs and excise. They sought to attract traders, a typical piece of legislation being Edward I's *Carta Mercatoria* of 1297. What is apparent as as whole is that large sections of the powerful were prepared to give quite high taxation revenues to the crown because they realized that their own interests were usually being served. Tocqueville was right to note that the English aristocracy and gentry manned local government and taxed itself. The level of infrastructural support and penetration was correspondingly high. A Confucian bureaucrat moved every three years and simply could not know enough about local conditions to serve a particular area well. Representation to a central assembly by local aristocrats created a different result.

The second general restraint on the arbitrariness is also the third general point to be made about the European polity. The complete 'formula' of the European dynamic is then that competition between 'long-lasting' states inside a larger culture encouraged the triumph of capitalism. Individual states did not exist in a vacuum. They were, rather, part of a competing state system, and it was that system, particularly the military organization it engendered, that played a considerable part in determining the character of individual states. Why was this?

A state system leads to a high degree of emulation. This emulation can be very clearly seen in artistic matters, but it is extended to the establishment of various scientific clubs in 18th-century France in conscious imitation of their English rivals. Such emulation is ultimately only possible between states which recognized each other as of approximately similar standing; empires do not tend to copy the culture of their small neighbours – mere barbarians! The reference to empires brings out other facts about a state system that prove beneficial for economic growth. A state system always had an inbuilt escape system. This is most obviously true in human matters. The expulsion of the Jews from Spain and the Huguenots from France benefited, and was seen to benefit, other countries and this served in the long term as a limitation on arbitrary government. Very importantly, capital was equally mobile. Thus, Philip II's abuse of Antwerp led, within a matter of years rather than decades, to the rise of Amsterdam. In a brilliant passage making this point, McNeill has shown that repeatedly Philip II *wanted* to behave like an autocrat but the mobility of capital defeated him (McNeill 1982, Ch.1). This was particularly true of his relationship with Liège, the foremost cannon producer of late 16th-century Europe. When Philip pressurized them too hard, artisans and capitalists simply went elsewhere. A certain measure of decent and regularized behaviour was ensured by these means. However, perhaps the fundamental mechanism at work was that of military competition. The positive impact of competition on European society can most dramatically be seen in the modern world. The revelation of German industry applied to war in 1870, for example, sent a ripple of anxiety and counter-measures throughout European capitals; states were forced to rationalize their societies in order to survive. Yet state competition was responsible for rationalizing European societies before the age of industry. Consider again the German case. Dramatic defeat by Napoleon was ascribed not to greater industrial development, but to the impact of an ideologically motivated citizen army. The reform group around Hardenburg (including Scharnhorst and Gneisenau, and with Clausewitz as their greatest intellectual figure) realized that serfs could not provide such an army; the reforms of 1807, 1811 and 1818 changed the Prussian social structure at a stroke. The purpose of such changes was military, but the commercialization of agriculture that resulted was economically beneficial. This mechanism was at work in Europe roughly from 1100, when the multi-state character of Europe finally crystallized. Throughout the Middle Ages there was a breeding race to provide heavier, more effective cavalry, and other great changes were associated with the rise of bowmen and pikemen, the adoption of gunpowder and the consequent need for new Italian defences, the vast increase in army size in the 17th century, and the creation of a citizen-army during the French Revolution. Each of these changes necessitated money, and it was the search for funds that necessitated the king calling his Estates, and raising funds by providing the infrastructures mentioned.

As noted, the European state became able to generate far more power than its imperial rivals: thus the France of Louis XIV probably had as large an effective army as Ming China, even though the population was only 20 million, not about 150 million. This raises an important and interesting question. The organic quality of the European state arose from its having to accept and co-operate with other elements in civil society. However, why was it that the more powerful European state did not turn inwards in order to establish something more like an imperial system? Roughly, European absolutism represents just such a move, and it is important to stress how unsuccessful it was. It is conventional to compare absolutist France with England in order to give the impression of greater strength in the former case. This is mistaken, since English society generated more power *without* an absolutist façade; it proved this in defeating France in war on every occasion except one in which they met in the 18th century. This returns us to the question of competition. No state could afford to stand alone without risking defeat. It is hugely significant that by the middle of the 18th century France was sending its intellectuals to England and was in other ways trying to copy her secrets. All this suggests that there must be a prime mover amongst the states in order to get competition to work in the first place. In fact, there were several prime movers in European history, the torch of progress being passed from Italy, to Holland and to England. The last of these played a highly significant part as such a torch-bearer, and it seems no accident that this state possessed a powerful and, crucially, *centralized* estates system which insisted on the state remaining organic during the absolutist period. It is important to stress this, since the reaction to the discovery that imperial strength hides feet of clay has been to say that the European state was always more powerful. Put like this, the statement is misleading. Power operates in two dimensions, and the real contrast is between arbitrary government generating little power and the organic government of a civil society generating a great deal.

Reflections

The argument can be summarized in three propositions. First, extensive social interaction networks are needed for the market to flourish. In China, such extensive networks were provided by the polity. However, imperial rule was, perhaps could only be, based upon the negative tactic of preventing horizontal linkages that it could not control, and it was because of this that bureaucratic interference eventually proved deleterious for the economy. Thus, secondly, we can say that political fragmentation is a necessary consequence of the emergence of capitalism, *albeit that political fragmentation took place within the normative order, i.e. the extensive network provided by Latin Christendom.* Thirdly, a large part of the causation for the triumph of capitalism depended upon military competition forcing long-lasting states to interact strongly with their civil societies.

References

Anderson, P. 1974. *Passages from antiquity to feudalism*. London: New Left Books.
Brown, P. 1967. *St. Augustine*. London: Faber.
Burke, P. 1986. City states. In *States in history*, J. A. Hall (ed.). Oxford: Basil Blackwell
Cipolla, C. 1976. *Before the Industrial Revolution*. London: Methuen.
Duby, G. 1974. *The early growth of the Medieval economy*. London: Weidenfeld & Nicolson.
Elvin, M. 1973. *The pattern of the Chinese past*. Princeton: Princeton University Press.
Hall, J. A. 1985. *Powers and liberties: the causes and consequences of the rise of the West*. Oxford: Basil Blackwell.
Huang, R. 1974. *Taxation and governmental finance in sixteenth century Ming China*. Cambridge: Cambridge University Press.
Huang, R. 1981. *1587*. New Haven: Yale University Press.
Jones, E. L. 1981. *The European miracle*, Cambridge: Cambridge University Press.
McNeill, W. H. 1982. *The pursuit of power*. Oxford: Basil Blackwell.
Mann, M. 1986. The autonomous power of the state: its organs, mechanisms and results. In *States in history*, J. A. Hall (ed.). Oxford: Basil Blackwell.
Myers, A. R. 1975. *Parliaments and estates in Europe to 1789*. London: Thames & Hudson.
Postan, M. M. 1975. *Medieval economy and society*, London: Penguin.
Rodinski, W. 1983. *The walled kingdom*. London: Flamingo.
Weber, M. 1978. *The agrarian sociology of ancient civilisations*. London: New Left Books.
Wittfogel, K. 1957. *Oriental despotism*. New Haven: Yale University Press.

6 *The imperial form and universal history: some reflections on relativism and generalization*

JOHN GLEDHILL

State forms and the divergence of occidental history

A great deal of theorizing about the origins of the modern world has emphasized the contrast between the system of multiple competing national state units characteristic of the Occident and the encompassing imperial state systems of other arenas of civilization. This is, indeed, a point of common ground between Wallerstein and theorists who reject the economism of his explanation of European development in terms of the logic of uneven accumulation within a 'capitalist world economy', such as Skocpol (1979) or Mann (1986). What might be termed the dominant 'Anglo-Saxon' perspective on the transition to capitalism, with its focus on the role of the individualistic entrepreneur and market freedom, also faces an increasingly determined challenge from theories that emphasize the role of the state in producing the conditions for capitalist development (Holton 1985).

There are substantial differences of view on how far European development should be explained in terms of historically specific European feudal precursor forms, a more complex combination of prior historical conditions invoking the legacy of the Roman Empire of the West, or in terms of post-medieval conditions, including the effects of European expansion. The 'cultural' dimension of European development is scarcely exhausted by Weber's 'Protestant ethic' problematic, as indicated, for example, by the recent discussions of the longer-term role of Christian doctrine and the Church in the work of Hall (1985) and Mann (1986). A lot of recent work has stressed the limitations of concentrating the search for the social and cultural forces which would eventually produce modern capitalism on the world of the pre-industrial urban bourgeoisie. Cases for the priority of rural transformation have been argued, for example, by Merrington (1976) and Brenner (1977, 1982), whereas Kriedte's (1983) analysis of 'proto-industrialization' points to the way in which merchant capital was pushed to the countryside by urban guild restrictions. Hilton (1973, p. 235) has suggested that concepts of personal freedom articulated in rural class conflict may be as significant as urban patterns within the European socio-cultural matrix. However, despite all this diversity, there is continual renewal of the long-established tradition of juxtaposing some form of abstraction of European society, polity and culture and the structures of world-empires, so that varying systemic relations between the imperial form's cosmologies, political economy, social structures and forms of domination are postulated as ultimate blocks on developmental possibilities.

Whether we like it or not, most comparative social science invokes some form of disjunction between the Western and non-Western historical experience (Gledhill 1988a). The disjunction may be focused on different historical moments, ranging from the Classical world or the Christian epoch at one end, to the economic, social and political developments of the 16th or 19th centuries at the other, and it may also be constituted in a myriad of different ways, reflecting different appreciations of the 'essence' of 'modernity' and underlying theories of social change. The centrality of the disjunction was given in the historical process that created the 19th-century disciplinary framework of social sciences institutionalized into a professionalized academic system which is now worldwide.

Social anthropology, created to produce the knowledge of 'other cultures' required for the fulfilment of the Western intellectual project – even as its subject-matter was simultaneously rejected by the newly founded core disciplines – has succeeded only imperfectly in achieving a critical awareness of the intellectual baggage that it absorbed from sociology. Wedded to the notion of the autonomy of social relations, and, consequently, of 'societies' as bounded entities, anthropology is still grappling with the real historical nature of its traditional objects of study (Wolf 1982). A strong contemporary reassertion of relativism and a focus on 'interpretation', though often apolitical and a means of avoiding engagement with contemporary macro-social realities, is not in principle inconsistent with sensitivity towards large-scale historical interactions and the impact of capitalist expansion, since most anthropologists who are interested in the realities of class relations and politics in the contemporary Third World are also eager to chisel away at the inverted Eurocentrism of the radical sociology of development. Herein lies a major problem. If knowledge of 'the other' is simply orientated towards illuminating the 'difference' represented by the West, then the exercise immediately short-circuits the process of comparative analysis. Just as the qualitative variety in sociocultural transformation – the substantive form of development – within the contemporary 'Third World' is reduced to the inconsequential by both the normative evolutionism of traditional modernization theory and the theory of 'the development of underdevelopment' alike, so the past history of humanity becomes simply a laboratory for exploring the Western experience – whether the aim of the analyst is to explain the 'triumph of the West' or to critique it.

In this chapter, I use material on the late prehispanic Inca and Aztec empires in the New World to illustrate some of the tensions which exist between a strongly relativizing view of culture and history and attempts to place particular cases in a more general comparative context. In my contribution to the second published volume based on the Congress symposium (Gledhill 1988b), I use this discussion as a baseline from which to develop some further points on the comparative analysis of processes of class and state formation by considering the Spanish-American society created by European colonization of the same regions.

Culture and ideology in the evolution of the New World empires

That post-colonial sources often impose European conceptions on aboriginal institutions is hardly open to dispute and, though this problem is perhaps most acute in the sphere of understanding indigenous cosmologies, the very fact that more mundane aspects of native society may only be fully intelligible in terms of those cosmologies exacerbates problems of interpretation.

The relationship between archaic power systems and cosmological models has long been recognized and analysed in such classic modern work as Wheatley's *pivot of the four quarters* (Wheatley 1971) or Zuidema's (1964) study, *The ceque system of Cuzco*. However, observation of a relationship can lead to conclusions of widely differing import in terms of general theory. For example, consider Dumont's (1970, p. 3) classic attack on the notion of 'social stratification' (and 'inequality') as a basis for analysing the Indian caste system:

> The adherents of a less radical sociology then accuse us of falling into 'culturology' or 'indology' and of losing sight of comparison, which, in their eyes, is sufficiently guaranteed by concepts like 'social stratification' and by the mere consideration of the similarities which allow phenomena taken from different types of society to be grouped together under a common label. But such an approach can only ever achieve the general, as opposed to the universal, and with respect to our goal of comparison it represents another short-circuit . . . Why should we travel to India if not to try to discover how and in what respects Indian society or civilisation, in its very particularity, represents a form of the universal? In the last analysis, it is by humbly inspecting the most minute particulars that the route to the universal is kept open.

As the universal, Dumont's analysis posits individualism versus holism, equality versus hierarchy. Hierarchy is seen (Dumont 1970, p. 252) as:

> a fundamental feature of complex societies other than our own, and a principle of their unity; not their material, but their conceptual and symbolic unity.

In Dumont's view, the specific case of India represents the realization of an ideal-type of hierarchy, in which power is encompassed by status, and *artha* (action conforming to self-interest) by *dharma* (action conforming to universal order), through the relationship between *Brahman* and *Kshatriya* in the Hindu caste structure. Dumont's procedure may, of course, be taken as confirming the truth of the assertion that anthropology's real objective (and starting-point) has always been that of understanding the Occident, and that avoidance of all ethnocentrism is impossible, since anthropology exists in order to construct an 'otherness' which is intelligible in and for Western eyes. However, such a conclusion does not detract from the argument for striving to combat ethnocentrism: it is simply a warning against self-delusion.

Some Marxist writers, such as Wolf (e.g., 1982), are perfectly willing to concede that hierarchic ideology is integral to societies based on the 'Tributary Mode of Production' and that the way 'domination is inscribed into the structure of the universe' in such systems – among which he includes Christendom – has important implications, implications which transcend the conscious legitimation and power strategies devised by particular élites, and the appearance of coexistent or even competing models in a particular 'civilizational orbit'. For example, China had 'no organized church': Confucianism's socially exclusivist role as the state dogma of the *literati*, and concomitant refusal even to attempt to comprise a 'totalizing' belief system answering the 'eternal questions', guaranteed the coexistence of other religions of more popular and salvationist bent, though the sponsorship of Buddhism as a state religion under the Sui and T'ang in the 8th century AD can be seen as a response to the apparent failure of Confucianism in terms of imperial objectives (Eisenstadt 1969, pp. 55–9). Wolf (1982, p. 83) notes:

> . . . the dominant supernatural order, working through the major holders of power, encompasses and subjects humanity. At the same time, the ideological model displaces the real relation between power-wielding surplus takers and dominated producers onto the imagined relation between superior deity and inferior 'subject' . . . The problem of public power is thus transformed into a problem of private morality, and the 'subject' is invited to win merit by maintaining order through the regulation of his own conduct. This displacement also embodies a contradiction. If public power falters and justice is not done, the ideological ties linking subject and supernatural are also called into question. The rulers lose legitimacy; the mandate of Heaven may pass to other contenders, or people may begin to assert the claims of their segmental morality against the official apparatus of mediation. Yet the arguments proffered in support of these claims will center upon the nature of the imaginary tie between subject and supernatural, not upon the nature of domination anchored in 'other than economic means' [of surplus extraction].

The construction of broad concepts like the 'tributary mode of production' or 'hierarchic society' does not, of course, itself lead to answers to dynamic and developmental questions of a more specific kind. In the case of imperial states, we are faced with the perennial questions of explaining the cyclical processes of empire formation and collapse, particularly salient to the apparently highly unstable supra-regional hegemonies of the New World, with their marked phases of political fragmentation. We are also faced with the fundamental issue of how far it is possible to produce a general theory of empire formation. At one extreme we have an account of empire formation and collapse as a structurally determined phenomenon corresponding to a model of social reproductive dynamics within world-systems suggested in the formulations of Ekholm & Friedman (1979, 1985), which emphasize the similarities between ancient and modern 'global systems'. At the other pole, an implicit teleology of pursuit of maximum power as civilization's contribution to human nature is seen as being refracted through varying ecological-geographic, social and cultural realities.

One recent work on the New World which focuses on the specific and the cultural is the study by Conrad & Demarest (1984), who seek to analyse the Aztec and Inca empires in terms of the notion of 'ideological adaptations'. Their objective is twofold: to explain why the Mexica and the Inca, rather than one of the innumerable other potential contenders for supra-regional power in the pre-imperial phase of decentralization, succeeded in becoming an imperial power in the face of seemingly rather more-promising contenders for that role, and to demonstrate that the ideological innovations that gave the two emergent powers the edge shaped both the nature of imperial expansion and the social, political and economic contradictions which emerged as the long-term material implications of these ideologies were realized.

Thus, for example, the 'inchoate' form of Aztec imperialism, with its weak administrative incorporation and unconsolidated conquests, is explained as an implication of the warfare–human sacrifice complex which linked the Mexica patron god Huitzilopochtli, promoted to identification with aspects of Texcatlipoca and Tonatiuh (spring–summer sun–warrior sun), to the divine mission of staving off cosmic destruction by feeding the sun with sacrificial victims: if provinces were not in a position to rebel, they could not continue to act as a source of sacrificial victims. The imperial cosmologies–ideologies themselves are seen as partly the result of unconscious shifts or borrowings from a wider and ancient cultural repertoire, but primarily as the product of conscious efforts on the part of emergent ruling groups to rework elements of that repertoire in order to realize their political goals. The emergent ideology responds, in the first instance, to rulers' strategies for consolidating power and legitimizing increasing social distance and economic stratification, though the expansionary process itself is seen as sustained by material and social incentives which can be offered to lower levels of society. It is the 'ideological adaptation' which determines which societies will become successful imperialists. Whereas this expansionary dynamic, once installed, creates material demands that reinforce it, such as dependence on tribute for provisioning the patronage structure, the imperial ideology is also seen as the prime determinant of an irreversible pattern of maladaptation in the long term: stabilization is incompatible with the inner logic of the system, at least in these two cases.

It is certainly valuable to examine the extent to which the cultural logic of power systems induced 'maladaptive' development trajectories in ancient civilizations. Sharer's (1973) model of the Classic Maya collapse, based on the hypothesis that Tikal attempted to install a Teotihuacán-style political economy in the Peten after the 'hiatus' associated with the collapse of the highland centre, would provide another illustration of an argument of this type from the Mesoamerican literature, though Sharer's analysis works in terms of a much wider framework of intersocietal interactions. It is also worthwhile trying to answer the question why the Aztecs ate people, and Conrad & Demarest's (1984) answer to this question is certainly infinitely preferable to the ethnocentric idiocies of Harris and others (Harris 1977). It seems that Aztec expansionism intensified the cult of human sacrifice to an unprecedented degree, though material culture evidence alone demonstrates that it was also central to the state religion of Tula. A number of other analyses have argued that beyond the role of the Huitzilopochtli myth as a unique cultural paradigm, the intensification of human sacrifice under the Aztecs corresponded to the particular instability of centre–periphery relations in this period. The weakness of Aztec hegemony, and their imperfectly suppressed latent feelings of 'inferiority' as a group of Chichimeca origin, created a kind of 'cosmic paranoia' that was answered both psychologically and pragmatically in the 'theatre of terror' surrounding the Templo Mayor, where the lords of subject states were obliged to witness the slaughter of their own people (Carrasco 1982, pp. 185–6).

What is perhaps more significant from the point of view of distinguishing the historically particular from the more general is the way the mythic material associated with the Quetzalcoatl legend signifies the way in which auto-sacrifice and other-sacrifice represented a point of articulated tension in Mesoamerican cosmology which was quite openly expressed within Mesoamerican élite society in the post-classic period. We might conceivably discount the sources which claim that the Texcocan élite rejected the practices espoused by their partner Tenochtitlan as tainted by post-conquest rationalizations, but it is less easy to discount the detail and consistency in the sources which treat the (self-evidently late post-classic) theme of the conflict between Quetzalcoatl (in his aspect of Quetzalcoatl Topiltzin, human ruler and culture hero) and the gods Texcatlipoca and Huitzilopochtli. After Quetzalcoatl rejects the sorcerer's demands for human sacrifice, he is tricked (through his own vanity and sensual weakness) into drunkenness and incest, and subsequently he leaves Tollan with his followers . As Carrasco (1982, p. 175) suggests, it is likely that this story was taught in the *calmecacs*, the priestly schools of Tenochtitlan and the other cities of the Aztec empire. It is an ambiguous story: on the one hand, Quetzalcoatl Topiltzin, the paradigm of creative rulership, beauty and perfection, whose myth is that of all political legitimacy and the 'exemplary centre' of Mesoamerican civilization, is shown to be a flawed human being confounded by his own sensuousness and sexuality, giving way to the more powerful and astute Texcatlipoca–Huitzilopochtli. On the other hand, Quetzalcoatl's fall is also the fall of Tollan itself, a slide from cosmic harmony towards chaos and 'pathetic disintegration' (Carrasco 1982, p. 178).

Carrasco's analysis postulates that the Mexica were still more innovative in cosmological terms than Conrad & Demarest (1984) suggest, in the sense that their ideologues sought to produce an alternative cosmogeny to the repetitive archetype of successive cosmic destructions inherited from the earlier Mesoamerican tradition. In positing the world age of the 'Fifth sun' as a synthesis of its predecessors, their cosmogeny placed Tenochtitlan at the centre of universal space–time in a way which posited an end to cyclical catastrophe (Carrasco 1982, pp. 168–70). If the late post-classic version of the Quetzalcoatl Topiltzin myth seems, at one level, to be serving the interests of Mexica hegemony in terms of this new cosmogeny, at another level it might be seen as subversive of the claims of that hegemony. In the cosmogeny of the 'Fifth Sun' the Mexica élite not only made themselves hostage to the impact of continuing revolts against their hegemony, defeats in border wars and the succession of 'natural catastrophes' which marked the terminal decades of the empire's history, but to the unforeseeable reaffirmation of the 'truth' embodied in the older tradition of Quetzalcoatl by the arrival of the Spaniards. Though the scenario for the unfolding of this 'mythic drama' was prefigured in the more structural sociopolitical tensions revealed in the Quetzalcoatl discourse, and might have been realized through a series of purely 'internal' historical events, there could be no clearer testament to the 'material' force of cosmology in the management of politics.

Perhaps the kind of account that Conrad & Demarest (1984) give is too conjectural. The conscious harnessing of human sacrifice to an imperial cult, whose linking of Huitzilopochtli with the sun, and human sacrifice with cosmic order, gave the Mexica a sense of collective identity and turned their expansion into a 'divine mission', appears to have been a possibility open to other polities of the late post-classic. Conrad & Demarest in effect conclude that, given the failure of several earlier attempts at empire formation in the period, the key to Aztec success lay in hitting on the right ideological formula at the right time: i.e. after the defeat of Azcapotzalco and the appropriation of this mini-empire's land and tributaries by the *Tlatoani* and warrior élite opened up new class relationships and underpinned internal concentration of power. To some extent it may be necessary to see the rise of the Aztecs as a very particular case, in the sense that the Aztecs were a 'marginal' group forced to locate themselves cosmologically in a world of hegemonic 'high culture'. Yet it seems possible to make a much more general analysis of the relationship between the Mesoamerican cosmology of 'exemplary centres', the continually reworked and refashioned mythic material associated with Quetzalcoatl, the cyclical instability of supra-regional hegemonies in the area, and the rise of 'marcher lords' on the periphery of the core areas of urban civilization, an analysis which might also hold lessons for other areas where there are similar cosmological patterns at a more abstract level, such as Mesopotamia. 'Tollan' remained a living reality for various Mesoamerican centres even in periods of maximal political fragmentation. In this sense, whatever the vicissitudes of individual political hegemonies, and despite the massive upheavals in population distribution and settlement pattern which characterized Mesoamerican prehistory, some of which might conceivably have been related to the shattering of cosmic worlds, the development of urban culture, from the days of Teotihuacan onwards, was a larger, cumulative process implicating many individual 'societies': together with the urban socio-economic infrastructures of trade and agricultural technologies, the preservation of this 'cultural' understanding of rulership and the significance of ceremonial places set limits on the kind of social 'devolution' which could occur within the larger system.

To take 'culture' seriously is not, I think, necessarily to embrace idealism. The rise of Tenochtitlan, built on an island, brought a significant change to the urban settlement pattern of the Valley of Mexico: the different communities of this traditional 'heartland of cities' were relocated towards the lakeshore and a truly integrated symbiotic economic macro-region developed, with the lacustrine transport network at its centre and the lakeshore cities acting as 'gateways' for controlling the flow of goods from Tenochtitlan to subordinate centres in their hinterlands (Hassig 1985, pp. 144–9). Although it is important to stress that Triple Alliance sponsorship of major public works in the spheres of productive and transportation infrastructure as well as ceremonial began after the initial establishment of Tenochtitlan hegemony over the Valley (Brumfiel 1983, pp. 274–5), and to perceive the importance of *non-agricultural* production in this pattern of development, the new lake-orientated economy centralized around Tenochtitlan–Tlatelolco was also dependent on the innovations in the sphere of agricultural technology represented by the *chinampas* or 'floating gardens' (Boehm de Lameiras 1986, pp. 288–93, 1988). Conrad & Demarest (1984) themselves also note, for example, that the actual pattern of Aztec expansion corresponded to an independent political-economic rationality on the part of the state: key rare resource provinces were brought under control, like the Guatemalan cacao-producing region of Soconosco, whereas intervening territories were bypassed.

It is perhaps pointless to debate the significance of these different dimensions of the rise of the Aztecs in a simple 'cause and effect' manner, since they are so closely intertwined. It is certainly simply wrong to discount the role of religious ideology by adopting the traditional evolutionist perspective of a transition from 'theocratic' to 'militaristic', 'secular' domination, for reasons I explore in more detail elsewhere (Gledhill 1988a). The fact that, as Eisenstadt (1969) notes, the rulers of ancient states may come to pursue increasingly 'autonomous' and 'secular' political goals, and their societies become more socially differentiated, does not make religious hierarchy a less encompassing structure, as Conrad & Demarest's discussion of the strategies of the Aztec and Inca élites demonstrates in an exemplary fashion. Nevertheless, the explanatory emphasis throughout their discussion is on the specific conditions for

Mexica hegemony, and the extent to which the state ideology was the key to the specific form of long-term contradictions which developed in the social formation. The question to which it may not provide an adequate answer is simply: what *is* the social formation in this case?

Noting the *de facto* development of Tenochtitlan hegemony within its 'Triple Alliance', Conrad & Demarest (1984) treat the problem of empire formation as a matter of the innovations or adaptations of individual socio-political units. They thus ignore the way in which ramifying alliances between dynastic groups within the Basin of Mexico city-states underpinned the progressive, cumulative consolidation of a pan-basin aristocratic stratum, creating the conditions under which manipulation of cross-cutting ties could become an increasingly effective technique for political centralization, while favouring the 'inchoate' structure of the imperial core, in which city-states were subordinated and turned into tributaries, but left under the control of local dynastic groups whose legitimacy was intertwined with that of the dynasty of the imperial centre by virtue of their common encompassment by the principle of Toltec descent (Calnek 1978, 1982, Brumfiel 1983). An individual *tlatoani* might be executed, but the subsequent restoration of the dynasty and the strengthening of the class position of the *pipiltin* against their local commoner population was an inevitable consequence of the logic of the system as it had evolved during the pre-imperial phase.

The key to successful empire formation lay in consolidation of hegemony in the Basin of Mexico, something that Azcapotzalco failed to accomplish: united, the Basin was a natural expansionary centre (Katz 1978). It can therefore be argued that the structural process of progressive enlargement of hegemony was dependent on the evolution of the larger city-state alliance structure (rather than an individual state's ideological innovations). Of its very nature, such a process required *time*: the region had experienced a massive loss of population in the period of 'Toltec' hegemony, and the fragmented city-state pattern was not simply a devolution from a previously more centralized and unitary state organization in the region, but the result of recolonization of the area by a variety of different groups. It was not simply political hegemony which was being negotiated in the growing violence of confrontation between city-states, but the nature of the relations between ruler and ascriptive aristocracy, and lord and subject, which would characterize the emergent social system.

In its earlier stages, before Moctezuma Xocoyotzin's attempt to centralize and bureaucratize through rigidifying the status structure (Gledhill 1984, pp. 141–2), the empire offered both material benefits and, most significantly, hierarchic status advancement to members of intermediate groups such as the craft and merchant corporations – even commoners were promoted for valour. Again, it is important to stress that religious status entered into all the emergent gradations of late post-classic society, and all the 'corporate groups', commoner *calpultin* as much as *pochteca* merchant guilds, were both internally hierarchized as well as differentiated in terms of wealth and economic stratification. Furthermore, the subject population was differentiated into specific, named strata, such as the *tecpapouhque*, as distinct from the ordinary *macehualtin*, whose relative rank was defined in terms of the nature of the services they provided to higher strata (Offner 1984, p. 139), that is, hierarchically *in the strict sense*. However, developments at the level of the 'internal' stratification systems of the late post-classic, and the realization of empire formation itself, depended on the development of mechanisms which overcame the segmental structure of city-state dynastic politics. Thus, it seems undesirable to extract a particular city-state ideological complex from the larger cosmology by which it was encompassed, even if we concede that innovation within the larger complex is a significant element in the emergence of a hegemonic centre. Nor should we ignore the way in which changes in the structure of domination between lord and subject depended on a longer-term process of transformation cross-cutting city-state domains.

One might perhaps argue that, in a structural sense, the 'core' of the Aztec empire remained multicentric, despite the dominance of Tenochtitlan, and Moctezuma II's attempt to impose further centralization. Hassig (1985, pp. 92–103) argues that an emphasis on the deficiencies of the Aztec imperial form is premised on an inappropriate equation of 'empire' as a general form with territorial control. Seen as a 'hegemonic' rather than territorial empire 'sacrificing depth of control and extraction for breadth', the continuing existence of largely autonomous local governments and the frequency of revolt in the Aztec case might seem less of an index of 'inferiority' relative to more territorial forms. As Mann (1986, pp. 137–46) has pointed out, in considering the problem of military and political logistics in the ancient world more generally, early empires were perforce 'empires of domination' rather than territorial empires. In any event, whatever our judgement on the place of the Aztec case in the more universal history of the imperial form, focusing on the particular cultural complex that underpins the expansion of a particular centre at a particular phase in the long-term developmental sequence of an arena of 'civilization' tends to obscure the relationship between a particular episode and larger cyclical and secular processes.

'Political economies' and class formation

Cosmologies are more than simply ideological 'shells' that encapsulate more fundamental and more-'material' relationships: even if the Spaniards' religious mission was tempered by the conscious admission that 'where there is no gold, the Church does not enter' (Frank 1972), the social history of Latin America would undoubtedly have been fundamentally different had it been colonised by a north-western European power in a later epoch (Gledhill 1987). However, the nature of prehispanic empire in the New World also reflects other structural conditions and processes which emerge from the adoption of alternative perspectives. In the highland Mesoamerican case, a number of different theoretical approaches have drawn out the significance of the prehispanic market-place network

(Sanders *et al.* 1979, Berdan 1978, Gledhill & Larsen 1982, Hassig 1985). This factor also provides one of the possible axes on which we might hang an explanation of some of the contrasts between Mesoamerica and the Andes, notwithstanding the different constructions that can be put upon Murra's 'vertical control' model of Highland Andean exchange systems (Murra 1975, Browman 1978, Bradby 1982, Spalding 1984). A noteworthy feature of the development of empires and shifts in the location of centres in Mesoamerica seems to be the way in which this process articulates with changing distributions of population and the changing structures of inter-regional trade systems. That the market centre of Tlatelolco seems to predate the formation of the city of Tenochtitlan which incorporates it also seems significant.

It has been argued that inter-regional economic integration via exchange in the ancient world was, in general, weak, and that empires (politico–military incorporation) therefore constituted the only possible means of large-scale social integration (Mann 1977, p. 288). In opposition to those who view 'economic development' as the work of decentralized social forces, universalizing what I have already noted may not be an entirely appropriate view of European development, Mann insists that political decentralization brought economic recession, if not regression, and that it was the 'compulsory co-operation' instituted through 'empires of domination' that provided the conditions for cumulative social transformation (Mann 1986, pp. 146–61). On the other hand, his own argument that 'the economic base of civilisation, five per cent above the margin of subsistence, is also of considerable meaning to the actors themselves' (Mann 1977, p. 272), might suggest that, although the absence of the thoroughgoing breakdown of rural self-sufficiency at both regional and household level characteristic of the industrial capitalist era has significant implications for the type of macro-social relations between classes, and centre and regions, which typify pre-capitalist formations, resources flowing through larger spatial and societal networks take on a particularly strategic importance from the élite point of view. Whatever the precise form in which such control is effected, it can function both as a mode of securing the co-operation of local power-holders and of provisioning a military apparatus of centralized power. To this extent at least, the issue may be relevant to understanding the processes underlying the formation and consolidation of empires.

This last point leads to further issues: the dialectics of centralization and decentralization in the appropriation of the social surplus product and formation of class relations within ancient societies. The existence of a decentralized system of market-place exchange and merchant wealth accumulation (albeit not 'merchant capitalism', but wealth accumulation which was ultimately largely 'consumed' in ceremonial and encompassed by hierarchy) was something to which the Aztec state structures had to adapt, despite the elaboration of new apparatuses of political control over these pre-existing decentralized organizations. In both Highland Mesoamerica and the Andes it is also possible to point to the emergence of new categories of dominated persons and modes of surplus appropriation as a fundamental social reality beneath the process of imperial expansion and indeed, linked to it.

In the Inca case, there is a clear distinction to be made between 'state sector' appropriation of surplus and the personal domains of emperors, which became the property entrusted to the *panaqas* formed after the ruler's death. The *panaqas* were corporations that maintained the land and other property of the dead emperor for their own support and the maintenance of the cult of his mummy. They were made up of the male descendants of the emperor who were not chosen as successor to his political powers but continued to enjoy access to high offices of state, and women who were frequently wives of the incumbent Inca, so that *panaqas* continued to have an interest in the imperial succession through the matrilateral link in the next generation (Patterson 1985b). The 'freezing' of land and dependent labour in the *panaqas* created a long-term contradiction in the sense that the incoming ruler was forced to create a new property base for himself *de novo*, whereas the *panaqas'* continuing interest in power was a source of repeated conjunctural conflict. The Inca system of dynastic succession and property inheritance was a critical element in the development of the political economy of the empire, but most analysts have focused on the significance of a particular structural shift in the course of the development of the social formation, associated with the growth of the *yanacona* and other categories of persons removed from their enclavement in the local *ayllu* community. For example, Murra (1980) describes the overall trend as a transition from 'corvée to retainership', and Schaedel (1978) as a shift from a 'redistributive' to 'feudal–despotic' phase.

However, the precise nature and implications of such shifts are crucial, particularly from a longer-term perspective in which attention to the cyclical processes of empire formation and collapse has to be balanced against the assessment of relatively irreversible social changes. As Patterson (1985a) has pointed out, we can learn little about how (and indeed, why) a particular social formation develops and is transformed by adopting a simplistic evolutionist formula such as 'the appearance of social classes and private property' – concepts which are of limited universal value unless qualified and more tightly specified (Gledhill 1988a). His own analyses emphasize the way in which successive Inca rulers sought solutions to the problem posed by their initial dependence on the support of the *panaqas*, and progressively shifted to strategies involving alliances with the élites of non-Inca ethnic regions, creating the conditions for the formation of a class structure that was distinct from earlier patterns of social hierarchy.

As a result of his reorganization of the administrative and religious apparatus of the state, Pachakuti, victor of the dynastic struggle which preceded Inca expansion beyond the Cuzco Valley, curbed the power of his father's and brothers' *panaqas* by focusing state religion on, and alienating land and labour for the maintenance of, the Temple of the Sun and a system of state shrines (*wak'as*), demoting the religious sites associated with the adversary *panaqas* and effectively preventing them from accumulating additional resources in the newly incorporated areas of the expanding empire. Pachakuti's ultimate successor, Topa'Inka, faced with a new problem in the form of his father's *panaqa*, directed his attention to the zone of expansion, establishing alliances with non-Inca *wak'as* and political élites. The implication of this new tactic was not simply a check on the power of other *panaqas*, but an enhancement of the ability of his non-Inca allies to extract surplus from their own people, and the beginnings of a class structure cross-cutting existing hierarchic patterns and ethnic divisions.

The final victor of the new round of succession conflict which followed Topa'Inka's premature demise in turn responded to the implications of the strategy of his predecessor in a way which reinforced and deepened this latter tendency. Huayna Capac made grants of land and retainers to local 'ethnic' chieftains (*kurakas*), in order, Patterson suggests, to undercut the strength of the previous alliances between his father's *panaqa* and the *wak'as*. This gave them the means to overcome the limitations on their wealth-accumulation possibilities imposed by their established relations to their communities, and at the same time bound them to Inca domination, at least in the medium term, since the danger of such a strategy is clearly that a transformation of local power relations will ultimately promote feudalization. At the same time Huayna Capac appropriated new land for his own *panaqa* and the state, using a programme of state-directed colonization (and the creation of Murra's state-controlled 'vertical archipelagos') to consolidate an extended state political-economic sector.

Though the overall proportion of the Andean population involved in such shifts may not have been large (Spalding 1984, p. 102), an increasing number of people were being extracted from their ethnic communities and transformed into state or noble retainers in the late Incaic period. Spalding (1984, pp. 87–8) suggests that *mitmaq* colonists sent to serve in distant zones of the 'state archipelagos' slipped into becoming more tied to state institutions gradually as the bonds linking them to their communities of origin dissipated. One of the most significant shifts may have been the way the inhabitants of rebellious provinces were reintegrated into imperial society through resettlement programmes, creating 'a permanent state military force outside the structure of *mit'a* service by local ethnic groups' (Spalding 1984, p. 103). Patterson links Huayna Capac's use of state-managed lands to create a full-time standing army in the North to the ensuing pattern of dynastic conflict. In the succession crisis which followed the death of Huayna Capac, the empire split on a north–south axis in a way that reflected some of the effects of the preceding processes: Huascar was supported by the *wak'a* on the central Peruvian coast with which Topa 'Inka had been particularly closely aligned whereas Atahuallpa had direct control of the northern army.

In these processes we might detect a double trend in the direction of long-term 'feudalization'. First, there is a tendency towards the detachment of persons from their 'traditional' rural communities, and the development of new forms of surplus extraction based on personal dependence and semi-servile relationships. It is important to stress that *yanacona* existed in the heartlands of the future Inca empire in the pre-

Incaic period, and were also to be found in more distant areas dominated by petty chiefdoms which were subsequently incorporated into the empire, such as the Quito region of Ecuador (Salomon 1986, pp. 127–9). Though they were tiny societies, with maximum populations of a couple of thousand souls, the degree of internal stratification in the Quito chiefdoms was by no means inferior to that of the larger polities to the south, though we must bear in mind that their apparent 'archaism' may be deceptive, and that it might be an error to see them as an 'autonomous' development (Gledhill 1988a). The degree of rank degradation suffered by those holding *yana* status in Quito does not seem to have been great: some were polygamous (Salomon 1986, p. 129). Nor do they appear to have been war captives or refugees. However, what makes the development of the retainer stratum under the empire seem something with further implications is the way it augments the ability not simply of the state, but also of the various elements of the 'ruling class', to extract surplus independently of the tributary relationship with the encapsulated kin communities of 'free commoners'.

The same trend is evident in Mesoamerica, where it is possible to understand the variety of such forms of relationship, and the endless gradations between statuses, in considerable detail. Even 'slaves' (*tlacotin*) do not constitute a single, unitary category, but are clearly distinguishable from agrarian 'serfs' (*mayeques*), people lacking membership in a landholding *calpulli* corporation who became private tribute-payers to their *pipiltin* lords, free from obligations to the state unless they worked on land owned by a public official in his private capacity (Gledhill 1984, pp. 138–41, Offner 1984, pp. 135–42). Prebendal 'office land' and patrimonial holdings are clearly distinguished in the native terminology.

The second 'feudalizing' tendency is a trend towards a gravitation from centre to periphery as the empire expands, because the strategy for binding local power-holders to the centre, or rather to the emperor, creates the conditions for increasing appropriation of wealth throughout the empire as the process of class-formation cross-cuts the division between subjugating and subjugated ethnic polity. Though the Inca emperors developed increasingly sophisticated techniques for appropriating resources for the state, it is not at all clear that this was in complete correspondence with the maintenance of an imperial centre identified with old Cuzco and the original Inca dominant class. Though the imperial ideology was elaborated, and ethnic élites were given a considerable material incentive to acquiesce in the imperial form, the social identity of previous political units does not seem to have been diminished to any greater extent in the supposedly more 'integrated' Inca empire than in the Aztec case, and the dependence on alliances with groups outside the imperial centre seems only to have exacerbated the structural problems created by inter-*panaqa* conflict.

The use of resident hostages at Cuzco as a 'back-up' control system, reminiscent of the Tokugawa *Sankin Kotai* system in Japan, perhaps indicates the kind of compromises such a strategy entails. Cuzco itself remained a ceremonial centre, dedicated to the consumption of surplus in the form of sacrifice at the *wak'as*, though the fact that Tenochtitlan was also *the* centre for craft production and trade did not in any way reduce the dedication to the elaboration of the cosmo-magical 'symbolism of the centre' of this astonishing urban artefact. Emphasis on 'centralization' in the Inca case has obscured the fact that the provincial *wak'as* retained their autonomy, and offered oracular predictions favourable to the tranquillity of the empire only as long as the self-serving representatives of the deities were supplied with sufficient material incentives (Spalding 1984, p. 101). Despite the Incaic census system and the dispatching of 'administrators' to the provinces, provincial administrative centres as revealed by archaeology were, it appears, places devoted primarily to the political consumption of wealth and the ceremonial negotiation of relations between Inca and non-Inca élites (Morris 1982) – in other words, we have the type of 'indirect rule' system characteristic of 'empires of domination'. Given the social conditions underlying this structure, Huayna Capac's successors would have faced considerable difficulties in pushing towards greater rationalization and centralization of the imperial apparatus.

In the Aztec case, the significance of inter-dynastic alliance networks in the consolidation of Aztec hegemony within the Basin of Mexico has already been noted. It can be seen that this process also corresponds to processes of class formation cross-cutting formal political divisions: marriage alliances were cemented by assignments of land (Offner 1984, p. 126), and 'largesse' (tribute redistribution) towards *lower ranking* allies in other dynastic groups was a key element of Aztec statecraft – another tactic of subverting existing hierarchic relations in pursuit of centralization (Calnek 1978, p. 467). Aztec monarchs also made land grants which added to the existing patrimonial domains of the nobility, in a situation in which wealth accumulation was already decentralized and the share of the surplus available to the state sector correspondingly reduced. Moctezuma Xocoyotzin's attempt to centralize by restricting bureaucratic office to the *pilli* category did not necessarily entail an increase in the absolute *class* power of the aristocracy and may, in fact, have been intended to achieve the opposite: after the mid-15th century tribute collection was increasingly bureaucratized under Tenochtitlan control and taken out of the hands of local lords. However, the 'reform' did inevitably add additional tensions to the centrifugal tendencies already created by the peculiar nature of the relationship between the 'exemplary centre' and all the polities it incorporated, not simply geographically distant 'peripheries'.

Conclusions: imperial states in universal history

If we look beyond the late prehispanic empires of the New World, either forward into the colonial period or sideways into a broader comparative framework, it seems readily apparent that the struggle between the state and the landlord classes over the appropriation of the social surplus tends to become fundamental to imperial politics, though it may be complemented by other forms of factional conflict among the élite. The creation of imperial bureaucracies that are dependent on the state in a fundamental sense is the favoured strategy of centralizers – whether the route taken is the absolute form of domination represented by slavery, or the 'promotion' of intermediate groups in terms of status hierarchy. However, such strategies seem to be difficult to maintain in perpetuity in the ancient world: prebendal systems tend to degenerate into feudalized forms, as offices become hereditary and land and dependent labour are appropriated as patrimonial domain. For example, in China, the T'ang systematized administration through the *literati* through the 7th to 9th centuries AD, but this rolling back of the power of 'traditional' nobility did not endure, since the bureaucracy succeeded in transforming itself into another type of land-owning nobility, a situation which persisted until the Ming embarked on the road towards recentralization in the 14th century. The Chinese style of centralization and decentralization was associated with a cycle of 'agrarian reform': the state rolls back landlordism to recreate a 'free peasantry', thereby securing their surplus labour, product and military services for itself, then, as the tax burden rises, the state itself contributes to the processes which underpin the re-expansion of landlord power (Gledhill 1984, p. 138, Wolf 1982, p. 55).

Of course, it would be naive to pretend that the rural society which existed at the time of the Ch'ing abolition of serfdom in the 18th century, following centuries of commercial development and transformation of class structures towards mercantile relationships between landlord and peasant, was not radically different from that which had existed at the time of the Ch'in and Han. The imperial cycle of centralization and decentralization was transformative, and the direction of the transformation was towards a transition from 'status' to monetized class relationships and proprietary wealth based on the combination of land-ownership and office-holding. At the same time, we might observe that the recreation of 'the free peasant smallholding' has also been a feature of certain patterns of political centralization in the Occident: France is the obvious case. Brenner has attributed the different agrarian developments and forms of political centralization characteristic of England and France, respectively, to the greater unity and solidarity of the feudal aristocracy in England, in comparison with the 'relative disorganization' of their French counterparts, so that in the English case a strong monarchy was the product of a strong aristocracy, and a decentralized system of surplus extraction, developing into agrarian capitalism, was maintained before and after the feudal crisis. In later 13th-century France, declining seigneurial revenues, consequent on successful peasant resistance to landlordism, create the conditions for a new form of monarchical centralization based on the progressive gravitation of the lordly class towards the royal administration, and the replacement of an ineffective decentralized mode of surplus extraction with a more effective, centralized mode (Brenner 1982, pp. 253–64). Skocpol's comparison between the French, Russian and Chinese Revolutions is premised on the notion that there is a meaningful parallel to be drawn between 'proto-bureaucratic' imperial states in the Occident and the Orient, precisely in terms of the contradictory nature of the relationship between the state and decentralized class power (Skocpol 1979, p. 49). She suggests that the French Revolution has more in common with the Chinese Revolution than it had with the English Civil War, and that the characterization of the French and English cases as 'bourgeois revolutions' representing parallel movements towards capitalism within a unitary European trajectory of development is false.

In the end, the location of the Inca and Aztec empires in 'world historical time' may not be too problematic. Yet though it can obviously be argued that conditions in the post-medieval European multiple-state civilizational arena as a larger totality were very different from those obtaining in other contexts, a point Skocpol herself emphasizes, and the implied comparison between France and China is in many respects superficial, an absolute association between a unitary 'West' and 'modernity', based on a teleological process of 'reading history backwards', may not be the best approach for assessing the extent to which formations such as the Spanish-American empire were in themselves the harbingers of a new world-historical epoch.

References

Berdan, F. 1978. Tres formas de intercambio en la economía Azteca. In *Economía, política e ideología en el México prehispánico*, P. Carrasco & J. Broda (eds), 77–95. Mexico: Nueva Imagen.

Boehm de Lameiras, B. 1986. *Formacíon del estado en el México prehispánico*. Zamora: El Colegio de Michoacán.

Boehm de Lameiras, B. 1988. Subsistence, social control of resources and the development of complex society in the Valley of Mexico. In *State and society: the emergence and development of social hierarchy and political centralization*, J. Gledhill, B. Bender & M. T. Larsen (eds), Ch. 5. London: Unwin Hyman.

Bradby, B. 1982. 'Resistance to Capitalism' in the Peruvian Andes. In *Ecology and exchange in the Andes*, D. Lehmann (ed.), 97–122. Cambridge: Cambridge University Press.

Brenner, R. 1977. The origins of capitalist development: a critique of neo-Smithian Marxism. *New Left Review* **104**, 25–92.

Brenner, R. 1982. The agrarian roots of European capitalism. In *The Brenner debate: agrarian class structure and economic development in pre-industrial Europe*, T. H. Aston & C. H. E. Philpin (eds), 213–327. Cambridge: Cambridge University Press.

Browman, D. L. 1978. Toward the development of the Tiahuanaco state. In *Advances in Andean archaeology*, D. L. Browman (ed.), 327–50. The Hague: Mouton.

Brumfiel, E. M. 1983. Aztec state making: ecology, structure and the origin of the state. *American Anthropologist* **85** (2), 261–84.

Calnek, E. E. 1978. The city-state in the Basin of Mexico: late prehispanic period. In *Urbanization in the Americas from its beginnings to the present*, R. P. Schaedel, J. E. Hordoy & N. S. Kinzer (eds), 463–70. The Hague: Mouton.

Calnek, E. E. 1982. Patterns of empire foundation in the Valley of Mexico, late Postclassic period, 1200–1521. In *The Inca and Aztec states, 1400–1800; anthropology and history*, G. Collier, R. Rosaldo & J. Wirth (eds), 43–62. New York: Academic Press.

Carrasco, D. 1982. *Quetzalcoatl and the irony of empire: myths and prophecies in the Aztec tradition*. Chicago: University of Chicago Press.
Conrad, G. W. & A. A. Demarest 1984. *Religion and empire: the dynamics of Aztec and Inca expansion*. Cambridge: Cambridge University Press.
Dumont, L. 1970. *Homo Hierarchicus: the caste system and its implications*. London: Weidenfeld & Nicolson.
Eisenstadt, S. N. 1969. *The political systems of empires: the rise and fall of the historical bureaucratic societies*. New York: The Free Press.
Ekholm, K. & J. Friedman 1979. 'Capital', imperialism and exploitation in ancient world systems. In *Power and propaganda: a symposium on ancient empires*, M. T. Larsen (ed.), 41–58. Copenhagen: Akademisk Forlag.
Ekholm, K. & J. Friedman 1985. Towards a global anthropology. *Critique of Anthropology* **5** (1), 97–119.
Frank, A.G. 1972. *Lumpenbourgeoisie. Lumpendevelopment*. New York: Monthly Review Press.
Gledhill, J. 1984. The transformation of 'Asiatic' formations: the case of late Prehispanic Mesoamerica. In *Marxist perspectives in archaeology*, M. Spriggs (ed.), 135–48. Cambridge: Cambridge University Press.
Gledhill, J. 1987. State and class formation in Mexico, 16th to 19th centuries: frameworks for comparative analysis. In *Power relations and state formation*, T. C. Paterson & C. W. Gailey (eds), 128–54. Washington DC: American Anthropological Association.
Gledhill, J. 1988a. Introduction: the comparative analysis of social and political transitions. In *State and society: the emergence and development of social hierarchy and political centralization*, J. Gledhill, B. Bender & M. T. Larsen (eds). London: Unwin Hyman.
Gledhill, J. 1988b. Legacies of empire: political centralization and class formation in the Hispanic-American world. In *State and society: the emergence and development of social hierarchy and political centralization*, B. Bender. J. Gledhill & M. T. Larsen (eds). London: Unwin Hyman.
Gledhill, J. & M. T. Larsen 1982. The Polanyi paradigm and the dynamics of archaic states: Mesopotamia and Mesoamerica. In *Theory and explanation in archaeology: the Southampton conference*, C. Renfrew, M. J. Rowlands & B. Segraves (eds), 197–229. London: Academic Press.
Hall, J. 1985. *Powers and liberties: the causes and consequences of the rise of the West*. Oxford: Basil Blackwell.
Harris, M. 1977. *Cannibals and kings*. New York: Random House.
Hassig, R. 1985. *Trade, tribute and transportation: the sixteenth century political economy of the Valley of Mexico*. Norman: University of Oklahoma Press.
Hilton, R. 1973. *Bondsmen made free: medieval peasant movements and the English rising of 1381*. London: Methuen.
Holton, R. J. 1985. *The transition from feudalism to capitalism*. London: Macmillan.
Katz, F. 1978. A comparison of some aspects of the evolution of Cuzco and Tenochtitlan. In *Urbanization in the Americas from its beginnings to the present*, R. P. Schaedel, J. E. Hordoy & N. S. Kinzer (eds), 203–14. The Hague: Mouton.
Kriedte, P. 1983. *Peasants, landlords and merchant capitalists: Europe and the world economy 1500–1800*. Leamington Spa: Berg Publishers.
Mann, M. 1977. States, Ancient and Modern. *Archives européenes de Sociologie* **18**, 262–98.
Mann, M. 1986. *The sources of social power: a history of power from the beginning to A.D. 1760*. Cambridge: Cambridge University Press.
Merrington, J. 1976. Town and country in the transition to capitalism. In *The*

transition from feudalism to capitalism, R. Hilton *et al.*, 170–95. London: New Left Books.

Morris, C. 1982. The infra-structure of Inca control in the Peruvian Central Highlands. In *The Inca and Aztec states. 1400–1800; anthropology and history*, G. Collier, R. Rosaldo & J. Wirth (eds), 153–71. New York: Academic Press.

Murra, J. V. 1975. El control vertical de un máximo de pisos ecológicos en la economía de las sociedades andinas. In *Formaciones económicas y políticas del mundo andino*, 59–115. Lima: Instituto de Estudios Peruanos.

Murra, J. V. 1980. *The economic organization of the Inka state.* Research in Economic Anthropology Supplementary Publication No. 1, Greenwich: JAI Press.

Offner, J. A. 1984. *Law and politics in Aztec Texcoco.* Cambridge: Cambridge University Press.

Patterson, T. C. 1985a. Exploitation and class formation in the Inca state. *Culture* **5** (1), 35–42.

Patterson, T C. 1985b. Pachacamac: an Andean oracle under Inca rule. In *Andean prehistory and protohistory: papers from the second annual Northeast conference on Andean archaeology and ethnohistory*, D. P. Kvietok & D. H. Sandweiss (eds), 159–76. Ithaca: Cornell University Press.

Salomon, F. 1986. *Native lords of Quito in the age of the Incas: the political economy of North Andean chiefdoms.* Cambridge: Cambridge University Press.

Sanders, W. T., J. R. Parsons & R. S. Santley 1979. *The Basin of Mexico: ecological processes in the evolution of a civilization.* New York: Academic Press.

Schaedel, R. P. Early state of the Incas. In *The early state*, H. Claessen & P. Skalnik (eds), 289–320. The Hague: Mouton.

Sharer, R. J. 1973. The Maya Collapse revisited: internal and external perspectives. In *Social process in Maya prehistory*, N. Hammond (ed.), 532–52. New York: Academic Press.

Skocpol, T. 1979. *States and social revolutions: a comparative analysis of France, Russia and China.* Cambridge: Cambridge University Press.

Spalding, K. 1984. *Huarochirí: an Andean society under Inca and Spanish rule.* Stanford: Stanford University Press.

Wheatley, P. 1971. *The pivot of the four quarters.* Edinburgh: University of Edinburgh Press.

Wolf, E. R. 1982. *Europe and the people without history.* Berkeley: University of California Press.

Zuidema, R. T. 1964. *The ceque system of Cuzco: the social organization of the capital of the Inca.* Leiden: E. J. Brill.

7 *Factional competition in complex society*

ELIZABETH M. BRUMFIEL

Social complexity is conventionally defined in terms of the number of *unlike* parts in an integrated whole. Such parts might be functionally specialized units that contribute complementary goods and services to the whole, or they might be horizontally differentiated socio-economic strata in a non-egalitarian state. The interaction of unlike parts is an important process in the development of complex societies. However, I have recently been concerned with the importance of *like* parts in complex society. Like parts often exist as functionally and socially undifferentiated *factions*. Aztec ethnohistory suggests that such factions provide an important dynamic for change in complex societies. This chapter explores some aspects of this dynamic and suggests ways of identifying factionalism in the archaeological record.

Previous definitions of factions have emphasized their lack of formal structure. For example, Bujra (1973, p. 133) defines factions as 'politically oriented quasi-groups whose members are recruited on diverse social principles by a leader'. Also, according to Lewellen (1983, p. 109), 'factions tend to be informal, spontaneous, leader–follower groups organized for a particular purpose and disbanding when that purpose is accomplished or defeated'. However, to understand the dynamics of factions in complex society, it is most useful to focus upon the fact that the factions within a society are structurally and functionally identical groups which, by virtue of their similarity, compete for resources or positions of power or prestige, or both.

Structurally similar groups use resources in similar ways; therefore, they may compete for resources, but structural similarity ensures that the competition will be non-revolutionary in intent. The objective of factional competition is to achieve a favourable allocation of existing benefits; factions hope to gain more while their competitors gain less. Participants tend to conceptualize factional competition as a zero-sum game. This is one factor contributing to the often noted lack of ideological commitment or coherent social programme in factional competition (Bujra 1973, p. 136). Another factor is that structurally similar groups are likely to hold similar ideas about what should be done and what can be done. Thus debate centres on the relative legitimacy of similar claims, not the relative merits of substantially different programmes.

Because it is non-revolutionary in intent, factional competition has been regarded as non-revolutionary in consequence. It is seen as a temporary response to changing conditions (Bailey 1969, p. 52) or as an impediment to constructive, meaningful social action (Seigel & Beals 1960, p. 415).

However, given the proper environmental and social context, factional competition expands in scale and intensity until it transforms the conditions of its own existence. It can then be a major force in social transformation.

Factionalism in complex society

Disputes are universal in human society but factions are not. Disputes over land, breaches of exchange obligations, etc., develop into factional competition only when other resolutions to the dispute are not available. In some cases disputes may be resolved by group fission; other disputes may be resolved by a mediated settlement acceptable to both parties. In still other cases the dispute may not be resolved, but parties to the dispute are unable to recruit supporters or divert resources to their cause. The likelihood of these alternative outcomes depends on the social and environmental contexts within which the dispute occurs. For example, fission is the probable outcome if land is freely available and no complex economic or ritual interdependence has developed among group members (Bujra 1973, pp. 141–3). Mediated settlement is probable if an oligarchy of elders or nobles monopolizes political power. The ability of disputants to mobilize resources for their conflict is likely to be limited if they lack resources and if those who control resources have no interest in supporting them.

Factional competition in complex society is probably rooted in the same kinds of disputes that arise in tribal societies – disputes over land, inheritence, marriage contracts, etc. To these disputes at the lower level are added disputes among ruling élites: disputes over rights to surplus extraction, and to positions of power and prestige. Factions develop as commoners align themselves with élite patrons in the hopes of channelling resources to their own disputes while élites support their clients' interests as a means of mobilizing resources for their own élite pursuits. Thus, society is divided by cleavages that cut vertically rather than horizontally; factional competition prevails over class conflict.

Prior to Aztec rule (1250–1430), Central Mexican society seems to have been permeated by factional competition. This is evident in the high level of political violence. Early Aztec history is marked by numerous incidents of usurpation and regicide, of polities fissioning or simply disintegrating because of internal conflict (Brumfiel 1983, p. 268). The source of factional competition can be found in the political and economic structure of the Early Aztec polities.

In both the pre-Aztec and Aztec periods, the small city-state was the most basic political unit (Sanders 1956, 1968, Soustelle 1961, Gibson 1964, 1971). City-states contained populations of from 5000 to 50 000 people, and they covered areas of from 80 to 200 km (Sanders 1968, p. 91, Sanders *et al.* 1979, pp. 151–2, Hicks 1982, pp. 231–2). Each city-state was governed by a paramount (*tlatoani*) who ruled by virtue of his membership in the local royal lineage. He was assisted by a group of nobles that included his own children and the descendants of past rulers, his vassal lords (*tetecutin*) and the descendants of past vassal lords (Carrasco 1971, pp. 351–4). This élite stratum constituted less than 10 per cent of the regional populations (Cook & Borah 1963, p. 243). Support for the élite was highly decentralized. The ruler was supported by the tribute and labour of 'free' commoners, but he also received produce and labour from commoners attached to his patrimonial estates. Vassal lords and a few lower-ranking nobles also held patrimonial estates that assured their support (Carrasco 1976, 1978). These estates supplied nobles with foodstuffs, cloth, domestic service and an array of other goods (Guzmán 1938, Carrasco 1977, Hicks 1982, pp. 238–41). The lower-ranking nobles who held no estate lived as dependents in the households of their higher ranking relatives (Carrasco 1976, pp. 22–3). Commoners were food producers and craftsmen. Some resided in proximity to the ruler's palace in the central town of the domain; others lived in surrounding villages and hamlets (Sanders *et al.* 1979, p. 153, Hicks 1982, pp. 231–2). Commoners were organized in corporate groups (*calpulli* or *tlaxilacalli*) sharing joint liability for tribute goods and service, and supplying contingents of soldiers in time of war. In return for their services to the élite, the *calpulli* or *tlaxilacalli* was granted land which it distributed to its members in small subsistence plots (Carrasco 1978, p. 30).

In the absence of a regional state, these arrangements generated a great deal of factional competition in the upper stratum. Significant differences of wealth, power, and prestige separated nobles who were the heads of noble estates (paramounts, vassal lords and a few lower-ranking nobles) from those who held no endowment. At the same time, noble estates were scarce resources. All land and commoner labour were claimed by existing noble estates; there were no 'free' resources which an enterprising noble might organize into a new establishment. Patrimonial estates could be obtained only by inheritence or by taking an estate already in existence and dividing its assets in two. Because of the rules of cognatic inheritance and noble polygamy, numerous candidates contested the inheritence of domains and patrimonial estates, each supported by a different coalition of affines and maternal kinsmen (cf. Carrasco 1984). Though one candidate prevailed, disappointed nobles continued to seek coalitions of support that would enable them to win an inheritance. At interregnums the control of noble estates might be contested all over again as incumbents and unsuccessful pretenders lent their support to different royal princes. Upon his installation, the successful prince could be expected to repay his supporters by recognizing the legitimacy of their inheritance claims or by creating new estates for them.

Within the commoner stratum, factionalism was expressed in persistent ethnicity (cf. Van Zantwijk 1973, 1985). Use-rights to agricultural land were legitimated by reference to a group's myth of origin, a migration myth which ended in some paramount granting lands to the group and its leader (who was thereby ennobled) in exchange for vows of fealty (for example, Chimalpahin 1965, pp. 72, 145–6, 148–50). Tied to their commoners by bonds of ethnicity (but not kinship), lords were expected to be protective of their interests and moderate in their demands for tribute goods and labour. If not, commoners could throw their support to some other noble competitor, or they could resume their migration, settling on new lands under a new lord in some other domain. Because they supplied tribute in peace and soldiers in war, immigrant commoners were always well received (Brumfiel 1983, pp. 269–70). In a sense commoners enjoyed more open access to the resources which they required than did nobles; consequently, factional competition was less intense among them.

Although the same structural principles were present throughout central Mexico, they operated under different ecological conditions in different regions, producing different results. In the southern valley, intensive chinampa agriculture provided an expanding resource base and a quickly growing commoner population. This made it possible to resolve heirship disputes among nobles through fission rather than intensified factionalism. The typical city-state in the chinampa zone contained three or four co-rulers (each governing his own lands and people). Together, they could manage crises of succession arising in any one of the royal lines. In the rainfall-dependent agricultural zones of the middle valley, rulers tried to resolve élite competition through expansion rather than through fission and political involution. Middle-valley paramounts sought to conquer and incorporate neighboring domains which could then be distributed to victor's own non-inheriting nobles or joined to the victor's tribute base (Brumfiel 1983, p. 269).

The intensity of political competition in the middle valley, both within and between city-states, seems to have impelled local rulers to forge military alliances between towns which were sealed by intermarriage. Figure 7.1 records marriage alliances between city-states in the Valley of Mexico before Aztec state formation in 1428. It indicates that inter-city marriage alliances were mostly confined to the middle valley, i.e. the region of rainfall-dependent agriculture where rulers engaged in expansionary warfare. In contrast the city-states of the southern valley seem to have confined alliance-building to the multiple ruling lineages within a single community. For example, Xochimilco was a town of regional importance (Parsons *et al.* 1982a, pp. 75–9 Hodge 1984, pp. 81–97), but not a single instance of marriage linking Xochimilco to another city-state appears in the standard historical sources for prehispanic Mexico (Alva Ixtlilxochitl 1975–7, *Anales de Tlatelolco* 1948, Chimalpahin 1965, *Crónica Mexicayotl* 1949, etc.). The same is true for Amecameca. Only Chalco among the southern city-states seems to have been drawn into the middle valley sphere of élite intermarriage and alliance building.

The middle-valley pattern of inter-city warfare and marriage alliance was self-intensifying. Marriages between allied towns intertwined the genealogies of the different ruling lineages and resulted in coalitions that cut across the boundaries of city-states. Consequently, local factions assumed regional proportions. By 1400, the middle and northern valley was dominated by two regional coalitions, one centred on Tezozomoc, the incumbent ruler of Azcapotzalco, the other focused on Ixtlilxochitl, the

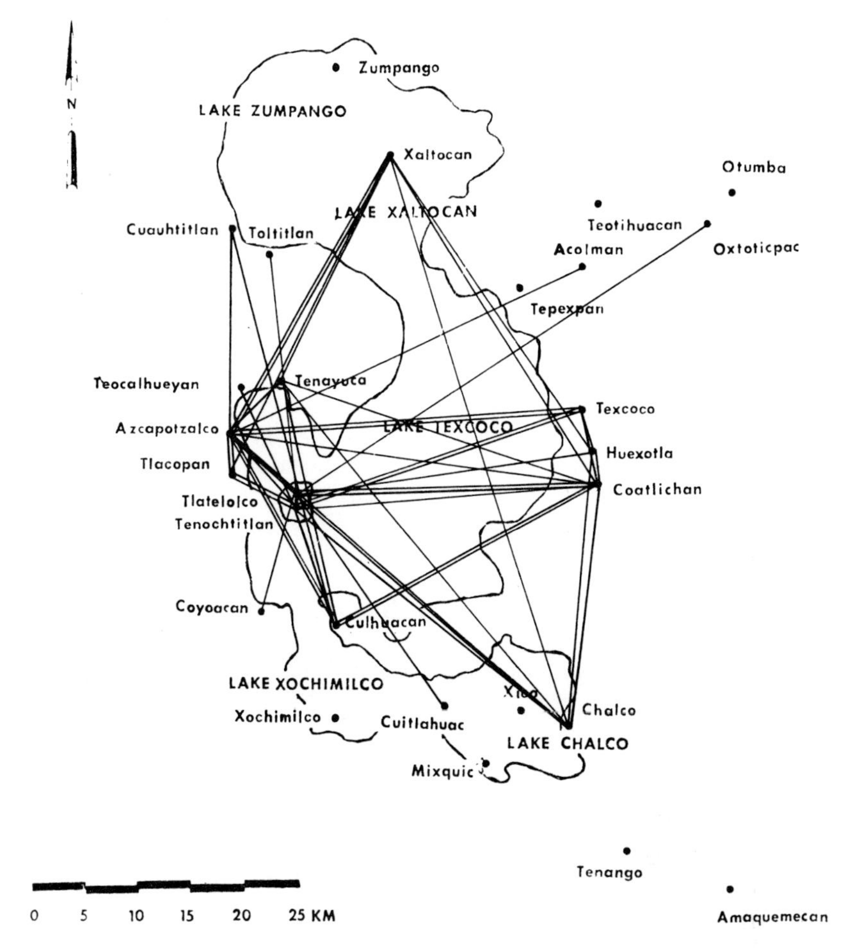

Figure 7.1 Marriage alliances in the Valley of Mexico during pre-Aztec (S.I.3) times.

incumbent ruler of Texcoco. The depth of the factional competition is evident in the following description of Tezozomoc's final attack upon Texcoco:

> There was such great confusion, not only within the city of Tetzcuco but in all the other cities, towns, and places of the domain, for some called the name of Ixtlilxochitl and others that of the tyrant [i.e. Tezozomoc], such that fathers took one side and sons the other, and even between brothers and kinsmen there was confusion and division. (Alva Ixtlilxochitl 1975–77, II, p. 45.)

Factional competition had by this time transformed the conditions of its own existence. Regional factionalism synchronized political violence. The violence removed an entire generation of political leadership by death or exile. Without these leading figures, factional alignments and coalitions fell into disarray. There was a power vacuum in the Valley of Mexico which was quickly filled by the Aztec state. The state played upon continuing factional competition at the local level, supporting local princes who were most willing to go along with state policy. The earlier web-like systems of regional alliance were replaced by a centralized system of political patronage. Having centralized power at least temporarily, the state could expand the resource base of the élite through intensified surplus extraction from the commoner stratum and through imperial expansion. These resources were then used to construct a more open system of hierarchy for the élite. The new system, based on achievement in warfare, could potentially admit as many qualified individuals as existed. Nobles no longer had to squabble over the limited number of positions of worth at the heads of traditional noble estates (Brumfiel 1987a). The old impetus to factional competition was lost, and when élite factionalism reappeared it was structured along new lines (centre–periphery, cf. Smith 1986) and moved according to a new dynamic.

Identifying factionalism in the archaeological record

Just as other political processes can be detected archaeologically (cf. Pollock 1983), sustained factional competition should leave an imprint in the archaeological record. This section discusses certain aspects of factionalism that affect material culture. The discussion concludes with a series of observations as to how factional competition may be reflected in Valley of Mexico ceramics from the pre-Aztec and Aztec eras.

Success in factional competition requires coalition building. It requires the amassing of loyal supporters and powerful allies and patrons. Since opposing factions draw members from the same pool of candidates, they must compete to build their coalitions. They do so through the manipulation of symbols, symbols that are used to interpret reality through the classification and evaluation of persons and events (cf. Douglas & Isherwood 1977, pp. 65–7). These symbols are displayed and manipulated in ritual events; the more intense the factional competition, the more frequent and elaborate will be the symbolic displays. Thus, factional competition should be archaeologically evident in the abundance and elaboration of artefacts used in such events.

The character of factional competition has some specific implications for stylistic variation in symbolically meaningful artefacts over time and space. Because factions are not differentiated by their social programmes and because their competition focuses on the relative legitimacy of their claims, competing factions should not be differentiated stylistically. All competing factions should use the same symbolic vocabulary to state their claims of legitimacy. Archaeologically, regions drawn into factional competition should produce symbolic artefacts in a single regional style. Factions try to make themselves appear better, not different. This also suggests that they will be conservative in their choice of symbolic vocabulary. They will state their claims using traditional markers of legitimacy. Archaeologically, factional competition should produce large quantities of elaborate artefacts, but with little stylistic innovation over time.

The pre-Aztec inhabitants of the Valley of Mexico developed an elaborate array of élite goods which were displayed and manipulated in ritual events that served as the idiom of factional competition (Hicks 1981, Brumfiel 1987a). These included many articles of dress and personal adornment: richly embroidered textiles, jewellery crafted from precious stones and metals, feathered adornments and mosaics. Unfortunately, most of these items were made of perishable or highly valued raw materials and are not, therefore, likely to be preserved in the archaeological record. Other items of élite consumption served as parts of the domestic establishment. Housing, household furnishings, food, drink, tubes of tobacco, flower garlands and domestic staffs that included servants, musicians and entertainers were manipulated in ritual displays that Smith (1987) calls 'household consumption rituals'. As he suggests, the ceramic vessels used for the service of food and drink at consumption rituals are one archaeologically visible gauge of such activity.

The service of food and drink accompanied a wide variety of politically significant social interactions in late prehispanic Mexico. Feasts and entertainment marked the births, marriages, and deaths of household members, and in noble families these were matters of considerable political importance (Sahaguń 1950–69 Bk 4, pp. 97, 122, Bk 8, pp. 129–30, Durán 1967 II, pp. 123, 297, 1971, p. 122). Feasting and entertainment also marked succession to the rule of city-states and noble houses (Durán 1967 II, pp. 311, 326, Zorita 1963, p. 95, Carrasco 1966). Feasts were held at regular intervals to facilitate the internal administration of political units. For example, the rulers of kingdoms held feasts several times a year to distribute foodstuffs and currency to their administrative and service staffs (Alva Ixtlilxochitl 1975–7 II, p. 105, *Anales de Cuauhtitlan* 1945, p. 35, Broda 1976, Carrasco 1977), and the heads of *calpulli* groups hosted gatherings of commoners to deliberate their common affairs (Zorita 1963, pp. 109–11). Deities were periodically honoured by feasts in the home or palace, and these feasts often conveyed manifestly political messages (Durán 1967 II, pp. 92, 118, 172, 193, 257, 292, Sahagún 1950–69 Bk 2, p. 47, Bk 4, pp. 56, 870). Food, flowers and tobacco were customary gifts of hospitality, extended to both diplomatic envoys and guests with less overtly political intentions (Alva Ixtlilxochitl 1975–7 I, p. 441, Durán 1967 II, pp. 276, 292, 338, 353, 392). Since consumption rituals so frequently served as a means of expressing and manipulating political alliances and coalitions, the vessels which mark them also provide an indirect measure of the intensity of factional competition (Brumfiel 1987b).

Focusing on the abundance and elaboration of serving vessels in the Valley of Mexico in pre-Aztec and Aztec times, it should be possible to validate our discussion of factionalism in the archaeological record by confirming the following predictions.

(a) In pre-Aztec times, stylistic differences should separate the middle and northern valley which was a single area of factional competition from the southern valley which was not a part of that region.
(b) In pre-Aztec times, serving vessels should be more abundant and more elaborately decorated in the middle and northern valley, where factional competition was intense, than in the southern valley where disputes could more often be resolved by fission.
(c) There should be little stylistic change in pre-Aztec ceramics, but

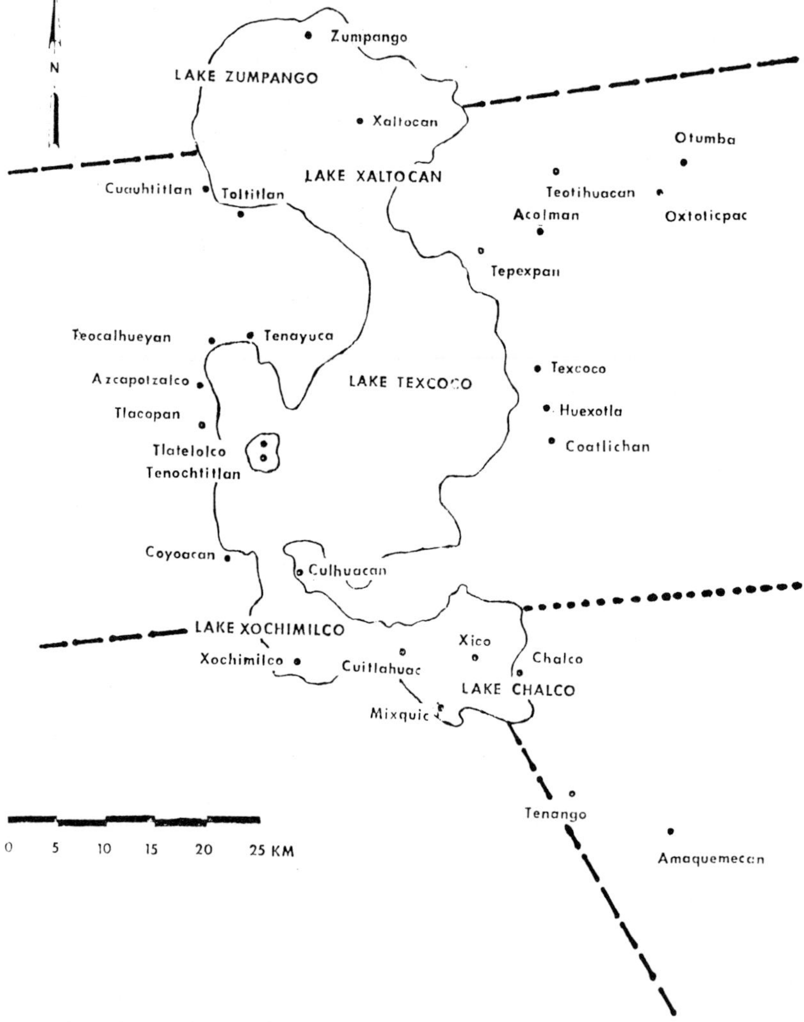

Figure 7.2 The incidence of Aztec II Black-on-Orange pottery in the Valley of Mexico. Aztec II is absent in the northern valley, common in the middle valley, and rare in the southern valley. There are scattered pockets of Aztec II in the Chalco-Amaquemecan region.

> change and innovation should be rapid during the Aztec era, particularly in Tenochtitlan. In the Aztec capital, a new prestige system developed which centred on feasting and competitive gift-giving among private citizens (Brumfiel 1987a). This did not involve competition for traditional offices requiring legitimation in traditional terms. Rather, it was an open system of prestige consumption where trendiness was valued and innovation was frequent.

The first of these predictions is partially validated by what is already known of Valley of Mexico ceramics in pre-Aztec times. Parsons *et al.* (1982a, p. 372) report that the Valley of Mexico is divided into three ceramic regions in pre-Aztec (S.I.3) times: a northern region defined by an assemblage that lacked any significant Aztec I or II Black-on-Orange; a central region characterized by an assemblage in which Aztec II Black-on-Orange (and Black-on-Red and Black-and-White-on-Red?) was dominant; and a southern region with an assemblage dominated by Aztec I Black-and-Orange and Chalco Polychrome (Fig.7.2).

Figures 7.1 and 7.2 reveal that the distribution of Aztec II Black–on-Orange in the Valley of Mexico closely parallels the pattern of intercommunity intermarriage. Little Aztec II pottery is found north of Xaltocan, the northernmost community in the marriage alliance network, and Aztec II pottery is almost absent from the lakebed communities lying south of Culhuacan. The coincidence of Aztec II pottery with intercommunity marriage alliance is not perfect; some Aztec II pottery occurs at Amecameca and Tenango in the south-east corner of the valley, an area that does not appear to have intermarried with communities in the middle valley. However, overall Aztec II Black-on-Orange is shared among communities linked by élite intermarriage; in this particular case historical records enable us to verify that ceramic style coincides with a regionally demarcated network of social interaction under conditions of political fragmentation and factional competition.

The competitive character of interaction is suggested by the high incidence of decorated pottery in the Aztec II ceramic zone (Table 7.1). The frequency of decorated ceramics in middle-valley collections consistently falls between 25 and 45 per cent of the ceramic assemblages. In contrast, the frequency of decorated ceramics in the southern valley is much lower: 6–7 per cent in collections from Xico and Xochimilco, and 13 per cent in mixed Early–Late Aztec materials from Chalco. Factors other than factional competition may have contributed to the high frequencies of decorated ceramics in the middle valley. For example, if the middle valley was a more integrated market region than the southern valley, competition between ceramic producers would have been more intense, resulting in an increased production of elaborately decorated vessels (cf. Feinman 1980). Some evidence of extensive regional marketing in the middle valley does exist. Green obsidian from Pachuca, in the far north-eastern corner of the Valley of Mexico, occurs in high frequencies (80 per cent) in pre-Aztec middle valley contexts (Noguera 1935, p. 162, 1970, Brumfiel 1980, p. 464), whereas in southern valley contexts the

Table 7.1 The incidence of decorated ceramics in the Valley of Mexico in pre-Aztec (S.I.3) times.

Site	Incidence
THE MIDDLE VALLEY	
Oxtotipac	37% of all sherds
Tepexpan (Parsons 1966)	45% of all sherds
Huexotla, Early Aztec units (Brumfiel, unpublished data)	45% of all rims
National Cathedral, Level IIIb (Piña Chan 1950)	43% of all sherds
Culhuacan (Litvak 1962)	25% of all rims
THE SOUTHERN VALLEY	
Xochimilco, excav. 1 Levels 8, 9,10 (Noguera 1970)	7% of all sherds
Xico Early Aztec units (Brumfiel, unpublished data)	6% of all rims
Chalco Levels 1–8 (O'Neill 1963)	13% of all sherds

frequency is lower (less than 30 per cent; Parsons *et al.* 1982b, pp. 155, 210). However, Smith's (1979) central place analysis of the Valley of Mexico argues against the existence of an integrated market system before the era of Aztec dominance, and it seems doubtful that producer competition could account entirely for the high proportions of decorated pottery in pre-Aztec middle-valley contexts. It seems likely that these high proportions can at least partially be attributed to the very frequent negotiation of social status through interaction in domestic contexts (i.e. the palaces of rulers and vassal lords), such negotiations being necessitated by the constant presence of credible rival factions.

Whether factional competition was associated with relatively slow rates of stylistic change in the pre-Aztec assemblages cannot be verified with data that are currently available. However, this preliminary assessment of stylistic distribution and elaboration of ceramics in the pre-Aztec Valley of Mexico suggests that factional competition does leave a predictable imprint on the archaeological record. As more adequate means of identifying factional competition are developed, we will be better able to assess the importance of competition between functionally similar factions for the emergence of social complexity.

References

Alva Ixtlilxochitl, F. de 1975–7. *Obras históricas*. E. O'Gorman (ed.). México, D.F.: Universidad Nacional Autónoma de México.

Anales de Cuauhtitlan 1945. In *Códice Chimalpopoca*, P. F. Velazquez (transl.), 1–118. México, D.F.: Universidad Nacional Autónoma de México.

Anales de Tlatelolco 1948. S. Toscano, H. Berlin, & R. H. Barlow (eds). México, D.F.: Antigua Libreria Robredo de Jose Porrua e Hijos.

Bailey, F. G. 1969. *Stratagems and spoils*. New York: Shocken.

Broda, J. 1976. Los estamentos en el ceremonial mexicana. In *Estratificación Social en la Mesoamérica prehispánica*, P. Carrasco *et al.* (eds.) 37–66. México, D.F.: Instituto Nacional de Antropología e Historia.

Brumfiel, E. M. 1980. Specialization, market exchange, and the Aztec state: a view from Huexotla. *Current Anthropology* **21**, 459–78.

Brumfiel, E. M. 1983. Aztec state making: ecology, structure and the origin of the state. *American Anthropologist* **85**, 261–84.

Brumfiel, E. M. 1987a. Elite and utilitarian crafts in the Aztec state. In *Specialization, exchange and social complexity*, E. M. Brumfiel & T. K. Earle, (eds), 102–18. Cambridge: Cambridge University Press.

Brumfiel, E. M. 1987b. Consumption and politics at Aztec Huexotla. *American Anthropologist* **89**, 679–86.

Bujra, J. M. 1973. The dynamics of political action: a new look at factionalism. *American Anthropologist* **75**, 132–52.

Carrasco, P. 1966. Documentos sobre el rango de tecuhtli en los Nahuas tramontanos. *Tlalocan* **5**, 133–60.

Carrasco, P. 1971. Social organization of ancient Mexico. In *Handbook of Middle American Indians*, Vol. 10: *Archaeology of Northern Mesoamerica, Part 1*, G. F. Ekholm & I. Bernal (eds), 349–75. Austin: University of Texas Press.

Carrasco, P. 1976. Los linajes nobles del México antiguo. In *Estratificación social en la mesoamerica prehispánica*, P. Carrasco *et al.* (eds), 19–39. México, D.F.: Instituto Nacional de Antropología e Historia.

Carrasco, P. 1977. Los señores de Xochimilco en 1548. *Tlalocan* **7**, 229–65.

Carrasco, P. 1978. La economía del México prehispánico. In *Economía política e ideología en el México prehispánico*, P. Carrasco & J. Broda (eds), 15–76. México, D.F.: Nueva Imagen.

Carrasco, P. 1984. Royal marriages in ancient Mexico. In *Explorations in ethnohistory: Indians of central Mexico in the sixteenth century*, H. R. Harvey & H. J. Prem (eds), 41–81. Albuquerque: University of New Mexico Press.

Chimalpahin, D. F. 1965. *Relaciones originales de Chalco Amaquemecan*, S. Rendón (transl.). México, D.F.: Fondo de Cultura Económica.

Cook, S. F. and W. Borah 1963. Quelle fut la stratification sociale au centre de Mexique durant la première moitié du XVIe siècle? *Annales, économies, sociétés, civilisations* **18**, 226–58.

Crónica Mexicayotl 1949. A. León (transl.). México, D.F.: Universidad Nacional Autonoma de México.

Douglas, M. & B. Isherwood 1977. *The world of goods: towards an anthropology of consumption*. New York: W. W. Norton.

Durán, D. 1967. *Historia de las Indias de Nueva Espanã*. A. Garibay (ed.). México, D.F.: Porrua.

Durán, D. 1971 *Book of the Gods and rites and the Ancient Calendar*, F. Horcasitas & D. Heyden (transl.). Norman: University of Oklahoma Press.

Feinman, G. 1980. *The relationship between administrative organization and ceramic production in the valley of Oaxaca, Mexico*. Unpublished Ph.D. dissertation, Department of Anthropology, City University of New York.

Gibson, C. 1964. *The Aztecs under Spanish rule*. Stanford: Stanford University Press.

Gibson, C. 1971. Structure of the Aztec empire. In *Handbook of Middle American Indians*, Vol. 10: G. F. Ekholm & I. Bernal (eds), *Archaeology of northern Mesoamerica, Part 1*, 376–94. Austin: University of Texas Press.

Guzmán, E. 1938. Un manuscrito de la colección de Boturini que trata de los antiguos señores de Teotihuacán. *Ethnos* **3**, 89–103.

Hicks, F. 1981. Merchant barrios and the balance of trade in prehispanic Mesoamerica. Paper presented at the 80th Annual Meeting, American Anthropological Association, Los Angeles, California.

Hicks, F. 1982. Texcoco in the early 16th century: the state, the city and the *calpolli*. *American Ethnologist* **9**, 320–49.

Hodge, M. G. 1984. *Aztec city–states*. (Memoirs, No. 18). Ann Arbor: The University of Michigan Museum of Anthropology.

Lewellen, T. C. 1983. *Political anthropology*. South Hadley, Massachusetts: Bergin & Garvey.

Litvak, J. 1962. Un montículo excavado en Culhuacán, en 1960. *Tlatoani* **16**, 17–31.

Noguera, E. 1935. La cerámica de Tenayuca y las excavaciones estratigráficas. In *Tenayuca*, 141–201. México, D.F.: Departamento de Monumentos Artísticos, Arqueológicas e Históricas.

Noguera, E. 1970. Exploraciones estratigráficas en Xochimilco, Tulancingo y Cerro de la Estrella. *Anales de Antropología* **7**, 91–130.

O'Neill, G. C. 1963. *Postclassic ceramic stratigraphy at Chalco in the Valley of Mexico*. Unpublished Ph.D. dissertation, Department of Anthropology, Columbia University, New York.

Parsons, J. R. 1966. *The Aztec ceramic sequence in the Teotihuacan Valley, Mexico*. Unpublished Ph.D. dissertation, Department of Anthropology, University of Michigan, Ann Arbor.

Parsons, J. R., E. Brumfiel, M. H. Parsons & D. J. Wilson 1982a. *Late prehispanic settlement patterns in the Southern Valley of Mexico: the Chalco–Xochimilco region*. (Memoirs, No. 14). Ann Arbor: University of Michigan Museum of Anthropology.

Parsons, J. R., E. Brumfiel, M. H. Parsons, V. Popper & M. Taft 1982b. Late prehispanic chinampa agriculture on Lake Chalco-Xochimilco, Mexico. Mimeo report on file, The University of Michigan Museum of Anthropology, Ann Arbor.

Piña Chan, R. 1950. Estratigrafía en los terrenos adyacentes a la Catedral Metropolitana, *Tlatelolco a Través de los Tiempos* **11**, 67–92.

Pollock, S. 1983. Style and information: an analysis of Susiana ceramics. *Journal of Anthropological Archaeology* **2**, 354–90.

Sahagún, B. de 1950–69. *Florentine codex: general history of the things of New Spain*, A. Anderson & C. Dibble (transl.). Santa Fe: School of American Research.

Sanders, W. T. 1956. The central Mexican symbiotic region. In *Prehistoric settlement patterns in the New World*, G. R. Willey (ed.), 115–27. (Viking Fund

Publication in Anthropology, No. 23). New York: Wenner-Gren Foundation.

Sanders, W. T. 1968. Hydraulic agriculture, economic symbiosis and the evolution of states in central Mexico. In *Anthropological archeology in the Americas*, B. J. Meggers (ed.), 88–107. Washington, DC: Anthropological Society of Washington.

Sanders, W. T., J. R. Parsons and R. S. Santley 1979. *The Basin of Mexico: ecological processes in the evolution of a civilization.* New York: Academic Press.

Siegel, B. J. and A. R. Beals 1960. Pervasive factionalism. *American Anthropologist* **62**, 394–417.

Smith, M. E. 1979. The Aztec marketing system and settlement pattern in the Valley of Mexico: a central place analysis. *American Antiquity* **44**, 110–25.

Smith, M. E. 1986. The role of social stratification in the Aztec empire: a view from the provinces. *American Anthropologist* **88**, 70–91.

Smith, M. E. 1987. Household possessions and wealth in agrarian states: implications for archaeology. *Journal of Anthropological Archaeology*, **6**, 297–335.

Soustelle, J. 1961. *Daily life of the Aztecs*, P. O'Brien (transl.). Stanford: Stanford University Press.

Van Zantwijk, R. 1973. Politics and ethnicity in a prehispanic Mexican state between the 13th and 15th centuries. *Plural Societies* **4**, 23–52.

Van Zantwijk, R. 1985. *The Aztec arrangement: the social history of pre-Spanish Mexico.* Norman: University of Oklahoma Press.

Zorita, A. de 1963. *Life and labor in Ancient Mexico*, B. Keen (transl.). New Brunswick: Rutgers University Press.

8 *Sensuous human activity and the state: towards an archaeology of bread and circuses*

SUSAN KUS

> Quelle que soit sa forme juridique, quelle que soit la philosophie sociale qui pretend en fonder l'existence, l'Etat est, métaphysiquement, un défi lancé à la mort, une négation de l'éphémère, un pont jeté entre le passé et l'avenir.
>
> (de Heusch 1962, p. 15)

Luc de Heusch (1962, pp. 15–16) has remarked that a study of politics must ultimately make reference to a comparative history of religions. It is within the domains of religion and politics, domains of both activity and representation, that a culture lays out its ontology and its logic of principles of force and power. Such principles of force and power are intimately tied to those of order and creation. Religion and politics define the degree and quality of the responsibility, be it conceived on the cosmological, moral, social or historical plane (Eliade 1959, p. 93), that a society is willing to accept in the creation and maintenance of the world it inhabits. This is a 'creation' not only in the figurative sense of the word, in the sense that humanity 'creates' the world it inhabits by investing it with order and meaning. This term must also be considered in its literal sense, a sense which can involve issues from humanity's collaboration in the creation of the cosmos (Eliade 1959, p. 93) to the creation of political structures through revolutions and the drafting of constitutions.

The study of indigenous primary state formations is a particularly interesting domain in which to explore the quality of the responsibility that societies are willing to shoulder in the creation of the worlds that they inhabit. I am not particularly interested in offering a tight definition of the state. I use the term 'state' as a shorthand to refer to a cultural situation wherein an interface between a cosmological and a religious order of activity and representation, and an emerging domain of political concepts and activities, provides the context for the definition of the responsibility referred to above. This is a context where members of a society are increasingly confronted by material and structural 'concretions' of a sociopolitical apparatus; where such things as permanent political offices, full-time bureaucratic specialists, and buildings reserved for public administrative affairs provide the experience of a permanent sociopolitical apparatus and routine. Such an experienced material presence finds a counterpart in a field of representations where concepts of a political order are 'reified' (in Marx's sense of the term), as well as partially 'disembedded' from more encompassing orders of cosmos and kinship.

Certain cases of indigenous state formation are particularly challenging and informative, for several reasons. In such cases, through the use of oral traditions and historical documents, we can gain some direct access to indigenous sociopolitical theory and ideology. Further, because of the physical scale of such societies, one can hope to gain a lively sense of the quality of human thought and social labour that is invested in the structuring and creation of these states. That is, one can appreciate the human scale of such cultural acts.[1] As members of contemporary state organizations whose presence is so heavily felt, social scientists have too often lost the quality of this scaling to the logic and vocabulary of systems theory, reified social institutions (e.g. 'the economy' or 'the administration'), and abstract material-economic principles (Kus 1985). In a sense our experiences as members of a state make it difficult for us to conceptually hold onto a notion of 'social praxis', let alone act upon such a notion. What is suggested in the following argument is that such a notion may have been more readily available to members of emergent state formations. The primary state formation of Imerina in central Madagascar will serve as the focus of the following discussion (see Fig. 8.1).

The interior of Madagascar witnessed complex social change and indigenous state formation somewhere between the 16th and the 18th centuries AD, depending on one's definition of the state and interpretation of available archaeological remains. A Jesuit missionary to the island, Père Callet, collected more than 1000 pages of Merina oral traditions (in the Merina dialect of the Malagasy language), collectively called the *Tantaran'ny Andriana* (*L'Histoire des Rois*). The central focus of these traditions is the recounting of the exploits of the Merina ruler (*mpanjaka*), Andrianampoinimerina, in his successful attempt to pacify the Merina population and to unify Imerina into a single state. The dates traditionally assigned to his rule are AD 1794 to 1810. Père Callet collected his traditions between 1865 and 1885. Some of his informants were direct descendants of the companions of this star diplomat and warrior (Delivré 1974). These traditions have been the subject of a careful preliminary analysis by Delivré (1974). Through his work and others (for example, Ayache 1976), it is possible to argue for the authenticity and traditional quality[2] of certain themes within the *Tantara* (as the traditions are referred to for short), certain themes that involve the nature of indigenous political activity and thought during and subsequent to the reign of Andrianampoinimerina.

In this chapter I explore certain aspects of indigenous sociopolitical theory in Imerina of the 18th and early 19th centuries AD. This exploration will serve as the basis of my argument – that a simple notion of theocracy, as traditionally defined, is insufficient to describe the ideological concerns of pristine states. Such a limited conceptualization of power and political legitimation (images of mindless masses humbly submitting to the capricious will of graven images) and scholarly

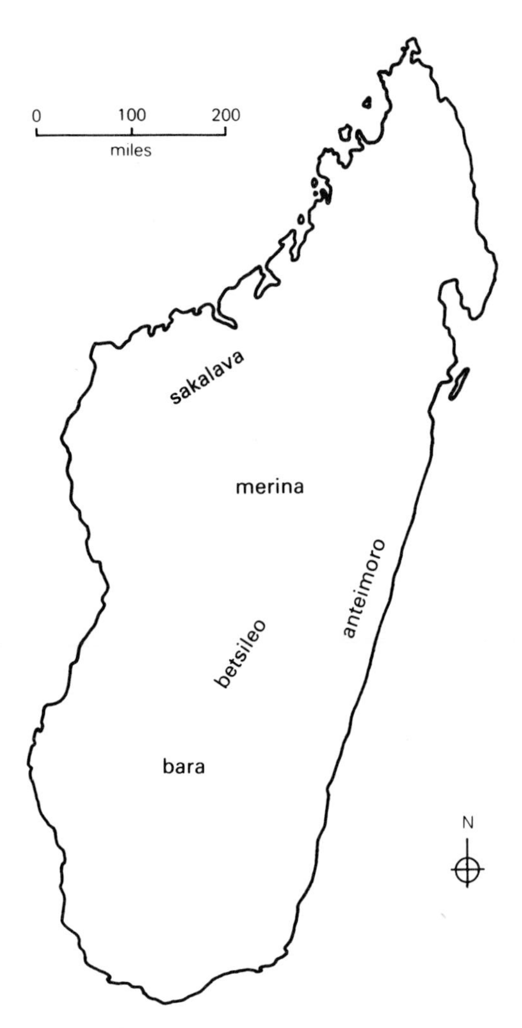

Figure 8.1 Some early states in Madagascar.

explanations of such cultural situations do not do justice to the social logic that defines and engages individuals in social and political relations beyond the level of immediate kinship ties.

Traditional Merina thought makes its share of appeals to god (*Andriamanitra*) and sacred idols (*sampy*) in an attempt to sanctify the world's order. Yet Merina thought contains much that is disconcerting if one wants to use the pair sacred and secular to contrast non-modern and modern religious and political thought.

The bringing of order to chaos is the quintessential creative act. The creation of the cosmos in traditional societies is the prerogative of the gods. Humanity finds a role in this creation, at times as collaborator in the original creative act, through the involvement of a mythic ancestor, at other times as guarantor of the established order in the continuing repetition of the primordial act of creation through ritual ceremonies of renewal. However, the social world is a contested domain. Humanity can concede its responsibilities within this domain, to become interpreters and imitators of the cosmological order that is seen to pervade and determine the social order (Kus 1982, Frankfort 1948). However, humanity can also accept responsibility for the creation of a social order. The most audacious wresting of this responsibility from the gods is effected perhaps through use of Marx's understanding of the nature of the social order as based upon collective human praxis without appeal to meta-social warrants[3] (Touraine 1977). However, it is argued below that the Promethean Merina are interesting forerunners as proponents of a theory of 'social praxis' used in the creation of a sociopolitical order.

The *Tantara*, though it concentrates on the activity of the Merina under the rule of Andrianampoinimerina, also contains a panorama of Merina history. Delivré (1974) has argued that the Merina of the early 19th century understood their history as an *evolutionary* history. It is an evolutionary history of the creation of a sociopolitical order. This order was given conceptual specificity in a political ideal of a unified kingdom, and this ideal was realized under the reign of Andrianampoinimerina.

Merina history, through the eyes of the oral traditions, begins with socially and politically 'undomesticated' original inhabitants of the interior of the island. These are the *Vazimba* who, naked and politically disorganized, were dispersed over the countryside. These *Vazimba* were eventually displaced or absorbed by the *Hova* who, to their credit, brought a modicum of sociopolitical order to the region in Weberian fashion by specifying an order of succession to political office. Class order was later imposed on the *Hova* by a ruling monarch. Originally this involved the creation of three noble or *Andriana* ranks, and the term *Hova* came to signify the commoner groups within Merina society. Subsequently the number of noble ranks was enlarged to six. However, even with the introduction of class organization to Imerina, the *order* within the sociopolitical domain was only tenuous and constantly disrupted by internal warfare.

The history of Andrianampoinimerina's ascension to power is the epiphany of the Merina social and political order. In this period the Merina had invested their history with a coherence and a direction. They had given time and the order of temporal events a direction by placing 'value on the future', as Eliade (1959) would say. The ideal of political unification was this value placed on the future. Political unification is presaged in the oral traditions of early Merina history when it is briefly experienced under the reign of Andriamasinavalona several generations before Andrianampoinimerina came to power; but it was the latter who finally and successfully realized this ideal.

The legitimacy of any sociopolitical *order* is based on it being just that – *an order*. One strategy for guaranteeing the permanence and continuity of a sociopolitical order is to place it within an 'ahistorical' order of a once-given pattern and its repetition (Kus 1982). That is to say that the activities of a sociopolitical order can be seen as a continuation and repetition of an original charter of the gods or a mimicry of a cosmological order. This is a situation that Frankfort (1948) argues is characteristic of the early state formation in the Nile Valley. In this riverine valley where early state development occurred in a situation of relative geographical isolation, and where the subsistence base was guaranteed by the annual renewal of cultivable soil by the flooding of the Nile, the representation of the sociopolitical order was embedded in that of the cosmological order. The representations of the pharaoh and the state were tightly intertwined with the divinities and temporal rhythms of 'natural phenomena' (e.g. sun, flood and harvest cycle). The ordering of a repetitive cycle provides a fairly secure base for conceptualizing permanence and continuity, but permanence and continuity are conceptually more problematic if change and innovation are to be envisioned as possibilities of sociopolitical activity. How does change not bring about disorder and chaos? How does innovation not engender discontinuity?

One way of introducing the possibility of creative social activity into the 'logic of the world order' is to conceptualize a 'natural' and a 'social' world that contains chaotic or disruptive elements. Thus, the possibility of disorder necessitates vigilant activity on the part of participants in a social formation. We can see such a logic in the Merina case if we look more closely at the Merina ideal of political unification and how the conceptualization of this ideal integrates the workings of the cosmological and the social orders.

Some four generations or so before Andrianampoinimerina's rise to power the Merina state was unified by the then reigning sovereign, Andriamasinavalona. As the historical tale runs, Andriamasinavalona could not and would not choose a successor from among his four eligible sons, despite the fact that there are traditional means to decide among heirs. For instance, one can watch how they arrange themselves in a room and choose the one who leans against the central pillar (Callet 1974 II, p. 10), or make them sleep in the same room and in the middle of the night enter this room with a light and see who sleeps with his head raised (Callet 1974 II, p. 13). If you prefer richer metaphors you can offer the potential heirs a series of gifts and interpret the significance of their particular choices (Callet 1974 I, pp. 560–62).

Not only would Andriamasinavalona not choose a single heir, he also refused to heed the advice of his counsellor, Andriamampandry. It is not without significance that this counsellor's name translates as 'the noble that creates calm or peace'. This counsellor warned Andriamasinavalona several times, and in very dramatic fashion, of the consequences of such a refusal. For instance, he appeared at the royal residence one day carrying a basket which contained four birds of prey (*voro-mahery*). When released these birds flew around and stirred up enough soot and dust to cover Andriamasinavalona, filling his eyes and throat, and covering dishes of rice, making his meal inedible. The 'peace-maker' commented that the incident was only a metaphor for what would happen to Imerina if it were divided into four parts (Callet 1974 III, p. 40). On another occasion Andriamampandry asked Andriamasinavalona to assemble his people. The 'peace-maker' then let loose a bull among the crowd. Many were trampled and injured, and some pregnant women were induced to abort. When Andriamampandry accepted responsibility for this act before the outraged sovereign, he explained that the destruction and loss of life that resulted from this act was negligible compared with what would happen to the Merina if Andriamasinavalona let four individuals exercise royal authority (Callet 1974 II, pp. 39–40). Unfortunately, Andriamasinavalona still stubbornly refused to designate a single heir, so it came about that war and famine continuously plagued the divided state (Callet 1974 II, pp. 36, 48–50).

Several generations later Andrianampoinimerina laid claim to the rule of the four districts of the divided state. The bases of his claim as presented in the *Tantara* are too extensive and involved to present here. Suffice it to say that these bases included not only a correct genealogy, but also the fact that Andrianampoinimerina liked to lean on central pillars and to sleep with his head raised. While genealogy and omens seem to have been clear in *designating* Andrianampoinimerina as heir to the state created by Andriamasinavalona, the *exercise* of this claim came through diplomatic acts and physical battles. These acts, according to the *Tantara*, were all directed toward the explicit goal of reuniting the divided state. It is the symbol of unity that plays a central role in the ideology and logic that Andrianampoinimerina used to legitimate his power and politics as described in the oral traditions. In direct discourse as presented in the *Tantara*, Andrianampoinimerina argued quite explicitly that political unity is the only way to bring peace and prosperity to a state plagued by disorder, famine, and warfare. The way to guarantee such peace was to have a single head of state (Callet 1974 II, p. 207).

Peace and prosperity are attendant upon unification. Without unification chaos and insecurity reign. Fear of brigands and continuous fighting between petty 'kingdoms' keep people from working in the fields and rice paddies and keep them away from markets. Political insecurity induces famine. This is the claim that is made for the period when Andriamasinavalona leaves a divided kingdom. One famine is said to have lasted for seven years (Callet 1974 I, p. 553).

Andrianampoinimerina was always claiming to wage battles, as well as to direct social labour in projects such as draining and dyking marshland areas, not for any personal gain, but for the welfare of the populace. In one piece of discourse he lays out this logic:

> . . . the core of the state ultimately is based on the work that renders the land productive since this is the way to ensure the well-being of the populace. I am happy to see your bright faces and foreheads without wrinkles because you are well-nourished. I am happy to see you are healthy and strong: my desire has found its realization. (free translation of Calet 1974 III, p. 173)

From this ideology or logic wherein political power is only legitimately held and exercised for the benefit of the population, it follows that Andrianampoinimerina can make the claim that his only 'real' enemies are natural disasters. These enemies include: (a) *rano voky*, the water that breaks [the dykes]; (b) *afo*, fire; (c) *mosary*, famine; (d) *havandra*, hail; and (e) *rivotra*, wind. People become accomplices of these enemies of the state when they perpetuate political chaos (by supporting a political rival), or when they refuse to act in united social effort to support the welfare of the state. This logic of a sociopolitical order, as ultimately interfaced with a natural or cosmological order, is further elaborated on in Andrianampoinimerina's social policy regarding the confrontation of these public enemies. These public enemies are to be fought through *united public* effort. Consequently, there is to be public upkeep of dykes. In case of fire all citizens are to answer cries for help. Industriousness on the part of all citizens, nobles as well as commoners, will ensure abundant harvests. For hail and wind, which are a bit more tricky to handle, Andrianampoinimerina also has a *social* solution. All citizens are to pay a tax to support full-time specialists to manufacture amulets against such destructive natural forces.

The argument that political disorder was an element of cosmological disorder for the Merina of the 19th century can be reinforced by citing several examples of the symbolic fusion of the political order and the order of physical nature. The first example is that of Kelimalaza, one of the royal fetishes said to have helped Andrianampoinimerina to unite Imerina (Callet 1974 II, pp. 435–6). This idol, which was carried into political battles, was also an idol associated with certain powers over natural phenomena. It allowed one to know when to plant rice, when the rains would come, and whether lightning would strike. It also allowed one to tell if there were alligators in a river (Callet 1974 I, p. 330). The second example is that of the custom of *mirary*. This was a solemn prayer that was chanted when a disaster, such as heavy rains, hail or strong thunder and lightning threatened the land (Callet 1974 I, p. 484). It was also chanted when soldiers were sent into battle (Callet 1974 I, p. 485).

There are two points to be culled from the previous discussion concerning the Merina conceptualization of the sociopolitical order that are important for the discussion to follow. They concern: (a) an indigenous notion of 'social contract', and (b) an indigenous notice of 'social praxis'.

In the Merina traditions that refer to the early history of the polity there is an understated recognition of the Merina population as the underlying source of political power and legitimation, a recognition that I am loosely referring to as a 'social contract'. In certain situations the population is said to have played an acknowledged role in the transfer of political power. In one instance an early ruling figure, Andriantsimitoviamindriandehibe, informs the population of his choice of successor. The oral traditions go on to say that:

> Conforming to this declaration of their father [the king] the people passed the royal authority into the hands of Andrianjakanavalondambo . . . (Author's translation of Callet 1974 I, pp. 532–3.)

In the discourses of Andrianampoinimerina, as presented in the *Tantara*, an even more explicit statement is given to the argument that political power is only held and exercised for the benefit of the population. One example of such discourse is:

> It is to the people that the king owes his right to govern, because if it is the case that the king wields great power in his position as sovereign, it is also the case that the people hold great power as the people. (Author's translation of Dandouau & Chapus 1953, p. 144.)

Indigenous Merina sociopolitical theory is not exceptional in this understanding of political power and its legitimate exercise. Examples from African states, chiefdoms of the Pacific high islands, and medieval European kingdoms of the overthrow of immoral rulers by a morally obligated populace should argue that in a number of pristine and pre-industrial states we can also find a concept of 'social contract' in indigenous sociopolitical theory.

Merina sociopolitical theory also incorporated a notion of social activity or 'social praxis' as necessary to the creation and maintenance of an ordered world. Such activity involved not only following vigilant 'maintenance' activities (e.g. upkeep of irrigation systems and regular payment of taxes), but also sociopolitical 'innovation'. The Merina saw their history not only as active, but as *progressive* and their social order as *perfectable*. The Merina reconciled the permanence of a sociopolitical order to the possibility of change within that order through the logic of a dynamic or evolving continuity (Delivré 1974).[4] The *Tantara* throughout its pages lists innovations attributed to its various rulers or *mpanjaka* (see Fig. 8.2). These innovations are mixtures of techno-economic inventions such as the introduction of cooked meat and guns to the Merina heartland, and social reforms primarily directed toward reworking and refining a system of class stratification. In the *Tantara*, on the one hand, there are the innovators whose deeds are recalled in detail. On the other hand, there are the rulers mentioned only briefly in order of their succession. These latter are individuals who have accomplished no memorable acts besides the maintenance of the status quo (Delivré 1974). The innovator *par excellence* in the *Tantara* is Andrianampoinimerina, and consequently the pages of the *Tantara* are filled with his exploits. When the *Tantara* speaks of the accomplishments of Andrianampoinimerina it is as if one is reading a classic anthropological text on the state. One is presented with a checklist of early state accomplishments, from the building of irrigation systems to tax and market reform. In the case of Andrianampoinimerina and the other innovators of the *Tantara*, their actions are presented as epiphanies of social *order*. Although their acts have specific and different historical content, they are more importantly manifestations of the essence of the social force of creation and thus demonstrate the fitness of the ruler to rule (Delivré 1974). Such *mpanjaka* are able to channel creative force and direct it toward perfecting the social system. Their acts recounted in the *Tantara* are steps toward actualizing an ideal of peace, prosperity and political unity.

Ruling Figure	Innovations
Rangita and Rafohy	regularize political succession
Andriamanelo	first *andriana* (noble) iron-working circumcision
Ralambo	use of the name Imerina firearms royal bath cooked meat cattle pens ranking of original three *andriana* groups
Andrianjaka	drained the Betsimitatatra royal funerary customs
Andriamasinavalona	first major unification of Imerina increased ranked divisions of *andriana*
Andrianampoinimerina	checklist of state innovations

Figure 8.2 Merina royal innovations.

The *Tantara* presents us with a history of creative and historical *acts*. Closer observation of who specifically are assigned roles as *actors* in this history is revealing as it concerns an indigenous notion of social praxis in Merina sociopolitical theory. The story of the Merina polity contained in the *Tantara* until the time of Andrianampoinimerina is a history where the social praxis that has created this history is vested in the Merina rulers. These rulers are not presented in the traditions as in any way deified. They are human figures whose actions serve to place them in the foreground of historical tales as heroic figures, and Imerina history at this time could be called heroic history according to Sahlins' (1983) use of the term.

Under the rule of Adrianampoinimerina the head of the Merina state continued to occupy the premier role as historical actor, but the body politic was explicitly acknowledged as contributing to the creation and maintenance of the state. The recognition of this active role of the population is evidenced in the traditional practice of the royal *kabary* as exercised by Andrianampoinimerina. The *kabary* was an address by the sovereign to the assembled populace. Such addresses were supposedly used to inform the populace of royal ordinances and projects to be undertaken. These addresses of the rulers often began with traditional formulae acknowledging their respect for the population as guarantors of the strength of Merina society. In the *kabary* of the early rulers of the Merina state the population is most often presented as passive witnesses to royal words and deeds, sanctioning the actions of the ruler by formulaic declarations of support.

However, under Andrianampoinimerina, the *kabary* was reconstituted as a powerful tool to gain public support in his military campaigns to unify Imerina and to underwrite the legitimacy of his claim to control the Merina state. There are several startling points concerning the practice of the *kabary* under Andrianampoinimerina as described in the oral traditions. Speech is a powerful force in traditional Merina society. To speak is to risk *tsiny*, to risk blame and censorship (Andriamanjato 1957, p. 14). If one presumes to speak in the presence of older individuals, one's parents or before the sovereign without lengthy and appropriate excuses for this presumption, one risks an early death (Callet 1974, p. 54) and the wrath of the ancestors. Yet the oral traditions referring to the period of Andrianampoinimerina's exploits contain lengthy and supposedly direct quotes not only of Andrianampoinimerina, but also of the population. The quotes from the speeches of the populace very rarely contain the prefacing formulaic excuses that such addresses demand, as if they have been edited out of the traditions to proceed more directly to the critical excerpts of the active dialogue between ruler and subjects.

These royal *kabary* of Andrianampoinimerina not only contain very explicit reference to the Merina population as ultimate retainers of political power, but they also often directly credit the population for the role that it played in placing Andrianampoinimerina at the head of a pacified and united Imerina. That is to say, that under Andrianampoinimerina, Merina history is no longer the simple history of the ruling nobles. The Merina populace are recognized by the sovereign for services rendered to the state. Delivré has said:

> There is then no more enviable situation [for a social group] than that of possessing a history, particularly when the sovereign himself gives it an official character through a solemn proclamation. (Author's translation of Callet 1974 III, p. 303.)

Andrianampoinimerina says as much in the oral traditions, though it is put a bit more poetically. Speaking to a group of Zanakandiamborona he says:

> If I give you money, it can be spent; if I offer you a *lamba* article of clothing, it can become torn. But here is what I give you, the memory of your worthy deeds will follow you always. (Author's translation of Callet 1974 II, p. 304.)

It is important to understand that the explicit acknowledgement in royal discourse of the Merina population as historical actors parallels the on-the-ground political strategy that Andrianampoinimerina used in gaining control of Imerina. As mentioned earlier, Andrianampoinimerina had legitimate genealogical claim to the rule of a united Imerina (Delivré 1974), but at the beginning of his political career he only held one of the four major political divisions of Imerina, the domain of Ambohimanga. Andrianampoinimerina eventually united and pacified Imerina through numerous military campaigns using *commoner* groups as his first and continuing base of popular and tactical support. Thus, there is a strong fit between the political strategy used by Andrianampoinimerina in his rise to power and its ideological presentation in the oral traditions.

Andrianampoinimerina's image in the *Tantara* does not conform to that of his heroic predecessors. He shares the historical stage with the Merina populace, and thus extends the notion of social praxis beyond the deeds of a ruling élite. Yet, this sharing of history is uneven for there is a division of labour between Andrianampoinimerina and his subjects – there is a division of intellectual from manual labour.

In the *Tantara* the *kabary* of Andrianampoinimerina are densely interspersed between descriptions of major military campaigns and organizational acts that resulted in the unification of Imerina. This alternation of speech and description in Merina history of this period emphasizes a counterpoint of *word* and *deed*. The following quotation of Andrianampoinimerina illustrates this historical quality of thought and practice:

> But for all the sovereign that I am, it is you, my people, who have assured my success; my mouth only indicated [the way] it is you that accomplished it. (Author's translation of Callet 1974 II, p. 71.)

Interestingly enough, at one point in the traditions, Andrianampoinimerina claims that it was through the force of persuasion that he unified Imerina, thus placing the extensive military operations he undertook in order of secondary importance. When Andrianampoinimerina attempted to extend his control beyond the heartland of Imerina into the Vakinankaratra (the region immediately to the south of Imerina) he is quoted as saying: 'I will take them through the means of speech and persuasion that allowed me to reunify Imerina'. (Author's translation of Callet 1974 II, p. 339).

It is perhaps even more interesting for the question of indigenous concepts of 'social contract' and 'social praxis' to ask, at this point, what are the constituent elements of the population that Andrianampoinimerina is so much in the habit of addressing and of sharing a division of historical labour with?

It will be recalled that one of the earlier forms of order brought to Merina society as discussed in the oral traditions is the establishment of a system of social stratification. Originally three noble groups were created, and subsequently the noble class was enlarged to six groups. Andrianampoinimerina's genealogical claim to Ambohimanga and to a united Imerina were based on a noble lineage. Yet often at times, if not most often, when Andrianampoinimerina addresses the population in the *Tantara*, little reference is made to the noble–commoner distinction. At one point he goes as far as saying: '. . . for me, they are all equal, the Merina' (author's translation of Callet 1974 III, p. 48). Another time he puts it more poetically: 'the Merina, my subjects, are like a piece of cloth [*lamba*] without front or backside, like the circular and uniform rim of a pot' (author's translation of Callet 1974 III, p. 89). However, before we have

Marx turning in his grave with the abolition of classes in ancient Imerina, I should point out that the situation is not that straightforward. This is evident in another poetic utterance of Andrianampoinimerina: '. . . the Merina are constituted as a braid of hair intermingled; but there are interstices nevertheless' (author's translation of Callet 1974 III, p. 28).

It might be possible to understand the complexity of the logic of the internal divisions of the Merina population by arguing that Andrianampoinimerina makes a distinction between a sociopolitical sphere of order and activity and a social but non-political, non-historical sphere of order and activity. In his addresses to the population, Andrianampoinimerina, for all his innovative energy, often says that he changes nothing concerning the traditions of the ancestors. This is as if to say that there is an underlying order to society that is fundamental to the constitution of that body. It is an order that is stable and is most often referred to in terms of rules of marriage. Andrianampoinimerina insists upon class endogamy on several occasions. However, when he is seen to address the nobles, which is not very often, it is to clarify the locus of political power in the state. Addressing the three original noble groups, the *Andrianteloray*, he makes it clear that though they are honoured as the source of Imerina's original rulers, they have no claim to the exercise of political power, i.e. they cannot aspire to the position of sovereign. Two of the additional noble groups, the *Zanakandriana* and the *Zazamarolahy*, are the direct kin of the sovereign. The sovereign designates the members of his kin that fill these two groups, and it is only the few members of the former group that are potential inheritors of his political power. When a new monarch assumes control the personnel of these two groups necessarily changes. Obviously this is a very clever manoeuvre, given what we know of the problem early states seem to be plagued by, of finding a means to guarantee peaceful transference of power upon the death of a sovereign.

The sixth noble group (not in order of ranking), the *Andriamasinavalona*, are the only group to exercise an important role in the political administration. They are the group that provided, from their ranks, spouses for the monarch, but they themselves could not inherit his office. However, what is interesting with regard to this group is that when Andrianampoinimerina wished to recompense certain commoner groups or, later when he expanded his rule beyond the Merina frontiers, non-Merina nobility for their roles in creating the Merina state, he placed them (if they accepted his offer) within the ranks of the *Andriamasinavalona*. In a sense the *Andriamasinavalona* are an honoured group of administrators and citizenry whose ranks were not solely entered by claim to a noble genealogy.

In the oral traditions it thus appears that, despite the persistence of the commoner–noble distinction, the population as it stands before the king in the domain of political activity is divided along lines other than class. The populace is addressed as a whole when the state is referenced in terms of its unitary, enduring essence. However, when the state is engaged in action or in social praxis, the population is assigned duties either along lines of geographical residence in a political district or they are more finely divided. These finer divisions are designated through the use of sobriquets that make reference to the great services such groups have rendered to the state and to the sovereign.

It could be argued that under Andrianampoinimerina's reign the Merina population served as guarantor of the continuity of the social essence that served as the *raison d'être* of the state ('social contract') as well as a source of creative political action ('social praxis'). In possessing a sociopolitical identity they constituted the creative force of the Merina state by not only participating in the creation of the state, but also existing as a testament to that order through the possession of a history of their role in the Merina state formation. It is the Merina population that came to serve as the base of the *dynamic continuity* (the 'bridge' of de Heusch in the opening citation of this chapter) of the Merina state in the early 19th century.

A Western history of ideas is willing to trace a concept of 'social contract' back only as far as the ancient Greeks, the Promethean culture heroes of Western democratic thought, and the concept of 'social praxis' is placed in a Marxist genealogy. However, the case of Imerina expands the context within which one might investigate the contents and functioning of such notions in the creation and maintenance of a sociopolitical order. This case further suggests an important question in the study of complex sociopolitical forms. Would it be possible to argue that notions of 'social contract' and 'social praxis', rather than being recent historical novelties, necessarily find a place in the conceptual–ideological field that defines questions of legitimacy and power in state-organized societies, societies where the logic of social relations surpasses the logic of kinship? If this is the case, if the logic of 'social contract' and 'social praxis' does find a place in the ideology of pristine states, then another interesting question is posed. How is the logic of such concepts played out in the material and social organization of such societies? That is, what are the consequences of such a field of representation for the non-ruling members of such societies?

If, in the indigenous sociopolitical theories and ideologies of emergent state formations, the well-being and consent of the social body is seen to serve as a justification for the existence of the state and a basis for evaluating the 'legitimacy' of a political regime, then it follows that some concessions must be made in directing social labour and surplus wealth towards the 'benefit' of the masses. Recent archaeological work on state formations concerned with defining and identifying the state in terms of class distinctions and exploitation has often been preoccupied with finding and studying archaeological vestiges of opulence and high culture (e.g. rich-baby burials, monumental architecture, human sacrifice and portrait art). Let me be clear here, I do not intend the last remark as a critique. In fact, I would argue that exploitation and classicism are fundamental to the existence of the state as we know it, and that the roots and forms of such logic and behaviour need to be brought into high relief to allow an effective critique of the state. Yet by urging that we look at the 'bread and circuses' that are offered to the masses by the retainers of political power and privilege, I do not intend to take an apologist's position with regards to the state.

Advocating an 'archaeology of bread and circuses' certainly sounds like a tongue-in-cheek remark. Yet I think this phrasing captures the point that I wish to make. On the one hand, the 'legitimacy' and tolerance of the state, its apparatus and its political élite by the general populace is dependent on the fact that the state and its directors guarantee a certain level of daily general well-being – the fat cheeks and wrinkle-free faces of the Merina, the affordability of the *baguette* for the French worker, garbage pick-up on a regular basis in Anytown, USA. Yet the state and its privileged members, on the other hand, have an interest in not only demonstrating that the state is functioning in an orderly fashion, but that it is functioning *well*. Thus, we find the state supplied '*chicha*' of the Incas, Roman circuses, and government grants for esoteric disciplines such as archaeology.

It seems to me that it might be interesting to theoretically pursue an archaeology of bread and circuses. One would need to understand the relationship between the indigenous ideology of early state formations and the material presence of the state as experienced by participants in such states. (This is a more specific formulation of the theoretical question that concerns the nature of the relationship between social representation and material social production.) Such research directions might help us to understand, on the one hand, how and at what cost the state is willing and able to 'buy' the consent of its members, and on the other hand, if and when an official ideology of 'social contract' and 'social praxis' can be employed for the unofficial goals of protest and revolution.

Notes

1 To be clear, I am not advocating a psychological reductionist explanation for the origin of the state. I am rather arguing that social actors operate not only in a world of physical and social 'laws', but also in a 'meaningful' world.

2 Ayache (1976) argues that Père Callet conceived of his task as that of an objective recorder of historical information rather than as offering critical commentary on historical documents.

3 Augé's use of the term 'meta-social warrants' refers to explanations of the social order that make ultimate reference to ahistorical laws of the physical universe be they enforced by God or discovered by Einstein, rather than to the nature of social and historical phenomena.

4 Eliade (1959) suggested that one way to envisage the possibility of change that does not bring disorder in its wake is to incorporate within the notion of change a dynamic principle of the creation order. That is, change can be seen as the progressive means to realizing an ideal future state.

References

Andriamanjato, R. 1957. *Le Tsiny et le Tody dans la pensée malgache*. Paris: Présence Africaine.

Ayache, S. 1976. *Raombana-l'historien (1809–1855)*. Fianarantsoa, Madagascar: Ambozontany.

Callet, F. 1974. *Histoire des rois (Tantaran'ny Andriana)*. Translated from Malagasy and ed. G. S. Chapus & E. Ratsimba. Tananarive, Madagascar: Edition de la Librairie Madagascar.

Delivré, A. 1974. *L'histoire des rois d'Imerina: interpretation d'une tradition orale*. Paris: Klinckieck.

Eliade, M. 1959. *The sacred and the profane: the nature of religion*. New York: Harcourt Brace Jovanovich.

Frankfort, H. 1948. *Kingship and the gods*. Chicago: University of Chicago Press.

Heusch, L. de 1962. Pour une dialectique de la sacralité du pouvoir. In *Le pouvoir et le sacré*, L. de Heusch (ed.). Bruxelles: Annales du Centre d'Etude des Religions.

Kus, S. 1982. Matters material and ideal. In *Symbolic and structural archaeology*. I. Hodder (ed.). Cambridge: Cambridge University Press.

Kus, S. 1985. Gods, kings, scholars and the state. Paper delivered at the 84th Annual Meeting of the American Anthropological Association, Washington, DC.

Sahlins, M. 1983. Distinguished lecture: other times, other customs: the anthropology of history. *American Anthropologist* **85** (3).

Touraine, A. 1977. *The self-production of society*. Chicago: University of Chicago Press.

9 *Anurādhapura: ritual, power and resistance in a precolonial South Asian city*

R. A. L. H. GUNAWARDANA

The process of urbanization makes its appearance in Sri Lanka, as it did in South India, much later than in the northern parts of the Indian subcontinent, although megalithic peoples enjoying access to the use of iron tools had been present in the island for a long time. Certainly by the 1st century BC urban settlements had already arisen in different parts of the island. Inscriptions written in the earliest form of the Brāhmī script refer to towns like Aba and Bama in the present Kurunāgala District, Bataśa, Nilaya and Śiva in the Kāgalla District, Kaśaba and Uti in the Ampārē District and Cita in the Kandy District (Paranavitana 1970, pp. 32, 41, 60–1, 63, 75, 81). Later epigraphic records datable to a period falling within the next three centuries or so mention towns like Naka, Magana and Palo in the Anurādhapura District, Kaḷaha in the Polonnaruva District and Bagu and Kaṭaka in the Kurunāgala District, (Paranavitana 1970, p. 89, 1983, pp. 23, 56). In his *Geographia* Ptolemy lists 11 places in the island, each of which he described as a *civitas*. These include Margana, Iogana, Sindocanda, Nubartha, Hodoca, Dionysiseu Bachi, Bocana, Abaratha, Procuri, Nagadiba and Anubingara. A twelfth place, Maagrammum which was clearly Mahāgrāma in southern Sri Lanka, was referred to as a *metropolis*. Evidently, according to his informants, these were all fully fledged cities. Two places, Modutti and Talacori, are described as *emporiu*, and four others as *portus* (Ptolemaeus 1966, pp. 136–7). Certain place names cited here, like Margana and Abaratha, are reminiscent of some places mentioned in the inscriptions. Both epigraphic and literary sources suggest that elements of urban life were developing in a widespread area within the island. However, Anurādhapura clearly emerged as the leading urban centre and, apart for a few decades when Sīgiri and, later, Polonnaruva became the residence of rulers, its dominance over the island persisted for about 12 centuries. In fact, Anurādhapura was one of the most durable centres of political power and urban life in South Asia. The study of Anurādhapura helps us to recognize some specific features of the South Asian city, and furthers our understanding of variant types of the pre-industrial city.

Anurādhapura gained prominence primarily as the city where the king lived. The innermost part of the city was reserved for the residential quarters of the royal family, and the site of the royal palace was supposed to be at 'the centre' of the city (*Vaṃsatthappkāsinī* 1935, I, p. 284). It was not a city which was initially laid out according to a plan, but one which grew over the centuries. Remains of the walls of the city do not conform to the regular rectangular outlines of the planned city. The Chinese pilgrim Fa Hian, who visited Anurādhapura in the 5th century AD and stayed there for two years, was clearly impressed with the city, and his account is perhaps the most detailed description of cities visited by him. He noted that there were in all four principal streets. All the streets and lanes were well-maintained and were 'smooth and level' (Fa Hian 1957, p. 47). However, as in the case of the city wall, in their layout the streets appear to have belied their origins. For instance, the main street, called the Ceremonial Street, started at the southern gate near the Thūpārāma, and it is said to have veered eastwards and then northwards (*Sumanṇgalavilāsinī* 1931, pp. 572–3). Clearly it followed the casual and meandering path of an unplanned street.

As we shall see later, in certain respects the city represents the demarcation of space on the basis of social criteria. The evidence from the *Mahāvaṃsa* and other accounts suggests that fine distinctions were made between different sectors of the city, depending on the identity of the social group that occupied each sector. Fa Hian found that there were two major groups within the inner city. As one would expect, there was a prominent group of merchants whose houses impressed the Chinese pilgrim as being richly adorned (Fa Hian 1957, p. 47). Some of these residents were probably foreigners. Trading groups of South Indian origin were resident at the city from pre-Christian times, and there were even instances when they captured political power and dominated the region (*Mahāvaṃsa* 1958, Ch. 21, vv. 10–11, Paranavitana 1970, pp. 7). In a statement that should attract attention in the planning of future archaeological excavations at Anurādhapura the *Mahāvaṃsa* (Ch.10, v. 90) refers to a separate quarter set apart near the western gate of the city for men of Mediterranean or Persian (*Yona*) origin. The chronicle is not explicit about whether this quarter was inside or outside the city walls but, certainly by the 5th century, the merchants had emerged as one of the most prominent of the groups resident within the inner city.

Fa Hian speaks of the second major group of city-dwellers as being wealthy 'householders', probably meaning that stratum whose affluence was based on agricultural resources. Within this category may be grouped the two powerful clans who dominated the political life of the city as well as the whole island for many centuries: the Lambakaṇṇas and the Moriyas. The rulers of the island usually belonged to one or the other of these clans. Thus, as much as Anurādhapura was the centre of royal power, it was also a centre of clan power. Quite often, especially during the initial phase of the process of state formation, it was the arena where bitter clan struggles were fought out. Sometimes, as when Iḷanāga ascended the throne at the beginning of the 1st century AD, members of one clan would be reluctant to acquiesce to the authority of a new ruler from the rival clan. In this particular instance, the members of the Lambakaṇṇa clan were so powerful that they were able to disrupt the ceremonies marking the king's elevation to power and, when he attempted to punish them, to detain the king within his palace and to carry on the administration by themselves. It was by escaping to South India to obtain foreign troops and by waging a protracted campaign with the southern part of the island as his base that Iḷanāga managed to recapture the capital and win back his throne. It is said that he proceeded to mete out punishments of unforgettable and bewildering ruthlessness to the clansmen who defied him, lopping off their noses and heels (*Mahāvaṃsa* 1958, Ch. 35, vv. 15–44). Iḷanāga's experience shows how weak the king's hold over the capital could be. To be successful a ruler had to ensure that the support he enjoyed from his own clan was more than lukewarm, and this was not sufficient. Some of the principal elements of the policies that the ruler had to follow related to a strategy of controlling the power of the noble clansmen in the city and of ensuring that there was no threat to his personal position from their midst.

It was probably in response to this need that another social group came to be introduced into the city, and the initial attempt probably dates back to the reign of Iḷanāga though the presence of this group became a regular feature only by about the 5th century. Kings needed a group of armed followers who would owe personal allegiance to them and provide them with reliable support in internal struggles. Foreign mercenaries best suited the need. Detachments of South Indian mercenaries often mentioned in later records of Anurādhapura, and their leaders gained prominence in the political life, some of them, like Potthakkuṭṭha, gaining such power as to become king-makers. Although Anurādhapura was a locus for intrigue and power struggle within the ruling class, it was also, as in the case of cities in most other parts of the world, 'an institutional expression of power' (Abrams 1978, p. 25), the symbol of the domination of the ruling class over the rural peasantry. Co-operation among members of the ruling class, especially the royal family and the scions of the two powerful clans, was essential for the perpetuation of this domination. Irrespective of the fact of which clan the king belonged to, the leadership of the army and the administrative organization was recruited from both clans. Thus, while a show of power and ruthless punishment could keep the members of the rival clan at bay for some time, in the long term it was essential for the king to win the co-operation of members of both clans. It is possible to say that the city symbolized and that, despite conflicts, city life fostered the unity of the dominant groups in the face of threats from outside.

Even by the 1st century BC the separate identity of the inner city and the need to demarcate it from its other zones by means of protective circumvallation was being realized. In fact, it was the inner city which was the city proper, and in the chronicles the term city was often used to denote this inner part. Kuṭakaṇṇatissa (41–19 BC) built the first city wall to a height of seven cubits and excavated a moat around it. He is also credited with the construction of a new palace (*Mahāvaṃsa* 1958, Ch. 34, vv. 33–4; *Vaṃsatthappakāsini* 1935, II, p. 628). From this point in time onwards, for more than a millennium, Anurādhapura remained a fortified city. Fortifications were strengthened in the time of Vasabha (AD 65–109) who enlarged the wall, raising it to 18 cubits, or more than double its former height, and added fortified gatehouses at the entrances. The recent archaeological excavations at the eastern gate of the city have revealed an imposing, strongly fortified gatehouse. Marking out the perimeter was a practice followed at both cities and rural settlements. Villages were usually enclosed by fences; fortified settlements, on the other hand, were enclosed by walls. Thus, circumvallation was not a feature that was peculiar to the city; but no locality without a circumvallation qualified to be called a proper city. The city was also a centre of commerce. Weber's observation (1958, p. 66) that not all localities where trade took place were cities is particularly relevant here. Commercial centres without protective circumvallation were not considered cities, but were merely called commercial villages (*nigama*) or settlements of merchants (*vānijagāma*). Thus, it is interesting to note that in Sri Lankan thinking, the city was characterized by the twin features of circumvallation and commerce.

The value of circumvallation lay primarily in its military uses in times of attack by South Indian invaders and provincial potentates intending to capture power over the entire kingdom. The chronicle describes how elephants sheathed in protective armour were goaded on to break down city walls and gates while the defenders stationed on the top of the wall counterattacked by hurling weapons and pouring down molten pitch on the attackers:

> Roaring like thunder he came, and with his tusks pierced the panel of the gate and trampled the threshold with his feet; and with uproar the gate crashed to the ground with the arches of the gate. The crumbling mass from the gate-tower that fell upon the elephant's back did Nandhimitta dash aside, striking it with his arms. (*Mahavaṃsa* 1985, Ch. 25, vv. 37–9).

These descriptions may be more representative of later times, when the fortified city had come into being, than the earlier period to which the author attributes them. Anurādhapura was besieged several times as it was during the rebellion of Silākāla in the 6th century. There were times when the city was sacked by foreign invaders. Troops despatched by the South Indian kingdom of the Pāṇḍya dynasty plundered it in the 9th century. If plunder was one of the motives of foreign invaders, the objective of local rebels was to take it over. Some of these rebels with power bases in the provinces, like Silākāla and Mahānāga, were successful in capturing the city. Until the end of the 10th century, when its pre-eminence was eclipsed by the rise of Polonnaruva, successful rebels always continued to rule from Anurādhapura, and it is correct to maintain that for more than a millennium this fortified city represented the power of the state.

The clear demarcation of the inner city by means of a city wall had, as we shall see later, other important political as well as social and economic implications. It even had an impact on the development of ritual. The inner city (*ätuḷ nuvara*) developed a clear identity that found expression in literary and epigraphic works. On the basis of a narrow literal interpretation of a passage in the *Jātakaṭṭhakathā*, Hocart (1928, p. 150) concluded that the inner city was 'the royal enclosure' or the palace-complex. While the Pāli and Sanskrit terms denoting the inner city (*antopura, antaḥpura*) were also used in certain contexts, as in this text (*Jātaka* 1964, IV, p. 472), to indicate the area where the royal family lived, it does not necessarily mean that the inner city was limited to members of the royal family. Epigraphic records (*Epigraphia Zeylanica* 1912, II, p. 23) indicate clearly that there were other establishments inside the city walls and Fa Hian's description cited earlier refers quite explicitly to other social groups living within the inner city. The growth in their numbers meant that, over the years, there was tremendous pressure on the limited amount of building land within the city wall. Land usable for building would have been among the first types of land to become a commodity.

Immediately beyond the city wall were located the major monasteries at Anurādhapura, with their *stūpas* and other shrines of massive proportions: the Thūpārāma and the Mahāvihāra to the south of the city, the Abhayagiri to its north, the Pubbārāma to its east, the Tapovana to its north-west and the Jetavana to its south-east. Even by the 5th century some of these were extensive establishments supporting large numbers of clerics. Fa Hian noted that there were 5000 monks at the Abhayagiri monastery and 3000 at the Mahāvihāra (Fa Hian 1957, pp. 46,49). At the height of its affluence it is likely that Anurādhapura supported about 10 000 clerics. The widely scattered ruins of the monasteries are, in fact, more extensive than the area within the city walls. A contemporary visitor to Anurādhapura could not but be impressed by the fact that it had been, among other things, a city of monasteries and clerics. The picture one forms of the ancient Anurādhapura is very much like that of the 'temple cities' of Thailand described by Wheatley (1971, p. 251). The 'encirclement' of the inner city by a ring of monasteries and the concentration of a mass of *religieux* at the city were encouraged by the majority of rulers. Although most monasteries had been well endowed with sources of income and some were quite rich, there were arrangements made for the provision of food for their inmates at the Mahāpālī, a special alms-hall situated near the palace. Fa Hian formed the impression that 5000 to 6000 clerics were being fed there daily (Fa Hian 1957, p. 47). The number of monks waiting for food would have varied and perhaps diminished as some monasteries became more prosperous, but the practice persisted until well into the last days of the capital. At the site of the Mahāpālī are to be found today gigantic containers for food, fashioned out of stone. This practice of giving alms to monks on a massive scale, acted out daily before the populace, was a perennial demonstration of 'conspicuous generosity' (Gunawardana 1981, p. 136) on the part of the king, though in fact the Mahāpālī alms-hall was being maintained on the income from a special tax on all grain brought into the city (*Epigraphia Zeylanica* 1912, III, p. 133).

The three main monasteries at the capital, the Mahāvihāra, the Abhayagiri and the Jetavana, represented the leadership of three different groupings of clerics, called *nikāyas*, with affiliated monasteries dispersed over many parts of the island. Each of these groupings had its own recension of the Buddhist Canon as well as a specific school of interpretation of the scriptures. The three main monasteries of the capital were the repositories for the preservation of these canonical traditions and the centres for the further elaboration of these different schools of Buddhist thought. Anurādhapura was thus the apex of three distinct hierarchical networks that linked a large number of monastic establishments located in different parts of the island. To members of these *nikāyas* who lived away from the capital, their main monasteries at Anurādhapura were the sources of inspiration.

The position that shrines located at Anurādhapura occupied in the ritual life of the island directs our attention to another major function of the city. It is possible to discern two characteristic features about the location of shrines hallowed by myth and important to the Buddhist faithful in the island. On the one hand, they appear to have been as widely dispersed as in Nāgadīpa in the northernmost part of the island, at Kalyānī in the west, at Sumanakūṭa in the central highlands, at Mahiyaṅgana and Dīghavāpi further to the east, and at Tissamahārāma in the south. Thus, the circuit of the pilgrim emphasized the integrity of the island. On the other hand, the location at Anurādhapura of the Tooth relic, two Bodhi trees sacred to the island's Buddhists as branches of the tree under which the Buddha reached enlightenment and the five main *stūpas*, namely the Thūpārāma, the Mahāthūpa, the Abhayagiri, the Jetavana and the Mariccavaṭṭi, meant that there was a heavy concentration of principal objects of worship at the city. Perhaps to a greater extent than the Indian cities of those times, Anurādhapura was clearly a city distinguished by imposing public monuments of religious significance. Thus, it was the foremost centre of ritual that attracted a steady stream of Buddhist pilgrims from different part of the island, as well as from centres of Buddhism in other parts of the world. It is noteworthy that ritual attracted all Buddhists, the clerics as well as the laity, irrespective of sectarian divisions. It may also be added that there was clearly a dialectical relationship between this ritual function of Anurādhapura and its political function as the capital. While the central position it occupied in ritual bolstered its political position, the patronage of rulers living there was the main factor behind the growth of the number of shrines and imposing religious monuments which attracted the pilgrims.

There were some nunneries within the inner city, and we know that one of these was located by the Ceremonial Street (*Epigraphia Zeylanica* 1912, II, p. 23). Fa Hian (1957, p. 47) records that there were special halls at the head of the four main streets where preachers addressed the faithful on days set apart for religious activity in the lunar calendar of the Buddhists. Such activities may have been meant for residents of the inner city. The daily procession of monks to the Mahāpālī alms hall was an important event that linked the inner city with religious life outside. However, the location of the major monasteries in the outer urban zone meant that the ritual activities of the Buddhists were carried out mainly in the area outside the city gates. From about the 4th century AD the kings began to take steps to enhance the importance of the inner city and, in particular, the palace grounds in the ritual life of the Buddhists. The Tooth relic brought to the country during this century was housed not in one of the major monasteries, but in a shrine located within the palace grounds. Every year the relic was taken in a grand procession to the Abhayagiri monastery where a festival was held in its honour. It was kept there for 90 days and then brought back with great ceremony (*Cūlavaṃsa* 1925, Ch. 37, vv. 92–7, Fa Hian 1957, p. 48). Another major ritual event centred on the golden image of the missionary Mahinda, which was similarly housed in a shrine near the palace from where it was taken annually to the Mihintalē monastery and the Mahāvihāra for an extended festival in its honour (*Cūlavaṃsa* 1925, Ch. 37, pp. 68–90). By the 5th century Upatissa I had initiated the practice of holding regular festivals in honour of a Buddha image that has been also housed within the palace grounds (*Cūlavaṃsa*, 1925, Ch. 37, vv. 201–2). This was most probably the same as the shrine of the Buddha Dīpaṅkara mentioned in the time of Moggallāna I (AD 495–512), who brought into the shrine another cult object of great significance to the Buddhists, the Hair relic of the Buddha (*Cūlavaṃsa* 1925,Ch. 39, vv. 51–5). In the 6th century King Silākāla introduced a fifth cult object to the palace grounds when he built a shrine for a sacred Buddhist text brought from North India. Ritual stipulated for it included an annual procession to take it to the Jetavana monastery, where it was kept for some days (*Cūlavaṃsa* 1925, Ch. 41, vv. 37–40). Apparently, these arrangements continued into the last decades of the history of the Anurādhapura kingdom. It is interesting to note that the kings had, through deliberate acts, turned their palace grounds into a sacred precinct. By about the 5th century AD it was being claimed that the legendary missionary Mahinda had extended the boundary of the Mahāvihāra to incorporate the inner city, together with the residences of the leading lineages (*majājana*), within the sacred area (*Dīpavaṃsa* 1879, Ch. 15, vv. 6–32).

The organization of ritual implicitly recognized the distinction between the inner and the outer city while emphasizing the linkages between the two. The circumambulation of the inner city was incorporated as a part of certain important rituals. A ritual held at times when grave calamities like drought, famine and plague threatened the kingdom involved the recitation of the *paritta*, Buddhist incantations believed to possess miraculous protective power. The monks who performed this ritual first walked down the Ceremonial Street and then, during the course of an entire night, walked around the city wall with their right shoulders turned towards it (*Cūlavaṃsa* 1925, Ch. 37, vv. 194–6). Evidently, as in the case of the rituals of the Tooth relic during the period of the Kandyan kingdom (Seneviratne 1978, p. 85), for those who performed this ritual the inner city was a symbolic representation of the entire kingdom. Thus, the ritual unity of the kingdom was emphasized in the rituals of the city. It may have been noted that some of the rituals described above linked the leading monasteries of the three *nikāyas* with the palace which had become the repository of some of their main cult objects. Through the main monasteries the palace thus became linked with three extensive networks of monasteries scattered over the island. At the same time the fact that the main part of the major festivals took place at the relevant monasteries ensured that mass gatherings mostly took place outside the inner city, without exposing the residents of the palace to too many risks. Similar arrangements involving the location of shrines outside the fortified area for reasons of security are observable in other parts of South Asia (Kulke 1982, p. 25).

These rituals were not limited to those of the Buddhist faith. The *yakṣa* cults had been fostered by rulers from a very early time. The shrine of the *yakṣinī* Vaḷavāmukhī had been located within the grounds of the ruler's residence where, each year, sacrifices were made to her while the *yakṣa* Cittarāja was accorded the place of honour at an annual festival in which the ruler took part. The shrine of Cittarāja was by the reservoir Abhayavāpi, to the west of the city, and the shrine dedicated to the *yakṣa* Kālavela was to the east. The shrines of several other cults, like those of Pacchimarājinī, Vessavaṇa and Vyādhideva together with a hall meant probably for Brāhmanical sacrifices, were located by the western gate. Hindu shrines were found at several places in the outer city. To the north and north-west of the city there were several Jaina monasteries, settlements of Brāhmanas, Hindu temples and shrines for the *nāga* cult (*Mahāvaṃsa* 1958, Ch. 10, vv. 84–102, Gunawardana 1979, pp. 212–21). Thus, the ritual life of the city was, as would be expected, cosmopolitan and not limited to any one religion though, of course, Buddhist ritual activity was by far the most popular and, in fact, the dominant. Some of the festivals in the city would have been connected with local cults that emphasized the individuality of the city. In this respect the cult of the city god (*puradevatā*) was perhaps the most important. The *Mahāvaṃsa* informs us that the shrine of the god was located within the grounds of the Mahāvihāra to the south of the city at a site especially suitable for battles against the enemies of the city (*Mahāvaṃsa* 1958, Ch. 25, vv. 82–7). The study of these developments in ritual provides an interesting insight into the relations between the polity and religion in the Anurādhapura kingdom. The capital with its special Ceremonial Street had become a 'ceremonial centre' (Wheatley 1971, pp. 225–40) where a series of rituals and festivals took place each year. It was the major venue for the performance of ritual in the island. A new development in this respect was the re-allocation of ritual space, which in effect elevated the palace grounds to the apex of certain ritual networks. If, on the one hand, mass ritual activity of the Buddhists, which had earlier been largely confined to the outer city, clearly penetrated into the life of the inner city, incorporating even the palace grounds within its network, on the other hand it is equally clear that, in this process, ritual was pressed into the service of the state and transformed into state ritual (Seneviratne 1978). Rituals performed in the city, Buddhist as well as non-Buddhist, added a religious aura to political authority and were symbolic devices that helped to legitimize political power in ancient Sri Lankan society. The city of Polonnaruva was to take over this ceremonial function after the fall of Anurādhapura (Smith 1980). Paradoxically, religion also had a limiting effect on royal authority. Over the centuries monasteries accumulated a considerable degree of immunity from official interference. By the 9th and 10th centuries royal officials were not expected to enter monastic precincts for official business.

The observation made by de Coulanges (1956, pp. 126–7) that the ancient city was a sanctuary for worship was certainly applicable, at least to the zone immediately outside the city wall occupied by the monasteries. As will be evident later, the restrictions on royal power operative within this particular zone were sometimes demonstrated in a dramatic manner when royal officials attempted to arrest wanted men who had sought asylum within monastic precincts.

It is difficult to gain a clear understanding of some of the functions of the city without paying attention to 'settlements located immediately outside the gates' (*dvāragāma*), which formed an important part of the outer city. Four such settlements were affiliated to Anurādhapura, and it appears that a good part of the commercial activities at the capital took place within these settlements. Inscriptions have preserved for us the names of two of these settlements: one was Kalahumanaka located beyond the northern gate, whereas the Mahabataka settlement was to be found just outside the eastern gate. Both were mercantile settlements in which guilds providing banking facilities were to be found. In fact, the two inscriptions cited recorded permanent endowments made at these guilds, with the stipulation that the annual interest accruing from the two deposits was to be used perpetually for prescribed purposes (*Epigraphia Zeylanica* 1912, III, pp. 177, 250). As noted earlier, some of the foreign merchants had taken up residence close to the western gate, but the identities of the settlements on the west and the south of the city are not known. As purveyors of consumables, moneylenders and recipients of cash deposits yielding interest, these mercantile settlements appear to have performed some of the service functions required by the city.

Some of the basic services needed by the citizenry were provided by the rulers or the city administration. In the reign of Vasabha (AD 65–109) several ponds were built to supply water to the residents of the city and these ponds were fed by a network of subterranean conduits (*Mahāvaṃsa* 1958, Ch. 35, v. 98). Archaeological excavations in the area to the south of the city have brought to light the intricate system of clay pipes that supplied water to the Mahāvihāra from the Abhayavāpi reservoir. Anurādhapura had several parks, though some of them, like the Ran Masu Park to the south of the city, would have been reserved for the use of royalty. Amenities at the city included institutions for medical care. In the 4th century Upatissa I provided maternity homes, hospitals and homes for the crippled and the blind (*Cūlavaṃsa* 1925, Ch. 37, v. 182). There are references in the inscriptions to two hospitals being constructed in the 10th century. One of these was built by a certain General Sena close to the Ceremonial Street, whereas the other, built by King Kassapa V, was located near the southern gate (*Epigraphia Zeylanica* 1912, I, p. 46, II, p. 22). It is interesting to note that special attention had been paid to the organization of sanitary arrangements. A large workforce was detailed with the task of keeping the city clean, while a separate group removed the night soil from the city. A third and a fourth group were entrusted with the duties of removing the dead and looking after the cemetries (*Mahāvaṃsa* 1958, Ch. 10, vv. 91–2).

Such extensive and detailed arrangements would have created a need for administrative organization to supervise and to ensure that they functioned smoothly. These responsibilities were vested in an official of considerable power, the Warden of the City or the *nagaraguttika*, who was, however, appointed by the king (*Mahāvaṃsa* 1958, Ch. 10, vv. 81–2). Among the duties of this official were the maintenance of security within the city, and the apprehension and punishment of thieves and burglars. He was also expected to keep a check on the people who entered the city during the night, and to ensure that they were actual residents of the inner city (Ellawala 1969, pp. 122–3). Certain towns were administered by *nagara-bojhikas*, who probably enjoyed wider authority (Paranavitana 1970, p. 81). Other officials associated with the administration of the city were the city accountant (*gaṇaka*) and an employee called *nagaravudika* (Paranavitana 1970, pp. 18, 85, 1983, p. 90). The second term, which has been rendered into English as 'city architect', most probably denoted the office which was entrusted with the extensive duties of maintaining the public works within the city, as well as perhaps the construction of new works within the city limits. The presence of an accountant points to a situation of the city having its individual income, expenditure and accounting system. This suggests a development of some basic civic institutions with their specific individuality. The concept of the town as an individual corporation capable of taking collective decisions is embodied in two inscriptions set up by the citizens of Aba to record collective donations made to the *saṅgha* (Paranavitana 1970, pp. 75–6). It is likely that, at least in some towns, the leading lineages were associated with the civic administration. The reference to the eight lineages of the city of Uti (Paranavitana 1970, p. 41) probably relates to such an institutional arrangement. Similarly, in later times there were towns like Padaviya that were dominated and administered by mercantile corporations (Velupillai 1971, pp. 53–5; Pathmanathan 1982, pp. 19–20). However, in the case of Anurādhapura, it seems more possible that the city was closely under the control of royal officials.

The style of life in the city of Anurādhapura represented a standard very much above what was available outside. However, it is very likely that the amenities provided by the city were limited mainly to those living within the city walls. In this sense the city wall represented an important symbol of social demarcation. Even among the merchants, it was the rich and the powerful who lived within the inner city, while the residences of the lesser folk would have been located in one or another of the four outer mercantile settlements. It is specifically stated that a separate area outside the city wall had been allocated for the dwellings of the huntsmen who provided the city with its meat requirements (*Mahāvaṃsa* 1958, Ch. 35, v. 98). Similarly, the quarters of the workforce employed in occupations of 'low' ritual status were located in a zone outside the city wall and at a considerable distance away from it. Workers such as street-cleaners, porters who carried corpses and night soil, and keepers of cemeteries, were recruited from the *caṇḍāla* caste, which had the lowest ritual ranking, and they were settled in a special zone outside the city wall and to the north-west of the public cemetery. Distinctions between this group and their superiors were maintained even after death: there was a separate cemetery for them (*Mahāvaṃsa* 1958, Ch. 10, vv. 93–4). It would thus appear that the city represented an arrangement of space in accordance with a notion of the hierarchical order of society and that, apart from political status, membership of noble clans and economic position, ideas of ritual status influenced the allocation of people to zones within and outside the city. However, an important distinction has to be noted at this point. The arrangements outlined above, though they reflect to some extent the influence of caste ideology, did not in their totality represent an attempt to mark out zones within the city in strict adherence to Brāhmanical caste rules. It is particularly noteworthy that the settlements of the Brāhmaṇas were also located well outside the limits of the inner city. This would have been most unlikely if the Brāhmanical ideas were being strictly followed. It is perhaps correct to say that in its spatial arrangements Anurādhapura represented and affirmed the order of Sri Lankan society, with its special traits and peculiarities. The description in the *Mahāvaṃsa* presents us with the arrangements which were to be found at a time probably in the later history of the evolution of the city, but the author would have us believe that these arrangements had been in existence from its very inception. By his time, the ideas basic to these spatial arrangements were deeply rooted in society.

The observations made by the French traveller François Bernier, who visited India in the 17th century, have had a lasting impact on European conceptions of the South Asian city since he wielded a deep influence on the theoretical work of a host of prominent writers, including Richard Jones as well as Marx and Engels (Gunawardana 1976). Bernier noted that the economies of cities like Delhi and Agra were almost totally geared to supplying the needs of the royal court and the exceptionally large army that the Mughal emperors maintained. The dependence was so great that whenever the king left on a long journey with his court and the army, the city became virtually empty. Bernier contrasted the Asian city he had seen with European cities which flourished as centres of productive activity. 'Workshops occupied by skilful artisans would be vainly sought for in Delhi', he remarked. For him, Delhi was primarily 'a military encampment', (Bernier 1914, pp. 220–54). Marx followed this lead in characterizing the larger type of Asian city as 'a princely camp' that was a 'superimposition' (*Superfötation*) rather than an institution organically linked to the economy. In the real economy the town and village remained undifferentiated. The city was the place where the king or the provincial potentate resided and spent the revenues in the form of 'labour funds' (Marx 1953, pp. 377, 382). The use of the term 'labour funds' (*Arbeitsfonds*) which was rejected in his later works (Marx 1961, pp. 609–11) is very reminiscent of the writings of Jones that Marx had studied. According to Jones, the labour fund in Asia consisted of the surplus from agriculture extracted by the ruler, and the city was the locus for the disbursal of this fund in exchange for services and luxury goods. Thus, the groups within the city who provided goods and services in exchange for shares of the fund were obliged to follow the officials who handled its disbursal, as Bernier had observed. Consequently, Jones theorized, the city in Asia lasted only as long as it remained a political centre (Jones 1852, pp. 74–7).

The theories outlined above represent some of the earliest European attempts to analyse and to understand the nature of the South Asian city. Despite the fact that they were based on an extremely limited factual base, they are of great interest, and provide useful insights which are relevant to our study. We shall first start with an aspect of this body of theory which is not applicable to the city we have described above. It may have been noted that Bernier and Jones emphasized the transient nature of the Asian city. Though his use of the term 'princely camp' seems to suggest that his position on this question was close to that of the other two writers, it is important to note that in the *Grundrisse* Marx (1953, p. 377) also spoke of trading cities of Asia and that in *Capital* he (Marx 1961, p. 340) refers to cities like Dacca which had been centres of textile production. The conditions that Bernier observed may in certain ways be applicable to some principal cities in North India from about the 13th century. Even with these qualifications as regards time and area, his picture appears to be exaggerated. Certainly Delhi or Agra of Mughal times cannot be held to be representative of the South Asian city in general. As noted earlier, one of the most striking aspects of the history of Anurādhapura is the durability of this city. In fact, it ranks among the most long-lasting urban centres in the ancient world. Mercenary troops were stationed in this city but, unlike the Mughal emperors, the Sri Lankan rulers did not possess large standing armies. In times of war they rather depended to a great extent on the militias raised by the nobility in the city and by the leading lineages among the rural landholders. Anurādhapura was not only a residence of the king – as already noted, it was also a monastic city. The presence of large monastic communities which together occupied an area that was more extensive than the inner city distinguishes this city from those described by Bernier. This meant that throughout its history there were multitudinous, permanent communities settled in the city who were not tied to a peripatetic mode of life dictated by the wanderings of a king and his court. In fact, it may be noted that the distinction between the royal camp (*kañdavura*) and the city (*nagara*) was known and given expression in Sri Lankan literature. In a cosmological description found in a medieval text on popular Buddhism, the lower *suddhāvāsa* heavens are compared with royal camps: when a Buddha is alive they are occupied by Brahmas, but in the absence of a Buddha they disappear. As we shall see later, the same text goes on to discuss the characteristics of a city (*Karmmavibhāga* 1961, pp. 110, 158). Thus, in their thought, South Asians distinguished their cities clearly from princely camps. In fact, most South Asian cities, and certainly Anurādhapura, cannot be grouped under the category of princely camps that would suddenly become desolate when the king marched out with his army.

Despite their shortcomings, the early European theorists direct our attention to a number of functions of the city as a centre of political power, a locus for the concentration of the agricultural surplus, and a centre of consumption. Marx (1953, p. 382) specifically pointed to the role of location in the development of trading cities. Some of these ideas were to be elaborated later in the work of Werner Sombart and Gordon Childe. Sombart's concept of the 'consumption city' which received objects of consumption not in exchange for its own products, but on the basis of politico-legal claims (*Rechtstitel*) in forms such as taxes or rents (Sombart 1916, pp. 142–3), is particularly helpful in enabling us to understand aspects of the functions of Anurādhapura . When Jones spoke of 'labour funds' disbursed within the Asian city, he referred only to taxes collected by the ruler. Taxes probably represented the largest segment of the resources that flowed into the city, but this was not the only type of income. Ownership of irrigation works and land was well established in this society from about the beginning of the Christian era. Payments made in kind or cash for irrigation water (*daka baka*) as well as for the fish harvested from the reservoirs (*maji baka*), and the share turned in by the cultivator to the owner of the field (*bojakapati*), were the main sources of income for the propertied classes. The monastic community and the wealthy landholders living within the city walls were the two main groups at Anurādhapura who benefited from this type of income. A third type of property, mercantile wealth, made its appearance increasingly felt during the first seven centuries AD, which saw the expansion of foreign trade and an increase in the use of coins. The presence of mercantile wealth would mean that while retaining the concept of the 'consumer city' we have to modify Sombart's model: in addition to *Rechtstitel*, exchange did, to some extent, come into play as one of the mechanisms which ensured the supply of consumer needs within the city.

Weber's emphasis on the role of the market in the city (Weber 1958, pp. 66–7) seems at first inappropriate to the characterization of the premodern city, in particular the premodern city in Asia. However, it is quite interesting to note that the author of the early medieval Sri Lankan text cited earlier represents a parallel approach. For him, the city differed from the village on account of two criteria: (a) by circumvallation, and (b) by being a place where shops (*āpaṇa*) were to be found. According to this text, mercantile settlements belonged to an intermediate category, being places where shops were to be found but circumvallation was absent (*Karmmavibhāga* 1961, p. 110). It is most interesting to note that, according to this line of thinking, urban status was marked by the coincidence of the symbolism of military power and the demarcation of social space, as represented by the city wall and the prevalence of relations of commercial exchange. In particular, the fact that cooked food was sold in the city would have clearly distinguished the city from the village. The *Samantapāsādikā* (1924, II, pp. 380–1) refers to establishments where meals were being sold (*vikkāyika-bhattapacanaghara*) and to shops that specialized in the sale of cooked meat (*sunaghara*) and sweetmeats (*pūvaghara*). The use of coins in many different transactions had become quite well-known at Anurādhapura at a very much earlier time. Coins have been found at sites in the city in layers dated by archaeologists to a period between 200 BC and the beginning of the Christian era (Sirisoma 1972, p. 150). While this dating has not so far been substantiated by C^{14} material, there is no doubt that coins were in wide use by the 2nd century AD. Inscriptions attest to their use in a number of different types of transactions, including the sale and purchase of irrigation works and land, deposits in guilds in expectation of a return in interest payments, and donations made to religious institutions. The *Samantapāsādikā*, the 5th century translation into Pāli of a commentarial work written earlier in the old form of Sinhala, is probably representative of the same period as the inscriptions. This text attests to the fact that, by that time, the use of coins had become common in transactions involving the purchase of items of everyday use like axes, pottery alms-bowls used by monks, and fish, as also for settling judicial fines and payments made by peasant cultivators to owners of land and irrigation works (*Samantapāsādikā* 1924, I, pp. 380–1, IV, p. 698). The references to items like axes and bowls are of particular interest. The text describes situations in which customers intending to make purchases would visit the workshops of craftsmen to obtain products of their choice and then make the payment in coin. There were several settlements of craftsmen in the vicinity of the city, including a village of potters to its south, a village of carpenters and a village of lapidaries to its west, and a village of brickmakers at a short distance from its walls (*Vaṃsatthappakāsinī* 1935, II, pp. 483, 655, *Epigraphia Zeylanica* 1912, IV, p. 222). Thus, although Anurādhapura does not appear to have been a city known for its craft production, it was apparently a centre of consumption which stimulated petty commodity production to meet the needs of its residents. References to villages of craftsmen cited above are of particular interest, since they indicate that craft production took place outside the city. At a very early period in the history of Anurādhapura, certain types of craft production, like the manufacture of beads, did take place at sites which were later to be occupied by the inner city (Deraniyagala 1972, p. 139), but urbanization and circumvallation were evidently accompanied by the transfer of the centres of production to zones outside the city wall. It would appear that satellite settlements scattered around the city were the primary loci where this type of craft production took place. Some of the products of the satellite settlements, like those of the lapidaries, would have been meant for circulation within the prestige sphere of the local economy as well as for export. The documents cited above suggest that the use of coins was penetrating into the rural areas, but clearly ports and cities were the focal points where such new economic relations were evolving. They were the centres from which this expansion of new media of exchange took place. In this sense, Anurādhapura and other cities in the island were centres that demonstrated the path of future change in that society. However, we have to remind ourselves that, as in the Roman Empire, which was linked with Sri Lanka by trade, monetized exchange occupied only a small part of this economy, and that the circulation of goods depended largely on the mechanisms of taxation, rent and other payments made in kind.

The inner city was primarily a residence for non-producers, and it is correct to say that the ideal type of city-dweller was the wealthy man of leisure. A good proportion of city-dwellers at Anurādhapura were monks who were prohibited by the dictates of Buddhist monastic discipline from involvement in agricultural production. Thus, in an economic sense, Anurādhapura would seem to fall into the category of what Finley has called the 'parasitic city' (Finley 1973, p. 140). The colourful and emotive term 'parasitic' carries the implication that the city drained the resources of society and hampered its growth. An observation of Marx on conditions in precapitalist economies including those of Asia, which he represented in less dramatic phraseology, follows a parallel line of thought, but deserves special consideration since it permits certain important distinctions to be drawn in this regard. It was his view that accumulation could take place in such economies in the form of treasures and expansion in the scale of production, but consumption and reproduction generally kept pace with the increase of production. Thus, while emphasis was laid on the fact that production was geared primarily to internal consumption, Marx also made allowance for the capacity of these societies for a certain degree of growth. It was his view that production and reproduction could continue 'on a progressively increasing scale'. It is particularly significant that, according to his view, this process did not assume the form of the accumulation of capital, not because of parasitic consumption, but because the producer was not alienated from his means of production (Marx 1961, p. 598).

Growth in the pre-industrial economy was to be observed primarily in agriculture, but this does not mean that cities played no role in this development. The expansion of the city to some extent reflected the growing efficiency of the administrative apparatus in the collection of the surplus or the strategic importance of that particular location in trade networks, or both, but it primarily reflected the growth of the productive capacity of agriculture with new technologies such as irrigation. Like the early city in the Mediterranean region, Anurādhapura was not totally divorced from agriculture. It had its hinterland in the Malvatu river basin which supplied it with its basic requirements in food. In fact, the area immediately around the city provided a model of intensive agriculture with massive irrigation reservoirs that ensured an adequate water supply for two or three crops of rice each year. These patterns were distinct from the patterns of marginal agricultural production in those rural areas that were based on non-irrigated swidden crops. One of the dimensions of urban growth has to be understood in terms of a process of affiliation of village settlements to the city. These subsidiary settlements were linked with the city by economic, political and ritual bonds as well as by irrigation networks. Thus, the 'city' as well as its dependent villages formed a single unit, like the classical city described by Marx, which had the arable land surrounding it as its *territorium* (Marx 1953, p. 378).

The dependence of the city on the hinterland for its sustenance had significant implications for investment and growth. Irrigation works represented one of the most important types of property controlled by monasteries and wealthy groups living in the inner city. There is evidence suggesting that some of the profits from trade, too, tended to be invested in the construction or purchase of irrigation works (Gunawardana 1985, pp. 232–3). Here we see the same pattern of conversion of commercial wealth into other sources of income and status that has been observed in many different types of societies (Friedman & Rowlands 1978, p. 235, de Ste Croix 1981, pp. 120–2). While the irrigation work controlled by these social groups were mostly of small or medium scale, the king was the leading entrepreneur responsible for the construction of the largest types of irrigation reservoirs and canals. In constructing these works, some of which assumed gigantic proportions, the kings were not merely providing public works for the general welfare of their subjects. Apart from helping to win popular acclaim, these activities brought more tangible and substantial benefits. First, state intervention in the construction of large-scale hydraulic works contributed to the intensification of agricultural production and helped to increase the tax revenue. In addition, it helped to secure a further share of the agricultural produce in the form of irrigation dues and proceeds from fishing. Secondly, in those times when demography perhaps played the decisive role in determining the outcome of political struggles, large-scale irrigation works attracted settlers from marginal agricultural areas and provided the preconditions for future concentrations of population. In the hands of the rulers, irrigation activity was an effective mechanism that they could use to manipulate population densities and other resources in their kingdom in a manner which would be consonant with the prevalent system of the distribution of power. It was by maintaining a heavier concentration of population in their base areas that the rulers of Anurādhapura could ensure the perpetuation of their dominance over the other parts of the kingdom. That such a strategy was followed is evident from the fact that there is a heavy concentration of state-sponsored irrigation activities in two core areas. Of these two areas, as would be expected, it was the area immediately surrounding the capital that received the greater attention. The irrigation potential of the hinterland of Anurādhapura was exploited to the maximum and, in the 5th century, supplementary sources of water were being sought. The Kalā Oya, a river at a considerable distance to the south of the city, was dammed and, from the reservoir that was formed, water was diverted to the city along a canal 85 km in length. It was in the area around the city in the upper reaches of the river Malvatu, where four large irrigation reservoirs and an elaborate network of canals were located, that the most intensively exploited agricultural lands in the island were to be found. It will have been noted that, although Anurādhapura was a city of consumers, it was also an institution that contributed to the development of productive forces by attracting investment in irrigation works to its vicinity. Thus, while it is correct to say that growth in premodern society in Sri Lanka took place primarily in the agricultural sector, areas of the highest agricultural productivity were located in the immediate vicinity of the cities. The city, together with its hinterland, was a model for irrigation development and agriculture based on higher technology but, for obvious reasons, emulation of this model by provincial centres was not favoured by the rulers of Anurādhapura.

The emergence of large-scale irrigation works had other social and political implications. As in the Middle Eastern irrigation societies studied by Adams (1973, p. 24), such irrigation systems enlarged the agricultural base of the cities and, while bringing about a closer integration between the city and its hinterland, they also contributed towards strengthening the power that the king and the propertied classes wielded over the surrounding settlements of agriculturists. If irrigation permitted intensive agriculture and higher productivity, it also placed in the hands of the entrepreneurs additional means for the exploitation of the surplus. By exercising their control over the sluices and thereby the supply of irrigation water, the owners of irrigation works could and did force peasants to pay their dues. The predominant position that irrigation property occupied in this type of society was such that it enabled the entrepreneurs in irrigation activity to collect a share of the surplus even in situations where the agriculturist owned the land he cultivated. Investment of labour in the construction of irrigation works was in a certain sense analogous to investment in the means of production in capitalist society. If irrigation property may thus be considered a type of 'capital', it was a peculiar and primitive type of capital, in that it did not totally alienate producers from their means of production or develop under conditions of free wage labour. Further, the increase in grain production that irrigation facilitated did not bring about a trend towards petty commodity production in agriculture in any significant way. However, it was a type of 'capital' which converted a natural resource into an exchangeable commodity, alienated the agricultural producer from one of the elements essential for the productive process and ensured a regular return on the investment. The position that Anurādhapura and several other Asian cities occupied as the main strongholds of social groups that controlled this special type of property endowed these cities with a specific character which distinguished them from premodern cities in Europe and many other parts of the world.

In addition to being a centre of ritual for the hinterland as well as the whole island, Anurādhapura was also the foremost centre of cultural and intellectual activity of the time. In fact, the distinction between city and the village was conceived in political as well as cultural terms. The main monasteries at the capital were in a privileged position that enabled them to perform the intellectually vital, creative role expected of them. Monastic life freed a large number of clerics from the need for involvement in productive physical labour, and provided them with the leisure for intellectual pursuits. Monks from the provinces looked up to monasteries at the city as the premier centres of intellectual activity in the land, and the aim of aspiring scholars among them was to continue their studies at the capital. The major monasteries maintained close contact with foreign centres of Buddhism. Similarly, scholars from distant places like Kashmir, South India, the Bihar–Bengal area and China visited Anurādhapura, attracted by the standards of Buddhist scholarship for which these monasteries were renowned, as well as by rare manuscripts in their libraries. Buddhaghosa, who translated the Sinhala commentaries into Pāli specifically for the use of the international community of Buddhist scholars, and Fa Hian, who obtained manuscripts from the Abhayagiri monastery which were later translated into Chinese, were two of the best-known among such visitors. In particular, the Abhayagiri monastery was a centre where a significant attempt was made to undertake a comparative study of the main variant schools of South Asian Buddhism (Gunawardana 1979, pp. .247–57).

The monasteries at the capital also performed an educational function that attracted students from among both clerics and laymen. The substantial body of literary works written during this period were, with a few exceptions, produced at this city. As usual with cities elsewhere in the world, Anurādhapura patronized the painter, the sculptor and the architect. It is particularly noteworthy that this city was the primary location to which objects that may be described as containers of diverse cultural influences, whether it be literary and philosophical works from the neighbouring subcontinent, pottery from China, or coins and medallions from Rome, were brought for use, for careful study and, sometimes, for emulation. In this sense the city functioned as a contact point for the absorption and dispersal of external cultural influences. Hence, the 'culturally regenerative' role, which Hoselitz (1955, pp. .285–90) highlighted, appears to be equally applicable in this context, at least up to about the 8th century AD when a noteworthy change in the patterns of external relations appear to have taken place (Gunawardana 1985, pp. .230).

It is also important to note that the culture represented and propagated by the city was pervaded by an ideology which was politically significant. The massive monuments in the city glorified the Buddha and his teaching, but they were also testimony to the liberality of the kings. The ideal political order portrayed in the chronicles written by monks was one that supported the political integrity of the island under the sway of the rulers of Anurādhapura. Obeyesekere (1963, p. 142) has pointed out that the hierarchical structure of what he has termed the Sinhalese Buddhist pantheon 'is consonant with a social structure based on a hierarchy of caste'. To an equal if not greater extent the hierarchical elements in the structure of ritual reflected and buttressed the structure of political power. The poorer elements, like the craftsmen and those engaged in occupations with lower social status were, as noted earlier, assigned to the peripheral urban zones which were outside the city wall and away from it. Through its layout and arrangements the capital city brought out in stark terms the distinctions between the powerful and the humble in the Sri Lankan society of this period. The ideology of ritual status provided the justification of these arrangements. If the inner city symbolized the kingdom in ritual, it was implicit in this idiom that in social terms it was the powerful and wealthy residents of this enclosed space who represented the kingdom. From a very early date religion played a role in the development of structural elements of the thought process amenable and manipulatable in the wielding of power. The Buddhist concepts of the good life with emphasis on discipline or *sīla* and certain aspects of the theory of *arma* theory of *arma* which stress one's own responsibility for one's plight could be manipulated to secure subordination and to discourage resistance. The role of religion was particularly prominent in the formative phase of the state, when ritual helped to link dispersed rural communities with the emerging centres of political power (Gunawardana 1982, p. 27, Kulke 1982, p. 17). Thus, like the administrative and legal systems in the functioning of which the city played a central role, the literary, artistic and other intellectual activities of the city and the rituals that if fostered generally tended to conform to and propagate, rather than diverge from, an ideology which was conducive to the perpetuation of the political order prevalent at the time. However, this is not to imply that religion consistently played a centripetalizing role in all periods of Sri Lankan history. As will be evident later, certain elements in religious ideology and ritual were instrumental in curtailing royal authority and were also incorporated and utilized in the development of centrifugal forces.

A relevant question that may be raised in this context is whether the city posed no threat to royal power. The history of the city in Sri Lanka was not totally a history of urban passivity of the type that Elvin (1978, p. 88) emphasized with reference to premodern China. In the earlier part of the history of the city, challenges to royal power generally arose not from among the most exploited strata of society, but from men of power within the city walls and from the monks who lived in the immediate vicinity. As in the case of political struggles in ancient Greece (de Ste Croix 1981, p. 288), instances of open political resistance to the power of the rulers of Anurādhapura in which a significant measure of success was achieved were, apart from the two noteworthy instances discussed below, those in which leadership was provided by individuals from the ruling class. The lower classes generally constituted the expendable fighting force, manipulated and coerced into struggles within the dominant stratum and, hence, they merely provided 'the pedestal' for conflicts (Marx 1958, p. 248) that did not bring benefits in terms of their fundamental interests. Struggles for succession among members of the royal family were frequent. Sometimes as in the reigns of Iḷanāga and Jeṭṭhatissa (AD 266–76), the occasion for resistance was opposition to a successor to the throne on the part of a faction of nobles. In the first instance resistance was followed by capture of power which lasted three years while, in the latter case, the recalcitrant nobles who favoured another contender were immediately suppressed. There were also instances when factions of nobles gained greater success in capturing power. Such *coups d'état* were witnessed in the reigns of Vijayakumāraka (AD 247), Saṅghatissa (AD 251), Mittasena (AD 432) and Dhātusena (AD 477). In about the 7th century kings faced a threat from another group in the city when the commanders of the mercenary troops became the virtual rulers and began to appoint their own nominees to the throne.

The relationship that generally prevailed between the king and the Buddhist *saṅgha* was close and mutually accommodating. It would be correct to suggest that it helped to strengthen the hold of the rulers over their subjects, but in certain instances the clerics were a source of protest and resistance to royal authority. The ideology propagated by the monks in their writings had a restrictive influence on royal power, in that they decried injustices and excesses on the part of the king. These views were consonant with the interests and attitudes of the noble clansmen. The Sri Lankan state centred on Anurādhapura may be described as a system which provided for the sharing of power between the ruler and these powerful lineages. In this system it is possible to detect a relationship between the mobilizatory capacity of the rulers and the nature of their specific objectives (Gunawardana 1985, pp. 237–8). The distinction that has been drawn between 'power to' and 'power over' (Miller & Tilley 1984, p. 5) is particularly useful for understanding this situation. Thus, a king who was overwhelmingly successful in obtaining the support of his subordinates to divert resources and marshall the labour necessary for massive hydraulic works that were welcomed as beneficial would find powerful factions arraigned against him when he punished a member of the nobility or a group of monks in a manner that was perceived as excessive. There was at least one instance, in the case of Dhātusena cited above, where such resistance was sufficiently strong to depose the king. Monasteries enjoyed immunities from royal intervention, and any infringement of these rights was resisted by the monks. Protest and resistance on the part of the clerics usually took the form of acts symbolic of disapprobation, like public rejection of alms and donations, or an exodus of monks from the capital. Such protests sometimes led to violence. In the reign of Mahāsena a noble in the service of the king rose in revolt in opposition to the persecution of a main monastery, and the king was obliged to change his policy. This revolt was also led by a prominent personage from the city, but it was based on the outlying provinces.

The petering out of the trade with the Mediterranean region, and the emergence of powerful South Indian states that sought to increase their share of the regional trade, affected the fortunes of the rulers in the latter part of the history of Anurādhapura as the capital. Certain kings of the time were reduced to severely straitened financial circumstances. It is against this background that one has to examine the rise of new attitudes towards the city and the new roles that certain urban groups began to play. This phase witnessed the rise of rural potentates and, as in the case of the Inca state described by Patterson (1986), they resisted the hegemony of Anurādhapura by refusing to pay tribute and daring even to besiege the city. For a short time the city was, in fact, captured and held by the insurrectionist rural chiefs (*Cūlavaṃsa* 1925, Ch. 48, v. 95). Parallel to these developments was the rise to prominence of rural shrines located at a considerable distance from the capital, like Sumanakūṭa, which grew into a major centre of ritual attracting pilgrims. It was also during this phase that a sect of Buddhist monks who were opposed to life in the city emerged as a leading and influential group. They extolled the ideal of living in the forest. This phenomenon did not lead to an exodus of monks from the city, but the 'forest-dwellers' were immensely popular among the laity, and came to enjoy much greater authority than those living in the city. The movement promoted a trend that affected the position of the city as the foremost centre of religious authority.

The 10th century witnessed two incidents of greater activation on the part of the ordinary citizens of Anurādhapura in a new role of opposition to authority. These incidents are of particular interest since they question the popular view of the ever-passive Oriental city rigidly controlled by despots. It was evidently the lesser folk who took the initiative in what was perhaps the most widespread incident of urban protest in premodern Sri Lanka. The residents of Anurādhapura are said to have joined the soldiers and men from the hinterland to rise in protest when royal officials entered into a monastic precinct, violating its rights of immunity. This monastery, located close to the city, was the seat of a sect of Buddhist monks who were known to be particularly virtuous. The description in the chronicle suggests that it was a tumultuous and disorganized uprising of a popular nature. It soon assumed a violent character and, though the men involved in it did not have the capture of power as an objective, it was so widespread that it reduced the king and his men to helplessness. The mob swarmed up to a monastery where the king had gone and 'threatened him'. Then they gave chase to some royal officials and beheaded them. Certain officials, including some of the king's closest kinsmen, escaped the wrath of the mobs only by leaping over the wall and fleeing from the city. The uprising subsided only after the monks forgave the king and returned to the capital (*Cūlavaṃsa* 1925, Ch. 53, vv. 14–27). At the end of the 10th century, the mercenary soldiers staged a rebellion with the most serious repercussions for the city. Deprived of their pay for a long time, they took up arms against the king and besieged his palace, forcing him to flee. The king continued to remain in the southern part of the island while mercenary troops from Keraḷa and Karṇṇāṭaka, together with local men, are said to have ruled the north (*Cūlavaṃsa* 1925, Ch. 55, vv. 5–12). This paved the way for South Indian intervention and brought about the final collapse of the political power of Anurādhapura. It is not possible on the basis of the available sources to unravel the varied factors behind these events, but the religious associations of the first incident are unmistakable. It is particularly noteworthy that these two incidents do not appear to fall easily within the usual category of factional struggle led by a member of the upper stratum of the ruling class with the aim of capturing the throne.

The preceding account of Anurādhapura helps us to understand some of the multifarious functions of this city which lasted for an exceptionally long period. Anurādhapura was initially an unplanned city, but in the course of its growth it incorporated ritual and social distinctions in the arrangement of space. In addition to being a political centre, it was a city of monasteries and, as such, it was a centre of religious and intellectual activity. It was also the foremost centre of ritual for the entire island. In several senses of the term, Anurādhapura was the 'exemplary centre' (Geertz 1980, p. 124) for the people of the island. In fact, one of the most salient aspects of city life that emerges from our study is the pervasive emphasis on ritual. Ritual appears to have been a primary mode through which the theme of domination and subordination and, even if intermittently and less emphatically, the counter-theme of domination and resistance found recurrent expression. There was an inverse relationship between the efficacy of the administrative machinery available to the rulers at various times and the importance they accorded to ritual in the polity. What Wheatley (1971, pp. 257–67) has termed the 'centripetalizing function of the ceremonial centre' would have been crucial, particularly in the formative phase of the state and in the final phase of Anurādhapura as the capital. The latter period witnessed trends towards political disintegration and increasing attempts on the part of provincial leaders to assert their power. At the same time the city, with its separation of zones, fortifications, the massive gates, impressive residences within the inner city and arrangements to control movements into this area, was an institutional expression of power. It symbolized not only the power of the king and his officials as Wittfogelian theory would have us believe (Wittfogel 1957, pp. 34–42), but also the power of the noble clans and, later, the power of the propertied elements. The arrangements in the city reflected and also helped to strengthen the power of the social groups living in the inner city. However, there were rare but noteworthy interludes of brief duration when those from the peripheries of the city took the initiative to play a part that turned out to be decisive in the history of the city as well as the polity. Like most ancient cities, Anurādhapura was a consumer city, but it promoted petty-commodity production in crafts. It was the function of the city as a centre of commercial transactions that was recognized by ancient writers as one of the fundamental features of the urban settlement that distinguished it from the village. More than any of its other characteristics, it is perhaps its relationship with irrigation activity that marks out Anurādhapura and similar cities of Asia from their counterparts in other parts of the world. By directing investment towards the improvement of irrigation facilities of its hinterland, the city furthered the development of agricultural production. Anurādhapura was the seat of men with interests in irrigation property, and its fortunes were inextricably linked with the functioning of the intricate system of reservoirs and canals that surrounded it.

References

Abrams, P. 1978. Towns and economic growth: some theories and problems. In *Towns in societies: essays in economic history and historical sociology*, P. Abrams & E. A. Wrigley (eds). Cambridge: Cambridge University Press.

Adams, R. McC. 1973. The natural history of urbanism. In *The sociology of the city*, S. Halebsky (ed.). New York: Charles Scribner's Series.

Bernier, F. 1914. *Travels in the Mogul empire*, A. Constable (trans.). London: Oxford University Press.

Coulanges, F. de 1956. *The ancient city*. New York: Doubleday Anchor Books.

Cūlāvaṃsa 1925. W. Geiger (ed.). London: Pali Text Society.

de Ste Croix, G. E. M. 1981. *The class struggle in the ancient Greek world*. London: Duckworth.

Deraniyagala, S. 1972. The citadel of Anurādhapura 1969: excavations in the Gedige area. *Ancient Ceylon*, Vol. 2. Colombo: Department of Archaeology.

Dīpavaṃsa 1879. H. Oldenberg (ed.). London: Williams & Norgate.
Ellawala, H. 1969. *Social history of early Ceylon*. Colombo: Department of Cultural Affairs.
Elvin, M. 1978. Chinese cities since the Sung dynasty. In *Towns in societies: essays in economic history and historical sociology*, P. Abrams & E. A. Wrigley (eds). Cambridge: Cambridge University Press.
Epigraphia Zeylanica 1912. Colombo: Archaeological Survey of Ceylon.
Fa Hian 1957. Buddhist-country-records. In *Chinese accounts of India*, S. Beal (trans.). Calcutta: Susil Gupta.
Finley, M. 1973. *The ancient economy*. Berkeley: University of California Press.
Friedman J. & M. J. Rowlands 1978. Notes towards and epigenetic model of the evolution of civilization. In *The evolution of social systems*, J. Friedman & M. J. Rowlands (eds). London: Duckworth.
Geertz, C. 1980. *Negara: the theatre state in nineteenth-century Bali*. Princeton, New Jersey: Princeton University Press.
Gunawardana R. A. L. H. 1976. The analysis of precolonial social formations in Asia in the writings of Karl Marx. *The Indian Historical Review* **2** (2).
Gunawardana R. A. L. H. 1979. *Robe and plough: monasticism and economic interest in early medieval Sri Lanka*. Tucson: Association for Asian Studies.
Gunawardana R. A. L. H. 1981. Social function and political power: a case study of state formation in irrigation society. In *The study of the state*, H. J. M. Claessen & P. Skalnik (eds), The Hague: Mouton.
Gunawardana R. A. L. H. 1982. Prelude to the state: an early phase in the evolution of political institutions in ancient Sri Lanka. *The Sri Lanka Journal of the Humanities* **8**.
Gunawardana R. A. L. H. 1985. Total power or shared power? A study of the hydraulic state and its transformations in Sri Lanka from the third to the ninth century A.D. In *Development and decline: the evolution of sociopolitical organization*, H. J. M. Claessen, P. van de Velde & M. E. Smith (eds). Massachusetts: Bergin & Garvey.
Hocart A. M. 1928. Town planning (subsection of Archaeological summary). *Journal of Science* **1**, Section G. Colombo: Archaeological survey.
Hoselitz, B. F. 1955. Generative and parasitic cities. *Economic development and cultural change* **3**.
Jātaka 1964. V. Fausboll (ed.) London: Pali Text Society, Vol. 4.
Jones, R. 1852. *Text-book of lectures on the political economy of nations, delivered at the East India College, Haileybury*. Hertford.
Karmmavibhāga 1961. M. Vimalakīirtti & N. Sominda (eds). Colombo: Gunasena.
Kulke, H. 1982. Legitimation and town-planning in the feudatory states of central Orissa. In *Städte in Südasien: Geschichte Gesellschaft Gestalt*, H. Kulke, H. C. Reiger & L. Lutze (eds). Wiesbaden: Franz Steiner Verlag.
Mahāvaṃsa 1958. W. Geiger (ed.) London: Pali Text Society.
Marx, K. 1953. *Grundrisse der Kritik der politischen Ökonomie*. Berlin: Dietz.
Marx, K. 1958. The eighteenth Brumaire of Louis Bonaparte. In *Marx and Engels, Selected works*, Vol. 1. Moscow: Foreign Languages Publishing House.
Marx, K. 1961. *Capital*, Vol. 1. Moscow: Foreign Languages Publishing House.
Miller, D. & C. Tilley 1984. *Ideology, power and prehistory*. Cambridge: Cambridge University Press.
Obeyesekere, G. 1963. The great tradition and the little tradition in the perspective of Sinhalese Buddhism. *Journal of Asian studies* **22** (2).
Paranavitana, S. 1970. *Inscriptions of Ceylon*, Vol. 1. Colombo: Department of Archaeology.

Paranavitana, S. 1983. *Inscriptions of Ceylon* **2** (1). Colombo: Department of Archaeology.

Pathmanathan, S. 1982. The cities of medieval Sri Lanka, 1000–1250: centres of dynastic power, religious authority and commercial activity. *Seminar for Asian Studies*, Discussion Paper No. 1, Peradeniya.

Patterson, T. C. 1986. Tribes, chiefdoms and kingdoms in the Inca empire. Paper presented to the annual meeting of the American Anthropological Association, Philadelphia, December 1986.

Ptolemaeus, C. 1966. *Geographia*, R. A. Skelton (ed.). Amsterdam: Theatrum Orbis Terrarum.

Samantapāsādikā 1924. J. Takakusu & M. Nagai (eds). London: Pali Text Society.

Seneviratne, H. L. 1978. *Rituals of the Kandyan State*. Cambridge: Cambridge University Press.

Sirisoma, M. H. 1972. Coins [Appendix to Deraniyagal 1972]. *Ancient Ceylon*, Vol. 2, Colombo: Department of Archaeology.

Smith, B. L. 1980. Polonnaruva as a ceremonial complex: Sinhalese cultural identity and the dilemmas of pluralism. In *Studies in history of Buddhism*, A. K. Naraian (ed.). Delhi: B. R. Publishing Corporation.

Sombart, W. 1916. *Der Moderne Kapitalismus*, Vol. 1. Munich: Duncker.

Sumaṅgalavilāsinī 1931. W. Stede (ed.), London: Pali Text Society.

Vaṃsatthappakāsinī 1935. G. P. Malalasekera (ed.). London: Pali Text Society.

Veluppillai, A. 1971. *Ceylon Tamil inscriptions*, Vol. 1. Peradeniya: Royal Printers.

Weber, M. 1958. *The city*. New York: Free Press.

Wheatley, P. 1971. *The pivot of the four quarters: a preliminary enquiry into the origin and character of the ancient Chinese city*. Edinburgh: Edinburgh University Press.

Wittfogel, K. 1957. *Oriental despotism: a comparative study of total power*. New Haven: Yale University Press.

10 *Monastery plan and social formation: the spatial organization of the Buddhist monastery complexes of the Early and Middle Historical period in Sri Lanka and changing patterns of political power*

SENAKE BANDARANAYAKE

The most substantial body of artefacts that have survived from the Early and Middle Historical period (EMHP) in Sri Lanka (c. 250 BC to AD 1300; see Table 10.1) are the skeletal remains of Buddhist monastery complexes widely distributed throughout the country. We may estimate that there are between 2000 and 3000 such monastery sites, containing a total of between 50 000 and 75 000 individual structural units, dating mostly from the MHP. The excavation and documentation of these complexes has gone on for nearly 100 years and, understandably, is still far from complete. The best-known and most important concentrations are found around the principal politico–urban centres of the EMHP, particularly the ancient cities of Anurādhapura (3rd century BC to 10th century AD) and Polonnaruva (11th to 13th centuries).

The buildings in these monastery complexes were largely residential, with centrally located ritual and 'ecclesiastical' structures. They had brick masonry substructures and timbered superstructures, with the marginal use of stone for internal columniation and external detailing. Very little has survived of the original decoration, and nothing whatsoever of the superstructures, other than tile debris. However, the surviving substructures and ground plans of individual units and complexes tell us a great deal about the technology, planning mathematics, architectural symbolism and social meaning of these monuments, which represent the most significant and extensive material remains of the cultural product and cultural 'symbolism' of the society of the EMHP.

As far as the existing evidence indicates, Sri Lankan Buddhist monastery types show a relatively continuous history of development throughout the EMPH. Monastery sites at major centres such as Anurādhapura, which was in continuous occupation from about the second half of the 1st

Table 10.1 Chronological and cultural sequence for Sri Lanka

Date	Period	Phase	Society	Polity	Economy
−20,000 −10,000	PREHISTORIC PERIOD		band and tribal society		mesolithic food gathering
−1,000	PROTOHISTORIC PERIOD				incipient food production sedentary iron age farming irrigation
−300	PHEH		social differentiation rank & stratified soc. early state formation		
0	EARLY ANURADHAPURA PERIOD	EHP-1 Early Historic Phase 1	EARLY 'FEUDAL' SOCIETY - 1 -	unified all-island kingdom with regional divisions	primary urbanisation trade phase 1
+300					major irrigation & archit. complexes
	SIGIRIYA EMHP	EHP-2 Early Historic Phase 2	- 2 -	↑ centripetal tendencies dominant	↑
+650	LATE ANURADHAPURA PERIOD	MHP-1 Middle Historic Phase	MATURE 'FEUDAL' SOCIETY	↓	trade phase 2 ↓
+1250	POLONNARUVA PERIOD	MHP-2		end of unified kingdom	end of major irrigation & archit. complexes
	'SHIFTING CAPITALS' PERIOD	Late Historic Phase 1 LHP-1	LATE 'FEUDAL' SOCIETY - 1 -	multiple polities ↑ centrifugal tendencies dominant	secondary urbanisation trade phase 3
+1500	KOTTE PERIOD	LHP-2			
	KANDY PERIOD LHP	Late Historic Phase 2	- 2 -	anti-colonial wars and partial occupation ↓	tertiary urbanisation trade phase 4
+1800				total colonial occupation	beginnings of modern transition
MODERN TRANSITIONAL PERIOD					

millennium BC to the end of the MHP and beyond, are stratified to a depth of 4–5 m or more and show evidence of successive phases of constructional activity. The present surface or immediate subsurface remains belong mostly to the MHP, and especially to its later phases. Previous investigations (Bandaranayake 1974, 33–133) and recent excavations at Anurādhapura and elsewhere (Wikramagamage *et al.* 1983, 1984, Ratnayake 1986, Bandaranayake 1984a, 6, pp. 48–65) confirm that these later structures are at least locationally and sometimes morphologically related to earlier forms. In rare examples, such as the 'meditation monasteries', it is possible to reconstruct a detailed typological evolution extending over a period of several centuries (Bandaranayake 1974, pp. 127–30). However, in general we can only propose certain broad lines of development, based on fragmentary evidence from excavations and surface documentation.

This chapter puts forward a broad categorization of monastery forms, and locates them in a sequential pattern of development. However, our principal interest is not in establishing a descriptive typology and chronology of EMHP monastery forms – although that itself is a preliminary and still incomplete task – but in proposing an interpretative hypothesis linking:

(a) the spatial disposition of the ritual and residential units of various monastery types; and
(b) periodic changes in this disposition; with
(c) the changing patterns of power relations within the general social order itself, and particularly with regard to the interplay of 'centripetal' and 'centrifugal' tendencies in the evolution of the Sri Lankan polity.

Apart from the fact that, quantitatively speaking, the monastic remains constitute one of the most important sets of archaeological data relating to the EMHP, there are two further reasons why they are suitable material for such interpretations: first, the spatial organization of a monastic unit or monastic complex is based on a strict geometry, ultimately involving the demarcation of relationships and hierarchies, and therefore displaying clear patterns of ritual and social status, ranking and linkage; and secondly, architectural character of the monasteries, as the most extensive group of EMHP structures rendered in permanent materials, directly reflects not only their ideological and symbolic function, but also the important socioeconomic and sociopolitical role of the *saṅgha*, the Buddhist monastic order. The *saṅgha* constitutes one of the three component parts of the composite or triadic ruling group that was a specific feature of the Sri Lankan social formation in historical times.

The technics of the spacial organization itself were clearly based on a mathematical module (Bandaranayake 1974, p. 266). Recent investigations of buildings at Polonnaruva have shown the precision of the planning mathematics employed there, and the extensive use of a square modular grid, with the central square invariably coinciding with the ritual centre of the structure (Nakagawa 1986). Moreover, the ensuing lateral or radial 'compartmentalization of space' is often combined with the axial orientation of gateways, pathways, entrances, central buildings, etc. Thus, in any unit or complex of units there is both a symbolic and an actual hierarchical progression from the periphery to the centre, passing through a series of intermediate stages, some of which are occupied by subsidiaries.

When such a spatial disposition is found in a residential complex – or, more strictly, a sacro-residential complex – occupied by a highly organized religious élite, it tells us a great deal about the pattern of relationships existing within that group, and especially about conscious and ordered perceptions of these relationships. Moreover, when that pattern is replicated at a number of locations and is subject to systematic variations through time, and when these variations conform to similarly ordered changes in the broader political structure, we may justifiably pose the question of whether the spatial organization of the monastic complexes is related to patterns of power distribution within the polity as a whole.

The monasteries of the EMHP were clear manifestations of the ideological, sociopolitical and socio-economic position of the monastic order. Their architecture and spatial organization were highly visible and tangible expressions of that situation. Along with the king, the *saṅgha* seems to have enjoyed the special privilege of building in permanent materials. As the 'state religion' (Rahula 1956, pp. 62–77), Buddhism formed the dominant ideology throughout the historical period, a position very similar to that prevailing in other Mahayana or Theravada Buddhist countries such as Tibet, Burma and Thailand. The *saṅgha* enjoyed a particularly close relationship with the state. As Rahula (1956, pp. 75–6) succinctly describes it:

> The monasteries formed the centres of national culture, and *bhikkhus* were the teachers of the whole nation – from prince to peasant. They helped the king to rule the country in peace. It was the duty of the *bhikkhus* according to the Vinaya to side with the kings. They used their influence over the masses to support the kings who, in return, looked after their interests.

Their ideological position gave them considerable political and social influence and they enjoyed, in certain periods, varying degrees of immunity from the fiscal and juridical authority of the royal officials. Economically, as great land-owing institutions, embodying a form of private ownership of land, they were directly involved in production and in the appropriation of surplus, and they therefore had an independent economic existence. As for their connections with the secular élite, evidence from EHP-1, the MHP and the LHP and other parallel situations elsewhere in Asia (for a review of this evidence, see Bandaranayke 1984b, pp. 5–9), indicates a close interrelationship between the *saṅgha* – especially its higher ranks – and the secular, land-owing nobility and gentry. It was exclusively from these latter social groups that the royal officials were drawn, and also at least a substantial section of the *saṅgha* itself (Kotelawele 1978, Ilangasinha 1983).

The society of the historical period appears to be dominated by a closely interlocking, triadic structure, as mentioned above, of (a) king and officials, (b) *saṅgha* and (c) secular nobles and gentry, who are also in competition and conflict among themselves over the division of power and resources. A model of such a formation has been presented earlier (Bandaranayake 1984b, pp. 13, 15–16), drawing attention to the interplay or oscillation between 'centripetal' and 'centrifugal' tendencies, and the varying degrees of centralization and decentralization of authority that were brought about by this interplay. The Sri Lankan polity achieved a high degree of centralization as early as the last two centuries BC, and the concept of a centralized state dominates both traditional political thinking and symbolism, and modern historiography. However, the phenomenon of an all-pervading centralization that lasted through the entire historical epoch is now being challenged, and new conceptualizations such as 'interplay' or 'oscillation' models are being suggested in its place (e.g. the concept of 'a galactic polity'; Tambiah 1976).

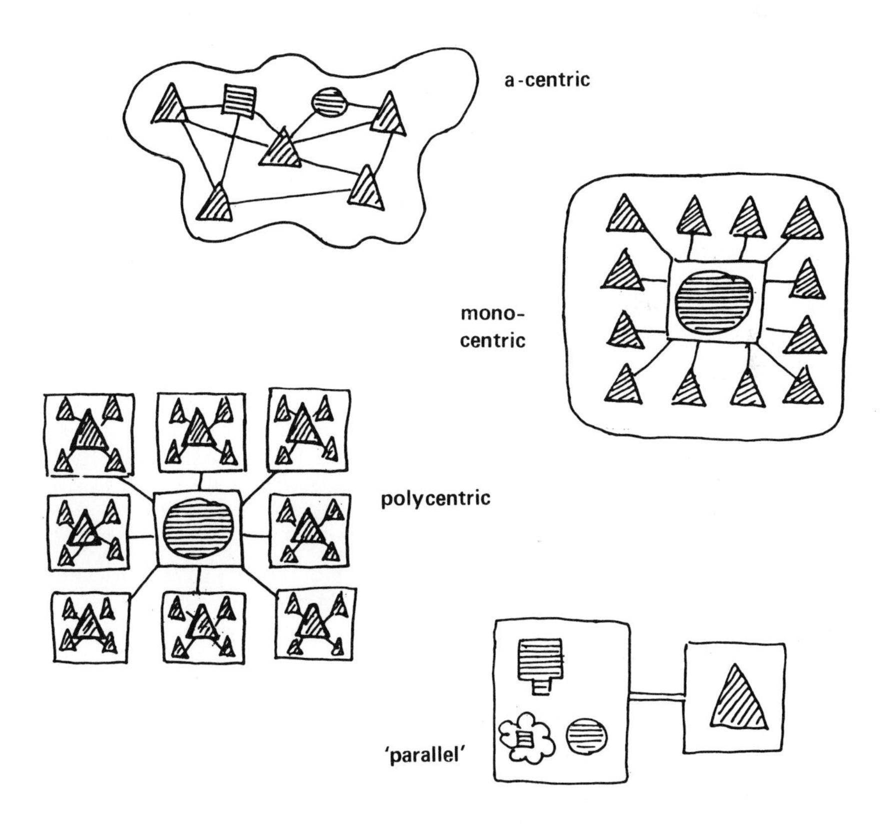

Figure 10.1 Basic monastic plan types (schematic).

Archaeological investigations provide useful evidence to test and support such as approach. The monastic remains of the EMHP provide just such a body of data. The changing configuration of the monastery plan through the EMHP seems to coincide in its broad evolutionary history with the changing pattern of power relations in the society at large.

In general, we may point out to four basic modes of spatial organization which prevail in the monastic layouts of the EMHP:

(a) the *a-centric* plan in which the monastic residences are dominant and there is no centralization of the overall monastic layout;
(b) the *monocentric* plan, in which the monastic complex is systematically organized around a single, expressively dominant, ritual centre;
(c) the *polycentric* plain in which an older, dominant centre remains but several subsidiary centres also appear, creating, as it were, a dynamic tension between the ritual core of the monastery and its peripheral residential units; and
(d) the '*parallel*' plan, in which there are single or multiple residences appearing alongside a ritual complex, the whole forming an independent or semi-independent micro-unit, capable of being integrated into a macro structure or of remaining autonomous without changing its basic character.

All four types are diagrammatically represented in Figure 10.1. The division of the EMHP into four major phases (Table 10.1) also incorporates distinct stages in the evolution of the Sri Lankan polity. The appearance or disappearance of the various monastery types that have so far been identified (Bandaranayake 1974, pp. 33ff, Basnayake 1983) can be systematically related to these phases (Fig. 10.2).

Thus, in the earlier half of EHP-1 – or what is now referred to as the Protohistoric-Early Historic (PHEH) transition – marked by the existence of a number of small kingdoms, principalities or other formations, i.e. before the emergence of a centralized state, the monastery is essentially an *a-centric* and organic form (Fig. 10.3). Significantly, this period also sees the monasteries as the focus of a conspicuous display of patronage by the dominant social groups of the groups of the period. These social groups, who are clearly 'the owners and controllers of wealth and political power and the dispensers of religious and economic patronage' in this society, have a variety of ranks and titles, amongst which royal titles and personages are not outstanding, as they are in later periods.

In contrast, EHP-2 sees the appearance of a highly centralized state and, at least in the metropolitan monasteries of Anurādhapura, the emergence of the *centric* plan (Fig. 10.4). In these the monastery is dominated by a central ritual structure, usually a *stūpa* of colossal proportions, the residential units being placed around it in a square or circular arrangement. This process, which may have had its origins in EHP-1, develops through EHP-2, reaching a culmination early in the 4th century AD. How completely this applies to the metropolitan monasteries, and whether it applies to suburban or provincial monasteries, has to be determined by

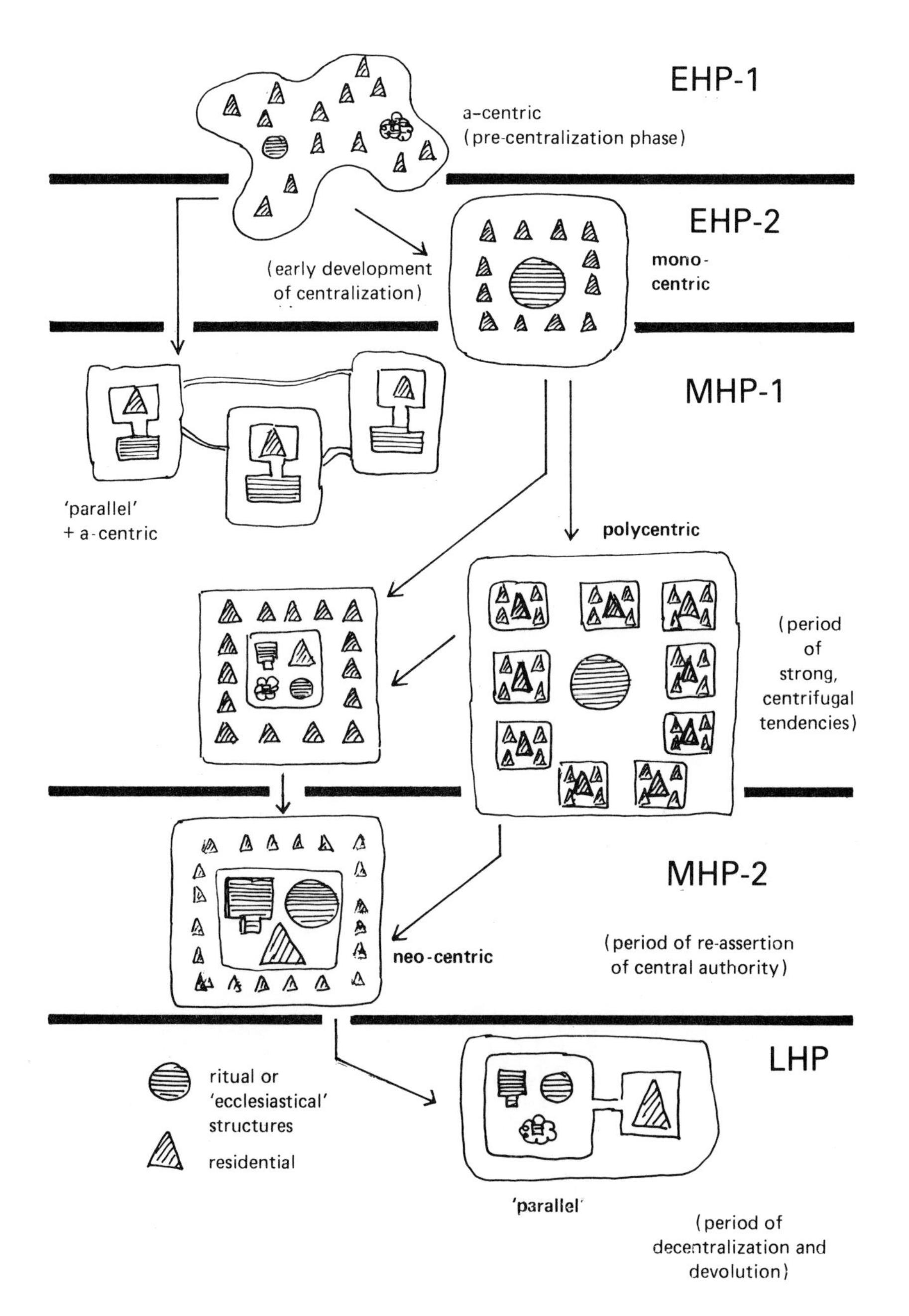

Figure 10.2 Development of monastic plan, 3rd century BC to 18th century AD (schematic).

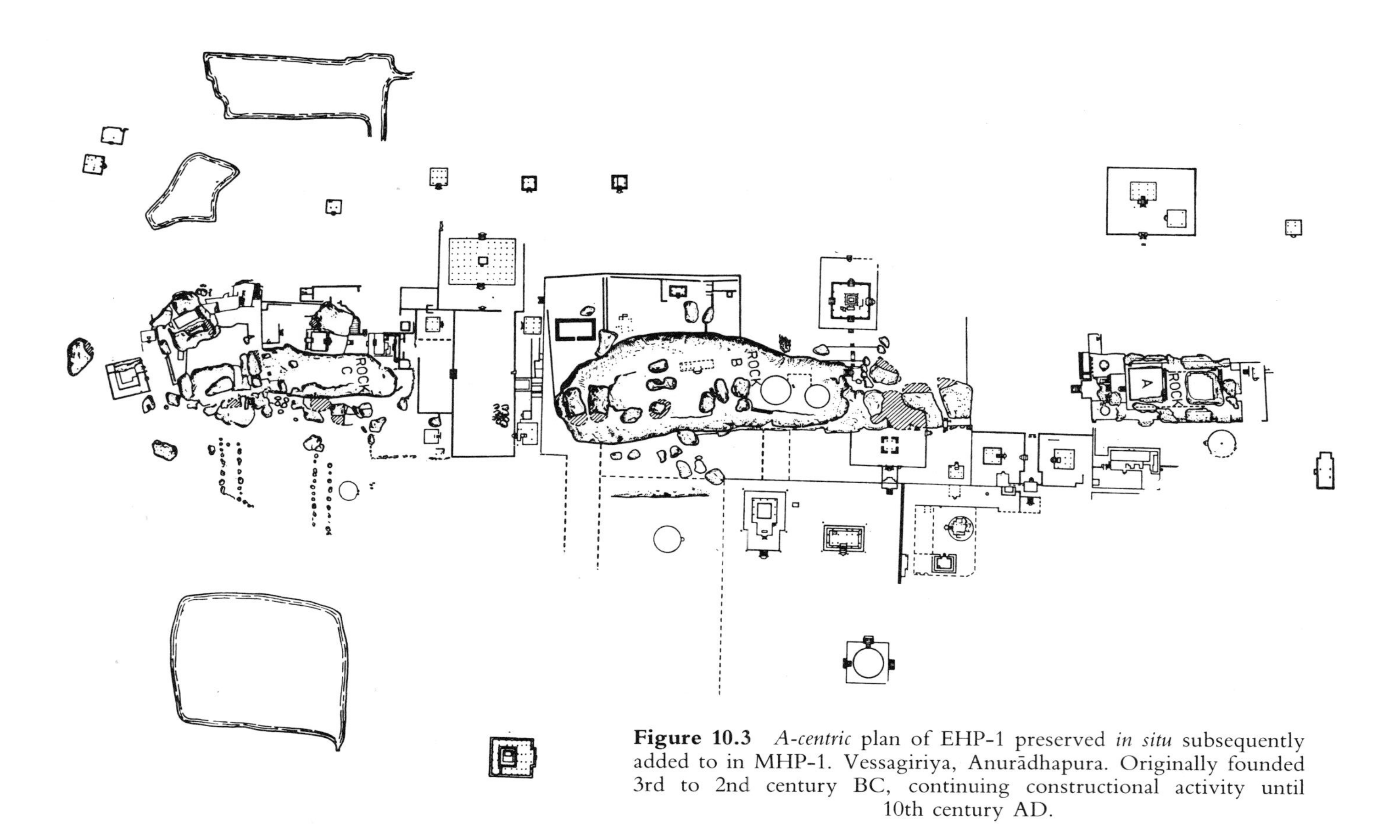

Figure 10.3 *A-centric* plan of EHP-1 preserved *in situ* subsequently added to in MHP-1. Vessagiriya, Anurādhapura. Originally founded 3rd to 2nd century BC, continuing constructional activity until 10th century AD.

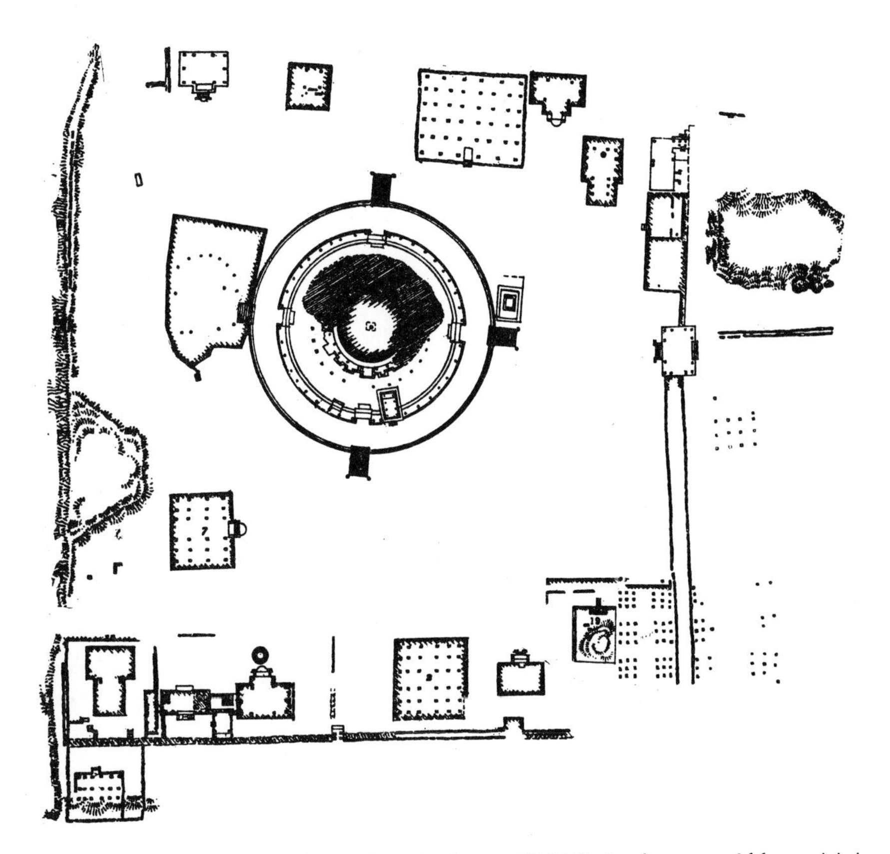

Figure 10.4 MHP-1 version of *centric* plan at EHP-2. Lankarama, Abhayagirivihara, Anurādhapura. Original foundation uncertain, but probably 3rd century BC to 1st century AD; present surface monuments *c.* 7th to 9th century (?).

future excavations. The remains of EHP-2 are deeply buried, unlike many EHP-1 sites, which for topographical reasons are more readily accessible.

Similarly, early MHP-1 is an even more obscure phase. However, remains at certain sites – where topographical conditions have prevented deposition from covering MHP-1 structures, or where recent excavations have revealed monastery layouts of the 6th and 7th centuries (for example Bandaranayake 1984, p. 48) – seem to indicate that the developments of this phase anticipate those of the late MHP-1 phases. However, taking MHP-1 as a whole we may say that it is marked by two major phenomena:

(a) the enormous expansion of wealth, social and political influence, ritual and organizational complexity, and architectural development and elaboration, as far as the Buddhist monastic order is concerned; and

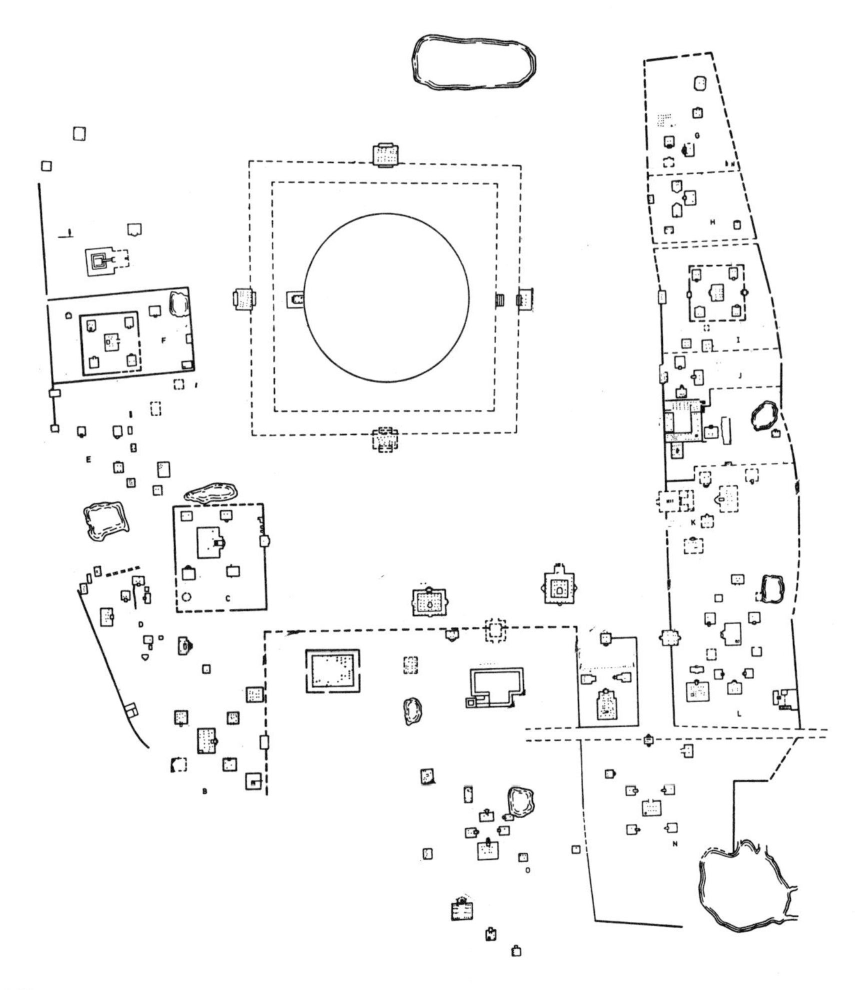

Figure 10.5 Superimposition of *polycentric* plan of MHP-1 over *centric* plan of EHP-2. Jetavanavihara, Anurādhapura. Circa 4th century AD.

(b) the dominance of centrifugal and devolutionary tendencies in the polity and the society as a whole.

The comparatively large number of monastery sites and forms known from this period relate as much to the nature of the cultural product as the improved conditions of preservation and retrieval. There is little doubt that the monastery forms reflect these specific developments. Amongst the distinctive features of the monastery layouts of this period are:

(a) the emergence of the *polycentric* plan, which displays a dynamic spatial equilibrium between the centripetality of the early (*centric*) monasteries and the newly dominant centrifugal elements (Figs 10.5–7) and

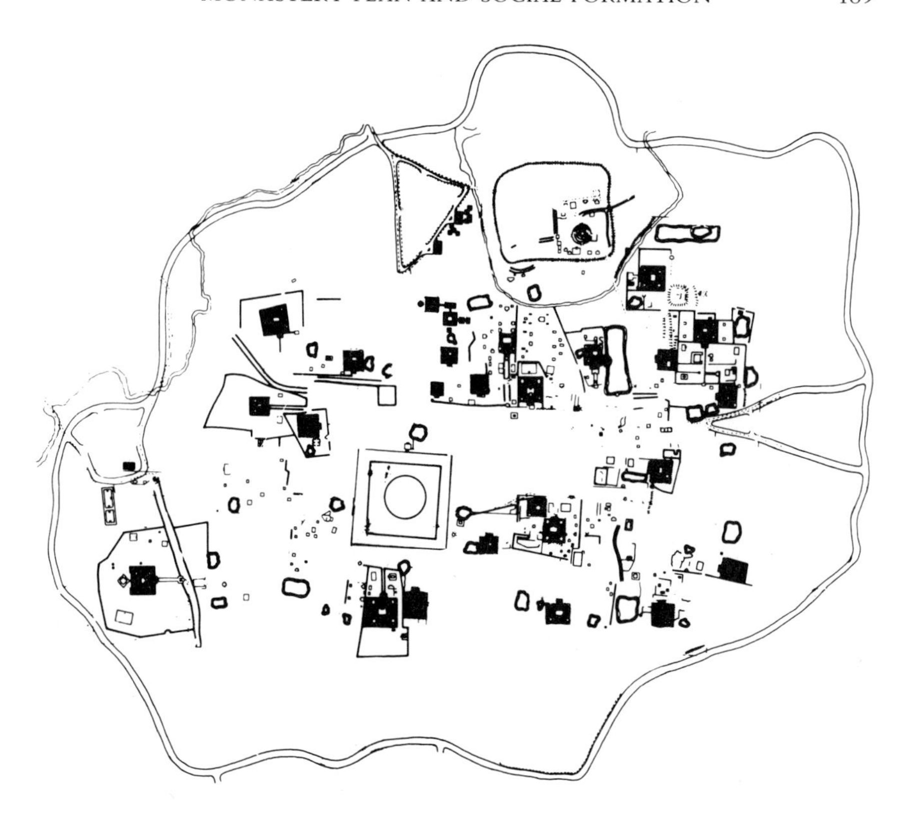

Figure 10.6 *Polycentric* plan of MHP-1 superimposed on an EHP-1 'core'. Abhayagirivihara, Anurādhapura. Originally founded 1st century BC; surface and immediate subsurface monuments 8th to 10th century AD.

(b) the evolution of elaborate and structured expressions of *a-centricity*, as seen in the meditation monasteries.

In this later type, the monastic unit itself is a freestanding or independent form, displaying a version of what we have called a '*parallel*' plan, i.e. a balanced counterposition between the ritual or ecclesiastical aspects, on one side, and the residential aspects, on the other side, without the dominance of either over the other. At the same time these units are often brought together in a single area in a loose *a-centric* cluster, sometimes connected by formally planned avenues. There is an avoidance of linear geometry in the communication lines between monastery units and of any spatially expressed dominance of one unit over another. However, the individual unit, while not displaying any centralization of status, is marked by a high degree of geometric formality, suggesting a strictly controlled internal community. The entire conception is therefore suggestive of a structured decentralization of status and authority, within a system of strict rules and interlinkages.

Figure 10.7 Archaeological remains of the central precinct of a Buddhist monastic unit or 'college' in the Abhayagirivihara at Anurādhapura (see also Fig. 10.6). The main building in the centre of the photograph is the residence of an abbot or high priest presiding over one of the many component units of an elaborate *polycentric* monastery of the MHP-1, 8th to 10th centuries AD. The scale of the central building is indicated by the size of the standing figures near the entrance.

MHP-2, in sharp contrast with MHP-1, sees the return – at least in the major urban monasteries of Polonnaruva (Basnayake 1986, Figs 4, 6 & 8)[3] – to a relatively simple *centric* or *neo-centric* plan (Fig. 10.8). This incorporated some of the developments of the earlier periods, such as the increasing monumentality of ritual and ecclesiastical structures. At the same time it sees the complete disappearance of the *polycentric* residential units, which form such a dominant feature of MHP-1. This is clearly related to developments in the *saṅgha* organization of the 11th and 12th centuries, where royal intervention brings about the establishment of new monastic rules and a reassertion of central authority. It also reflects the increased emphasis on central political dominance, especially in the second half of the 12th century, during a phase when the challenge to the centre was particularly strong.

A comparison between EMHP developments and those of the less well-known Later Historical period (LHP) helps to throw the earlier periods into clearer relief and to continue the same line of inquiry into the post-13th century era. The beginnings of the LHP in the 13th century mark a major transition in Sri Lankan history. The most visible manifestation of the historical changes that took place at this time is the shift in the main

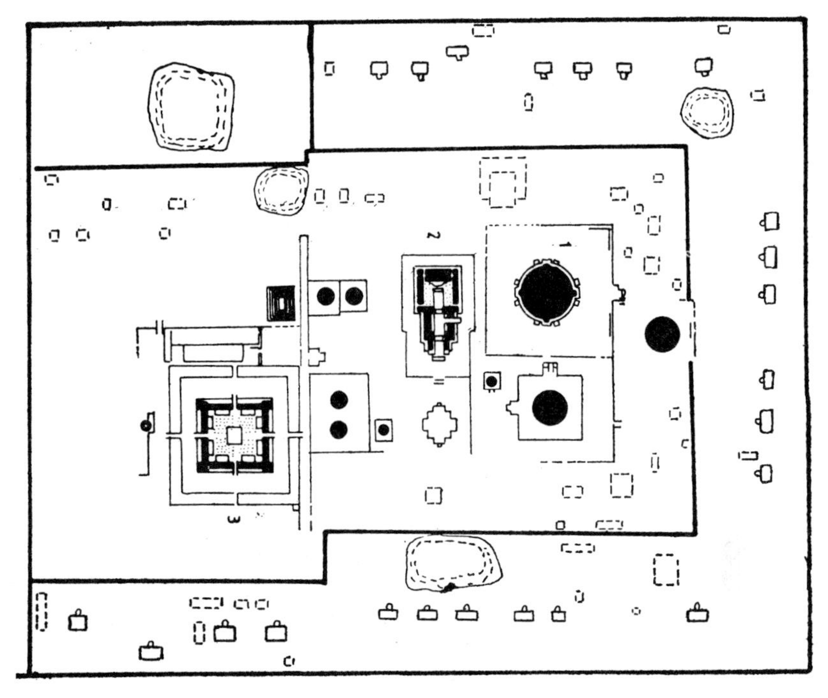

Figure 10.8 *Neo-centric* plan of MHP-2. Alahanaparivena complex, Polonnaruva, 12th century AD (sketch).

centres of political, economic and cultural activity from the dry-zone plains of the north-central and eastern regions to the wet lowlands of the south-west, the central highlands and the arid north. A most significant development was the decentralization of political authority and, therefore, of patronage, resulting in the disappearance of the monumental complexes and the dissolution of the monumental style that characterized the civilization of the EMHP. Conventionally viewed by historians as a period of decline, a loss of momentum affecting the entire civilization itself, more recent interpretations suggest instead a transition to more complex and varied forms of polity connected with underlying changes in social and economic organization, and with a process of 'secondary' urbanization.

The inevitable consequence of such a deep-rooted transition was a change in the nature of cultural production. As far as the Buddhist monastery was concerned, this involved a change in the use of materials, in form and technology, and especially in its spatial organization. The evidence relating to LHP-1 is much less clear than that for LHP-2, but what generally emerges from meagre archaeological data and from more extensive studies in architectural history is the appearance of monastery forms which display versions of the 'parallel' plan.[4] We may see in this a reduction of the elaborate hierarchical arrangements of the MHP-1 and MHP-2 monasteries to a basic plan in which a single residential compound stands in counterposition to a clearly demarcated ritual complex.

In a very general way we may observe that this new orientation reflects the sociopolitical developments of the LHP, in that it allows such a basic unit to either remain autonomous, supported by its own regional and 'manorial' economic base, or to form part of a network of linkages established between localized units which retain varying degrees of autonomy within their own contexts. In fact, the reduction-to-basics character of this LHP monastery allows it to adapt to different organizational, economic and political configurations without changing its essential form. At the same time late expressions of the *polycentric* plan appear in a few LHP-2 examples, as in the Malvatta and Asgiriya monasteries in Kandy. This exemplifies, in a way different from what is demonstrated in the '*parallel*' plan types, the '*polycentricity*' of the feudal power relations of the period. Appropriately, this phenomenon is restricted to the 'headquarter' monasteries of the two chapters into which the Buddhist *saṅgha* of the 18th century is divided.

In conclusion, we may say that what emerges from a long-term view of changes in the spatial organization of the Buddhist monastery complexes of Sri Lanka over a period of nearly two millennia is a significant correlation with the changing configurations of relationships within the social formation of the historical period. Our characterization of that social formation and our understanding of the major transitions that took place within it during its long historical trajectory are still at a very preliminary stage of development. The present level of generation of archaeological data with regard to the monastery forms is also extremely unevenly developed. The generalizations that are being put forward here in an interpretative hypothesis linking:

(a) the spatial disposition of the ritual and residential units of various monastery types; and
(b) periodic changes in this disposition; with
(c) the changing patterns of power relations within the general social order itself, and particularly with regard to the interplay of 'centripetal' and 'centrifugal' tendencies in the evolution of the Sri Lankan polity

are a contribution towards general theories of the social organization of space and the nature of relations within historical social formations. They can be tested only by further archaeological investigations and theory-based studies in social and cultural history.

Notes

1. With the exception of the central mountain region and the wet, perennial rainfall zone of the south-west, which only became areas of major historical importance in the Late Historical period.
2. The only exception to this is in the subsidiary units of certain monasteries which occupy an apparently subordinate position off the main avenue leading to a major unit, but even these replicate the plan of the 'parent' monastery , although on a reduced scale.
3. Although there is no basic change in the nature of cultural production from MHP-1 to MHP-2 (e.g. in its most significant formal qualities, symbolism or in technology and the use of material), the period during which substantial constructional activity was undertaken in MHP-2 was a relatively brief phase, limited to the second half of the 12th century. The study of the developments of MHP-2 is therefore almost restricted to the major urban monasteries of Polonnaruva. The evidence for the emergence and dominance of the *neo-centric* plan is therefore less extensive than for the trends exemplified in the far more complex body of data from the much longer periods of constructional activity in MHP-1.
4. The *parallel* plan adopted in the LHP is quite different from that seen in the meditation monasteries of MHP-1 (Fig. 10.9). The building types deployed in the few known monasteries of LHP-1 (Fig. 10.10) are similar to those found in the standard monasteries of the MHP, while in LHP-2 there is a considerable degree of change in form and materials.

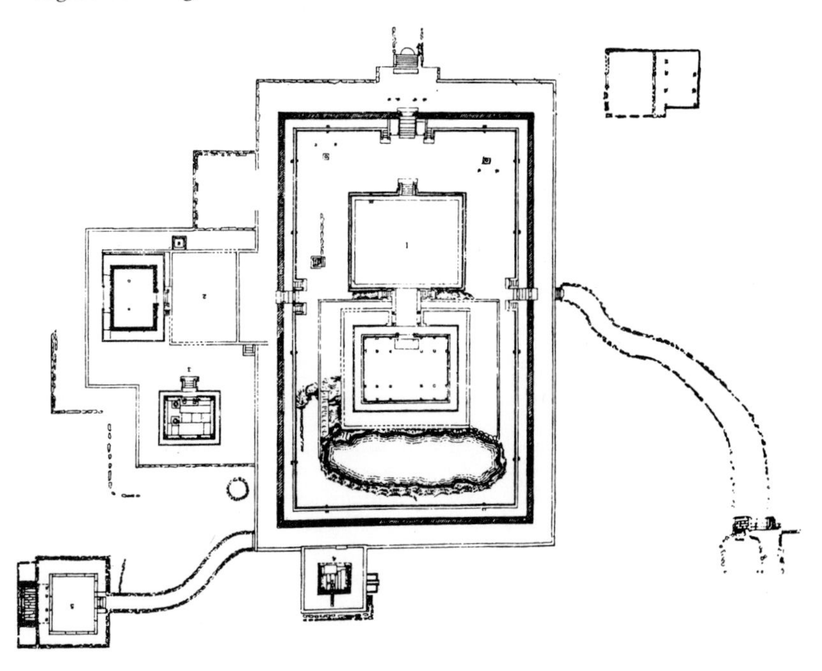

Figure 10.9 *Parallel* plan of MHP-1. 'Meditation monastery', Western Monastery H. Anurādhapura. 9th to 10th century AD.

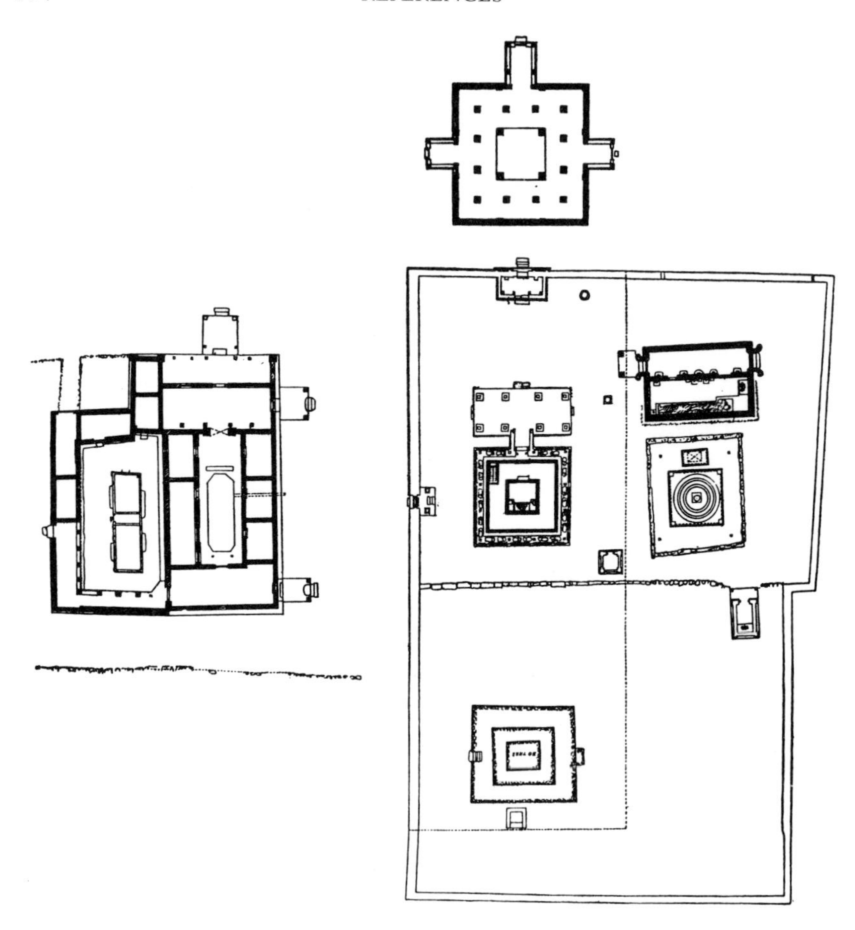

Figure 10.10 *Parallel* plan of LHP. Budumuttava, Nikavaratiya. Original foundation probably 13th to 14th century, reconstruction 18th to 19th century AD.

References

Bandaranayake, S. 1974. *Sinhalese monastic architecture; the viharas of Anuradhapura.* Leiden: E. J. Brill.

Bandaranayake, 1984a. *Sigiriya Project, first archaeological excavation and research report.* Colombo: Central Cultural Fund, Ministry of Cultural Affairs.

Bandaranayake 1984b. Problems in the classification of the historical societies of the Indian Ocean region in a taxonomy of social types: a review of the Sri Lankan situation. *Proceedings of the International Conference on Indian Ocean Studies, Section B*, 1–22. Perth: International Centre for Indian Ocean Studies.

Basnayake, H. T. 1983. Early Buddhist monasteries. *Samskrti* **17** (3), 51–61.

Basnayake, H. T. 1986. *Sri Lankan monastic architecture.* Delhi: Sri Satguru Publications.

Ilangasinha, M. 1983. Kinship and lineage in the Buddhist monastic order in mediaeval Sri Lanka. *Kalyani; Journal of Humanities and Social Sciences of the University of Kelaniya* **2**, 166–76.

Kotelawele, D. A. 1978. Nineteenth century elites and their antecedents. *The Ceylon Historical Journal* **25** (1–4), 204–14.

Nakagawa, 1986. Personal communication – illustrated lecture on systems of columniation and conjectural reconstructions of the Hatadage and Vatadage at Polonnaruva, at Postgraduate Institute of Archaeology, Colombo, March.

Rahula, W. 1956. *History of Buddhism in Ceylon*. Colombo: M. D. Gunasena.

Ratnayake, H. 1986. *Jetavanavihara project, first report* Colombo: Central Cultural Fund, Ministry of Cultural Affairs.

Tambiah, S. J. 1976 *World conqueror and world renouncer: a study of Buddhism and polity in Thailand against a historical background*. Cambridge: Cambridge University Press.

Wikramagamage, C., S. Hettiarachchi, J. Bouzek, J. Bren & P. Charvat 1983. Excavations at Abhayagiri Vihara (Ahuradhapura, Sri Lanka) in 1982. *Archiv Orientalni* **51**, 337–71.

Wikramagamage, 1984. Excavations at Abhayagiri Vihara (Anuradhapura, Sri Lanka) in 1983. *Archiv Orientalni* **52** (1), 42–74.

11 *A Buddhist monastic complex of the medieval period in Sri Lanka*

P. L. PREMATILLEKE

This chapter is concerned with one of the major monasteries of the medieval capital Polonnaruva, namely, the *Ālāhaṇa Pariveṇa*, a monastery which is significant for several reasons.

(a) The *Ālāhaṇa Pariveṇa* monastery constitutes one of the major excavation and conservation projects of the well-known UNESCO–Sri Lanka Cultural Triangle programme.
(b) Its layout exemplifies the maximum development of the ancient monastic complexes of Sri Lanka by a process of gradual synthesis of several important architectural characteristics from the monasteries of the early Anurādhapura period.
(c) This monastery happens to possess the largest sacred edifices of ancient times, which portray distinctive characteristics of ancient Sri Lankan religious architecture.
(d) The monastic complex, above all, is of intrinsic value for the study of religio-cultural associations that prevailed in medieval Sri Lanka.
(e) The monastery forms a link between the artistic and architectural traditions of the early Anurādhapura period (1st millenium), and the later centuries down to the end of the Kandyan period (19th century).

Buddhism has been firmly rooted in Sri Lanka since the establishment of the monastic order in the 3rd century BC, and remained the state religion of the Sinhalese monarchy. From the beginning the monarchy–*Sangha* relationship had been a complex one, giving expression to mixed feelings and sentiments at various times. Nevertheless, the literary and archaeological evidence of Sri Lanka show the extent of munificence showered, by the political authority, on the religious community almost continuously through Sri Lanka's history.

The tradition established by the contemporaries of the Buddha, such as monarchs and millionaires (*seṭṭhī*), ministers and the rest of the affluent society, was continued down the ages. The Asoka ideal of Mauryan times (3rd century BC) became the model of religious norms for his Sri Lankan counterpart Devanimpiya Tissa, and the Buddhist Order of *saṇgha* developed with ever-increasing fervour.

The chronicles, *Mahāvamsa*, *Nikāyasanghraha*, etc., are filled with accounts of royal patronage bestowed on the Order of Buddhist monks. Royalty was considered the *fides defensor* guarding the orthodox against heretical intrusions. The rulers vied with each predecessor in building monastic edifices and providing necessary amenities for the *saṅgha*. This resulted in the establishment of monasteries in all possible parts of the city. The *Mahāvihāra*, the centre of the orthodox Order, remained the mainstay of Buddhism. However, the intrusions of heterodox teachings from almost the beginning of the Christian era of breakaway groups such as the *Abhayagirivihāra* and the *Jetavanārāma*. The monastic edifices of Anurādhapura mainly centre around these three establishments.

Complex developments in the political authority and religious environment over a period of more than a millennium, and the resultant changes, led to the decline of the capital Anurādhapura. The Cola conquest in AD 993 dealt the final blow to this first capital city of Sri Lanka, while their hegemony in Polonnaruva for 77 years resulted in the emergence of the second great capital, exerting a major influence on the culture of Sri Lanka.

From about the 7th century, kings made Polonnaruva their base (hence the alternative name of the city: 'camp city' *Kandavuru Nuwara*), but the establishment of the capital city saw the emergence of a centre par excellence of political and religious authority in the island for about four centuries (10th–13th centuries AD). The infusion of new elements and structural transformations resulted in Polonnaruva and its culture undergoing a change from being essentially 'orthogenetic to a stage of being not yet heterogenetic', but a precarious combination of diverse elements, some of which were incorporated into a synthesis, others initially being rejected (Smith 1978). Many changes were seen in political and economic, social and religious forums within and without. The historical references and archaeological remains present a clear understanding of the synthesis of these elements, and it is with this background that one has to study the religious and cultural remain of Polonnaruva (Fig. 11.1).

The existing monastic remains in Anurādhapura and elsewhere clearly distinguish the planning methods adopted by the two groups, city dwellers (*gāmavāsī*) and forest dwellers (*vanavāsī*), which were in keeping with their religious practices. The monastic planning of the city dwellers indicates organically constituted monasteries with a great *stūpa* in each forming the central hub around which the dwellings and other related edifices were positioned. The monastic dwellings of the meditative, or *vanavāsi*, monks originally constituted rather inorganic cave dwellings with only a wall enclosing the front to form a living cell. However, the forest dwellers soon came to possess their own formal and organic monasteries, as evidenced by the 8th-century monasteries of the *Tapovana* (ascetic grove) group, now, popularly known as the Western monasteries (Hocart 1926). The plan constituted two large square terraces joined together by a wide gangway formed by a single slab of stone (hence the name 'double-platform' type). The rear platform contained a group of small cells for the monks to meditate in, the front one forming an open space, probably for use as an assembly hall. The entire edifice was surrounded by a stone wall with ponds and moats within it. It is noteworthy that whereas the monastic establishments of the city dwellers

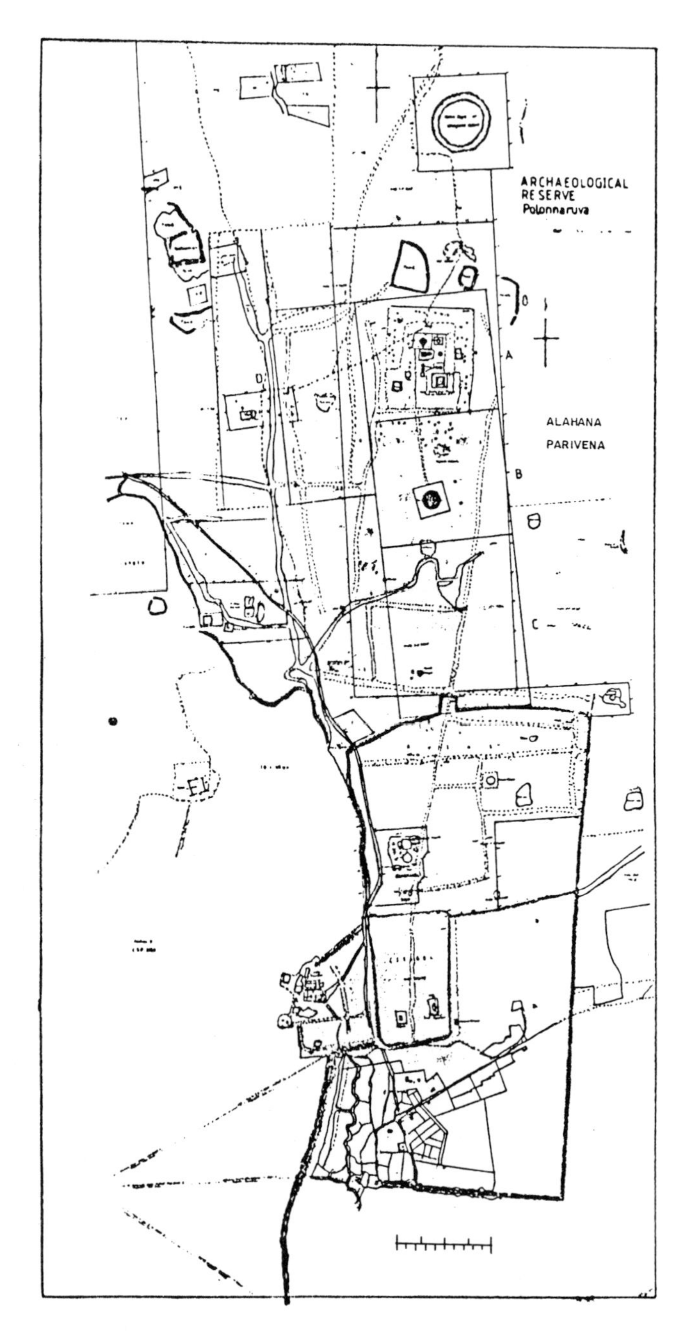

Figure 11.1 Ancient city plan of Polonnaruva.

closely follow the monastic planning and methodology of Indian prototypes, the double-platform plan of the forest dwellers constitutes an indigenous architectural plan of ancient Lanka (Prematilleke 1964).

Yet another monastic plan of great significance, that developed in Anurādhapura, is of the type known as the *pabbatavihāra* (Fig. 11.2) (literally meaning 'hill-monastery'). These represent a preplanned organic monastery type often showing Mahayanist influence (Prematilleke & Silva 1969). The monastery plan needs to be studied here more elaborately than in the two monastic types discussed earlier, as this preplanned structure bears a close parallel to the monastic plan of *Ālāhaṇa Pariveṇa* in Polonnaruva, which is the subject of our study.

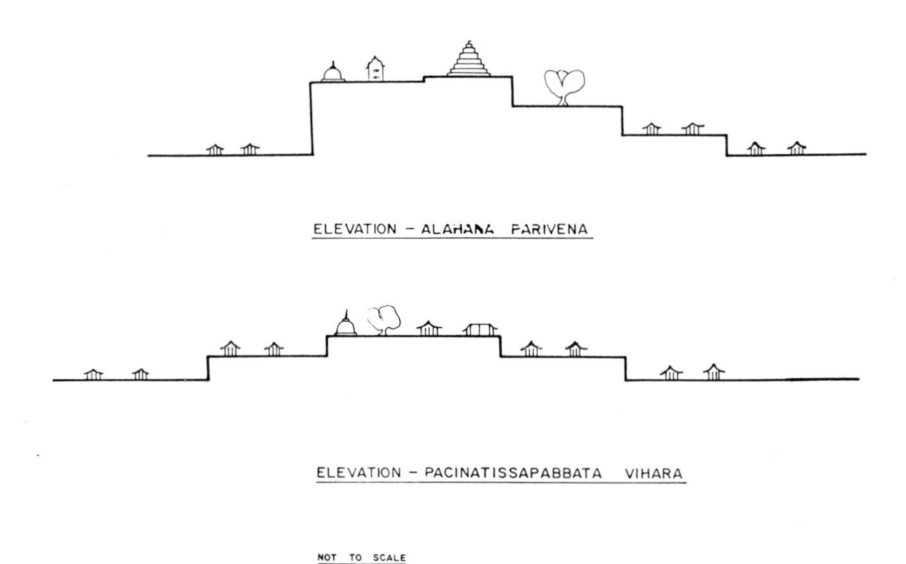

Figure 11.2 Pabbatavihara. Elevations

Several examples of the *pabbatavihāras* are found in Anurādhapura and elsewhere, eg. Vijayarama (Fig. 11.3), Pacinatissapabbata vihara, Puliyankulama monastery and Pankuliya, all situated on the outskirts of Anurādhapura, Dakkhina vihara in Sigiriya, Manikdena vihara, Magulmaha vihara in Lahugala.

Each of these sites formed a large quadrangle consisting of at least two or three concentric square terraces, surrounded by a moat. Hence the name moated monasteries (Bell 1891). The centremost top terrace contains the ritual and ecclesiatical edifices, the *stūpa*, Bo-tree shrine (*Bodhighara*), the image house (*Patimāghara*) and the chapter house (*Uposathaghara*). The terrace opens at the four cardinal points to the lower terrace, which was occupied by rows of living cells positioned at regular intervals, the frontage of the lowermost terrace being mostly confined to the refectory and bath (*Jantāghara*) meaning hot-water bath.

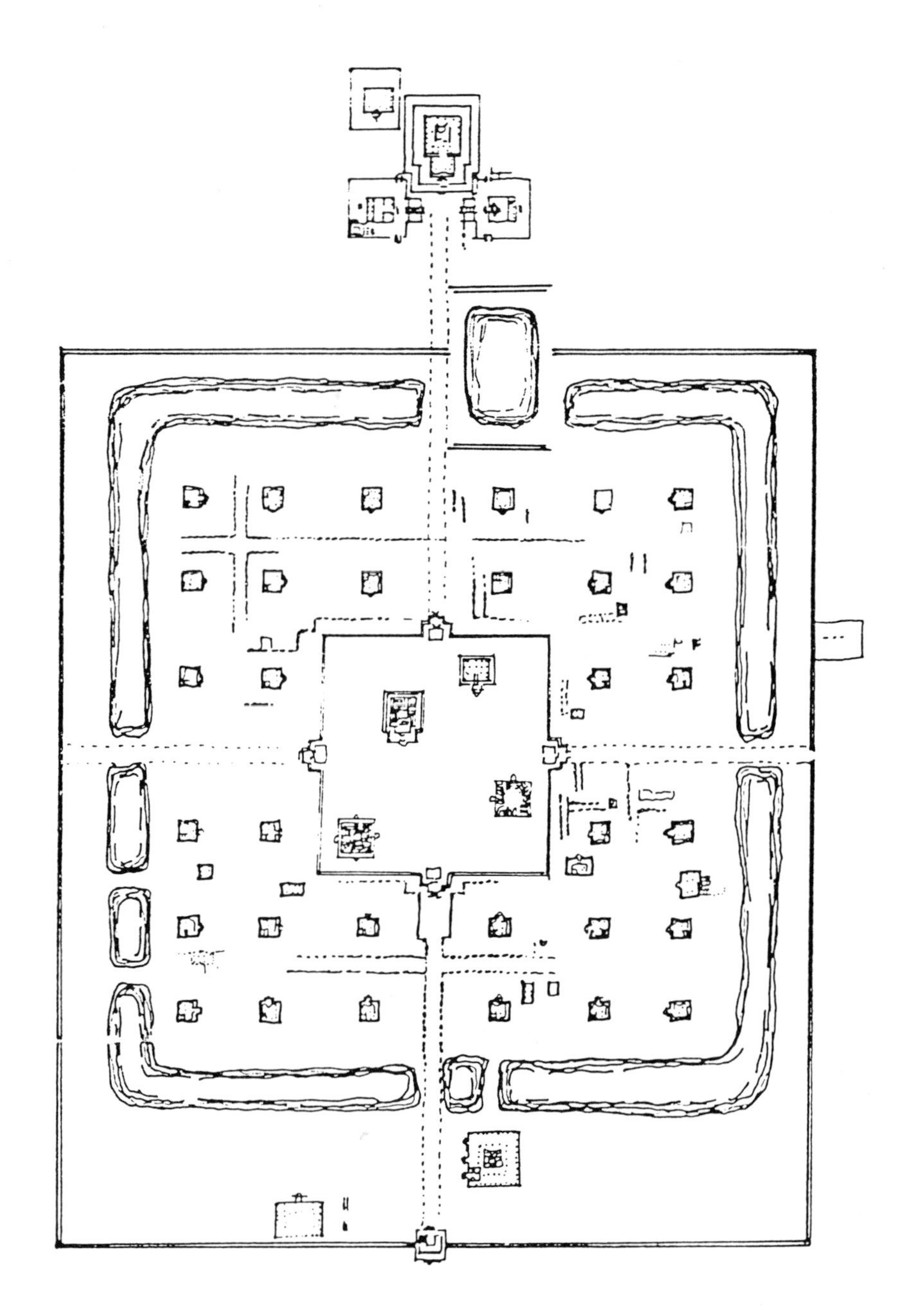

Figure 11.3 Vijayarama, Anurādhapura.

Although the monasteries are named *pabbata-vihāras*, these were not actually built on hills. They are terraced pyramids that enable one to evoke such a conception. A superficial similarity of this type may be seen in the pyramidal shrines of Indonesia.

The monastery type under discussion could, in one way, be considered a natural development of the Buddhist tradition of establishing sacred edifices on terraces marked by boundaries (*sīmā*), as reported in the Chronicle (*Mahāvamsa*). The arrangement of the cells on the four sides is obviously due to following the ancient Indian tradition, evidenced by the rock-cut as well as structural monasteries of Ajanta, Taxila, etc. (Dutt 1962). Here the cells that formed a continuous row around a central courtyard in the Indian prototype are positioned individually at regular intervals.

The arrangement of the four sacred edifices and the assembly (*sabhā*) together is referred to as Upapitha plan in *Manjusri*, a technical text on Buddhist architecture. The Buddhist monastery at Manikdena is the only example that contains actual remains of a *sabhā*, which is positioned at the centre of the terrace and which, according to the *Manjusri*, occupies the *Brahmapada*. The square stylobate with projections on four sides, situated in front of the *Lankātilaka* image house of the *Ālāhana* complex, has been conjectured to be a Bo-tree shrine (Bandaranayake 1974). Recent excavations did not support this hypothesis; it may be yet another instance of a *sabhā* edifice in the centre of the terrace.

The *Ālāhaṇa Pariveṇa* (crematory monastery) was so named because of its association with the site of cremation of prelates and kings. Continuation of this tradition down to the end of the Sinhala reign in Kandy is evident from *Ādhāhana Maluwa* monastery. The *Ālāhana* complex is located next to the northern boundary of the outer city limits of Polonnaruva, and was founded by the great king Parakramabahu I (AD 1153–86), who is credited with the foundation of several other large monasteries and the great irrigation reservoir, the Sea of Parakrama (Parakrama Samudra). *Ālāhaṇa Pariveṇa* remains the largest monastery of Polonnaruva, built on a monumental scale. A natural hillock had been fashioned into terraces on all four sides and the monastic complex built following the ancient traditions. The summit of the hill that forms the central platform contains the rituals and ecclesiastical edifices, namely, the *stūpa* (*Kiri-vehera*), the image house (*Lankātilaka*) and the chapter house (*Baddhasīmāpāsāda*). The fourth shrine, *Bodhighara*, however, is absent here. The lower terraces had been occupied by the dwelling quarters of the monks, *kuṭi* and *pāsādas*, refectories, kitchens, libraries, baths, toilets, wells, etc.

The monastic establishment under study is in a state of decay, having been exposed to the elements for about 800 years since the abandonment of the capital. Most of the edifices have been reduced to mere earth mounds, the only structure remaining in its original form being the *stūpa*, *Kiri vehera*. Even the solid brick-built structures such as the *Lankātilaka* image-house and the storeyed chapter house have lost their superstructures, and most of their functional and decorative components.

This monastery site has received the attention of several archaeologists (Bell, Hocart and Paranavitana) from the beginning of the 20th century, and over nearly eight decades the sacred and ecclesiastical structures, namely *Lankātilaka* and *Baddhasīmāpāsāda*, of the central terrace were cleared of debris and their remains were conserved. A small section of the lower terrace on the east side was also excavated, and its cellular structures were conserved. However, the major part of the monastery remained undisturbed until 1981, when a large-scale excavation and conservation programme was instituted under the auspices of the UNESCO–Sri Lanka Cultural Triangle Project. The excavations under this project were planned to expose the site comprehensively, except for the area which had already been disturbed by early archaeologists. The excavations hitherto completed have revealed much valuable data for the study of the monastic architecture and also the religious, cultural and social aspects of the period.

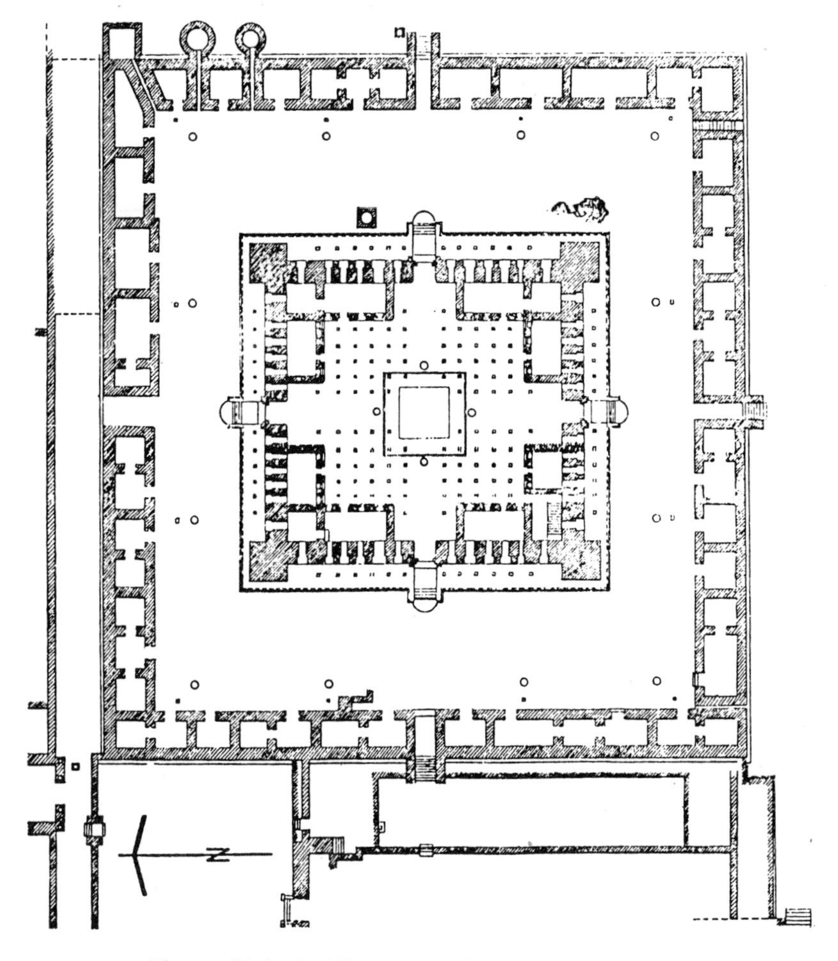

Figure 11.4 Baddhasīmāpāsāda, Alahana Parivena.

Although nearly eight centuries have elapsed since the abandonment of the capital and the consequent reduction of the buildings to a state of ruin, the excavations indicate that the accumulation of earth had been a slow process. This is attributable to the geological peculiarities of the site, which is formed of decayed quartzite bedrock almost to ground level. Sporadically spreads of gneiss formations are also seen. Most of the early phase structures are constructed on this stratum. Thus, unlike earlier sites such as Anurādhapura or Sigiriya, the *Ālāhaṇa Pariveṇa* does not possess more than three or four occupational layers. These are rather shallow, and together they relate to a short period of three to four centuries, the maximum depth of bedrock being not more than 80 cm. Layer 3 of the site was found to be the most productive stratum of the excavations, the deeper layers, if any, being formed by in-washed gravel deposits eroding through the upper terraces of the monastery (Prematilleke 1982).

The ritual and ecclesiastical structures forming the nucleus of the monastery on the topmost central terrace are noteworthy, and not only for their monumental character. The *stūpa* (*Kirivehera*) is the only extant edifice that remains preserved in its original 12th-century form. The image house, *Lankātilaka*, is the largest brick-built image shrine in Sri Lanka, measuring 38 × 20 m. The walls remain to a height of 17 m and would have been nearly 30 m when complete (Paranavitana 1954–5). This shrine, housing a brick-built Buddha image more than 12 m in height, constitutes a splendid example of the shrine type known as *Giñjakāvasatha* or '*Gedige*', which is built entirely of brick. The Thuparama in Polonnaruva exemplifies the design of this building when complete.

The chapter house, *Baddhasīmāpāsāda* is the largest structure of its type (Fig. 11.4). Located at the highest point of the hillock and commanding a grandiose view, it was a storeyed structure replete with all the amenities of a residential quarter. The ground floor comprising a central platform and surrounding cells was designed for the conduct of fortnightly ecclesiastical ritual preparations. The bath and toilets, urinals, etc., are located separately in a corner of the main terrace. The cells, both square and oblong in plan, which constituted the dwellings of the monks, are arranged on the lower terraces in a fairly regular order. These probably contained an upper floor of timber construction.

Apart from these, the Cultural Triangle excavations during the last four years have revealed two more important structures: a small chapter house and a hospital structure (Prematilleke 1982). The chapter house (Fig. 11.5) is smaller (16.40m × 13.60 m) than *Baddhasīmāpāsāda*, and is built within an enclosure. The edifice facing east has boundary stones at the four corners, evidence which supports its identity. The square moonstone is a departure from the usual semi-circular ones. The edifice consists of a quadrangular room at the back, with a passage around it, and a front room that probably formed the area for conducting fortnightly readings of the vinaya texts. The unique feature in this chapter house is the separate bath-cum-toilet unit. The bath consisted of a pedestal for a large pot of water. A stone drain had been built beneath the brick-paved floor, to lead refuse water into a brick-built pit (Prematilleke 1982).

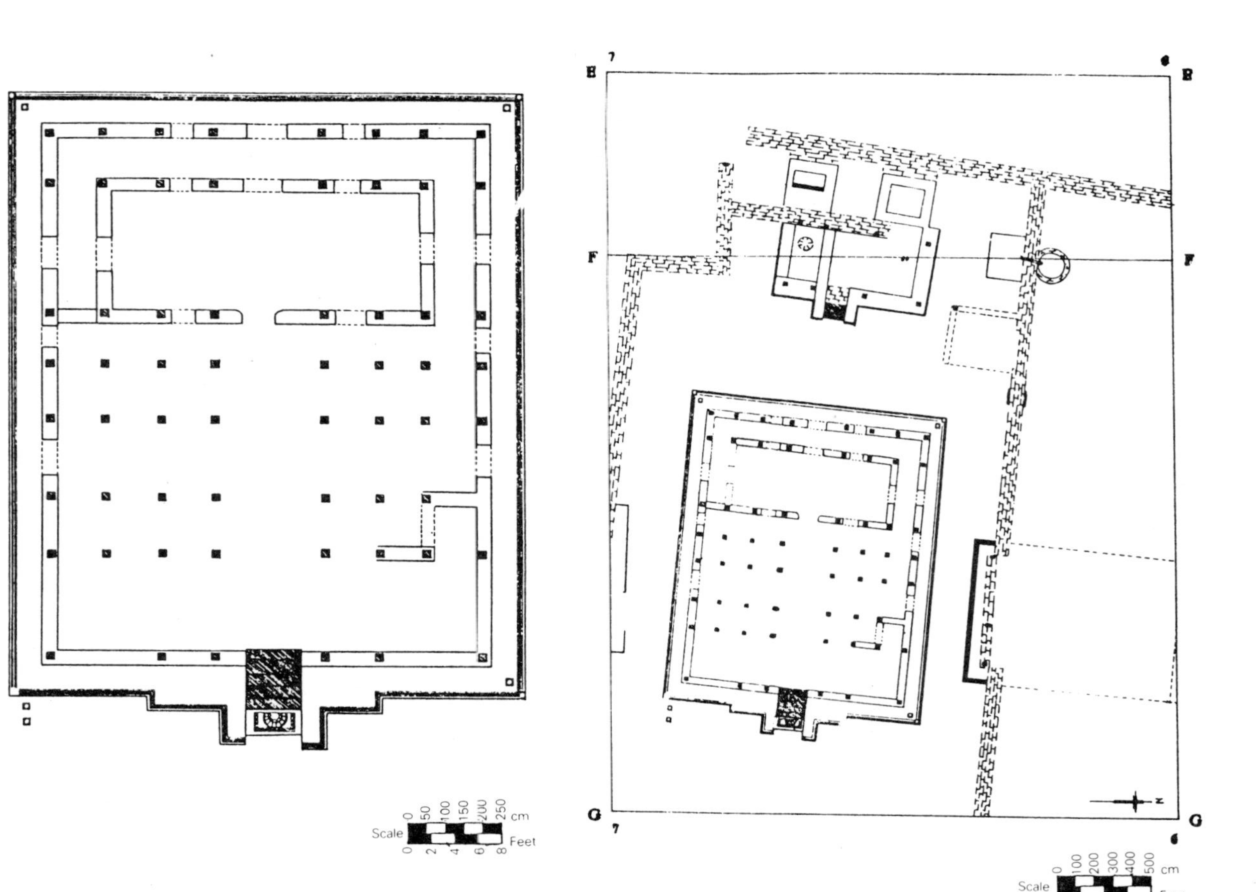

Figure 11.5 Chapter house (newly discovered). (a) Plan of the 'Simaghara' area. (b) Ground plan of the 'Simaghara'.

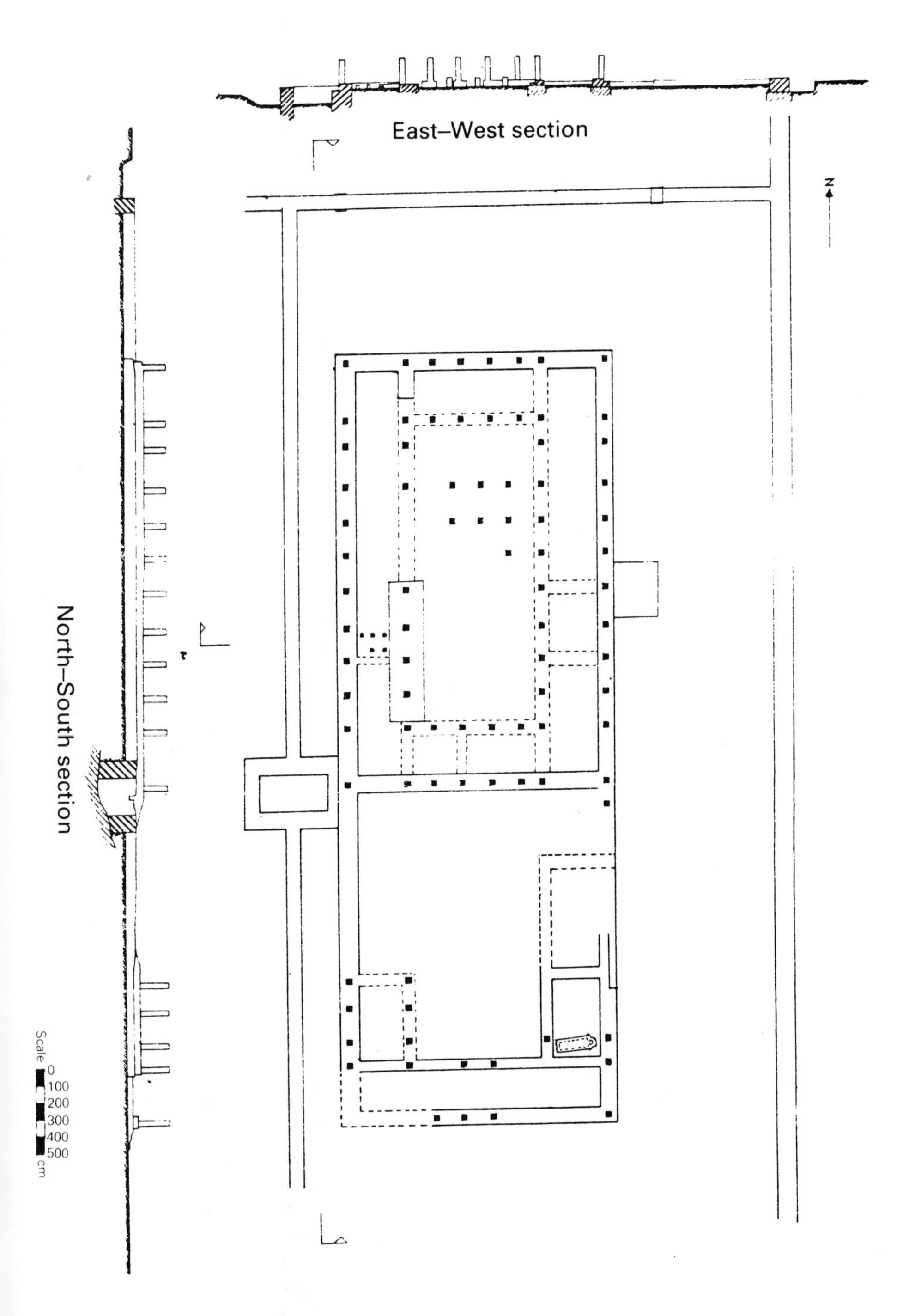

Figure 11.6 Monk's Hospital (newly discovered).

The excavations to the south of the main hillock revealed the first hospital building discovered from Polonnaruva (Fig. 11.6). Being located within the monastery, it would be correct to surmise that this is a monks' hospital. The structure is rectangular in plan (44.85 × 33.30 m) and is divided into two sections, the living area and the treatment area with refectory and toilet facilities. The living area consists of an inner court which bears stone stilts to hold a Buddha shrine, probably of timber construction (Prematilleke 1986). The living apartments were located around the court. The layout of the area set apart for the refectory and for medical treatment is similar. One of the rooms here contains a medicinal trough, hollowed out of a solid stone, in the shape of a human body (Fig. 11.7). These troughs were used to immerse the patients in medicinal oils and herbal juices, for the treatment of ailments such as rheumatism, snake-bites, etc. The practice of treating snake-bite patients with oil or herbal baths in wooden troughs is in vogue even today in *Ayurvedic* (native) medicine. The excavations at the hospital site also revealed several artefacts that threw light on the types of medical and surgical equipment used. Several medicine grinders and fragments of Chinese jars, some with stamped-in logos of the manufacturers, were also among the finds. These are products of the Sung period, and provide evidence for dating of the artefacts (10th to 12th centuries AD) (Prematilleke 1982). The hospital also provides concrete evidence for the continuance of the traditional practice of medical care used in early times as exemplified by the hospitals at Mihintale (8th century AD), Anurādhapura and Medirigiriya.

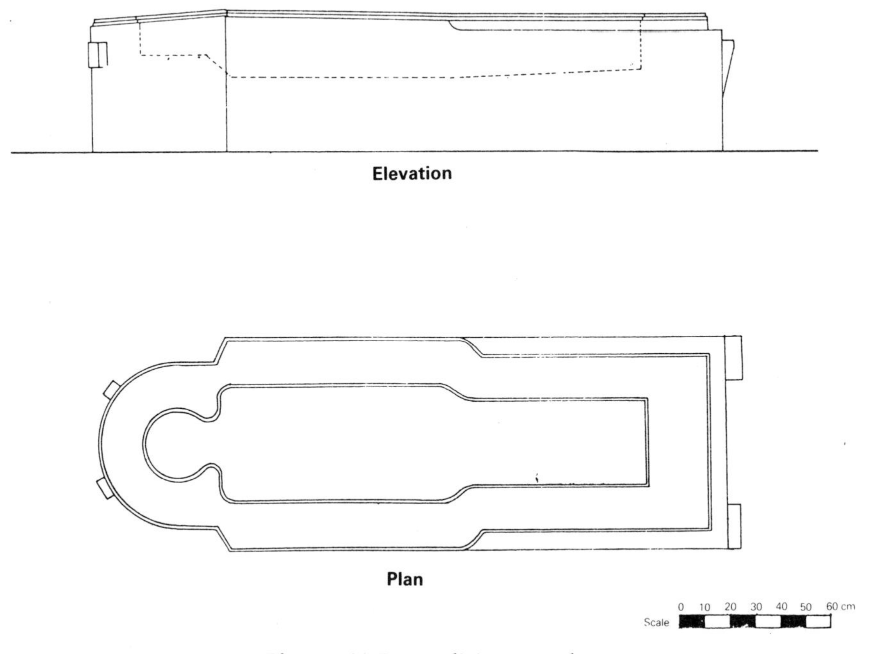

Figure 11.7 Medicine trough.

The recent excavations have exposed a wealth of materials that help reconstruction of the history of the monastery in particular and the Polonnaruva period in general. A mass of ceramics, both local and foreign, metal objects, glassware, stoneware, coins, beads and bangles, burial pots containing human bones and stone inscriptions are among the finds (Prematilleke 1982).

The local pottery of the *Ālāhaṇa Pariveṇa* is numerous and varied. These include begging bowls of Buddhist monks, refectory and kitchen utensils, lamps, stools and tiles. The typology of pottery in preparation will provide an insight into the evolution of potters' products through the ages. The imported items consist of Chinese ceramics, particularly of the Sung period (960–1279 AD). Some of these that carried the manufacturer's mark are quite valuable to the archaeologist. These objects demonstrate the relations which were conducted with China during this age. The metal objects range from weapons of all types to styli used for writing on palm leaves and copper plaques, helmets, chalices, lamps, etc. Hundreds of coins found here are issues of the Polonnaruva kings. Of particular interest and significance are the rare issues of smaller denominations of Parakramabahu. The earthenware pots of various sizes containing human bone fragments are of interest for the study of the significance of the monastery complex of *Ālāhaṇa Pariveṇa* as a cremation site (Prematilleke 1982). A fair number of epigraphical records were executed by the rulers of Polonnaruva, particularly Parakramabahu and Nissankamalla, both of the 12th century. These refer to various activities of the rulers, largely of a benevolent nature. A few of these records are of immense value in the study of the history and character of the monastery.

Besides the Buddhist remains, the monastery site accommodates a number of monuments dedicated to the worship of Siva. These follow the traditional Dravidian architectural forms of the Colas and Pandyans (Parnavitana 1954–5). The influence exerted by Dravida norms of architecture and decorative norms on the existing Buddhist tradition is fairly evident. Nevertheless, this late synthesis has not marred the continuation of the indigenous styles that had evolved through the preceding centuries.

It is noticeable that the western part of the *Ālāhaṇa Pariveṇa* monastery is studded with many Hindu shrines. Perhaps this area had been occupied by the Colas before the establishment of the second great capital of the Sinhala monarchy. The numerous bangle pieces and beds, quite similar to the many Dravidian artefacts discovered in the area, further suggests their habitation in this locality.

The surface evidence and excavated stratified data point to the occupation of the monastery for a period of about four centuries, though the literary evidence takes the period of foundation of Buddhist monasteries in Polonnaruva to the 8th century (Paranavitana 1954–5). The structural evidence and occupational layers indicate a characteristic process of building over the sites of older edifices which could have perished from natural causes or been devastated by enemies. There are instances where monastic cells were constructed over filled-up wells or refuse pits of an earlier era. In the 12th century a large number of monuments built by

Parakramabahu have been attributed to his successor, Nissankamalla, who is credited with the largest number of epigraphical records enumerating his own benevolent contributions to Buddhism. In several instances building materials from an earlier period are found which have been used for the construction of structures of the succeeding age. This is most evident in the re-use of stone pillars, stairways, etc. Sometimes pillars bearing inscriptions of about the 10th century have been found used as reinforcements on later structures.

The foregoing evidence in respect of the *Ālāhaṇa Pariveṇa* brings out many salient features of a medieval Buddhist monastic complex. It has already been noted that the *Ālāhaṇa Pariveṇa* had been so named by the chronicler because the monastery had been used for the cremation of monks and royalty. The small *stūpa* mounds scattered over the site are evidently such edifices, enshrining the ashes of the dead. However, recent evidence from excavations tends to support the use of the area as a cremation ground even before the establishment of the monastery. For instance, a pillar inscription bearing 10th-century script, discovered at the eastern end of the monastery, refers to the boundaries of the areas set apart for cremation of the dead (Prematilleke 1982). The Cola occupation of this area before the founding of the monastery has already been referred to. Among the burials discovered one was that of an infant, which indicates the use of this cemetery for the laity at some previous time. Thus, new evidence supports the existence of a cremation ground at the site and, even after building the monastery, its function as a cemetery was continued, but was limited to the *Sangha* and royalty.

The monastic layout of the *Ālāhaṇa Pariveṇa* is evidence for the furthest continuation for the monastery plan of the *pabbata-vihāra* type noted above. The excavations around the central terrace revealed the arrangement of the dwelling cells in a somewhat regular order. The southern area apparently formed separate quadrangular cells together with the monks' hospital.

However, the *Ālāhaṇa Pariveṇa* complex does not indicate all the features of a preplanned monastic complex as seen in such sites as *Pācinatissa-pabbata vihāra*. There is no moat running round the vihara at the lowest terrace level. The four paths at the four cardinal directions are also absent at *Ālāhaṇa*. In having the monastery built on a hillock, with several tiers below accommodating the living cells, the *Ālāhaṇa* shows a *pabbata-vihāra* in its natural setting.

The central edifices such as *Lankātilaka* and the *Baddhasīmāpāsāda*, depict the zenith in the development of plans and designs found in the smaller and unpretentious buildings of the earlier period. The distinctive architectural features at this stage seem to be a successful blending of local idiom with extraneous Dravida norms. 'Elaboration of detail at the expense of form', a characteristic of stylistic variation found in India, may also be noted in medieval Lanka. The South Indian preference for over-ornamentation or ornate character found its full expression in the image shrines of Polonnaruva.

The Cola occupation and the resultant construction of Hindu shrines accounts for the particular character of medieval Polonnaruva art and architecture. Decorative features on the exterior wall, representing *pāsādas* with figures of *Brahmas* and Gods, and the characteristic *kudu* and *Pañjara* motifs, are found amidst the ornamental norms of Buddhist architecture of Polonnaruva as exemplified by the *Thupārāma*, *Lankāyilaka*, and *Tivanka* image house (Paranavitana 1954–5).However, the basic architectural principles do not seem to have been changed by this synthesis as is evident from Polonnaruva. The Dravida norms of buildings, their plinth types, pillars, etc., as found in the Hindu shrines, are distinctly different from Buddhist architectural styles (Paranavitana 1954–5). The structural principles such as vaulted roofs are also retained, as against the non-vaulted horizontal roof forms of the Dravidians. The corbel-arch continued even though the principles of the true arch appear to be known. The spanning of space in the totally brick-built image house combined the corbel and true arch forms. In brief, the architecture as presented by Buddhist and Hindu shrines of *Ālāhaṇa Parivaṇa* complex and elsewhere in Polonnaruva portrays a blending of decorative features, while remaining distinctive in basic building plan.

The *Ālāhaṇa* monastery complex epitomizes the religious symbolism of the early and medieval periods of Sri Lanka as seen in the strict institutionalization of the monks' Order through the intervention of the monarchy. The unification of the different schools or sects of the Order of monks (whose conduct was at a low ebb at the end of the early Anurādhapura period), through the royal authority of Parakramabahu, testifies to the previous divergence of religious thought. The Theravada system was well established during medieval times, but inscriptional evidence discovered during recent excavations (Prematilleke 1986) indicates the presence in the *Ālāhaṇa* complex of believers in the Mahayona doctrine. The existence of Hindu monuments both within and without the complex testifies to the religious tolerance that existed in the *Sangha* as well as the monarchy.

The affluence and self-sufficiency achieved during this period in terms of food and shelter, and the trade relations that were established with India, Arabia, South East Asia and China, must have had beneficial effects on monastic life, as indicated by large monastic complexes such as the *Alāhaṇa Pariveṇa*, which would easily have accommodated two to three thousand monks. Numerous artefacts such as imported ceramics, especially Sungware from China, a newly discovered bronze chest probably of Arabic origin, gilt bronze objects, glassware and beads, etc. all indicate the intensive and cordial relations that the political and religious authorities had with the other countries during medieval times.

The abandonment of the capital at Polonnaruva in the 13th century, and its shift from the dry zone to the wet zone in the south-western part of the island, seem to have caused lasting changes in the religious sphere. A new socio-economic order introduced through the influence of the Western world brought about a revolution in religious thought. The early period of monastic architecture virtually ended in Polonnaruva, and new trends in religious architecture are exemplified by the 14th-century image shrine of *Lankātilaka*, in the Kandy district. This new synthesis may be related to the architectural styles of Vijayanagara in India, which were direct successors of the Pallavas and Cola architectural idioms.

References

Bandaranayake, S. 1974. *Sinhalese monastic architecture*, Leiden: Brill.

Bell, H. C. P. 1891. *Archaeological Survey of Ceylon Annual Report.*

Dutt, S. 1962. *Buddhist monks and monasteries of India.* London.

Hocart, A. M. 1926. *Memoirs of the Archaeological Survey of Ceylon* **3**.

Paranavitana, S. 1954–5. The art and architecture of the Polonnaruva period. *The Ceylon Historical Journal* **5**.

Prematilleke, P. L. 1964. *Religious architecture and sculpture of Ceylon (Anuradhapura period).* University of London, unpublished Ph. D. thesis.

Prematilleke, P. L. 1982a. First Archaeological Excavation Report, Ministry of Cultural Affairs, Colombo.

Prematilleke, P. L. 1982b. Second Archaeological Excavation Report. Ministry of Cultural Affairs, Colombo.

Prematilleke, P. L. 1982c. Third Archaeological Excavation Report. Ministry of Cultural Affairs, Colombo.

Prematilleke, P. L. 1986. Fourth Archaeological Excavation Report. Ministry of Cultural Affairs, Colombo.

Prematilleke, L. & R. Silva 1969. A Buddhist monastery type of ancient Ceylon showing Mahayanist influence. *Artibus Asiae* **30**.

B. Smith, 1978. *Religion and legitimation of power in Sri Lanka.* Chambersburg, Pennsylvania.

12 *Value, ranking and consumption in the European Bronze Age*

KRISTIAN KRISTIANSEN

It has been generally observed that in the early sequence of bronze technology, the deposition of artefacts in ritual hoards is more frequent than in burials (Kristiansen 1987). In this chapter, I propose that ritual hoarding is distinguished from burial ritual by the fact that it is linked primarily to a communal ideology, and represents a different form of *value* from that associated with the burial of outstanding individuals. A difference in value is also expressed in the context of deposition. Hiding artefacts at sacred places, for example, in bogs and in rivers or under large stones, can be contrasted with the public display of wealth offered by the family or group in the burial ritual. Thus the change from ritual hoarding to burial deposition would seem to indicate important social and ideological changes in the evaluation of status.

The social aspects of consumption

The Early Bronze Age of northern Europe is characterized by a rather simple tool kit which replaced already existing stone and flint forms, such as axes and later daggers (Kristiansen 1987). Important new configurations were introduced with the bronze lance and the long sword, this latter innovation representing an important new element in warfare, which must be expected to have had some social implications. Female prestige goods are absent during the Early Bronze Age, but there are a series of developments in this area which emerge following the introduction of new complex weapons and male prestige goods. Here also, a variety of new ornament types are introduced.

We can thus observe two trends:

(a) a development from general forms of prestige goods towards more specific forms; and
(b) a development from male dominance in the employment of prestige goods in social and ritual consumption towards a more balanced male–female relationship.

It has often been argued that these developments reflect a technological evolution in specialist skills. Although this cannot be totally ruled out, I believe that we should rather see technology as a dependent variable that responds to social needs. Technology does not determine the development of status diversity. It can be argued rather that, following the initial phase of the application of bronze technology, there existed a constant potential, but that this was not realized until the demands for more complex forms arose at the level of consumption.

The question then is, how are we to understand this development towards technological and typological complexity? Without going into detail, it can be argued that it represents a development from more general forms of rank linked to traditional prestige goods towards the emergence of social complexity expressed in new and more specific forms of prestige goods. In the initial phase these prestige goods of bronze imitated those of stone and were channelled into the communal ritual sphere. Here they coexisted for some time along with traditional prestige goods of stone, bone, etc., that were still employed in burial consumption. Prestige goods of bronze were thus excluded from individual consumption and competition. However, this pattern was broken through the consolidation of supplies of bronze. Bronze now became employed in burial consumption and, as we shall see, it further became involved in the development of social hierarchy. In northern Europe this is reflected in the establishment of ritual chiefs who were separated from chiefly warriors in burial equipment, and also in terms of their function in relation to actual warfare. Chiefly swords, as opposed to those of the warriors, were rarely used or sharpened. Chiefly swords are heavy and full hilted, whereas warrior swords are lighter and flange hilted. Similar distinctions may be made with respect to female prestige goods.

This is a completely different pattern from that found in the Early Bronze Age. The interesting question now becomes, what were the mechanisms which made such a development possible? I believe that the key to this puzzle may be found in the impact of ideology.

The ideological context of value and ranking

As has already been noted, it is a significant feature of the early phase of bronze technology that prestige goods of bronze were employed within the traditional communal ritual, but are not found as grave goods. There is no indication that new rituals or belief systems were adopted, and continuity and tradition appear to be stressed through the imitation of stone and flint forms. Bronze axes further indicate a rather close relationship between subsistence production and prestige goods production, in that they could be employed both as tools and as prestige goods. This employment of bronze axes in the realms of both subsistence and communal ritual indicates the forms of control held by the local community. Chiefs were not able to monopolize and sustain either subsistence or ritual on a permanent basis.

A few hundred years later the situation is completely changed. By now bronze axes have disappeared as prestige goods. They have been replaced by a variety of new personal prestige goods. For males these are linked to warfare and ritual, and for females to personal adornment. Prestige goods are separated from the sphere of subsistence production which is now under the control of chiefly families as the economic basis for their monopoly of alliances and the exchanges of these prestige goods in bronze. A new elaborate religious system, with a complex set of ritual paraphernalia, has developed which may have been used to legitimate these privileged positions of power and prestige. This interpretation is further supported by new and more efficient weapons and a new organization of warfare. Chiefs are thereby able to demonstrate their power and superiority in two ways:

(a) by employing new ritual spheres, which they controlled, as a means to mediate in the provision of access to these new goods; and
(b) by acting as war-leaders, through their access to weapons and military technique, which they also controlled.

The origins of these changes may be located in the spread of two related phenomena: the lance and long sword, and a new ideology of aristocratic warfare that formed part of a new religion. The spread of the long sword should not be considered merely as a technological and military innovation, however important it appears to have been with respect to these spheres. The long sword was also part of an ideologically charged military complex that spread from the Eastern Mediterranean and Asia Minor throughout Europe during the first half of the second millennium. Also associated with this complex is the use of war chariots and stools as symbols of chiefly dignity.

It was this combination of new efficient weapons and the ideology of a warrior aristocracy that allowed leading individuals to separate themselves from the community and sustain and legitimize their new positions. The monopoly of ideological information subsequently came to achieve an important function in the continued legitimation of the chiefly aristocracies throughout the European Bronze Age.

Conclusion

I propose that traditional tribal and communal belief systems and systems of minor ranking were gradually undermined and manipulated by the establishment of long-distance exchange networks. These linked the tribal groups of Europe together in a new prestige-goods ideology. When the system was amplified by a combination of new military innovations and a matching ideology of ruling élites, the foundation was laid for the development of new tribal hierarchies. Such an explanation puts the long-disputed evidence for so-called Mycenaean influence in northern Europe into its proper perspective. It was clearly the manipulation of such social and ideological value systems that triggered social evolution. The impact of the subsistence economy was only determining in the sense that it set barriers. Such barriers are evidenced in the regional cyclical developments of exchange networks and consumption based on local cycles of over-exploitation and ecological deterioration, but the dynamics of the system was rooted in the social and ideological organization of society. In particular distinct forms of value expressed in the circulation of material items are crucial for understanding the transformation of social rank in this period.

Reference

Kristiansen, K. 1987. From stone to bronze: the evolution of social complexity in northern Europe, 23,000–1,200 BC. In *Specialization, exchange and complex Societies* E. M. Brumfiel & T. Earle (eds), 30–51. Cambridge: Cambridge University Press.

13 *Marxist perspectives on social organization in the central European Early Bronze Age*

SIMON MAYS

Introduction

Following the rise of the so–called 'New Archaeology', there was a marked increase in the number of archaeological studies attempting to understand social organization, and explain social change, in prehistory. Various theoretical approaches have been used, but the one which is considered here is the Marxist perspective. This standpoint has been used in the analysis of a wide range of social forms, from Palaeolithic hunter-gatherers (Gilman 1984) to late prehispanic Mesoamerican civilizations (Gledhill 1984). Marxist models have also been used in studies of social organization in the European Early Bronze Age (for example Otto 1955, Gilman 1981).

A central aspect of the Marxist approach is its emphasis on the role of exploitative relations between social subgroups as a cause of social change. A problem here is that it is difficult to know to what extent the concept of exploitation can be applied to past social forms. For instance, it could be argued that an emphasis on exploitative relations as a cause of social change is appropriate for analysing the civilizations of classical Greece and Rome. De Ste Croix (1975, p. 57) has commented that:

> the essential problem in every civilised country is how to extract a sufficient surplus from the primary producers in order to give at least some people enough leisure time for government, the arts and sciences, and other necessities and luxuries of civilised life. The technological level of the Greco-Roman world was a great deal lower than is generally realised . . . . In such a society, unless everyone is to have to work nearly all the time, some means has to be found of screwing a substantial surplus out of the lowest class. The Greeks and Romans, among other means, employed slaves for this purpose.

Thus, in this case, exploitation (in the form of slavery) was necessary to sustain the society, hence a Marxist model would seem to be appropriate here: a consideration of the exploitative relationships between social classes would be vital for understanding social organization and social change.

But what of smaller-scale societies, in which no such large body of non-producers exists? Here, it could be argued, exploitation of the primary producers is not a necessity for sustaining the social system, so there are no *a priori* grounds for assuming the existence of exploitative social relations in precapitalist societies.

Amongst Marxist-oriented anthropologists and social scientists there is disagreement concerning the extent to which the concept of exploitation can be applied to pre-capitalist societies. For example, in those social formations termed segmentary lineage societies by anthropologists, Meillassoux (1981) and Rey (1975, 1979) clearly believe that definite forms of exploitation exist, a point accepted by Terray (1975, 1979) in his later work. However, Godelier (1977, Deluz & Godelier 1967) and Hindess & Hirst (1975), argue that it is not a feature of these social forms. They distinguish between appropriation of surplus, on the one hand, and exploitation, on the other; this allows for the existence of functional authority of the sort described by Sahlins (1958, 1968), and Netting (1972), among others.

In addition, ethnographic studies (for example, Bohannan 1958, Sahlins 1963, 1968, Fortes & Evans-Pritchard 1940, Howe 1978) seem to show that in many small-scale societies high-status individuals or chiefs may wield insufficient power to exploit their subjects.

Despite the above, many archaeological studies seem to make the assumption that exploitation was a feature of prehistoric societies. For example, Gilman, in a study of social organization in the European Early Bronze Age, takes as the starting point for his analysis the question, 'In spite of the fact that their actions do not serve common interests, how do élites establish and maintain control?' (Gilman 1981, p. 4), arguing that the assumption of an exploitative role for a social élite 'constitutes a more uniformitarian view of social process in stratified societies' (1981, p. 8). In Gilman's model the power of the social élite to exploit their subjects derives from control over subsistence resources.

A major aim of this chapter is to try to discern whether there is any archaeological evidence for the existence of exploitation in a society in an area of central Europe during the Early Bronze Age.

A useful operational definition of exploitation in the Marxist sense is due to Tilley. He defines it as 'a situation in which an individual or group of non-producers appropriates the surplus product created by the labour of direct producers, which is then harnessed to further the sectional interests of these non-producers' (Tilley 1984, p. 112). In this light it was thought appropriate to investigate the way in which a person's material existence varies with his or her social status.

It was also thought important to study the question of freedom of access to social positions. Many previous writers (for example, Otto 1955, Childe 1958, Gimbutas 1965, Gilman 1981) have associated the earlier European Bronze Age with the rise of hereditary social ranking, at least for higher-status individuals. Anthropologists have noted the relationship between the degree of freedom of access to social positions, and the amount of power wielded by an élite (and hence the degree to which they are able to exploit the rest of society). Comparing societies in which high status is achieved with those in which it is inherited, Terray (1975, p. 96) has said of the former that 'some of the exploited one day will become the exploiters, and the hope of such promotion inevitably reduces the sharpness of conflicts'. He also makes the point that, when social divisions are based on age and sex, it is easier for such divisions to be portrayed as 'natural', hence it is more difficult for the lower-status individuals to act as a class 'for themselves', i.e., to become conscious of themselves and thus have the potential for collective action in pursuit of their common interests. However, this sort of argument may also be applicable to the élite or chiefly class. It could be suggested that in cases where access to these high-status positions is via personal qualities or achievements, as opposed to being strictly hereditary, then this may tend to inhibit the élite from forming a class 'for themselves' and exploiting the rest of the community in pursuit of their own sectional interests. For example, among the Cuna of North-East Panama there are always rivals among the élite to the paramount chief. Hence, if a chief makes himself unpopular among his followers, then factionalization may occur and he may be supplanted by another chief: 'Thus one of the most effective limitations on what a chief can do is the scrutiny and resistance of other chiefs' (Howe 1978, p. 544). Hence, in this case Cuna chiefly power is severely limited by divisions and rivalries. This factor also helps to ensure the efficacy of several other social conventions, discussed by Howe (1978), which act to limit the power of a chief. The ultimate sanction behind all these is the removal of an undesirable chief from office; although this may not happen often, it is this possibility that ensures the efficacy of the social constraints on power. It will inevitably be rather easier to do this if there are rival chiefs with whom to replace him, rather than if the chiefs act as a class 'for themselves' and provide mutual support for each other's actions to safeguard their own sectional interests at the expense of the rest of the community. It is consistent with the arguments of Terray (1975, 1979) that chiefs will be more likely to act as a class 'for themselves' if they are united by ties of blood, than if they were a disparate group lacking such kinship ties. Hence, in the former case it might be expected that social constraints on chiefly power, of the sorts discussed by Howe (1978), might be less effective.

Elsewhere (Mays 1987) I have investigated aspects of diet and disease stress, together with a study of the distribution of physical labour within society. In this chapter some initial results are summarized concerning access to social positions and aspects of dietary variation with respect to social status.

Materials and methods

The database for this study comprises the material from the cemetery at Hainburg, in Lower Austria. The site lies near the south bank of the Danube, 11 km west of Bratislava. A total of 258 flatgraves were revealed by excavations in the 1930s, of which two were cremations. In terms of material culture it belongs to the Wieselburg or Gata group (Schubert 1973), a local subgroup of the Early Bronze Age Únětice culture. A typological study of the artefacts from the site (Schubert 1973) indicates that it belongs in the later part of the Early Bronze Age, Br A2 in Reinecke's (1924) terminology. It was probably in use sometime between about 2000 and 1800 BC.

Social organization was investigated primarily using this cemetery material. Univariate and multivariate statistical techniques were used to study the distribution of grave good types, and an investigation of energy expenditure in mortuary ritual was undertaken using an analysis of grave wealth.

Diet is an important aspect of an individual's physical conditions of life, and preferential access to valued food resources by higher-status individuals has often been thought to be an important aspect in studies of social complexity (for example, Fried 1967). In this light it was thought appropriate to investigate the way in which an individual's diet varies with social status. Chemical analysis for bone strontium was a technique used to investigate diet. In order to study the question of achieved versus ascribed social status, an analysis of patterning in inherited aspects of skeletal form was undertaken, and the results were compared with inferences made from the distribution of grave good types and grave wealth.

Analysis of diet

Differential access to valued food resources according to social status does seem to be a characteristic of some chiefdom societies (Hatch & Giedel 1985). Ethnographic and archaeological evidence suggests that in many cases meat constitutes such a valued resource (Schoeninger 1979, Brown & Blakely 1985). The meat : vegetable ratio of prehistoric diets may be investigated using analysis of bone strontium.

The behaviour of strontium in the biosphere is such that it undergoes fractionation through the terrestrial food chain. Meat therefore contains generally lower levels than vegetable foods (Schroeder *et al.* 1972). Research using laboratory animals (Rheingold *et al.* 1983) has demonstrated a firm relationship between dietary and skeletal levels of strontium; bone strontium levels thus vary with the meat : vegetable ratio of the diet. Studies suggest that in many cases strontium levels in bone from archaeological contexts can be thought of as indicative of those in life (Lambert *et al.* 1979, 1982, 1983, 1984, 1985, Mays 1983, Sillen 1981). Aspects of the results for the material under study indicate that this is also likely to be true for Hainburg. Bone was analysed for strontium using atomic absorption spectrophotometry.

Analysis of artefactual grave inclusions allowed the burials to be ranked on a continuous scale of wealth. In addition, analysis of the occurrence of certain imported artefactual types (e.g. amber beads) and sociotechnic items (*sensu* Binford 1962) allowed the isolation of a group of 31 burials which could be considered as distinct from the rest of the cemetery on the basis of both grave wealth and the type of artefacts they contained. Thus, in order to study dietary variation with social status, the way in which bone strontium varied with grave wealth for the whole sample was investigated, and the bone strontium content of the distinctive 'rich burials' was compared with that for the rest of the cemetery. In the analysis males and females were treated separately, since there is evidence for the existence of physiological differences in strontium metabolism between the sexes (discussion in Sillen & Kavanagh 1982).

Results

A scattergram of bone strontium against grave wealth was drawn up, and a regression analysis was performed on the data. This indicated that only 2 per cent of the variability in bone strontium was accounted for by variability in grave wealth for both sexes. Not surprisingly, in view of this result, no significant difference in mean strontium levels was found between the so-called 'rich group' graves and the rest of the cemetery, for either males or females. Thus, there is no evidence here of any status-related dietary differences.

Analysis of freedom of access to status positions

At Hainburg the mean wealth score for sub-adults (i.e. those aged less than 18 years) was only 48 per cent of that for adults, this difference being significant at the 0.5 per cent level. Furthermore, of the 31 'rich' graves only three were of sub-adults.

In the early application of the methodology of the New Archaeology to mortuary data, the finding of rich-child burials was interpreted as suggesting ascribed social status (for example Saxe 1970), since achievements at such an early age would have been negligible. However, there are indications that inferences here should be made with caution. Ethnographic evidence shows that differential treatment of young children may be due to different attitudes to death in these cases than to adult deaths, rather than to social status differences (for example, Ucko 1969, Pader 1982, p. 62). Furthermore, the death of a child of high-status parents may be used as an opportunity for the parents to display their wealth or social standing: rich-child burials may reflect not the child's social status, but that of its parents (Shennan 1982, O'Shea 1984, pp. 251–2). Braun (1979, p. 72) has argued that if the burial treatment of a child is expected to follow the social position of its surviving family, then at some point in life the mortuary treatment of an individual must shift to the representation of that individual's own social identities. Citing van Gennep, Braun argues that this shift often occurs around puberty. Hence, the interpretation of rich-child burials as primarily reflecting the social status of the parents would appear to be more applicable to young children than to adolescents. In this context it is interesting to note that the three sub-adults in the 'rich group' are all aged 6 years or less. It could be that burial by high-status parents might best explain their presence here, rather than ascribed social status. It is thus argued that the analysis of the grave goods suggests that social status is, at least primarily, achieved rather than ascribed.

Study of inherited skeletal traits

An individual's genotype, or genetic make-up, is manifested in his skeletal remains in two ways: metrical variation (i.e. variability in the size and shape of the bones) and non-metrical variation. This last takes the form of minor variations, such as additional foramina, variation in sutural patterns or presence of supernumary ossicles. In this study both metric and non-metric variation are investigated.

Both environmental and genetic factors play a part in determining skeletal form, so it was thought appropriate to select for use in the study only those metric and non-metric traits for which there is direct evidence that the genetic component in their causation is sufficient to render them useful for the study of genetic relationships between individuals in human skeletal series. A literature survey revealed 21 non-metric and 19 metric traits that fulfilled this criterion and were appropriate for study in the skeletal material from Hainburg. These aspects of skeletal variation were analysed using multivariate statistical techniques, and the results were compared with inferences concerning social status made from the analysis of mortuary variability. The results showed no evidence of an inherited component to social status at Hainburg.

Summary of results

Analysis for bone strontium revealed no significant dietary variation with social status. Analysis of the distribution of grave wealth and of non-metric and metric skeletal variation revealed no evidence of an ascribed component to social status.

Discussion

The results suggest that a traditional Marxist model of the sort described by Gilman (1981) may be inappropriate for this data set. The strontium analysis gave no indication of any inequalities in the distribution of food resources according to social rank, and the lack of an inherited component to social status argues against the vision of a permanently differentiated ruling élite.

The settlement data could be viewed as consistent with these results. It seems that a two-level settlement hierarchy existed in the transition from the Early to Middle Bronze Age in central Europe. Defended settlements are known, and it is possible that these formed some sort of regional centres (Vladár 1973, Točík & Vladár 1971, Oždáni 1986). However, these defended settlements appear to post-date the Hainburg cemetery: there seems to be an absence, in these sites, of artefact types characteristic of the Hainburg material, and many of the bronze artefacts (or stone moulds thereof) are of early Middle Bronze Age forms (e,g. the hoard of axe-heads at Nitriansky-Hrádok – Točík 1981 – or the stone mould for heart-shaped pendents, found at Veselé – Točík 1964. There is no evidence for any settlement hierarchy contemporary with the cemetery at Hainburg. What evidence there is seems to indicate small, undefended sites; for example, the settlement at Grossmugl (Beninger 1941). This lies in Lower Austria, about 65 km north-west of Hainburg, and the finds indicate that the two sites are probably contemporary (e.g. a spherical-headed bronze pin of the type characteristic of the later phase at Hainburg was found at Grossmugl). What were interpreted as six house plans were located in the excavation of this open settlement.

Calculations from cemetery data also point to small community size: using data from Nitra group cemeteries, Shennan (1975) estimated a community size of approximately 30–40 people. Thus, the settlement data also tend to argue against the sorts of social divisions implicit in Gilman's (1981) model.

It was therefore thought appropriate to explore the relevence of alternative social models to that of Gilman to the Early Bronze Age data. One such model is the segmentary lineage society: that in which there is rule by elders, and in which social status is achieved rather than inherited. It was thought possible that this type of model might be more appropriate to the data under study. In a Marxist perspective the position of high-ranking individuals within society is based on their control over access to valued resources. In a traditional Marxist model material items (such as subsistence goods) constitute these valued resources, but in these types of society it has been suggested (Meillassoux 1981) that elders achieve and maintain their position not via control of access to material goods, but by controlling the exchange of brides between communities. Meillassoux (1964, 1981) has studied this type of social organization among the Guro of the Ivory Coast. Women circulate between communities in exchange for material goods or bridewealth, which represents the future claim to a bride by the wife-giving community, rather than payment for the bride. The elders control these transactions; hence, possession of bridewealth distinguishes an elder from other members of the community. Thus, bridewealth goods represent both the rank of an elder and the promise of a woman for that elder's community. These goods tend to be durable luxury items, and Meillassoux (1981, Ch. 4) has shown how they may acquire general exchange value. He suggests that elders exert social control over subordinate males, or juniors, by controlling the distribution of brides. Divisions in this sort of society are thus based on personal qualities or achievements, and on gender.

As was briefly discussed above, Meillassoux (1981) claims that in these societies definite forms of exploitation exist, as does Rey (1979), though the latter seems to be discussing societies in which there is inherited components to social status. Terray (1975, 1979), although accepting the existence of exploitation, argues that it will generally occur to a lesser extent than in societies with a permanently differentiated élite, since all elders have once been juniors and, assuming achieved social status, all juniors have the opportunity to become elders.

In addition, the power of elders over women and low-status men may, in reality, be somewhat limited. Meillassoux, in a general discussion of social organization of this type, states that junior men may be consulted by elders over decisions that effect the whole community (Meillassoux 1981, p. 79), and he criticizes Rey (1975) for over-reliance on historical examples of lineage-based societies that had contacts with European slavers; here the elder's treatment of lower-status men was undoubtedly influenced by the Europeans' wish to purchase them as slaves. In these cases exploitative relations certainly existed between elders and juniors, but clearly it is not safe to extrapolate this finding to pre-contact societies. Meillassoux (1981, p. 76) also notes that women may occupy positions of status and authority in these societies, though he claims this is fairly uncommon.

In a study of lineage-based societies in the Ivory Coast and Ghana, Terray (1975) shows that the degree of exploitation may be variable: e.g. among the Abron and the Kulango, men do most of the work involving the cultivation of the staple crop, in contrast with the situation among the neighbouring Dida, though in both cases men and women eat similar diets regardless of who contributed most to the raising of the crop. Among the Duna of the Southern New Guinea Highlands there is little evidence of exploitative relations between the sexes in the subsistence sphere since 'approximately equal labour inputs are rewarded with equal shares in consumption' (Modjeska 1982, p. 85). The elder's authority generally seems to rest more on the respect and agreement of the rest of the community than on power as such; elders who attempt to misuse their positions to try and exploit others may fall from office (e.g. among the Dida, Terray 1972, p. 170). However, Deluz & Godelier (1967) and Godelier (1977) argue that exploitation is not a feature of this type of social formation, as do Hindess & Hirst (1975). The above writers argue that elders, rather than being exploitative, perform important co-ordinating and regulating functions, particularly in the subsistence sphere. It would therefore seem to be important to distinguish division of labour from exploitation. In a study in the New Guinea highlands, Sillitoe suggests that the nature of the sexual division of labour inhibits the rise of an exploitative élite and allows individual households to be fairly independent. Thus, the structure of the 'relations of production' (or the division of labour) may not facilitate exploitation but obviate it (Sillitoe 1985, p. 516).

The analysis of grave wealth at Hainburg showed that the graves of adult females were significantly (at the 0.5 per cent level) more wealthy than those of adult males, the artefacts in question generally being decorative items of dress (e.g. amber beads). Hodder conducted a study of groups in northern Kenya whose social organization is similar to that described above. He states that: 'From an elder's point of view, women should be displayed as objects of exchange. The main way in which this is achieved is through dress. By extensive decoration of the female body with beads, bangles and baubles, symbolic reference is made to prestige value' (Hodder 1985, p. 154). By analogy with this example, it could be suggested that at Hainburg the rich grave goods in the female burials symbolize their role in a bridal exchange network, and hence their value to the community.

In these types of society women tend to move between communities, going to live in the settlement of their husband's family on marriage (patrilocality; see Meillassoux 1981, Hodder 1985, Rey 1979). In this situation many of the men in a particular community would be closely related to one another (e.g. brothers would live in the same settlement), whereas this would be less so for the women (sisters might well go and live with husbands in different villages). Previous studies have demonstrated the utility of metric (Spence 1973) and non-metric (Lane & Sublett 1972) variation in human skeletal remains in the archaeological investigation of residence practices.

In the present case it was reasoned that in the case of patrilocal residence the variability in the non-metric and metric data under study would be expected to be greater for males than for females, reflecting the greater genetic homogeneity in males from a particular community. However, there proved to be no significant difference in the variability in this respect between the sexes.

It could be suggested that the lack of evidence here to support the hypothesis of patrilocality argues against the applicability of models such as that of Meillassoux to the Hainburg data. However, the assumption here is that our cemetery population represents all the dead from a particular prehistoric community. It could be, for instance, that women were transported back to their natal community for burial. Return of the dead for burial in their natal area seems a fairly common ethnographic finding: for example, among the Mesakin of the Sudan, a woman is generally buried back in her natal area, not in her husband's area where she spent most of her life (Hodder 1979, p. 165). Alternatively, a group of communities could use the same cemetery area; this too could account for the results obtained. The practice of endogamy would also be consistent with the results, but the data on settlement size would seem to indicate that exogamy would have been necessary to maintain the communities at the sizes postulated.

Summary

The preliminary findings presented above suggest the lack of an inherited component to social status, and no differential access to food resources according to social rank. There is no evidence for the existence of exploitation in this Early Bronze Age society. The above might be interpreted as inconsistent with the sort of traditional Marxist model suggested by Gilman (1981) for the European Early Bronze Age; it may be that a segmentary lineage model is more consistent with the data. However, interpretations made here may need to be revised in the light of further study of the material, since important areas, (e.g. the study of the distribution of physical labour) remain to be investigated.

References

Beninger, E. 1941. Die frühbronzezeitliche Dorfanlage von Grossmugl (Niederdonau). *Mitteilungen der Prähistorischen Kommission der Österreichischen Akademie der Wissenschaften* **4**, 49–89.

Binford, L. R. 1962. Archaeology as anthropology. *American Antiquity* **28**, 217–25.

Bohannan, P. 1958. Extra-processual events in Tiv political organization. *American Anthropologist* **60**, 1–12.

Braun, D. P. 1979. Illinois Hopewell burial practices and social organization: a re-examination of the Klunk–Gibson moundgroup. In *Hopewell Archaeology, the Chillicothe Conference*, D. S. Brose & N. Greber (eds), 66–79. Ohio: Kent State University Press.

Brown, A. B & R. L. Blakely 1985. Biocultural adaptation as reflected in trace element distribution. *Journal of Human Evolution* **14**, 461–8.

Childe, V. G. 1958. *Prehistory of European Society*. London: Penguin.

Deluz, A. & M. Godelier 1967. A propos de deux textes d'anthropologie économique. *L'Homme* **7** (3), 78–91.

De Ste Croix, G. M. 1975. Review of Westermann, W. L. 'The slave systems of Greek & Roman antiquity'. *The Classical Review* **7**, 54–9.

Fortes, M. & E. Evans-Pritchard 1940. Introduction. In *African Political Systems*, M. Fortes and E. Evans-Pritchard (eds), 1–23. London: Oxford University Press.

Fried, M. H. 1967. *The evolution of political society*. New York: Random House.

Gilman , A. 1981. The development of social stratification in Bronze Age Europe. *Current Anthropology* **22**, 1–23.

Gilman, A. 1984. Explaining the Upper Palaeolithic Revolution. In *Marxist perspectives in archaeology*, M. Spriggs (ed.), 115–26. Cambridge: Cambridge University Press.

Gimbutas, M. 1965. *Bronze Age cultures in Eastern and Central Europe*. The Hague: Mouton.

Gledhill, J. 1984. The transformation of Asiatic formations: the case of late prehispanic Mesoamerica. In *Marxist perspectives in archaeology*, M. Spriggs (ed.), 135–48. Cambridge: Cambridge University Press.

Godelier, M. 1977. *Perspectives in Marxist anthropology*. Cambridge: Cambridge University Press.

Hatch, J. W. & R. A. Giedel 1985. Status specific dietary variation in two world cultures. *Journal of Human Evolution* **14**, 469–76.

Hindess, B. & P. Q. Hirst, 1975. *Pre-capitalist modes of production*. London: Routledge & Kegan Paul.

Hodder, I. 1979. Social structure and cemeteries: a critical reappraisal. In *Anglo-Saxon cemeteries*, P. Rahtz (ed.), 161–9. Oxford: British Archaeological Reports (International Series) No. 82.

Hodder, I. 1985. Boundaries as strategies: an ethnoarchaeological study. In *The Archaeology of frontiers and boundaries*, S. W. Green and S. M. Perlman (eds), 141–59. New York: Academic Press.

Howe, J. 1978. How the Cuna keep their chiefs in line. *Man* **13**, 537–53.

Lambert, J. B., C. B. Szpunar, & J. E. Buikstra 1979. Chemical analysis of excavated human bone from middle and late woodland sites. *Archaeometry* **21**, 115–29.

Lambert, J. B., S. M. Vlasak, A. C. Thometz & J. E. Buikstra 1982. A comparative study of the chemical analysis of ribs and femurs in woodland populations. *American Journal of Physical Anthropology* **59**, 289–94.

Lambert, J. B., S. V. Simpson, J. E. Buikstra & D. Hanson 1983. Electron microprobe analysis of elemental distribution in excavated human femurs. *American Journal of Physical Anthropology* **62**, 409–23.

Lambert, J. B., S. V. Simpson, J. E. Buikstra & D. K. Charles. 1984. Analysis of soil associated with woodland burials. In *Archaeological Chemistry III*, J. B. Lambert (ed.), 97–113. Washington, DC: American Chemical Society.

Lambert, J. B., S. V. Simpson, C. B. Szpunar & J. E. Buikstra, 1985. Bone diagenesis and dietary analysis. *Journal of Human Evolution* **14**, 447–82.

Lane, R. A. & A. J. Sublett 1972. Osteology of social organisation: residence pattern. *American Antiquity* **37**, 186–201.

Mays, S. A. 1983. A biological approach to the study of mortuary data: a case study using the human skeletal material from the late Romano-British/Early-Saxon cemetery at Ulwell, Dorset. M.Sc. Dissertation, University of Southampton.

Mays, S. A. 1987. Social organisation and social change in the Early and Middle Bronze Age of Central Europe: a study using human skeletal remains. Ph.D. Thesis, University of Southampton.

Meillassoux, C. 1964. *Anthropologie économique des Guro de Côte d'Ivoire.* Paris: Mouton.

Meillassoux, C. 1972. From reproduction to production. *Economy and Society*, **1**, 93–105.

Meillassoux, C. 1981. *Maidens, meal and money*. Cambridge: Cambridge University Press.

Modjeska, N. 1982. Production and inequality: perspectives from central New Guinea. In *Inequality in New Guinea Highland Societies.* A. Strathern (ed), Cambridge: Cambridge University Press.

Netting, R. M. 1972. Sacred power and centralisation: aspects of political adaptation in Africa. In *Population growth: anthropological implications*, B. Spooner (ed.), 219–44. Cambridge, Massachusetts: MIT Press.

O'Shea, J. 1984. *Mortuary variability: an archaeological investigation.* New York: Academic Press.

Otto, K. H. 1955. *Die sozialökonomischen Verhältnisse bei den Stämmen der Leubinger Kultur in Mitteldeutschland.* Berlin: Ethnographische-archaeologische Forschungen III.

Oždani, O. 1986. Zur Problematik der Entwicklung der Hügelgräberkulturen in der Südwestslowakei. *Slovenská Archeológia* **34**, 5–96.

Pader, E. J. 1982. *Symbolism, social relations and the interpretation of mortuary remains.* Oxford: British Archaeological Reports (International Series) No. 130.

Reinecke, P. 1924. Zur chronologische Gliederung der süddeutschen Bronzezeit. *Germania* **8**, 43–4.

Rey, P. 1975. The lineage mode of production. *Critique of Anthropology* **3**, 27–79.

Rey, P. 1979. Class contradiction in lineage societies. *Critique of Anthropology* **4**, 41–60.

Rheingold, A. L., S. Hues & M. N. Cohen 1983. Strontium and zinc content in bones as an indication of diet. *Journal of Chemical Education* **60**, 233–4.

Sahlins, M. D. 1958. *Social stratification in Polynesia.* Seattle: University of Washington Press.

Sahlins, M. D. 1963. Poor man, rich man, big man, chief: political types in Melanesia & Polynesia. *Comparative Studies in Society and History* **5**, 285–303.

Sahlins, M. D. 1968. *Tribesmen*. Englewood Cliffs, New Jersey: Prentice-Hall.

Saxe, A. A. 1970. Social dimensions of mortuary practices. Ph.D. dissertation, University of Michigan.

Schoeninger, M. J. 1979. Diet and status at Chalcatzingo. Some empirical and technical aspects of strontium analysis. *American Journal of Physical Anthropology* **51**, 295–310.

Schroeder, H. A., I. H. Tipton & A. P. Nason 1972. Trace metals in man: strontium and barium. *Journal of Chronic Diseases* **25**, 491–507.

Schubert, E. 1973. Stüdien zur frühen Bronzezeit an der mittleren Donau. *Bericht der Römisch-Germanischen Kommission* **54**, 1–105.

Shennan, S. E. 1975. The social organisation at Branc. *Antiquity* **49**, 279–88.

Shennan, S. E. 1982. From minimal to moderate ranking. In *Ranking, resource and exchange*, A. C. Renfrew & S. J. Shennan (eds.), 27–32. Cambridge: Cambridge University Press.

Sillen, A. 1981. Strontium and diet at Hayonim Cave. *American Journal of Physical Anthropology* **56**, 131–7.

Sillen, A. & M. Kavanagh 1982. Strontium and palaeodietary research: a review. *Yearbook of Physical Anthropology* **25**, 67–90.

Sillitoe, P. 1985. Divide and no-one rules: the implications of sexual division of labour in the Papua New Guinea highlands. *Man* **20**, 494–522.

Spence, M. W. 1973. The study of residential practices among prehistoric hunter-gatherers. *World Archaeology* **5**, 346–57.

Terray, E. 1972. *Marxism and primitive societies*. New York: Monthly Review Press.

Terray, E. 1975. Classes and class conciousness in the Abron kingdom of Gyaman. In *Marxist analyses in social anthropology*, M. Bloch (ed.), 88–135. London: Malaby Press.

Terray, E. 1979. On exploitation, elements of an autocritique. *Critique of Anthropology* **4**, 29–39.

Tilley, C. 1984. Ideology and power in the Middle Neolithic of Southern Sweden. In *Ideology, power and prehistory*, D. Miller & C. Tilley (eds), 111–46. Cambridge: Cambridge University Press.

Točík, A. 1964. *Opevnená Osada z doby Bronzovej vo Veselom*. Bratislava: Slovenská Akadémai vied.

Točík, A. 1981. *Nitriansky Hrádok-Zámaček. Bronzezeitliche Befestigte Ansiedlung der Madarovce-Kultur*. Nitra: Archaeologický ústav Slovenskej Akadémai vied.

Točík, A. & J. Vladár 1971. Prehl'ad bádania v problematike vývoňa Slovenská v dobe bronzovej. *Slovenská Archaeológia* **19**, 365–422.

Ucko, P. J. 1969. Ethnography and archaeological interpretation of funerary remains. *World Archaeology* **1**, 262–80.

Vladár, J. 1973. Osteuropäische und mediterrane Einflusse im Gebiet der Slowakei während der Bronzezeit. *Slovenská Archaeológia* **21**, 253–357.

EUROPEAN EXPANSION, COLONIALISM AND RESISTANCE

14 *Orientalism and Near Eastern archaeology*

MOGENS TROLLE LARSEN

Mario Liverani, for his inspiration

In December 1931 an impressive new building for the Oriental Institute at the University of Chicago was inaugurated. This house contained offices for scores of scholars who worked as archaeologists and philologists in the field of the ancient Near East, libraries, a great lecture hall, and a fairly large museum where the finds from a number of excavations conducted by the institute, principally in Mesopotamia and Egypt, were on display. This was, and is, one of the most important and prestigious research institutions in the field.

Over the main entrance to this new building was placed a large relief (Fig. 14.1) which, in the words of James Henry Breasted, the first Director of the Institute, who also created the design for the relief, shows 'the transition of civilization from the ancient Orient to the West'. He offered an elaboration of the conceptual framework for this monument in an article entitled 'The task of the Orientalist and its place in world history', published in a book which commemorated the inauguration of the new building (Breasted 1933). The text itself goes back to a presidential address given to the American Oriental Society in 1919.

Figure 14.1 The large relief designed by James Henry Breasted over the door of the Oriental Institute at the University of Chicago.

Generations of scholars – including myself – have passed underneath this relief without really noticing it. It is a rather inferior work of art, but the message contained in it is of considerable interest, since it gives us a symbolic statement of the ideological underpinnings of much of the work that went on, not just in that particular building, but in all research institutes dedicated to the study of the ancient Near East.

The scene on the relief shows an ancient Egyptian scribe who hands over to a semi-naked Westerner a fragment of a relief with a hieroglyphic inscription. The Egyptian has a Near Eastern lion at his feet, the Westerner an American bison, and the fields behind these two men contain further figures and monuments which represent the traditions that each of the main characters represents. Behind the scribe are various ancient kings: Assyrian, Babylonian, Egyptian, Sasanian and Persian, and in the field above them some of their accomplishments: the palace at Persepolis, the Sphinx and the pyramids at Gizeh. This, then, is the ancient Near East which, through the Egyptian scribe, hands over to the West the essential element in civilization, the gift of writing.

The person who receives the heritage of the East is described in the Institute guide from 1931 as 'the vigorous and aggressive figure of the West'. He combines elements of Greek, Roman and modern art, and resembles the contemporary sculpture erected in Mussolini's Italy. He is clearly intended to represent the synthesis of the Western tradition as a man who is both a hero and a scientist. In the field behind him are the people he represents: Herodotus, Alexander, Julius Caesar, a crusader, a field archaeologist leaning on his spade, and, finally, the scholar in his study handling a newly excavated vase. Three buildings stand for this Western tradition: the Acropolis, a European cathedral and the US State Capitol at Lincoln, Nebraska, a modern skyscraper chosen here because it was built by the same engineering firm that was responsible for the Oriental Institute.

In this image we have represented the transfer of civilization from the ancient Orient to the West, and the ideological content becomes even clearer and more explicit in Breasted's (1933) article. According to him modern man, in his understanding of the past, stands face to face with a great gulf between:

> on the one hand the palaeontologist with his picture of the dawn-man enveloped in clouds of archaic savagery, and on the other hand the historian with his reconstruction of the career of civilized man in Europe. Between these two stand we orientalists endeavouring to bridge the gap. It is in that gap that man's primitive advance passed from merely physical evolution to an evolution of his soul, a social and spiritual development which transcends the merely biological and divests evolution of its terrors. It is the recovery of these lost stages, the bridging of this chasm between the merely physical man and the ethical, intellectual man, which is a fundamental need of man's soul as he faces nature today. We can build this bridge only as

> we study the emergence and early history of the first great civilized societies in the ancient Near East, for there still lies the evidence out of which we may recover the story of the origins and the early advance of civilization, out of which European culture and eventually our own civilization came forth. *The task of salvaging and studying this evidence and of recovering the story which it reveals – that is the greatest task of the humanist today.* (Breasted 1933, pp. 1–2)

This, then, was the programme for scholarly research which formed the basis for working in the Near East: Western man was looking for his own past, for an explanation and a description of how the world in which we live came to be. Breasted presented a unilinear, diffusionist view of world history, and the great ancient civilization of the Near East came to occupy a crucial and central position:

> From these civilizations as our base we are able to push backward up the centuries and connect with the prehistoric stages which preceded civilization and developed into it; while in the other direction we may follow down the centuries from the civilizations of the Near East to the Neolithic barbarism of Europe, which was stimulated into civilized life by cultural influences from the farther shores of the Mediterranean. In this vast cultural synthesis, embracing the whole known career of man, the civilizations of the Near Orient are like the keystone of the arch, with prehistoric man on one side and civilized Europe on the other. (Breasted 1933, pp. 10–11.)

If this picture represents 'the whole known career of man', then it is clear why the relief can forget about Chinese, Indian, Japanese and Arabic – not to mention African kings and their achievements. In such a view the study of the ancient Near East obviously becomes a vital task, but in fact all other cultures on the globe must be seen as deviations, aberrations, culs-de-sac, and Western civilization alone has the privilege of being the direct descendant of the very first civilization on Earth. The study of ancient Mesopotamia or Egypt is therefore of crucial importance, and it is obvious that excavations of, for example, palaces in Sri Lanka or temples in India, or for that matter monuments from the later phases of Near Eastern history must have a much lower priority.

Such attitudes have obviously informed much of the scholarship directed towards the ancient civilizations of the Near East. Countless books and articles have told the story of the search for 'the Cradle of Civilization', which European scholars expected to find in that area. This concept was closely related to the interest in the background for the Old Testament, and consequently Western religion, and there can be no doubt that this little-studied part of the Orientalist heritage has played a very important role for the way in which archaeological research in the Near East has been structured.

The ideas contained in Breasted's article have a long history in European thought. When Johann Gottfried Herder published his great work *Ideen zur Philosophie der Geschichte der Menschheit* between 1784 and 1791, he was writing at a time when practically nothing certain could be said of the ancient world; yet it was nevertheless clear to him that it was in the Near East that we should find the origin of innumerable human achievements in culture and technology. To him the ancient worlds were reduced to 'a few faded leaves which contain stories about stories, fragments of history, a dream of the world before us', but this '*Traum der Vorwelt*' pointed directly to a past which was in a sense the origin or precursor of our own:

> Wir wandern wie auf den Gräbern untergegangener Monarchien umher und sehen die Schattengestalten ihrer ehemaligen Wirkung auf der Erde. Und wahrlich, diese Wirkung ist so gross gewesen, dass wenn man Ägypten zu diesem Erdstriche mitrechnet, es ausser Griechenland und Rom keine Weltgegend gibt, die insonderheit für Europa und durch dies für alle Nationen der Erde so viel erfunden und vorgearbeitet habe. (Herder 1784–91, pp. 302.)

Already here, at the end of the 18th century, we are faced with the conviction that the basic cultural, social, technological and religious inventions were transmitted from the ancient Near East via Europe to the entire world.

In the 19th century, the time of Western hegemony over large parts of the globe, of colonialism and imperialism, a unilinear view of world history which marked out the Western civilization as the concluding glory of millennia of development obviously had a lot of attraction. This was a strong motive for the allocation of generous funds for excavations, as well as for the creation of large collections of antiquities in museums in the West, and later the setting up of academic posts, research programmes and educational systems in the universities.

Typical of this attitude are the sentiments expressed in 1898 by the founders of the Deutsche Orient Gesellschaft, who wanted to throw light upon 'those original conditions . . . where we find the roots of our own culture, our time-reckoning and starlore, our system of weight and measure, as well as important parts of the religious concepts which are contained in the Old Testament'.[1]

In Breasted's scheme religion does not even appear, and for him the story was one which showed how man 'raised himself by his own bootstraps', but, of course, the Christian faith was an important reason for the study of the ancient Near East in the eyes of other scholars.[2]

Especially in Germany in the period before World War I, the concern with the religious question developed (or deteriorated) into a series of radical attempts to build grand schemes of historical interpretation on the evidence from the ancient Near East. In the very young and rather obscure discipline of Assyriology a major debate arose, known as the '*Babel und Bibel*' controversy. The fundamental aim of this school of thought was to locate the Old Testament, and consequently the Jewish faith, in a Near Eastern cultural context – an effort that inscribes itself in the anti-Semitism of the time, and which concluded in a denial of the value of Old

Testament traditions for the Christian faith. Judaism was placed in a Near Eastern perspective, one religion among many, marked by a kind of parochial monotheism which contrasts harshly with the universal monotheism of Christianity. Surprisingly, it was possible for at least some of the scholars involved in these feats of scholarship to find a meaningful relationship between the worlds of the ancient Near East and modern Christianity. The Jewish world and its religion was bypassed, or jumped over, and the symbol of the direct connection between Babylon and Christianity became the Three Wise Men from the East who came to do homage to the Saviour in Bethlehem (Ebach 1986, Larsen 1987).[3] Another school, known as 'Pan-Babylonism', claimed that ancient Mesopotamia was the home of all myths, and this was further related to the fashionable concern with astral mythology, in particular solar myths. All myths everywhere in the world could be traced back to a system of belief which was first formulated and elaborated in Mesopotamia around 3000 BC, the only place where the entire system had ever been truly understood, so that the borrowed mythology of all other peoples represented more-or-less-distorted versions of the original system (Inden 1986).

In archaeology, the best known formulation of the idea of Near Eastern influences upon the development of European civilization is probably that offered by Gordon Childe, based on the same kind of diffusionist theory that is found in Breasted's article. Childe uses one of the common metaphors for historical development – the running river – as the basis for one of his most famous statements on this:

> If our own culture can claim to be in the main stream, it is only because our cultural tradition has captured and made tributary a larger volume of once parallel traditions. While in historical times the main stream flows from Mesopotamia and Egypt through Greece and Rome, Byzantium and Islam, to Atlantic Europe and America, it has been repeatedly swollen by the diversion into it of streams from Indian, Chinese, Mexican, and Peruvian civilizations, and from countless barbarisms and savageries. Chinese and Indian civilizations have indeed not failed to absorb currents from one another and from farther west. But, on the whole, they have hitherto discharged these into placid unchanging backwaters. (Childe 1954, p. 29.)

Another metaphor has been the torch of civilization, lit originally in the cities of the ancient Near East, and passed on from hand to hand until it ended in Greece and Europe. However, there was a built-in ambiguity, since the great civilizations of Mesopotamia and Egypt were seen both as the origins of Western cultural, social and religious traditions, and as the greatest contrast to the West – monolithic, despotic states compared with the individualism, democracy and entrepreneurial spirit of Europe. It seems clear that for a majority of the European historians and archaeologists who expressed views on this subject, from Hegel to Marx and beyond, the basic concern was to find an explanation of the uniqueness of the capitalistic West and its role in world history.

The uniqueness of Europe was explained in different ways, but in any event it is clear that the Near East with its 'Asiatic' traditions was a somewhat suspect and ambiguous foundation for the glory of Europe. Childe was concerned with the question of how Near Eastern influences were transformed in Europe, how basic technologies were diffused and used for new purposes in utterly different social and political contexts (see Rowlands 1987). The world of the Asiatic mode of production is in glaring contrast with the democratic society of Athens. The ancient Near East has all too often been analysed on the basis of such a set of preconceived ideas designed to uphold the prevalent view of the decadent, despotic Orient.

If it is agreed that the Orient represents stagnation and backwardness, and that the model for progress and evolution is the West, then modern Asia faces an uphill struggle in trying to catch up.[4] However, for the historian this view also actualizes the question of how, when and where the West became the West, and the traditional answer is of course that something utterly new came into the world with the Greeks. It is often assumed that they created their own culture more in opposition or in contrast to, than in inspiration from, the ancient civilizations of the Near East (Bernal 1987). Finley (1973) chooses to concentrate only on the worlds of Greece and Rome, and his reason for excluding the earlier ancient civilizations of Mesopotamia and Egypt from consideration is that they are so totally different that they really do not belong meaningfully in the same category:

> It is almost enough to point out that it is impossible to translate the word 'freedom', eleutheria, in Greek, libertas in Latin, or 'freeman', into any ancient Near Eastern language, including Hebrew, or into any Far Eastern language either, for that matter. (Finley 1973, p. 28.)

For the Europe of the 19th and early 20th centuries the Orient was alien, the symbol of 'the other'. It hardly needs pointing out that this view – which could be elaborated endlessly with countless cruder quotes – is related to the Orientalist tradition, as described by Said (1978, p. 11), who claims that 'all academic knowledge' about the cultures of the Orient 'is somehow tinged and impressed with, or violated by, the gross political fact', i.e. the reality of imperialism and colonialism.

European uniqueness is taken up again in the recent book *Before civilization* by Renfrew, which is presented as a re-evaluation of European prehistory in the light of the results of the new system of dates based on the carbon-14 technique. Prehistoric Europe is, in his interpretation, separated from the Orient by 'a fault line' that runs across the Balkans:

> the basic links of the traditional chronology are snapped and Europe is no longer directly linked, either chronologically or culturally, with the early civilizations of the Near East. (Renfrew 1976, Fig. 21, p. 116.)

This refers specifically to European prehistory, but Renfrew goes further and also suggests that the first civilizations in Europe, the Minoan culture of

Crete and the Mycenaean on the Greek mainland, were unrelated to the ancient Near East:

> I believe, indeed, that this first European civilization was very much a European development, and that most of its features can be traced back, not to the admittedly earlier civilizations of the Near East, but to antecedents on home ground, and to processes at work in the Aegean over the preceding thousand years. (Renfrew 1976, pp. 211–12.)

It is difficult to avoid linking this interpretation of the early 1970s with the political realities of the time, and especially with the strong desire felt in Europe to understand the subcontinent as an entirely autonomous entity. The independence of Europe as a cultural fact was established when it was also being attempted as a political fact, and the despotic 'East' of our own time is of course a well-established element in Cold War rhetoric.

It is understandable that all work done in the field of Near Eastern studies has been inspired by some version of the search for European identity and uniqueness. The diffusionist paradigm made this field into one of the central concerns of humanistic research, and in this way it seems to have given archaeology its special focus at a certain time. It represents an emphasis on continuity, and a kind of historical purpose which exists independently of 'events' and apparent historical change – a 'rootedness' or authenticity which connects the chaotic modern world with ancient culture. However, there was always the rival interpretation which saw the Orient as the home of despotism with monolithic political structures and a complete disregard for the individual; in brief, the antithesis of the democratic, egalitarian European society.

These concerns are still, of course, very much alive. A group of distinguished scholars has very recently conducted a discussion entirely within this framework in the journal *Symbols*, published by the Peabody Museum. Professor Kwang-Chih Chang started a debate in 1984 in an article in which he suggested that the traditionally accepted ideas about the beginning of civilization, in which man's control over nature and the development of technology played a large role, were 'fundamentally at odds with the ancient Chinese reality of a layered but interlinked world continuum, in which privileged humans and animals roamed about from one layer to another'. Chang felt that the traditional analysis has relevance only for 'European civilization and its Oriental precedents' which had achieved what he called 'a significant breakout' from 'the cultural pattern which characterised Chinese and Mayan civilization' (Chang 1984, pp. 20–1).

His ideas were largely adopted by Willey, a leading specialist in Central American and Mexican archaeology, who spoke of the 'Chinese–New World pattern of political ideology', which may have been 'essentially universal at one time, a time or a stage in which complex societies and states arose'. In fact, Willey suggested that the similarities between Chinese and New World cultural traits and ideology are to be understood as 'independent expressions deriving out of an ancient Palaeolithic mythological base', so we are dealing with issues of extremely broad significance and the 'Near Eastern breakout' is in need of an explanation. Willey offers a hint when he speaks of 'the great importance of the Near Eastern temple markets'. Both Chang and Willey emphasize the point that the choice between the two models of culture and ideology is still before us; in Willey's words, 'the struggle between monolithic control and the political diversification of power' (Willey 1985, pp. 17, 23).

One notices that the Near East in this sweeping analysis seems to have become a champion of progress, standing for a less oppressive political system and clearly pointing the way towards Western democracy. This is understandable in terms of the contribution offered by Lamberg-Karlovsky, for his entire argument was focused on the concepts 'equity' and 'justice', terms which he found to constitute the kernel of what he termed 'the Mesopotamian Social Contract'. He concludes:

> The 'moral obligation' imposed on rulers for constituting freedom, equity and justice are as old as the ancient palaces and temples of the Near East. Such 'moral' concepts continued to receive affirmation whether in the Acropolis of democratic Athens, the Magna Carta of King John, or the principles of Liberté, Égalité, and Fraternité of the French Revolution. As certain as these concepts are pivotal to Western Civilization, they are foreign to the political ideology of ancient Egypt, China, and India. (Lamberg-Karlovsky 1985, p. 23.)

However, the next issue of *Symbols* contained an article by Hammond, Professor Emeritus at Harvard of Latin Language and Literature, which brought back some order; it was entitled 'The Indo-European origin of the concept of a democratic society', and Hammond's central argument was expressed as follows:

> Chang posits only two conceptual patterns for primitive civilization, the Chinese, or shamanistic, shared with the New World, and the Mesopotamian . . . But the present comments would argue that in fact the concepts of government in early Greece, though perhaps early subject to Near Eastern (rather than Mesopotamian) influences, were basically distinct and derived from an Indo-European background. (Hammond 1985, p. 11.)

So here we have the fundamental elements in the old debate being brought forward again: Asiatic despotism, European uniqueness – and the ambiguous role of the ancient Near East, this time with the emphasis on aspects of the complex Mesopotamian sociopolitical structure which appear to make it more 'Western' and less despotic.

A radical – and perhaps somewhat disgusted – approach to this entire problem was adopted by the famous Assyriologist A. Leo Oppenheim, who gave his book, *Ancient Mesopotamia*, the defiant subtitle 'Portrait of a Dead Civilization' (Oppenheim 1964). His point was that the ancient world should be studied on its own terms, and that such an enterprise was relevant and meaningful without any further justification. However, his attitude has not exactly been the dominant one in the field.

The way in which the traditional frameworks have shaped the study of the ancient Near East can only be hinted at, for no investigation exists on which conclusions of any substance can be built. One simple observation – elaborated upon by Kohl in the next chapter of this book – is that, whereas it has always been legitimate, indeed of obvious importance, to study the origins of the Near East, with a correspondingly heavy emphasis on prehistory, Western archaeologists have shown little interest in those phases of Near Eastern history that come after the moment when the 'Torch of Civilization' had been passed on to the Greeks. What came after that time was presumably to be seen in terms of Childe's image of stagnant pools, whereas the mainstream rushed on into new and exciting areas in Europe.[5] Also, the research strategies have, of course, been shaped by European concerns, and anyone who has looked at the history of archaeological exploration in Iran will realize the importance of the idea of the search for the Aryans, their pottery, their buildings and their towns. The search for parallels to the Bible quite naturally played a large role for archaeologists who were excavating cities like Niniveh, Calah (Nimrud) or Babylon, which figured so prominently in the Old Testament.

These are relatively well-defined motivations, even though much remains to be done before we have reached an acceptable understanding of their relationship to such ideological fields as nationalism, colonialism, religious movements and the rampant anti-Semitism of the 19th and 20th centuries. However, the role of Orientalist attitudes in the development of the archaeological traditions in the area was much more subtly pervasive, and it shaped the priorities involved in the work, as well as the understanding of the finds. It is important that these questions be taken up and subjected to a critical evaluation within the disciplines working in the Near East, and there is no doubt that such work is going to have serious effects on the actual practice of archaeologists, philologists and ancient historians. Placing these disciplines in their proper context within the intellectual history of Europe and the West is a necessary precondition for any meaningful further development.

Notes

1 See *Orientalistische Litteratur-Zeitung* **1/2**, 36, note 1 (1898).

2 See, for instance, Albright (1957, p. 401, note 1): '. . . it is singularly one-sided to recognize that man's physical constitution is an elaborately designed structure which will at best require a vast amount of research to understand, but at the same time to insist that the emotional, aesthetic, and religious ideas and aspirations of man are idle vestiges of a savage past or are mere puerile superstitions. It is far more "reasonable" to recognize that, just as man is a being evolved by the eternal spirit of the Universe, so his religious life is the result of stimuli coming from the same source and progressing toward a definite goal. In other words, the evolution of man's religious life is guided by divine revelation'.

3 I have dealt with these questions in an article to be published with the papers from the conference 'The Humanities Between Art and Science', held by The Center for Research in the Humanities at Copenhagen University in 1986. See also Ebach (1986). The reference to the Three Wise Men comes from Delitzsch (1905, p. 48): 'so gewiss das Wort Goethes wahr bleibt, dass "der menschliche Geist über die Hoheit und sittliche Kultur des Christentums, wie es in den Evangelien schimmert und leuchtet, nicht hinauskommen werde", so können wir, die wir die altbabylonische Welt erforschen und die führenden Geister Babyloniens mit ernstem Eifer, ja mit Furcht und Zittern bestrebt sehen, Gott und die Wahrheit zu suchen, es nur freudig begrüssen, dass der Evangelist die babylonischen Weisen die ersten sein lässt, die an der Wiege des Christentums ihre Huldigung darbringen'.

4 See Marx (1853) (in Marx & Engels 1979, p. 76), where he writes of the British rule in India: 'England, it is true, in causing a social revolution in Hindostan, was actuated only by the vilest interests, and was stupid in her manner of enforcing them. But that is not the question. The question is, can mankind fulfil its destiny without a fundamental revolution in the social state of Asia? If not, whatever may have been the crimes of England she was the unconscious tool of history in bringing about that revolution'.

5 In this connection it is worth pointing out that for instance the Parthian rock reliefs which show Roman Emperors kneeling before Oriental monarchs as vanquished and subjugated prisoners, have been effectively erased from the European consciousness as images which contradict essential Western ideas (see for reproductions Herrmann 1977, pp. 87–94).

References

Albright, W. F. 1957. *From the Stone Age to Christianity. Monotheism and the historical process*, 2nd edn. New York: Doubleday Anchor.

Bernal, M. 1987. *Black Athena. The Afroasiatic roots of classical civilization*. London: Free Association Books.

Breasted, J. H. 1933. *The Oriental Institute*. Chicago: University of Chicago Press.

Chang, Kwang-Chih. 1984. Ancient China and its anthropological significance. *Symbols* (Spring/Fall), 2–22. Cambridge, Massachusetts: The Peabody Museum.

Childe, G. 1954. *What happened in history* 1982 edn. Harmondsworth: Penguin.

Delitzsch, F. 1905. *Babel und Bibel*, 3. (Schluss-)Vortrag. Stuttgart: Deutsche Verlags-Anstalt.

Ebach, J. 1986. Babel und Bibel oder: Das 'Heidnische' im Alten Testament. In *Die Restauration der Götter. Antike Religion und Neo-Paganismus*. R. Faber & R. Schlesier (eds), 26–44. Würzburg: Königshausen & Neumann.

Finley, M. 1973 *The ancient economy*. London: Chatto & Windus.

Hammond, M. 1985. The Indo-European origin of the concept of a democratic society. *Symbols* (December) 10–13. Cambridge, Massachusetts: The Peabody Museum.

Hermann, G. 1977. *The Iranian Revival*. Oxford: Elsevier-Phaidon.

Herder, J. G. 1784–91. *Ideen zur Philosophie der Geschichte der Menschheit*. Schmidt (ed.). Wiesbaden: R. Löwit.

Inden, R. 1986. Orientalist constructions of India. *Modern Asian Studies* **20**, 3, 401–46. Cambridge: Cambridge University Press.

Lamberg-Karlovsky, C. C. 1985. The Near Eastern 'breakout' and the Mesopo-

tamian social contract. *Symbols* (Spring), 8–24. Cambridge, Massachusetts: The Peabody Museum.
Larsen, M. Trolle 1987. Orientalism and the Ancient Near East. *Culture and History* **2**, 96–115. Copenhagen: Museum Tusculanum Press.
Marx, K. & F. Engels 1979. *Pre-capitalist socio-economic formations. A collection.* Moscow: Progress Publishers.
Renfrew, C. 1976. *Before civilization. The radiocarbon revolution and prehistoric Europe.* Harmondsworth: Penguin.
Rowlands, M. 1987. 'Europe in prehistory': a unique form of primitive capitalism? *Culture & History* **1**, 63–78. Copenhagen: Museum Tusculanum Press.
Said, E. W. 1978. *Orientalism.* New York: Vintage Books.
Willey, G. R. 1985. Ancient Chinese–New World and Near Eastern ideological traditions: some observations. *Symbols* (Spring) 14–23. Cambridge, Massachusetts: The Peabody Museum.

15 *The material culture of the modern era in the ancient Orient: suggestions for future work*

PHILIP L. KOHL

When Napoleon Bonaparte invaded Egypt in 1978 he not only was fascinated by its material remains, entombing himself briefly in the pyramid of Cheops, but also hoped that his 'social scientists' – the fledgling Orientalists and early ethnographers that he had assembled as part of his expedition – would study the Egyptian peasantry to provide insights into the social order of Pharaonic times. This was the dawn of Orientalism, that highly developed esoteric brand of colonially supported scholarship so richly and emotionally characterized by Said (1979). The East was defined as the Other: remote, inaccessible, unchanging, monolithic, and of primary scholarly interest for its unbroken historic heritage, which stretched back to form the foundation of Biblical and Greco-Roman civilization, the latter of which, in turn, was perceived as defining the beginnings of the Western tradition. Near Eastern archaeology clearly developed within this Orientalist framework. Rich, Layard, Rawlinson, Petrie, Botha, Place, de Sarzec, Schliemann and Koldewey – the early pioneers of archaeology in the eastern Mediterranean and Mesopotamia, as well as the eminently recondite fields of Assyriology and Egyptology – were loyal subjects (sometimes even administrators) of the expanding colonial powers, and were inspired by Biblical and classical accounts of the past.

Viewed from an historical perspective, such sources of inspiration are understandable and, of course, continue to motivate many archaeologists working in the Orient today. However, if we examine the development of 20th-century Near Eastern archaeology, we can detect the emergence of a new, seemingly more innocuous (i.e. less potentially hegemonic) and more objective stimulus, one influencing many anthropologically trained archaeologists. The archaeology of the ancient Orient fascinates us not primarily because of its potential for confirming or refuting stories from the Bible and classical literature, but because of its perceived evolutionary value. This archaeological record provides a key for understanding how it all began, how food production initially developed, how and when the state first arose or, more generally, how crucial cultural evolutionary steps were taken. After Braidwood organized his interdisciplinary team at Jarmo, numerous prehistorians went to the Near East to document the evolutionary record contained in its material remains. The point is not to indict or question the validity of this enterprise (a purely hypocritical undertaking for one proud to be a prehistorian interested in these developments), but to raise the uncomfortable question as to the extent to which the nearly exclusive prehistoric focus of anthropologically trained Near Eastern archaeologists has helped to perpetuate the still-vibrant Orientalist mode of understanding the Near East and, paradoxically, left unexamined the exceptionally important evolutionary leap or spurt into the modern era. When we excavate a 'typical' Near Eastern village farming community of the early Holocene or, better, when we conduct an ethnoarchaeological analysis of a 'typical' contemporary Near Eastern village, we are also continuing, however unwittingly, that grand tradition of Napoleon's scholars – viewing the Near East and its peoples as undifferentiated, unchanging and as having qualitatively transformed themselves only during the remote past.

Of course, Islamic archaeology constitutes a subfield of Near Eastern archaeology, but its relative underdevelopment in this context is significant. Later Arab remains have been bulldozed away to uncover the stratigraphically sealed, more desirable materials only in a few exceptional cases. Yet prehistorians blithely have searched for *tells* unburdened by later Islamic levels, or have conducted surveys that lumped potentially distinguishable Islamic occupations into one or two (early-late) subperiods which rarely were subjected to further intensive analysis. Occasionally, authorities in Middle Eastern countries which experience a revival of so-called neo-traditionalism demand that archaeologists focus on the Islamic past; such a request is often understandable and even long overdue, given the lack of previous work on Islam. In general, few Islamic sites have been excavated; the work that has been done has focused typically on the classical and early medieval, pre-Mongol periods – virtually ignoring the remains of the modern, post Vasco da Gama era. Emphasis has largely been placed on defining Islamic material remains from an art historical perspective, noting similarities in art styles and architecture across the vast area that was embraced early by the Islamic world or discussing stereotypic and abstracted features of the typical Islamic city (Grabar 1973, Lapidus 1969). Again it must be asked whether such a focus, however understandable in itself, also helps to perpetuate an Orientalist perception of Islam as monolithic, exotic and frozen in time.

That Islamic archaeology need not be so limited and can enrich our understanding of major historical developments is illustrated well by consideration of a striking example counter to the above generalizations: Whitehouse's intelligently conceived excavations of the Abbasid port city of Siraf, which flourished from the late 8th to the mid-11th centuries AD. This work has helped date more precisely the expansion of long-distance trade from the Islamic world east to China and south to East Africa, and it even helped Whitehouse and his colleagues to evaluate, in the light of incontrovertible archaeological data, the validity of Pirenne's famous thesis that the collapse of the ancient world, spread of Islam, and subsequent rise of the Carolingians were related phenomena (Hodges & Whitehouse 1983). More such work is needed not only for the Abbasid caliphate and Early Islam, but also for later periods, particularly those strongly affected by European influences on the East. The remainder of this chapter attempts to illustrate through selected examples and suggestions the *potential* of an historically informed Late Islamic archaeology, an archaeology which – when combined with other records of material culture – could document the extent and nature of Western economic and political expansion into a never-stable Orient.

The European capture of the Indian Ocean trade and the decline of inland cities that traditionally relied on overland caravan trade are certainly related developments, but the timing, extent and nature of this relationship could be clarified by archaeological research. Through historical data, Steensgaard (1973) attempted to show that qualitative changes in long-distance trading patterns only occurred after the Portuguese had been ousted by the Dutch and English in the early-17th century, that the overland peddling trade, which had been conducted for centuries, if not millennia, prospered throughout the 16th century only to decline precipitously with the arrival of the economically more progressive Dutch and English East India Companies. This rich thesis invites archaeological–material culture validation. Historic documents record the impressive scale of late overland caravans (one from Baghdad to Basra in 1610 consisted of 943 loads drawn by about 1100 animals, which transported about 300 tons and stretched for about 3 km (cf. Tekeli 1973, p. 250). Given the provision and logistic requirements of such movements of goods and animals, archaeological evidence should be able to pinpoint precisely when this trade entered its period of decline. Detailed distributional recordings and investigations of the caravanserais, which dot the Middle Eastern landscape, would not only confirm the chronology of this decline, but also show how sudden and ubiquitous a phenomenon it actually was.

An urban pattern of life in the ancient East began, of course, with Sumer, and the persistence of urbanism is an enduring feature documented by archaeological settlement surveys (for example, Adams 1981) and, for the modern period, by relatively complete historic records (for example, Issawi 1969). An archaeologist could examine the historic data documenting growth patterns of regional towns and capitals throughout the Middle East from c. AD 1800 onwards and contrast this record of urbanism during the period of Western colonialism with those documented for much earlier periods. Recently, Stone (1987) has attempted to detect similarities in both the physical structures and layout (narrow winding streets, *culs-de-sac*, walled compounds and quarters, etc.) and social neighbourhood groupings of the Old Babylonian city of Nippur with those supposedly typifying the ethnic compounds and precincts of the traditional Islamic *madina*. This ambitious and laudable effort at comparison satisfies less than it should, precisely because the typical Islamic *madina* is itself abstracted or removed from history, conceived within the ahistoric Orientalist mode. How much more intriguing and stimulating would have been the exercise of comparing the neighbourhoods of Nippur with, for example, those historically described for Early Abbasid Baghdad, both of which, in turn, could have been contrasted with records of Baghdad during the 19th century or even under the British Mandate. The record of urbanism in the Middle East is continuous, but it hardly reveals a pattern of continuous growth. Middle

Eastern cities were founded, waxed and waned, due to economic and political factors within a larger interacting world. Ninth-century Baghdad was considerably more prosperous and more developed than its 19th-century descendant. What features persist, and what are novel as one looks at Middle Eastern cities from the 16th to the 20th centuries? Historical and archaeological records could be combined to answer questions such as these. An archaeological and material culture analysis of the Middle East during the modern period can be distinguished in part from the historical archaeologies of many other areas of the world by the availability of documentation extending back nearly 5000 years. An evolutionary focus could be maintained as one examined the advent of Western capitalism and colonialism throughout the Middle East.

English's (1966) study of the integration of the city and countryside of Kirman province through the putting out or urban contracting of rural woven carpets was followed-up by an ethnographic analysis of one of the villages so tied to Kirman (Dillon 1976). Dillon, an anthropologist, questioned English's conclusion that the social relations of the area had fundamentally altered with the introduction of urban-financed carpet-weaving in the villages, arguing for little social development despite the appearance of a new petty capitalist mode:

> . . . capitalism (as an economic mode) was introduced into Kirman, perhaps as early as the 17th century, first in the form of the wool trade, and then later in the form of the shawl trade and finally in the late 19th century in the form of contract carpet weaving, or the putting out system. These new economic modes, however, changed the control of capital resources and the relations between classes (i.e. the socio-economic formation) very little. (Dillon 1976, p. 460.)

Such a thesis could be formulated as a potentially testable archaeological proposition. One could record shifts in the size and function of rural settlements in Kirman province during the past 400 years, and record the material culture concomitants of the introduction of the wool, shawl and, finally, contract carpet-weaving industries. Unfortunately, no Near Eastern archaeologist has yet attempted to study such a 'late' problem.

Similarly, archaeological–material culture data clearly could help us to understand differences between those areas of the Middle East that came under direct colonial rule (e.g. Algeria, Egypt and Syria) and those that were only indirectly or economically controlled (Iran, Afghanistan and Turkey) by Western powers. Abu-Lughod's (1971) study of Cairo has shown how the 'modern' city first emerged in the 1860s – or simultaneously with the opening of the Suez canal – and consisted of two halves: the traditional, densely crowded *madina*; and a new French-inspired, British-occupied western section. How does this bifurcation or physical mitosis compare in scale with the emergence of new centres (*Shahr-i Nau*) alongside the old cities (*Shahr-i Khuneh*) of Kabul or Herat during the second half of the 19th century? How does either pattern compare with the less directly dominated late 19th-century-Qajar capital of Teheran? Urban historians have assembled abundant materials that almost beg for anthropological comparisons and analyses by archaeologists attuned to an evolutionary appreciation of the advent of the modern era.

As Gordon Childe (possibly somewhat tongue-in-cheek) was fond of observing, archaeological data, unlike historical records, do not consciously misinform, and this advantage becomes particularly important when one is forced to evaluate the persistent prejudices of modern times. An historian writing in late-19th century England unabashedly characterized Russian expansion into Asia in the following terms:

> the Russian [mission], as viewed by those responsible for her policy, is neither to develop territory nor to refine people. Her destiny is to use that which she already possesses as a means by which further conquests are to be made, until, by dint of an ever-forward movement, she finds herself in possession, not of India, or of China or Persia, but of the whole Asiatic Continent, which under the military sway of an army, ruled by the great White Tsar, may once again control the destinies of the world . . . Little or nothing is done to encourage the development of trade: the great point kept in view is to constantly extend the government of the Tsar, without regard to the internal interests of the country or the requirements of its people. Her power of expansion is, in short, that of assimilation, and no attempt is made to benefit the condition of the people who are from time to time added to the population. (Krausse 1900.)

The assertion of this Cold War prototype could be evaluated through an objective consideration of the material culture record. What shifts in settlement location and growth are observed in Russian Central Asia between 1860 and 1900? How are the cities of Bukhara, Samarkand and Tashkent transformed during this period, and how do the changes that they experience compare with those wrought in earlier incorporated areas, such as Transcaucasia? Finally, and perhaps most intriguingly, how does the material documentation of colonial presence in the Russian Empire compare with that, for example, of British India? What would a controled comparison of the government buildings and urban layout of British-ruled Calcutta and the Russian-controlled administrative capital of Tiflis (now Tbilisi) reveal? This material culture record exists and should be studied to make such comparisons into the extent and nature of different types of colonial rule. For early Calcutta see, for example, the plans and glowing descriptions in Curzon (1925), as well as the broader historical account of Pearson (1954); for 19th-century Tiflis, see Suny (1986) with bibliography, and for graphic depictions of its 19th-century life and material culture, Gersamia (1984). Such a study could not, of course, itself disprove the assertion that Russian – relative to British – rule did not 'benefit the condition', 'refine the people' or 'develop the territory' of the conquered region. Such evaluations always involve value judgments that, inevitably, may be based on different criteria. These latter standards will necessarily be made more explicit through the empirical documentation of different kinds of material culture records; in so doing, blatant prejudices will be exposed and a more objective understanding reached.

Unfortunately, this chapter cannot answer the questions it has posed. The work still needs to be done. An evolutionary archaeology of the ancient Near East has so far been conceptualized only within an Orientalist mode that distances present realities from past concerns. This need not be true. It is perhaps uniquely the case in the ancient Orient that one can maintain one's interest in understanding broadly formulated evolutionary questions, at the same time examining and attempting to change the adverse effects of colonial rule.

References

Abu-Lughod, J. 1971. *Cairo: 1000 years of the city victorious.* Princeton: Princeton University Press.

Adams, R. McC. 1981. *Heartland of cities.* Chicago: University of Chicago Press.

Curzon, G. N. 1925. *British government in India: the story of the viceroys and government houses*, Vol. 1. London: Cassell.

Dillon, R. 1976. *Carpet capitalism and craft involution in Kirman, Iran: a study in economic anthropology.* Unpublished Ph.D. dissertation, Department of Anthropology, Columbia University, New York.

English, P. W. 1966. *City and village in Iran: settlement and economy in the Kirman basin.* Madison: University of Wisconsin Press.

Gersamia, T. 1984. *Old Tbilisi.* Tbilisi: 'Sabchota Sakartvelo' (in Georgian, Russian and English).

Grabar, O. 1973. *The formation of Islamic art.* New Haven: Yale University Press.

Hodges, R. & D. Whitehouse 1983. *Mohammed, Charlemagne and the origins of Europe.* Ithaca: Cornell University Press.

Issawi, C. 1969. Economic change and urbanization in the Middle East. In *Middle Eastern cities: ancient, Islamic, and contemporary, Middle Eastern urbanism: a symposium*, I. M. Lapidus (ed.), 102–21. Berkeley: University of California Press.

Krausse, A. 1900. *Russia in Asia: a record and a study 1558–1899.* London: Curzon Press (reprinted New York: Harper & Row, 1973).

Lapidus, I. M. 1969. *Middle Eastern cities: ancient, Islamic, and contemporary, Middle Eastern urbanism: a symposium.* Berkeley: University of California Press.

Pearson, H. 1954. *Eastern interlude: a social history of the European community in Calcutta.* London: Thacker, Spink & Co.

Said, E. 1979. *Orientalism.* New York: Vintage Books.

Steensgaard, N. 1973. *The Asian trade revolution of the seventeenth century: the East India Companies and the decline of the caravan trade.* Chicago: University of Chicago Press.

Stone, E. 1987 *Nippur neighbourhoods.* Chicago: University of Chicago Press (Studies in Ancient Oriental Civilisation, no 46, The Oriental Institute).

Suny, R. G. 1986. Tiflis: crucible of ethnic politics, 1860–1905. In *The city in late Imperial Russia*, M. F. Hamm (ed.), 249–81. Bloomington: Indiana University Press.

Tekeli, I. 1973. Evaluation of spatial organization in the Ottoman Empire and Turkish Republic. In *From madina to metropolis*, L. C. Brown (ed.), 244–74. Princeton: Darwin Press.

16 *Culture, identity and world process*

JONATHAN FRIEDMAN

The past decade has witnessed a marked change in the cultural state of the world that could not have been predicted in the 'progressive years' of the 1960s. In the increasingly crisis-ridden centres of the world system there has been an implosive loss of faith in the progress of 'civilization', and a corresponding explosion of new cultural movements, from cults and religious revival to primitivism, a new traditionalism, a striving for the re-establishment of a new culturally defined identity. All of this activity has been accompanied by an increasing 'national' and ethnic fragmentation in the centre – from Basques and Catalans to the Irish and Scots – and an exponential increase in cultural-based political movements, collectively referred to as the 'Fourth World': Amerindians, Hawaiians, the Melanesian Kastom movement, etc. In the following discussion I hope to be able to suggest some of the ways in which an understanding of this truly global phenomenon might be approached. Such an understanding is necessary if we are to come to grips with a process that has not only seriously affected our conditions of existence, but even our interests, values and desires.

Our first encounter with the phenomenon was within anthropology itself. In earlier work (Friedman 1977, 1982) I discussed what appeared to be a cyclical pattern of oscillation, within civilized cosmologies, between evolutionism, materialism and collectivism, on one hand, and primitivism, culturalism and individualism (a focus on the subject, not methodological or economic individualism) on the other. It appears that the process corresponds to a larger-scale cycle of expansion and contraction in world systems, not only in our own, but also in previous systems. This research was incited by an awareness that within anthropology there had occurred a major shift from the developmentalism and materialism that were dominant from the 1950s onwards to a growing culturalism and primitivism in the 1970s and 1980s. This was no mere intellectual development, no theoretical advance, but a broad shift in focus. Anthropologists such as Sahlins, who had been concerned with the issues of the evolution of the state and of political hierarchy in general, and whose position was generally one of technological or ecological determinism (Sahlins & Service 1960), have today become cultural determinists who see no continuity in social development (Sahlins 1976). A general loss of faith in progress, in the continued development of our own civilization has emerged. Some, like Harris, who have maintained their materialist stance (Harris 1968, 1978, 1981), no longer believe that evolution is a positive process, but envisage our history on Earth, rather like Hesiod, as a long and steep decline from a primitive state when there were not too many people and when everyone got his share of animal protein. If the late 1950s and 1960s were characterized by the development of a dominant cultural materialism, a New Archaeology, a Marxist anthropology, a development anthropology, today's emergent themes are culture as text, culture and identity, ideo-logics, culture and history, etc., all pervaded by a relativistic or even primitivistic standpoint (Geertz 1973, 1983, Clastres 1977).

Anthropology, as that subject which defines itself as knowledge of the 'other' of civilization, would seem to be the ideal reflective surface upon which to gauge transformations in our own identity, assuming that our construction of the primitive or traditional, or both, mirrors in a fundamental way our own self-construction. However, the changes in anthropology's object are identical to those that have in one way or another swept through not only the social sciences in general, but also the humanities, literature, art, pop-culture, youth movements, etc.

Daniel Bell, one of the doyens of American sociologists, provides a pattern strikingly similar to that of Sahlins and American anthropology in general. Beginning as a clear advocate of social development, moving gradually from the political left to the right, from class politics to the ideology of 'the end of ideology' to 'post-industrial' society (Bell 1973) to the 'cultural' contradictions of capitalism (Bell 1976), Bell has captured, in both his career and his analyses, the shift we have discussed. He expresses today the need to regain a cultural past and a traditional identity that are lost, if not impossible, in the emergent 'post-modernity' of today's capitalism (Bell 1980). The focus has shifted from class to ethnicity, from class to culture, from rationality to the need for religion.

History, as evidenced by developments in both Europe and the USA, is moving toward an historical anthropology, i.e. an attempt to recreate or penetrate societies and cultures of our own past. There has been a plethora of books on the history of death, sex and the family, and even such subjects as honesty, the origin of the monarchy, and the origins of French identity and English individualism. When the French historian Jacques Le Goff was asked recently in a television interview why books about medieval French society and culture have become so popular for ordinary people today, he answered quite candidly that there were three major reasons: (a) the emergence of a new primitivism; (b) an interest in discovering their cultural roots and (c) a renewed interest in the exotic. Expressed here is a search for primordial meanings, cultural roots, an attempt to find in the past that which anthropology finds in the geographically distant. The discovery that we, too, have an authentic culture, just as exotic and primitive as any tribal society in the anthropological literature, that we, too, have witches, rituals and tales susceptible to structuralist analysis, all of which can be found in the ordinary life of our own ancestors, is a true controversion of the modernism and developmentalism of yesteryear: 'Man's self-conscious will to destroy his past and control his future' (Bell 1976, p. 4). One is further reminded that the present position represents the inversion of an earlier anthropology to normalize the foreign – Condominas' (1962) ethnography *L'éxotique est quotidien* has today become 'le quotidien est éxotique'.

Within the humanities in general, in philosophy, literature and art, we witness the emergence of so-called post-modernism, expressed in numerous forms and media; directly in the work of Foucault (1966, 1967, 1975). Lyotard (1979) and Deleuze & Guattari (1972), in the art of Klossowski and Artaud, all expressive of a Nietzschian revolt against the death-like repression of a civilized culture and language, and indirectly in the work of numerous sociologists (Hirsch 1983, Berman 1982), anthropologists and critics. One anthropologist, Friedrich (1979, 1982) is a self-proclaimed post-modernist who, in striving to create a poetical anthropology (Tyler 1984), seeks the underlying primitive substrate of culture and language, denying emphatically the possibility 'that the discourse of one cultural tradition can analytically encompass the discourse of another cultural tradition' (Tyler 1984: 328), and asserting that only a deeper, poetic, understanding can grasp the truth of culture as a 'work of art' (Friedrich 1982: 2). This 'progressive' post-modernism is directly opposed in content to the cultural revivalism and neo-traditionalism discussed above, and might easily be associated with conceptual experiments in polymorphous perversity (Brown 1966) and pop-culture's 'pornotopia'. The opposition between the culturalist and post-modernist responses to crisis are rooted in the dual nature of the self-definition of civilization (Habermas 1975, 1981, 1983).

These shifts in intellectual culture are not isolated phenomena, but coincide with the very widespread emergence of a cultural politics, a politics of local autonomy, a reassertion of individual autonomy of traditional values, a protest against the homogenization of state–bureaucratic capitalism, against creeping mediocrity, mass-culture and uni-sex society. Even the women's movement has undergone such a change, where two of its major figures, one a conservative, Betty Friedan (1981), the other a radical, Germaine Greer, have both stressed the need to return to a more traditional domestic organization. Greer (1984) goes as far as to suggest that the species will most certainly die out if our present anti-reproductive freedom persists in the future. Her ideal model is the traditional extended family taken from an India whose development programmes are geared to its extinction in the name of progress and freedom, not least of women. All of this has often been referred to, sometimes pejoratively, but often positively, as the revolt of the middle classes (Illich 1983).

Youth culture has also undergone transformations that reflect tendencies that we have discussed above. Although the Birmingham School has done much to popularize the idea of cultures of opposition, the advent of punk has baffled the notion of class-based cultural expression (Hebdige 1983), since its content is an overall revolt against civilization, often making use of particularly post-modernist symbolism, often explicitly identifying itself with a lost primitivity, often closely associated with movements such as the 'urban indians' of Italy and with the squatters of the major European cities.

Here again, we find two kinds of primitivity, one a cultural traditionalism, a search for roots in the past or for models from the periphery, the other a more libidinous–aggressive soul of man awaiting its freedom from the chains of civilization, but also finding its roots in some distant pre-capitalist past (Foucault and Elias) or in more-contemporary primitive societies.

Crisis and the structure of civilized identity

In order to begin to understand what appear in some ways to be diametrically opposed reactions to the present crisis, post-modernism and traditionalism, it is necessary to gain some grasp of the structure or matrix of self-definition within which they occur, a grasp that might also account for both their opposition to a reinforced modernism characterized by a super-rationalism and to developmentalism.

From the point of view of culture, civilized identity may be conceptualised as a repertoire or structure of behaviour, manners, rules and ideas defining the properties of a centre as opposed to a periphery, temporal or spatial, or both, exhibiting a more 'primordial' character. The specificity of civilized culture is its formality and abstractness; the existence of a system of impersonally defined roles, contracts, wages, markets, or bureaucratic positions. It contains a model of the person as role-player, as a self-developing independent agent focused on the future and without interest in the past, a Goethian spirit, a modernist (Berman 1982). This repertoire is envisaged as an overlay, repressing if not emulsifying a more primordial stratum of human 'traditional' culture existing in a few remaining enclaves in the periphery of the civilized world and in the historical past of our own world (Diamond 1974). Often referred to in terms of 'primordial ties', *Gemeinschaft* is a way of life organized exclusively by direct personal relations where the social world and the cosmos are inextricably fused in a single structure of meaning. It is this 'authentic' culture that we have presumably lost in our civilized desolation (Sapir 1924). Furthermore, this culture is the expression of real human needs, for a meaningfully organized existence, a set of coherent values, the ultimate security that can only be provided by a community of personal relations. It is in this way that it can appear as a longing or even a political movement for the re-establishment of local community self-determination, ethnic autonomy, traditional values and fundamentalist

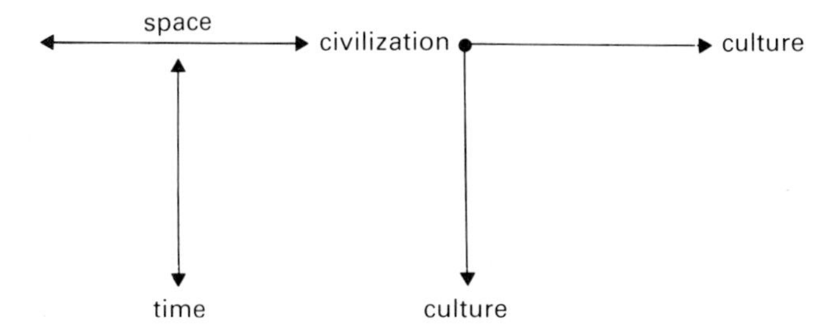

Figure 16.1 Civilized identity as the negation of culture.

religion. In this model, civilization – especially capitalist civilization – is the negation of culture, since the latter is defined as the concrete, face-to-face, communal, symbolically dominated life form of primitive and traditional (to a lesser extent) society (cf. Clastres 1977). The immanent structure of this definition of identity can be represented as in Figure 16.1.

The post-modernist image of civilized identity is largely similar to the traditionalist construct. The civilized state is similarly defined as a repertoire of abstract rules, of formal etiquette, etc., but this state is clearly identified with culture and not with its absence. Here it is conceived not as obliterating authentic culture, but as repressing nature, defined approximately in classical Freudian terms (Freud 1930). The primordial for the post-modernist is the primitive, the non-civilized, non-repressed non-adult. Where culture is identified with power it becomes synonymous with the super-ego of civilized man. In variants of Freudian-inspired sociology, such as the works of Elias (1982) and Foucault (1966), there is a clear tendency to identify pre-capitalist with pre-civilized and pre-cultural. Elias' feudal libido and Foucault's dualization of world history into pre- and post-Renaissance clearly exemplify a superego versus id view of culture promoted to the scale of universal history. A cursory knowledge of the anthropological literature, of course, discredits any such view – the 'civilizing process' is a central concern of primitive mythology (for example, Lévi-Strauss 1968).

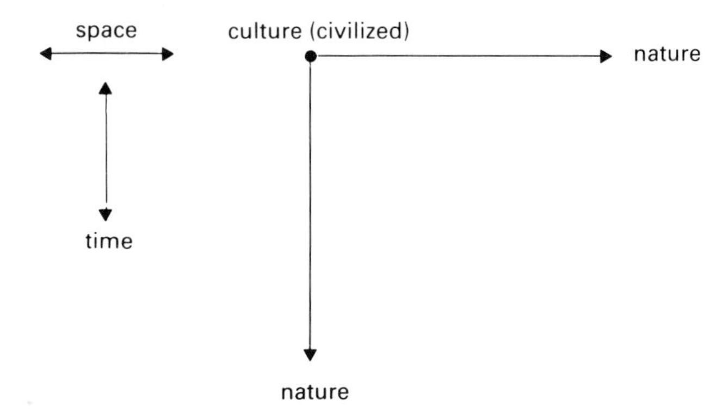

Figure 16.2 Post-modernist–traditionalist identity.

Here again, 'primordial' is located 'out there' or 'back then' – now nature instead of culture. It is again founded in basic human needs – not, however, for community, for meaning and for the directly personal, but for the full expression and elaboration of basic human desire, for the concrete, in the sense of the pre-linguistic, the pre-logical, of dream work, for communion (not community), in the sense of the obliteration of individual boundaries. The post-modernist structure of identity can be represented in a way analogous to the traditionalist structure (see Fig. 16.2)

Both the traditionalist and post-modernist structures of identity are opposed to the modernist position, the classical definition of civilized identity. In the latter, the abstract, the state and self-control are resolved into the rational and the progressive. Authentic culture tends to be seen as blockage and superstition, and is lumped together with the natural; the irrational, savage and the juvenile are also relegated to the spatial and temporal periphery of civilized identity.

The three variants of the structure of civilized identity can be summarized as follows:

Traditionalist–Culturalist
Civilization

1. abstraction
2. atomization–individualization: the dissolution of primordial ties.
3. disintegration of meaningfully organized existence
4. 'modernism' defined as the continual annihilation of the past in a process of on-going development of self-creation.

Authentic culture

1. concrete: social categories are elaborations on 'blood', sex, age, categories of nature, concrete thought in the Lévi-Straussian sense
2. direct interpersonal relations dominant; individual identity dependent on larger group, or at least its moral scheme
3. a structured meaningful scheme of human existence
4. tradition-bound social process, a stereotypic mentality based on the self-reproduction of fixed values

Post-modernist
Culture as civilization

1. élite (originally), bourgeois culture: production–repression
2. control by state, institutions and self
3. meaning organized around the autonomous individual, a 'middle-class' morality, independent spheres of social and cultural activity (work, home, leisure, art, etc.): Freudian model of ego–superego control as model for social order: rationality as dominant value, form dominant over content
4. mentality of individual (social) self-development, success, competition and 'status seeking'
5. abstract – socially as the dominance of a system of abstract roles and impersonal relations bridged by a formal etiquette: culturally as the dominance of form and formal relations, rationality and structure, i.e. control.

Nature

1. the primitive (primordial) liberated, the realm of 'desire', a culture based on the freed creativity of the human libido
2. absence of control, freedom of total expression

3. individual boundaries blurred, content dominates over form, absence of a superego–id hierarchy, activity boundaries blurred and dominated by the 'desire of the other', non-rational or arational value orientation
4. mentality focused on communion with the other, self as a fusion of mind and body, distinctions of sex, age and personality all polymorphized as the individual becomes one with his environment
5. concrete – the social based on the totalistic relation of whole people with one another: the concrete aspects of human and physical nature, the basic primordial qualities of the world are the subject of cultural elaboration and the creation of identities: the pre-logical, dreamwork aspects of thought are dominant

Modernist
Civilization
1. rationality and development as dominant principles
2. culture as bourgeois culture based on the code of individual liberty and the capacity for self-realization
3. meaning lies in movement (as in progress) itself, the future of liberated self-fulfilment
4. mentality of rational praxis applied to all the separate activities of life, equated with the values of fairness, basic equality and democracy, the goal of self-fulfilment through development
5. modernity as the cultivation of the new, the sophisticated and the capacity to change.

Culture–nature
1. barbaric or savage state: irrational, tradition bound and stagnant
2. traditional culture equated to the natural state, dominated by personal ties with all their oppression and unfreedom for the individual: society dominated by its past
3. meaning as religious, superstitious understanding of the world; irrational
4. concrete, juvenile mentality (*à la* Piaget), bricolage, engaged in stereotypic reproduction

There is another, purely technological, version of the modernist model, one that envisages the traditional and the primitive as equally rational and, in a sense, modern as the civilized. The difference between the two states of existence in this model is simply a question of the degree of techno-economic development. There is then an evolutionary continuum linking the primitive to the modern by means of a modernist dynamic rational adaptation to, and rational development of, techno-environmental conditions. This model, which negates the fundamental difference between us and them, which harbours a universalist humanism congenial to post-World War II liberalism and which provides the common ground for various forms of Marxism and other developmentalisms, might also be interpreted as the beginning of the dissolution of modernist identity. By denying the identity of rationality, development and the civilized state, it opens the door to cultural relativism. By negating the difference, it begins to negate itself.

The three kinds of self-definition (including the above variant of modernism) form a coherent structure of oppositions. In structuralist terms they can be reduced to transformations of a common civilized cosmology. Thus, the opposition of the traditionalist to the post-modernist is based on an opposition between the need to return to culture as opposed to nature. The opposition has numerous implications, i.e. the post-modernist might well define himself as future-oriented, his 'primitivity' lying in a psyche yet to be liberated, as well as in distant time and space, while the traditionalist has a more definite past in view. Just as traditionalism and post-modernism are reactions against modernism, the self-definition of modernism is opposed to both nature and culture. The three positions thus form a simple structure of the type shown in Figure 16.3.

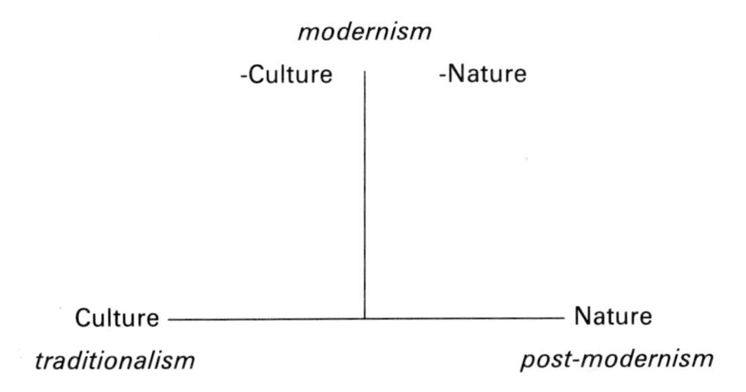

Figure 16.3 Three kinds of self-definition in a 'civilized' cosmology.

The structure in Figure 16.3 represents, of course, a set of extremes. In reality there are numerous areas of overlap among the three poles. It is in periods of crisis that the trifurcating nature of the structure becomes salient. Thus, if we conceive of the structured combination of the three poles as demarcating an identity space, then the emergence of traditionalism and post-modernism can be understood as expressions of the dissolution of civilized identity, whereas modernism is increasingly reinforced and even ritualized by those seeking to maintain a former identity. A better term than identity, here, might be identity-orientation.

What is essential here is that civilized identity has a specific construction, one that builds on an opposition between a self-in-the-centre and a periphery defined as Nature, traditional culture, the savage, the libido, i.e. a periphery 'out there' or a periphery within ourselves, or both. The identity crisis consists of the surging to the surface of that which is peripheralized within us, a closing in of that which is peripheralized outside of us; a search for meaning and 'roots' in the widest sense.

Fragmentation of the world system and the formation of cultural identity

The crisis of identity in the centre is expressive of a more general global crisis, as we have said. This crisis consists of the weakening of former national identities and the emergence of new identities; especially the dissolution of a kind of membership known as 'citizenship' in the abstract meaning of membership in a territorially defined state-governed society, and its replacement by an identity based on 'primordial loyalties', ethnicity, 'race', local community, language and other culturally concrete forms.

The tendency to cultural fragmentation is, in our view, not part of a process of development, of the emergence of a post-industrial order, an information society on a global scale. Rather, it is a question of real economic fragmentation, a decentralization of capital accumulation, an accompanying increase of competition, a tendency for new centres of accumulation to concentrate both economic and political power in their own hands, i.e. the beginning of a major shift in hegemony in the world system. The post-industrialization of the West is more a de-industrialization than a re-industrialization, the start of a probably terminal decline. As we have investigated the processes of cyclical expansion and contraction of global systems elsewhere, we need not go into further detail here (Ekholm 1975, 1976, 1977, 1980, 1984, Friedman 1976, 1978, 1982, Ekholm & Friedman 1979, 1980). Needless to say, the concept of post-industrial society is essential to the ideology of post-modernism, no matter what the explanation of the phenomenon (Bell 1973, 1976, Lyotard 1979).

The process of fragmentation has taken the form of movements for cultural autonomy, nationalist movements and ethnic movements, but also a general trend toward all forms of local autonomy and community self-control. At the highest level of segmentation, beneath that of the national state itself are nationalist–ethnic, ethnic and cultural autonomy movements.

Nationalist, or rather sub-nationalist, politics have become increasingly troublesome right here in the centre of the system. In 1957 Deutsch, in a mood of progressive optimism, stated that 'as far as minority groups within states are concerned, these appear not to be at all dangerous' (Deutsch 1957, p. 159). The belief in a pan-European society has for the most part faded today, in the wake of both national conflicts of interest, the ethnification of the nation state, and internal movements of Basques, Scots, Bretons, Flemish, etc., referred to in astonishment by a prominent researcher in the following terms: 'The recent reemergence and intensification of sub-national ethnic conflict in Western Europe and North America have come as a surprise to most scholarly observers' (Lijphart 1977, p. 46).

Thus, a development that was depicted decades ago as the 'integrative revolution' (Geertz 1963) in reference to the so-called 'modernization' process in the new post-colonial states of the Third World might just as well be depicted today as the 'disintegrative revolution' in reference to the system as a whole.

In both the centre and periphery of the world system there has been a rapid increase of ethnic-based movements for national autonomy. The situation can be summarized as follows:

(a) Where the population in question is only weakly integrated into a larger national state and the world system, a national movement may simply imply political and economic autonomy in a situation in which the local culture is fully a part of a total organization of life activities: for example the Shans and Kachin of Burma, the Iranian Kurds, the Naga of India, some lowland Indian groups of South America, etc. Most of these groups can be expected to be found in the periphery of the world system, where certain more marginal areas maintain a kind of modern tribal organization, and where others may have more traditional niches in larger regional systems dating back to early colonial or pre-Western periods. In such movements the local culture and identity are taken very much for granted, simply because there is no historical discontinuity between the present and the 'cultural' past.

(b) Where the group in question is fully integrated in the larger system, its identity is essentially dependent on a set of group symbols broadly defined as ethnic, anything from skin colour to language, to common descent or to a set of shared cultural practices, objects or beliefs. Nationalism here implies the establishment of a culturally distinct nation-state society that is essentially identical to other such state societies except for its ethnic distinctiveness. Here culture plays a crucial role in a great number of activities, but it does not enter into the process of material reproduction of the group. This kind of ethnic nationalism, often referred to as 'sub-national', is typical of the European situation, i.e. the situation of the centre of the world system where the entire population is integrated in a more-or-less homogeneous economic process of capital accumulation. Of course, it can occur anywhere in the system where the cultural sphere is separated from the process of reproduction.

(c) Where the group in question is again fully or partially integrated into the larger system, and its identity is again dependent on a set of common symbols, it may at the same time possess a cultural model of total life processes including material reproduction, which in turn becomes a central focus of the movement. This can occur in situations of either cultural continuity or discontinuity, i.e. where a cultural identity has been preserved in transformation or repressed in favour of an alternative identity 'imported' from the centre. Thus, there is no Basque model of a total life form, no Breton model of material existence, but there is a Hawaiian model of a total society, and a variety of North American Indian models of total ways of life. A movement organized around such a model can only occur where the model itself can be retrieved or reconstructed. Such a situation is one that we would also expect to find in peripheral areas where a pre-colonial = pre-civilized past is often preserved in the form of local traditions and European-constructed history and anthropology, all of which can be drawn upon at the appropriate moment. Such nationalisms as emerge here may not be comparable with the notion of nation-state, insofar as their specific cultural model implies a political organization of a completely different nature.

Nationalist movements are most lethal to the integrity of the current state organizations of the larger system, since their very existence implies the disintegration of the political units of which they are a part. Thus, they are the strongest form that the cultural crisis can take, expressing the reformation of sociopolitical identity along the lines of primordial loyalties at the very least, and the tendency to withdraw from the larger system ((c) above) at the very most.

Culture, in and out of the system

In order to understand the role that culture plays in the process of identity construction and deconstruction that we have discussed, it is necessary, in a preliminary way, to differentiate among the three ways that culture is implicated in the larger system. For the time being we refer to them simply as cultures I, II and III.

Culture I refers to that vaguest of all concepts of culture, that discussed and battled over by anthropologists since the inception of the discipline. Whether it refers to everything from agriculture to philosophy, or to the symbolic or mental orientations of society, is not as important in this context as the fundamental relation between the anthropologist, as representative of the centre, and his object, one that defines the 'objectivity' of anthropological description. Phrased in numerous ways as the privileged position of the scientific outsider, Culture I refers to an objective (in the sense of objectified) description of the content of the lives of the population 'out there' defined by its distance from 'us'. Now it is clear that this notion of culture is a product of the larger system itself, insofar as it can be understood as the observation of the periphery by the centre. Thus, objectivity is the potential product of a political relation. The degree to which the centre–periphery relation informs the content of our understanding of other cultures is clearly relevant, especially in the current crisis. However, our point here is simply to demarcate the notion of Culture I as 'objective' culture, the culture of the social analysis. As such, it refers to the specific properties of another society's system of meaningfully organized repertories of social action. This may include anything from dialect, gestures, styles of production and consumption to religious behaviour, symbols of identity and social values.

Culture II refers to that set of elements used by a population in its own self-identification. Rather than our identification of them, it refers to their identification of themselves. The specificity of Culture II is that it is a structure of identity in conditions where the population reproduces itself in essentially the same conditions as the rest of a larger sovereign population. Culture II thus corresponds, to what is usually known as the culture of ethnic identity. It is based exclusively on notions of commonality of language, 'blood' and descent irrespective of the nature of the social conditions in which it may be found. Culture II is as prominent in periods of global expansion as in periods of contraction. In the former, it is crucial in the formation of larger ethnic or minority blocks that can defend or advance their interests in the larger system, but there is clearly a tendency for economic success to weaken ethnic identity seriously as individuals find new and rewarding identities in the expanding career possibilities of the growing national society. In periods of contraction, ethnic or minority identity, or both, is something to fall back on, again for both economic defence and advantage, as well as for cultural and psychological security. The definitive characteristic of Culture II is its restriction to the function of identity, making it fundamentally adaptive to the national or global reproductive process.

Culture III is culture as the organizer of total life processes, including material reproduction. It defines itself in fundamental opposition to the larger system. Thus, although it contains the essential elements of cultural identity of Culture II, it also harbours a model of a different, 'former', society that can only exist external to the present system. As such, movements organized on the lines of Culture III do not stress the need for jobs, welfare and equal rights. Instead they demand a land base upon which to reinstate and practise their culture. Culture III is not organized for advantage within the system, but for exit from the system. As a political ideology it combines cultural identity with a culturally defined resistance to 'civilization'. It flourishes in periods of contraction. It may flare up in periods of expansion, which for the populations in questions are periods of marginalization, 'ethnocide ' and cultural collapse, but it is only in periods of civilizational decline that it can appear to be a superior ideology to that of the centre itself and that it can gather massive support for its goals. Since the ideology of such movements embodies notions close to those of the culturalists (traditionalists), an attachment to local community, close to nature, founded on the control of its own conditions of existence, based on direct personal relations, of extended family or kinship networks, or both, an absence of capital, even money, of the state and abstract forms of contract and wage, it has a strong appeal to both post-modernists and traditionalists in the centre, many of whom have become actively engaged in the struggles of such groups.

Culture and the global system

In the previous pages we have, by implication, been discussing the processes of disintegration of civilization. These processes do not leave a vacuum behind them: on the contrary, they would seem to imply a flowering of culture, of new identities and a search for a more concrete set of meanings for existence. Briefly, then, cultural-based identity would seem to vary inversely with 'modernity', i.e., with civilizational expansion (see Fig. 16.4).

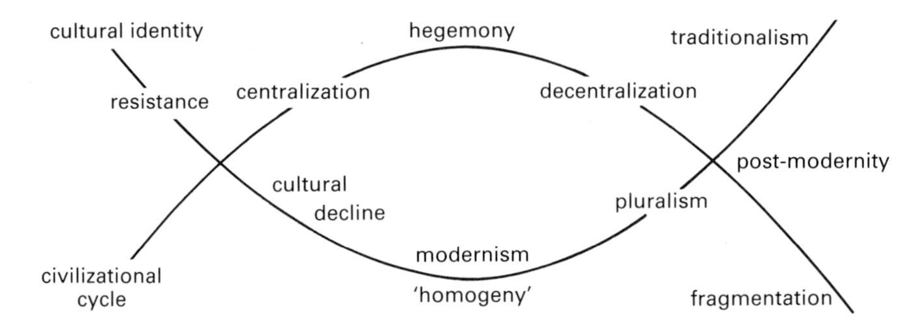

Figure 16.4 Civilizational cycles of hegemony and cultural identity

In periods of expansion (which at the highest level may characterize the centre as a whole, but which include numerous specific local expansion processes, even in periods when the centres are contracting – especially in areas variously referred to as semi-peripheries), there is a tendency for local self-reproductive systems to disintegrate and to become integrated into the larger colonial and international systems. This inevitably leads to breakdown of culture in the Culture III sense, often its transformation into Culture II. Ultimately there is a strong tendency to assimilation, to the increasing identification of individuals of aboriginal populations with the model of the centre, with a modernism that appears to be associated with success and which is itself successful. However, the catastrophic nature of world 'development' ensures that a large portion of the population of the system remains 'lumpenized' in conditions of extreme poverty in a state where Culture II remains dominant, if not by choice, then by stigma. Such partial processes of integration within the national state framework of modern capitalist civilization have long been optimistically discussed under the rubric of modernization, the 'passing of traditional society' (Lerner 1958) or the 'integrative revolution' (Geertz 1963). However, such discussion came not at the beginning of the process, but at its point of exhaustion.

The cultural decline characteristic of the periphery occurs simultaneously with the strengthening of modernist identity in the centre. This process is reversed in periods of contraction. As modernism collapses in the centre, there is an exponential increase of cultural identity, both at home and broad. At home there is a search for that which has been lost, and in the periphery for a cultural or even national autonomy previously repressed by the centre. Cultural identity, from ethnicity to 'way of life' flourishes at the expense of the system.

The analysis of the complex of phenomena in both centre and periphery, the interaction among the three cultures in the process of construction of cultural identity, and the relation between all of these processes and the material processes of global system in crisis are, we think, a fruitful and necessary approach to an understanding of a reality that until now has been totally elusive.

References

Bell, D. 1973. *The coming of post-industrial society.* New York: Basic Books.
Bell, D. 1976. *The cultural contradictions of capitalism.* New York: Basic Books.
Bell, D. 1980. *The winding passage.* Cambridge, Massachusetts: Alt Books.
Berman, M. 1982. *All that is solid melts into air: the experience of modernity.* New York: Simon & Schuster.
Brown, N. 1966. *Love's body.* New York: Random House.
Clastres, P. 1977. *Society against the state,* Oxford: Blackwell.
Condominas, G. 1962. *L'éxotique est quotidien.* Paris: Plon.
Deleuze, G. & F. Guattari 1972. *L'anti-Oedipe.* Paris: Editions de Minuit.
Deutsch, K. W. 1957. *Political community and the North Atlantic area: international organization in the light of historical experience.* Princeton: Princeton University Press.
Diamond, S. 1974. *In search of the primitive.* New York: Transaction.
Ekholm, K. 1975. System av sociala system och determinanterna i den sociala evolutionen. *Antropologiska studier* **14**.
Ekholm, K. 1976. Om studiet av det globala systemets dynamic. *Antropologiska studier* **20**.
Ekholm, K. 1977. *Om studiet av risgenerering i samhället och av hur risker kan avvärjas.* Göteborg: Aamarbetskommittén for långsiktmotiverad forskning, rapport II.
Ekholm, K. 1980. On the limitations of civilization: the structure and dynamics of global systems. *Dialectical Anthropology* **5** (2).
Ekholm, K. 1984. The study of risk in social systems: an anthropological perspective. Mimeo.
Ekholm, K. & J. Friedman 1979. 'Capital', imperialism and exploitation in Ancient World systems. In *Power and propaganda: a symposium on ancient empires.* Larsen (ed.). Copenhagen. (Republished in *Review* **6** (1) (1982).)
Ekholm, K. & J. Friedman 1980. Towards a global anthropology. In *History and underdevelopment,* Blussé, Wesseling and Winius (eds). Leiden.
Elias, N. 1982. *The civilizing process.* Oxford: Blackwell.
Foucault, M. 1966. *Les mots et les choses.* Paris: Gallimard.
Foucault, M. 1967. *Madness and civilization, a history of insanity in the Age of Reason.* London: Tavistock.
Foucault, M. 1975. *Surveillir et punir, naissance de la prison.* Paris: Gallimard.
Freud, S. 1930. *Civilization and its discontents.* London: Hogarth Press.
Friedan, B. 1981. *The second stage.* New York: Summit.
Friedman, J. 1976. Marxist theory and systems of total reproduction, Pt. I. *Critique of Anthropology* **7**.
Friedman, J. 1977. The social history of social anthropology. *Stofskifte* **1**.
Friedman, J. 1978. Crises in theory and transformations of the world economy. *Review* **2** (1).
Friedman, J. 1982. Catastrophe and continuity in social evolution. In *Theory and explanation in archaeology,* Renfrew *et. al.* (eds). London: Academic Press.
Friedrich, P. 1979. *Language, context and the imagination.* Stanford: Stanford University Press.
Friedrich, P. 1982. Linguistic relativism and poetic indeterminancy. Mimeo.
Geertz, C. 1973. *The interpretation of cultures.* New York: Basic Books.
Geertz, C. 1983. *Local knowledge.* New York: Basic Books.
Greer, G. 1984. *Sex and destiny.* London: Secker & Warburg.
Habermas, J. 1975. *Legitimation crisis.* London: Heinemann.
Habermas, J. 1981. Modernity versus postmodernity. *New German Critique* **22**.
Habermas, J. 1983. Neo-conservative culture criticism in the United States and

West Germany: an intellectual movement in two political cultures. *Telos* **56**.
Harris, M. 1968. *The rise of anthropological theory*. New York: Crowell.
Harris, M. 1978. *Cannibals and kings*. New York: Random House.
Harris, M. 1981. *America now*. New York: Touchstone Books.
Hebdige, D. 1983. *Subcultures*. London: Methuen.
Hirsch, J. 1983. Between fundamental opposition and realpolitik: perspectives for an alternative parliamentarianism. *Telos* **56**.
Illich, I. 1983. *Gender*. London: Marion Boyars.
Keesing, R. & R. Tonkinson 1982. Reinventing traditional culture: the politics of Kastom in Island Melanesia. *Mankind* (special issue) **13** (4).
Lévi-Strauss, C. 1968. *L'origine des manières de table*. Paris: Plon.
Lijphart, A. 1977. Political theories and the explanation of ethnic conflict in the Western World: falsified prediction and plausible postdictions. In *Ethnic conflict in the Western world*, Essman, M. (ed.) Ithaca: Cornell University Press.
Lyotard, F. 1979. *La condition postmoderne, rapport sur le savoir*. Paris: Plon.
Sahlins, M. 1976. *Culture and practical reason*. Chicago: University of Chicago Press.
Sahlins, M. and Service, E. (eds) 1960. *The evolution of culture*. Ann Arbor: University of Michigan Press.
Sapir, E. 1924. Culture, genuine and spurious. *American Journal of Sociology* **29** (4).
Tyler, S. 1984. The poetic turn in postmodern anthropology: the poetry of Paul Friedrich. *American Anthropologist* **86** (2).
Ziehe, T. & H. Subenrauch 1982. *Plädoyer für ungewöhnlisches Lernen. Ideen zur Jugendsituation*. Hamburg.

17 *The archaeology of colonialism and constituting the African peasantry*

MICHAEL ROWLANDS

Beside [Asia], Africa looks like a shapeless, uncouth giant. A flat cake without a form, vast and amorphous

Leo Frobenius

Introduction

For more than 30 years historians and archaeologists have worked to counteract primitivist ideas about the absence of change, the cultural backwardness and technical failure of Africa. In the 1950s it seemed as if little had changed to alter Hegel's view that 'Africa is not an historical continent; it shows neither change nor development . . . as we see them today, so have they always been' (*The philosophy of history*, p. 6). If it was still unproblematic for a modern historian to reiterate Conrad's horror in *Heart of darkness*, 'there is only the history of Europeans in Africa . . . the rest is darkness and darkness is not a subject of history' (Trevor-Roper 1963, p. 871), then the work of researchers in African history since has been both consciously and unconsciously guided by the quest to refute it and to represent the African past as a unique synthesis of oral tradition, archaeology and history, the autonomy of which was beyond doubt and would support the claim that Africa had made a privileged contribution to the diversity of human cultures (cf. Phillipson 1985, p. 10, Connah 1986, p. 6)

Either justifying or dispelling the desire of Europeans to reach out for an idea of what Europe is not, the 'primitive', the 'Orient', 'Africa' has been the hidden text in archaeological research, resulting in prioritizing certain work strategies and exhibiting a sensitivity to political issues that only recently have begun to impinge more forcefully on the consciousness of those working in the heartlands of the 'Great Civilizations'. Accounts such as Garlake's work in Zimbabwe (Garlake 1982), or Hall's in South Africa (Hall 1984) are graphic demonstrations that writing the past in Africa is always a politically mediated act. It is a sign of some success that writing on African archaeology can no longer be couched in such primitivist language as 'Africa during the late Pleistocene remained a kind of cultural museum in which archaic traditions continued without contributing to the main course of human progress' (Clark 1971, p. 181).

Yet there is a danger that an archaeology that continues to be defined by assessing Africa's position on an externally derived and 'universal scale of civilization' risks staying within it and thereby reproducing it in an inverted and potentially reinforced form. The concept of Africa is, after all, European in origin, and it has more to do with the construction of the civilized identity of the latter through its constitution of otherness than it has to do with explaining contemporary political and economic realities. To wish to argue that Africa has its own food-producing revolution(s), or independent iron-working traditions (Diop 1960), or that it lacked literate civilizations because its rich environments did not produce the constraints required for people to give up freedom (Phillipson 1985, p. 10), or that oral tradition based on speech is superior to and more authentic than literacy based on writing (Fage 1981) are symptomatic of the tendency to continue a long tradition of defining 'Africa in difference', and thus reinforcing its separateness from and potential inferiority to the rest of the world.

Moreover, it prevents the discipline engaging more constructively in understanding the origins of the discourses on African primitivism that it has so far attempted only to refute empirically rather than intellectually. In turn this failure inhibits recognition that underdevelopment in Africa is not of timeless origin, but is a result of a confused representation of a reality of recent origin: the product of the reorganization of local economies in the late precolonial and early colonial periods and, perhaps most significantly, a belief in the existence of an unreconstructed traditional African peasantry, sunk in ignorance and superstition, and incapable of change without external (i.e. European colonial) intervention. In the first part of this chapter I present a brief survey of some of the conditions which called into reality a certain kind of fiction called Africa; in the second part I argue that an historical archaeology of European contact can evade these snares and contribute to an historical archaeology of contemporary political and economic relevance.

The concept of Africa

The idea that Africa is an idea has an origin. Knowing what this is must be part of the process by which we understand how Europe reached backwards in time or outwards in space to discover what Europe is not (cf. Rowlands 1984). Europe, the Orient and Africa are thus concepts derived from the experience and internalization of their interaction rather than objective historical facts.

Since the beginnings of Western discourse on 'otherness' an idea has existed of an Ethiopia, or a Libya or an Africa that has allowed a 'primitive other' to be defined, distinct in its negativity from the broadly successful definition of the Orient in the European scale of thinking about such things (Said 1979, pp. 204, 208). It was relatively recently that 'Africa' came to be applied to the whole continent. The label of '*terra incognita*', by which the continent was known for so long, more aptly betrays a sense of absence, distance and a perception of the place as a void. Naming the place was a problem: Ethiopia, Libya, Sudan, Guinea, Niger, etc., have all been used at different times to refer to larger or smaller parts of this unknown land. Ethiopia is Greek in origin, and is first referred to in Homer as a place of 'sunburnt' people (*The Odyssey*, p. 2); Sudan is Arabic and has the same connotations of blackness (versus white). Africa comes from the Latin, and referred originally to the region around Carthage although its etymology is confused (Miller 1986, p. 10). Leo Africanus, whose *Description of Africa* first appeared in 1550, effectively spread to Europe the knowledge of Black Africa that Muslim traders had acquired over the centuries. Africa, as he describes it, is as distinct from the Islamic East as it is from Europe, and is inferior to both. In the Arabic myth of origin, Africa was created and derives its name from Ifricos, King of Yemen, who was the first to conquer and inhabit it and thus give it form (Miller 1986, p. 13). Its meaning as a place of separate colour and as a subjugated colony is thus established at an early stage in Western perception.

Miller gives a convincing account of the major elements that come to define Black Africa for 19th-century European civilization. This is the origin of the overtly racist definitions of Africa as 'black'; stripped of reason and moved only by a blind, sensorial desire. The civilizing standards of Egypt or Ethiopia are thus to be accounted for by their closeness to white Mediterranean civilizations, and hence their weakened status as African. Blackness is therefore nullity or absence; a depiction of void, which combines with a lack of reason; an absence of consciousness or logos (Miller 1986, p. 27). Hence, from Homer's sunburnt Ethiopians to Trevor-Roper's view of history, based on Conrad's *Heart of darkness*, the association of blackness with nothingness is at least consistent. Moreover, it justifies that the void has to be filled from the outside; the miraculous appearance of the white races in Africa inaugurates history and knowledge. After all, that which is dark can only be known by shedding light on it.

If Africa is separate, distant and a void, to Europeans it was also ambiguous and incoherent. For example, Homer's Ethiopia was both remote and delightful; a place of sensual pleasure (Snowden 1970, p. 148) and a place of monstrous troglodytes and other unhuman beings (Miller 1986, p. 26). Africa is at the same time a lost paradise and a hideous nightmare. This ambivalence in the writings of the Ancient World has been carried down the ages and received by us as double valency in all things African (Miller 1986, p. 32). Yet it is a dualism that cannot be sustained; its elements, polarized and apart, continually threaten to dissolve into each other. Distance and remoteness that combine monstrousness and the delights of fulfilment are collapsed in Africanist writing into a single idea; that of blackness. In 17th- and 18th-century writings, what comes through is a condensing of the association of colour with nullity. Africans are black, idolatrous, superstitious and given over to sinful pleasures, and it is all a consequence of an inability to control the passions (Hirschman 1977). Absence of control is documented by the absurd lengths to which Africans are said to go in superstitious devotions to objects and fetishes. Beliefs in idols, as objects worshipped in their own right rather than as symbols or reflections of an idea, clearly demonstrate an absence of reason and an incapacity for reflexive thought: 'Instead of a God of authority, repression and all-defining constancy, there is a god of released tension, wish fulfillment and malleability' (Miller 1986, p. 47). No wonder that Marx should use 'fetish' to describe the alienating practices of capitalist commodity production, and that Mauss would rapidly dismiss its anthropological relevance as a concept because it connotes only 'an immense misunderstanding between two civilisations, African and European' (Mauss 1969, p. 144).

In their identification of an object called Africa, Europeans experienced a fantasy of fulfilled desire in which the distinction between dream and reality was abolished. As a consequence the dogma emerges that Africa was the epitome of economic backwardness and the antithesis of European economic dynamism. For example, one of the justifications of colonialism in Africa was that it brought its peoples 'under the rule of law' (Richards 1985, p. 10). This dual valency of dream and reality, timelessness and backwardness, romanticism and monstrous contempt, still organizes Western popular perceptions of Africa, as well as the consciousness of some of its archaeological and ethno-archaeological practitioners.

Colonial representations

The economic backwardness of precolonial Africa had become firmly established colonial doctrine by World War I. Whereas European travellers from the 16th century had marvelled at the range of craft and agricultural products available in local markets (Skinner 1964), from the later 19th century into the 1920s and 1930s the tendency was to stress the predominance of the self-sufficient African peasant economy; and the dominance of agricultural production, its low yield and wasteful exploitation of the environment, due to a reliance on a primitive technology, lack of transport, communal land tenure and the extended family (Hopkins 1973, p. 9, Guyer 1984). Moreover, a number of anomalies from the standpoint of classical economic theory, notably the absence of a land market, the absence of labour time accounting and the idea that social rather than economic values were being maximized, served only to problematize further whether the 'native economy' could ever be rationally organized.

Different European colonial powers responded in different ways to the problem of what development meant in the African context. Cameroon in West Central Africa is of particular interest because it was under the colonial authority of Germany, Britain and France at different times. Like other West African colonies, it was created without a substantial white settler population, with quite explicit motives of economic exploitation through the use of force which should entail minimal administrative and military cost. When the German protectorate of Kamerun was declared in 1884 in order to defend the interests of German traders by preventing a trade monopoly of the Benue region by the British, a debate was already being pursued as to the proper nature of development under colonial rule, derived from German experience in Togo and South-West Africa (Stoecker 1986). The terms of the debate were already well known in Europe, where predominantly agricultural populations in Germany and Russia were perceived to be the main obstacle to economic development and, in particular, to the ideal of industrialization. At the turn of the 20th century Stalin's particularly brutal solution to the problem of the peasantry in Russia was not yet seriously contemplated. The 'peasantries' of Eastern Europe and Africa were uneasily associated as sharing a common problem of backwardness, and to be incapable of progress. Encouraging progress meant solving the central question of whether, in a predominantly agricultural population, development was best left to a *lasissez-faire* market principle which would encourage African small farmers to produce cash crops for the world market, or whether this was too unreliable, and rural food production to supply the towns and workers could only be organized by the state. In the first scenario the role of the colonial administration would be to encourage an entrepreneurial spirit among the owners of small farms, stimulate the flow of cheap labour to foreign capitalist-owned enterprises in the colony, raise revenue in cash to meet administrative expenses and break peasant self-sufficiency.

By the 1880s the liberalist view was under attack in Cameroon. This was partly due to what was widely perceived to be the non-capitalist rationality of African farmers. They were perceived to be incapable of development on their own. In part it was also technical problems encountered in transport, and the failure to break the monopolistic practices of coastal trading societies like the Duala, that together convinced representatives of the German trading companies that the forced appropriation of land and labour was the only path to successful development of the colony. Moreover, the decades from 1870 to 1890 saw a major industrial recession in Europe, the collapse of prices in primary tropical products (in particular palm oil) and the development of intense rivalry between the European trading companies to achieve increases in productivity at lower costs (Hopkins 1973). The main thrust of German expansion of the 1880s was directed towards the interior to bypass coastal trading monopolies, to develop the plantations and expand inland trade, and to solve problems in the supply of labour. The policy of imposing a fully developed capitalist economy on the colony was pursued vigorously in Cameroon in the 1880s and 1890s under the governorship of Von Puttkamer. He favoured direct taxation methods (a poll tax) to force Africans to work, and labour conscription, land expropriation and the establishment of large concession companies that were to be given exclusive rights to the products and labour of large areas of Cameroon, which they pursued often with the utmost brutality.

However, the alternative liberalist philosophy was never completely quashed. It gained increasing support in Germany as a result of the failure of plantations and concession companies to make significant profits (and in some case their success in making significant losses), and also as a consequence of a wave of genuine revulsion at the stories of brutal oppression that the missions, in particular, relayed back home. It was strongly believed that the worst aspects of the industrialized societies of Europe should not be reproduced in Africa. The colonies might instead be a haven for poor white German settlers to establish new farming settlements in Africa, alongside independent African farmers, and produce for a world market. This was not only an influential populist argument in Germany, it was also deemed by many to be the rational economic development for small-scale peasant farming populations in many parts of the world (cf. Richards 1985). Moreover, the costs of maintaining colonial rule by violence were becoming prohibitive, given that the promised economic profits were not forthcoming. However, the problem for those advocating the liberalist argument remained the supposed non-capitalist rationality of the African small farmer. There was no guarantee that indirect rule of the benevolent kind advocated would produce the desired results if the African peasantry was left to its own devices. This would require developing an African élite capable of recognizing its interests and setting an example for others, and also recognizing the benefits of education and religion.

Due to such pressures in Germany, Governor Von Puttkamer was recalled from Cameroon in 1906 and replaced by Governor Seitz, who pursued the ethical policy outlined above. This was effectively the beginning of the dogma that a traditional and anarchic African peasantry in Cameroon had existed before European contact and should be subordinated to the interests of a more powerful capitalist world economy. Seitz's policy, supported by the Basel Mission, was aimed at finding ways in which this could be effected as painlessly as possible. Seitz believed in setting up self-contained peasant communes in the German colonial protectorate, which would collect their own revenues and administer their own affairs (a classically German and Russian populist policy on how best to organize the peasantries of Eastern Europe, cf. Hussain & Tribe 1981). Seitz's intention was to protect Africans from excessive European exploitation, to avoid the need to rule by force, and to make the colony more self-sufficient and less under the financial control of the German Reichstag in Berlin. One aim was also to develop a new system of African political control in Cameroon, in which a small, educated, black African élite would be created to perform roles that until then had been filled by German expatriates. The same policy elsewhere in German colonial Africa was met with great hostility by white settlers, who probably correctly recognized that it would result in the creation of an educated African class capable of effective resistance to colonial rule. In Cameroon the absence of a significant white settler contingent meant that the opposition was muted and, if Germany had not lost its colonies after World War I, Cameroon might have been one of the first independent African states.

The ideological battle within the administration of German rule in Cameroon, as elsewhere in Africa, had its material effects as local African 'societies' battled to comprehend and resist what was being imposed on them (Chilver 1967). The question is, how do we gain some idea of these effects when the characterization of the African peasantry was itself a product of these debates? Debates, incidentally, that were not just limited to Africa, but originated as the 'agrarian problem' of the peasantry in Eastern Europe at the turn of the 20th century. The firm belief that countries with predominantly rural, peasant populations must find a different path to capitalist development from that experienced in Western European industralization was exported to Africa (Kitching 1984 cf. Mitrany 1954, Sabel & Zeitlin 1985). Moreover, by the time of World War I, the problem of the African small-scale farmer as non-rational and uninterested in commercial matters, embedded in mystical superstition and witchcraft, had become firmly established as the precolonial and pre-European contact 'reality' that colonial rule had to break for effective development to be possible. Not only did Europe therefore create the fiction of the African peasantry, it also then extrapolated the fiction into the African past as a natural reality that it was Europe's civilizing task to change and reform in order to make such populations amenable to capitalist development.

The archaeology of precolonial 19th-century Bamenda

In the confrontation of such opposing ideologies, the question is whether archaeology can form an independent basis for reconstructing the nature of late-precolonial African societies. In Cameroon the case is perhaps more open, in the sense that it was never the location of large precolonial African kingdoms that attracted numerous earlier European travellers, and whose accounts can be matched against later 20th-century colonial representations. We therefore have a more straightforward problem of assessing the archaeological and oral data available in the absence of a consistent literary history derived from European contact sources.

The case I describe is based on fieldwork carried out in the Western Highlands of Cameroon and, in particular, the Bamenda region (Fig. 17.1). This is a high-altitude savanna area (due to long-term human interference) which was first contacted by one of Puttkamers's contracted explorers, Eugene Zintgraff (cf Chilver 1961a). He was immediately impressed by the density of population and the resources of what came to be called 'the Grassfields', and worked assiduously to create the political conditions that would allow this to be used as a labour reserve for plantations on the coast, as well as a new opportunity of the production of cash crops and for trade by the concession companies. Yet the area had been vaguely known to Europeans since the 16th century as a supplier of iron spears and cutlasses to the coastal peoples around Rio del Rey (Ardener 1968, p. 87). In the 18th century relations between this area and the coast were strengthened through the slave trade, and the Grassfields regularly appear as a source of slaves to Europeans at Douala and Calabar (Warnier 1985, p 151). Perhaps the best general piece of evidence to indicate the extent to which the Grassfields had been incorporated into European-dominated trade circuits by the time of German colonization is the distribution of late-19th-century money forms (Fig. 17.2). When combined with evidence of types of transaction, this shows that the area was divided into three trading zones; one characterized by the distribution of cowries and dominated by traders from the Hausa emirates to the north; a second by the distribution of small glass beads of Mediterranean manufacture and distributed, particularly in the 18th and early 19th centuries, by French and Dutch traders through the port of Douala; and a third characterized by brass manillas that gained increasing importance during the middle and late-19th century, and were distributed by British traders through the port at Calabar. The Calabar trade gradually supplanted the Douala trade during the 19th century, and was beginning to compete effectively with the northern Hausa traders for products such as ivory, slaves, wild rubber, kola nuts and palm oil at the time of colonization (cf Chilver 1961b).

The degree to which local social exchange was transacted in foreign currencies by this period can be gauged by:

(a) Bridewealth payments and fines were made in brass rods at German contact; local market exchanges were conducted in either cowries or brass rods or their equivalents, and they could be exchanged at special border markets. Beads were no longer important except in very small transactions, but were used to decorate elaborate masquerade costumes, ancestral figures and calabashes of chiefdom nobilities. No separation of wealth items into spheres of exchange existed, and value could be stored and realized in any of these currencies. Hoards of brass rods and cowries are regularly found hidden on compound land to this day. Elders will account for them by saying that they would often acquire brass rods at times of the year when they did not want to use them, i.e. they were stores of wealth.

(b) A money–commodity–money circuit was standardized and extended to the sale of persons, in particular that of male slaves and boys to Europeans on the coast or for the internal slave trade. Female slaves were more likely to be bought locally and absorbed into complex marriage systems involving control by marriage lords over their offspring.

(c) Figures 17.3 and 17.4 show the expansion and contraction of these trading spheres throughout the 18th and 19th centuries. The Douala trade, which includes the areas with evidence of the earliest centralized chiefdoms, is shown to be in decline throughout the 19th century, while the Calabar trade expanded and was beginning to encroach on the dominant Hausa trade at the time of German conquest.

Although this evidence demonstrates that the Grassfields was a part of a larger European-oriented regional system, it says little about the nature of the incorporation or its effects. The archaeological evidence to be derived from a study of the history of iron production in the area gives a different picture of the organization of precolonial craft production and specialized production for exchange from the colonial view that Africans lacked technical skill and initiative.

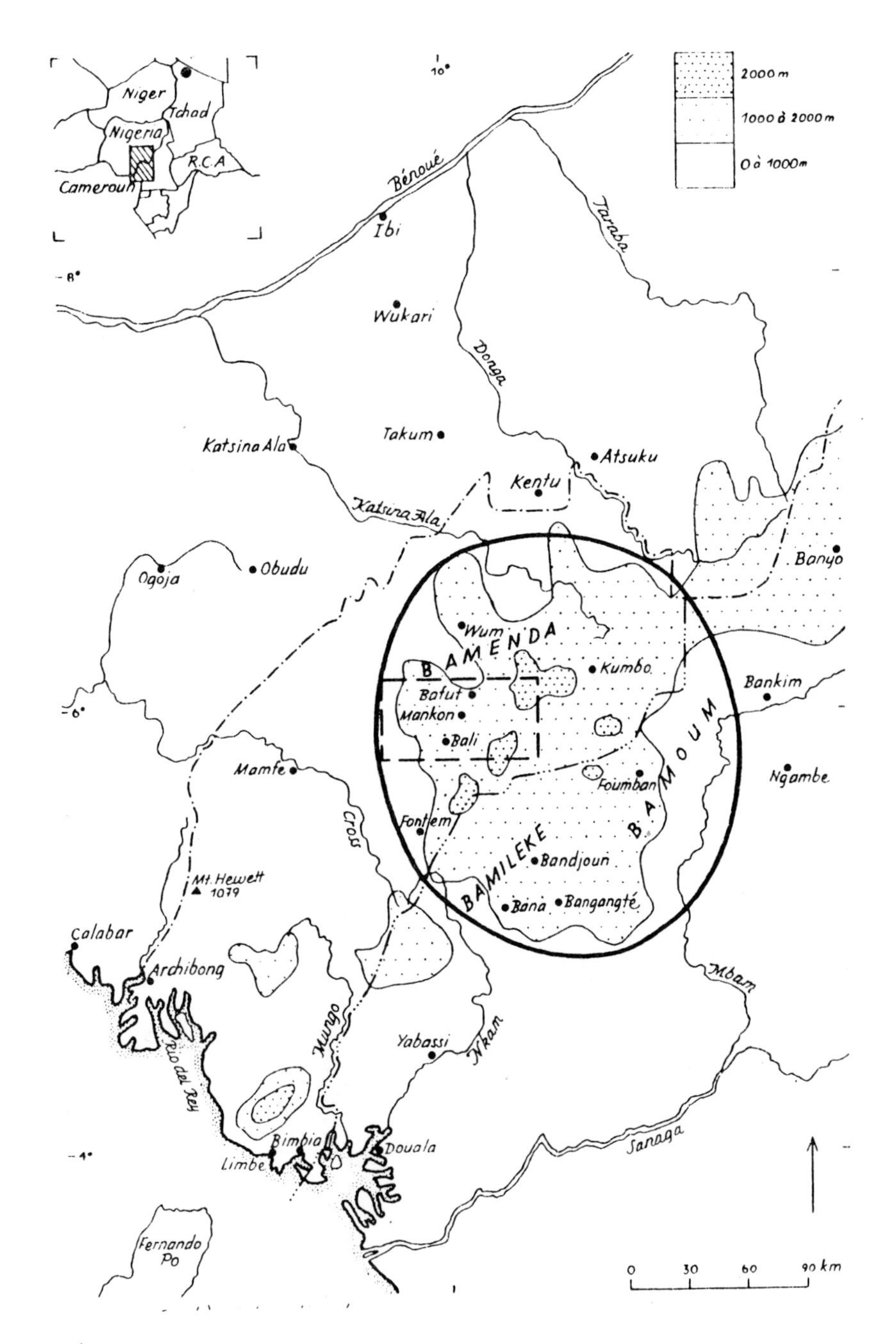

Figure 17.1 The 'Grassfields'.

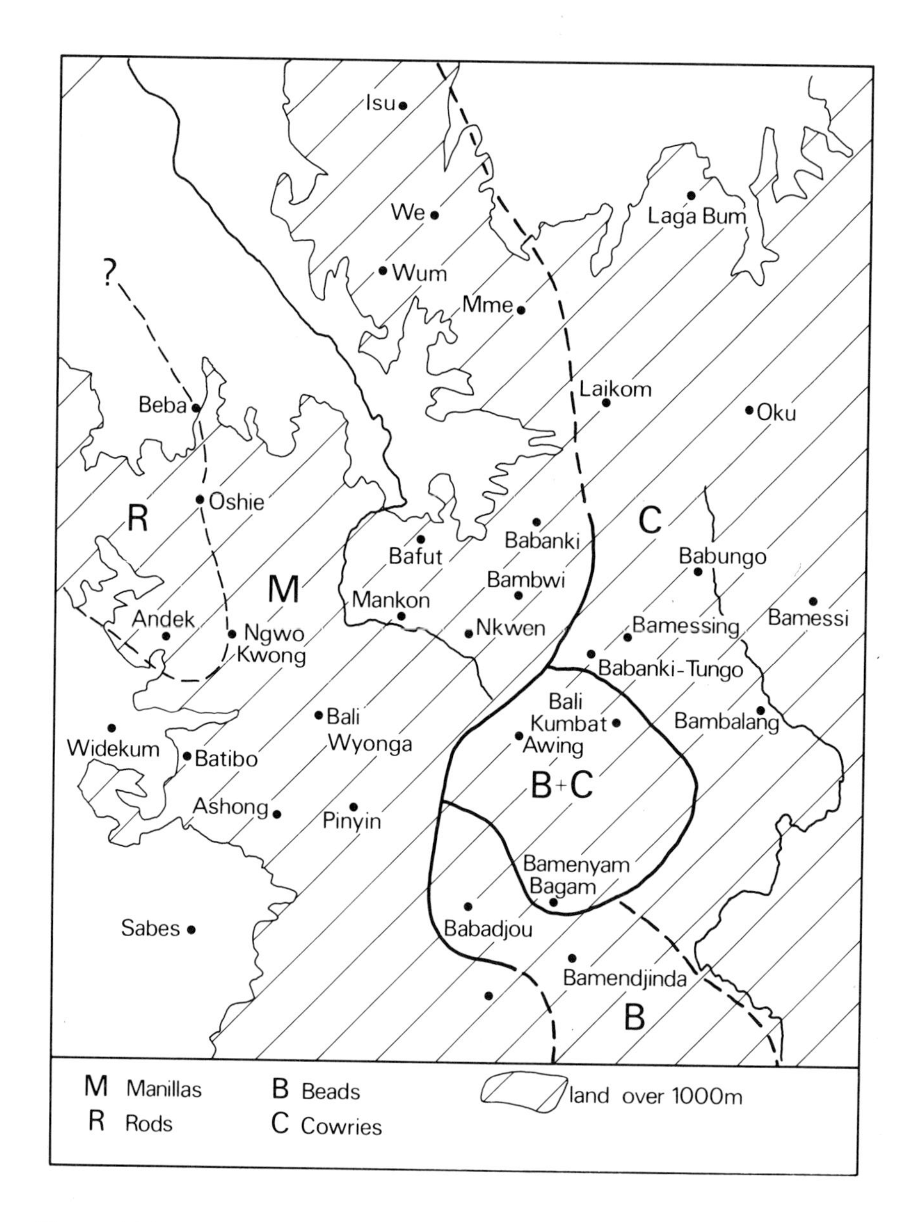

Figure 17.2 Monetary zones on the Bamenda Plateau c. 1890.

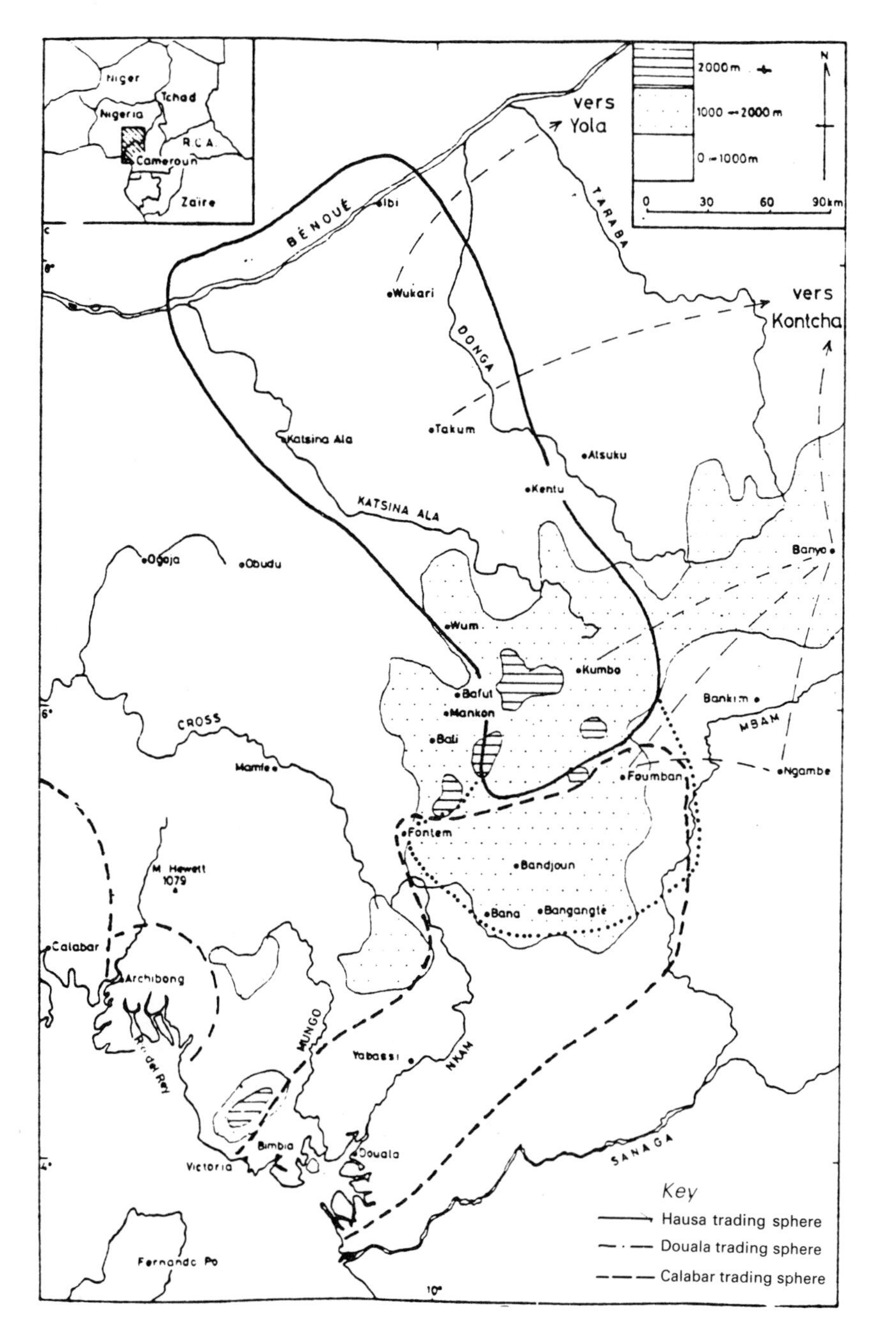

Figure 17.3 Trading spheres at the end of the 18th century.

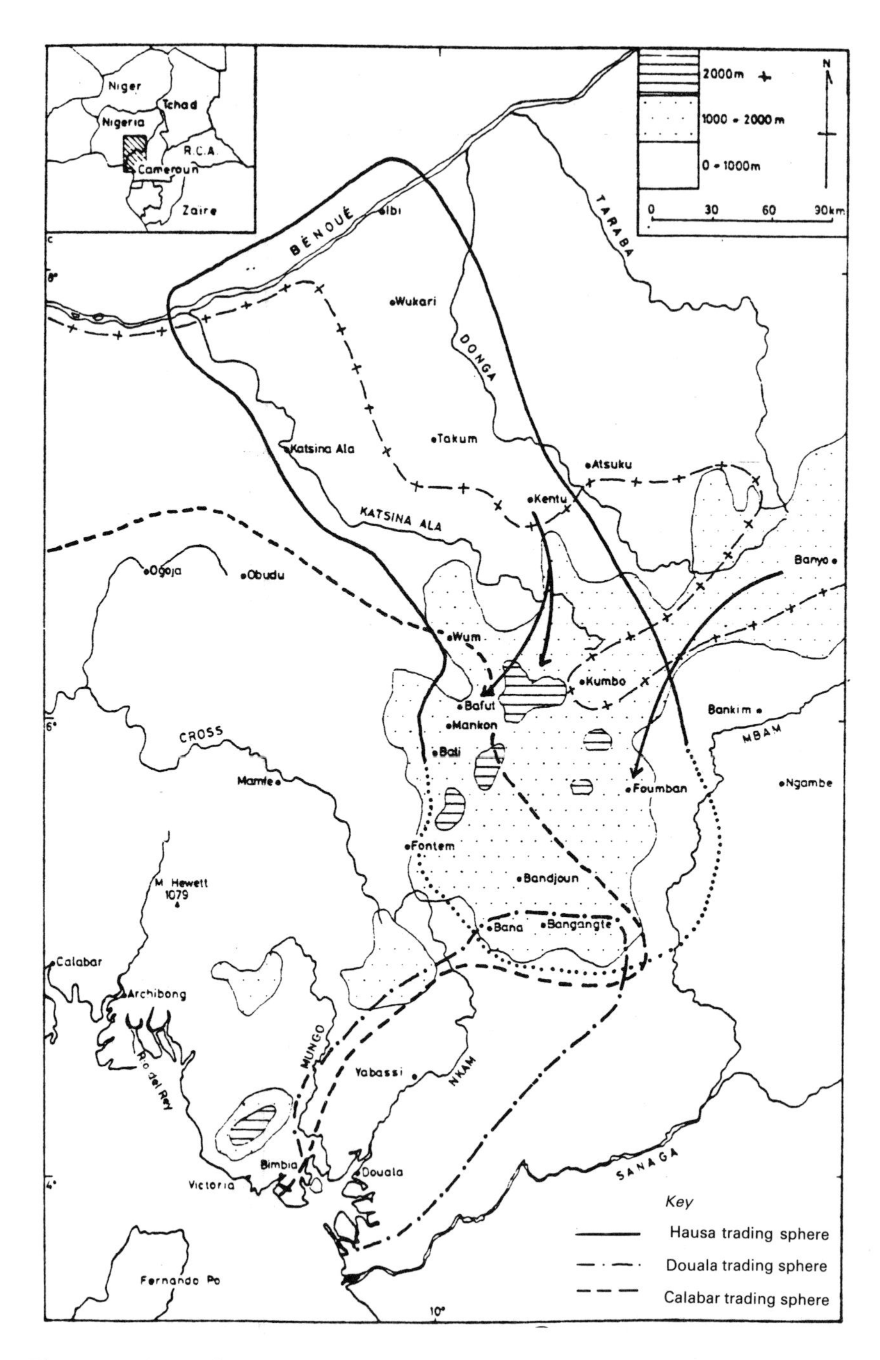

Figure 17.4 Trading spheres at the end of the 19th century.

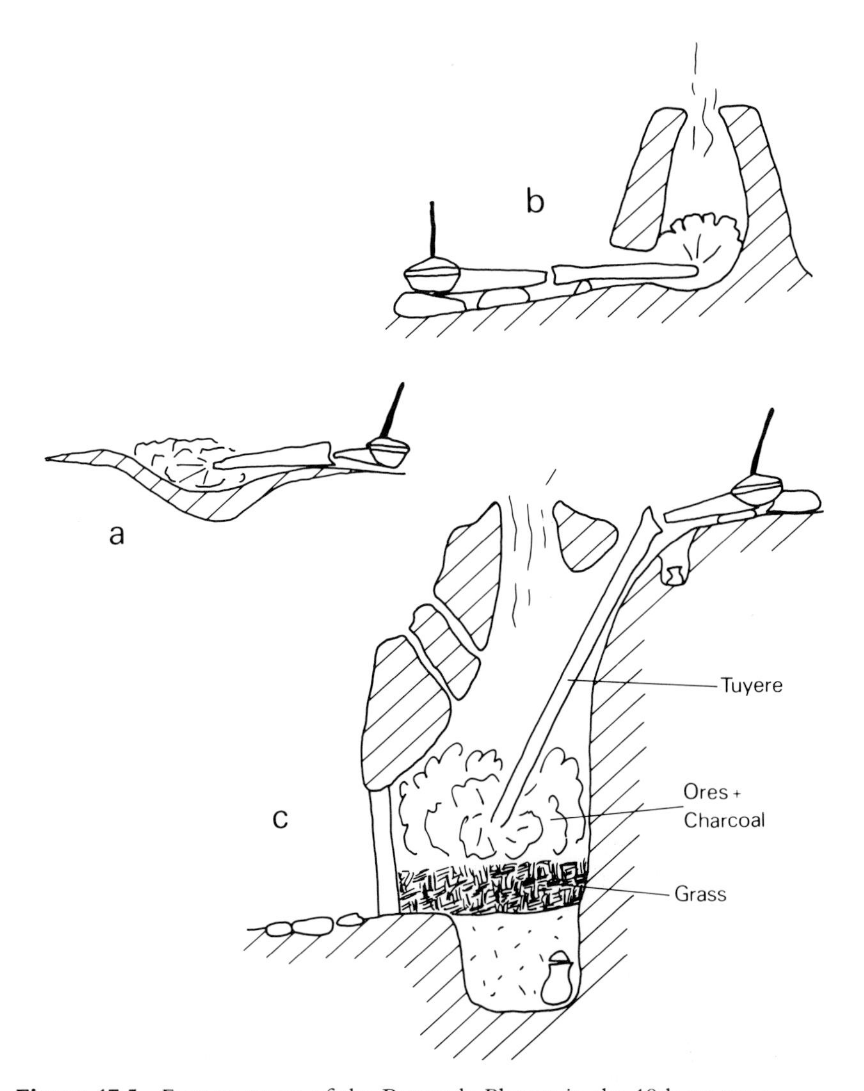

Figure 17.5 Furnace types of the Bamenda Plateau in the 19th century.

At the time of the German conquest, most villages were producing small amounts of iron, using a shallow bowl furnace technology (Fig. 17.5a). The 'primitive nature of the technology' was remarked upon by Zintgraff (Chilver 1961a, p. 10). The results of a field survey of ironworking sites and technologies and their scale of production shows that two other furnace technologies had been used to make iron, but were abandoned a short time before the German conquest (Figs 17.5 b & c). A low, cylindrical furnace using a double bellows seems to be the earliest and mot widespread form. Corrected carbon-14 dates for sites or associated material give a range of dates from the 3rd to 17th century AD (AD +

245 + 915; AD + 610 + 1260; AD + 1305 + 1669; Ly 3065-3067). This technology continued to be used to produce indigenous iron up until the 1940s in the more remote northern parts of the Grassfields (Jeffreys 1952). At some period, certainly no later than the 17th century, a larger 'clump-furnace' technology was developed that was capable of vastly increased rates of production (Fig. 17.5c). Some indication of the difference in scale of production that was introduced can be gauged from a comparison of the amounts of smelting debris remaining at the two types of furnace site:

	No. of chiefdoms	No. of sites	Vol. of debris(m^3)
cylindrical furnace	10	98	6 470
clump furnace	6	274	214 500

The clump-furnace technology is restricted to a number of village chiefdoms in the Ndop plain, and it replaced the earlier cylindrical-furnace technology. Moreover, all the later furnaces were located within the defensive boundaries of the chiefdom, whereas the earlier form has a more dispersed distribution (Fig. 17.6). Also, rituals of protection of compounds only include sites of the older furnace type and, where remembered, family heads still use them to identify ancient compounds where ancestors might be buried and require propitiation. The later type of furnace is not treated with the same respect, nor are women refused entry to such sites. This suggests that innovations in the iron technology coincide with the movement of settlement into defended sites, and the new furnace did not have the close association with compound land and property as the earlier type. Although the latter appears to have been lineage property and intended mainly to supply its members with iron, the former appears to have been organized at a village or chiefdom level for wider exchange. The iron produced also seems to have been of a superior quality. It is quite probable that these specialist iron producing chiefdoms of the Ndop plain were the source of the weapons and hoes said to have been favoured over European imports by coastal populations around Calabar in the 17th century (Ardener 1968, p. 87). Also, when Zintgraff visited the Ndop chiefdom of Babungo in 1889, he observed the technology, was presented with a sword and commented on the faultless quality of the iron being produced (Chilver 1961a, p. 21).

Although more accurate dating is a priority, the general sequence of iron-producing technologies suggests that these centres of specialized production and the system of regional exchange of which they were a part collapsed in the last two or three decades of the 19th century. The diffusion of an open-hearth-bowl technology was the devolutionary response by populations that were now no longer able to buy their iron hoes, spears and cutlasses at local markets or through trade friends, and had to re-invent a means of satisfying immediate needs (in particular, the male obligation to supply wives with hoes which otherwise would have

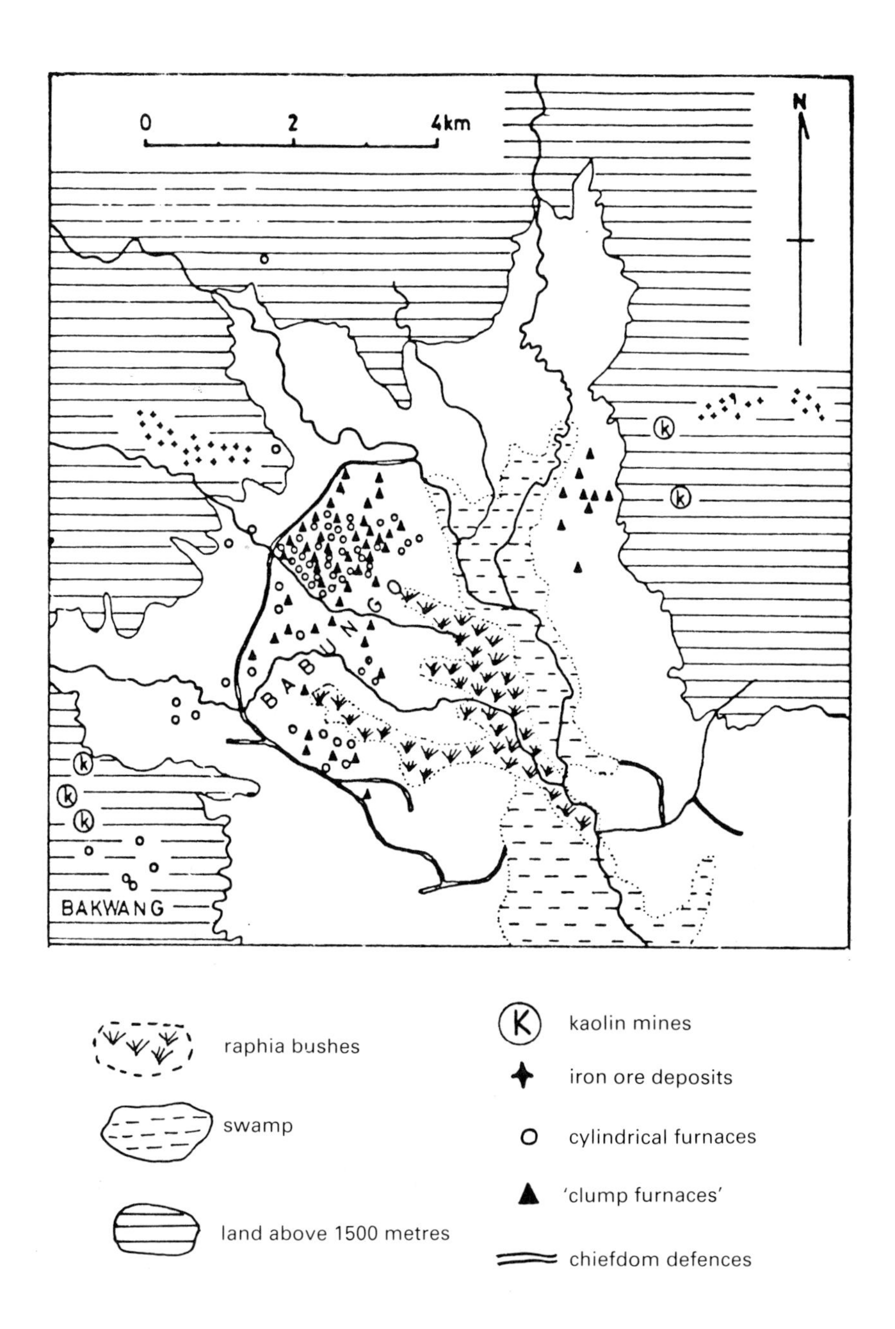

Figure 17.6 Distribution of ironworking sites, Babungo.

required brass rods to buy the European-imported forms). The devolutionary nature of the technology is underlined by the fact that easily available iron ores were no longer used, and smiths travelled to the older centres to mine and re-use the slag. The most likely explanation for the collapse of these specialist iron-working centres was their failure to compete with imports of European iron ingots and hoe blanks brought into the region in vast quantities from Calabar during the late-19th century (cf. Warnier 1985, p. 114).

However, it would be too easy to interpret these local transformations as a consequence of increasing European domination. The relationship between production and exchange, power and ideology in 19th-century Bamenda was more complex than this, and decline in one part of the region was part of a wider pattern of chiefdom competition and expansion to paramount status.

Chiefdoms, states and the regional system

According to oral tradition, the chiefdoms of the Grassfields in the 19th century were in a constant flux of political conflict, economic rivalry and competition for each other's population. Such rivalries still structure local contemporary politics, and there is little doubt that German colonization both interrupted and, for a time, facilitated a regional process of 'state formation' (Rowlands 1979).

When Zintgraff first established contact with the chiefdoms of the Grassfields in 1889, these processes had already reduced competition for paramount status to four contenders (Fig. 17.7). His policy was to use superior military technology to support one against the others in order to create a German client state – a policy that still figures in local politics as 'the Bali question'. Consequently, local forms of hegemony were reinforced (for example, Zintgraff's favoured partner chiefdom was given tribute rights over 30 formerly independent village chiefdoms in the 1890s, and punitive expeditions were directed against its rivals for paramount status). The German policy to create a client state in the Grassfields only reinforced a more general tendency towards the development of large concentrations of population in the centre of the plateau. (Rowlands 1979, 1986). Perhaps the most extreme version of this is to be found in the development of the kingdom of Bamum during the 19th century (Tardits 1980). This kingdom, situated in the Eastern Grassfields, contained about 70 000 inhabitants distributed over 8000 km^2, more than half of whom occupied a defended centre of 400 km^2, corresponding to the contemporary capital of Foumban. Figure 17.8 shows the distribution of settlement in Bamum before the concentration into the capital which, based on the accounts of ex-slaves and the dates of three expeditions into Bamum country by Fulani slave raiders, is said to have occurred in the reign of Fo'Mbuombue between c. 1824 and 1835 (Tardits 1980, p. 127). A middle- or late-19th-century date for a similar concentration of population around the palace site of Mankon, a smaller

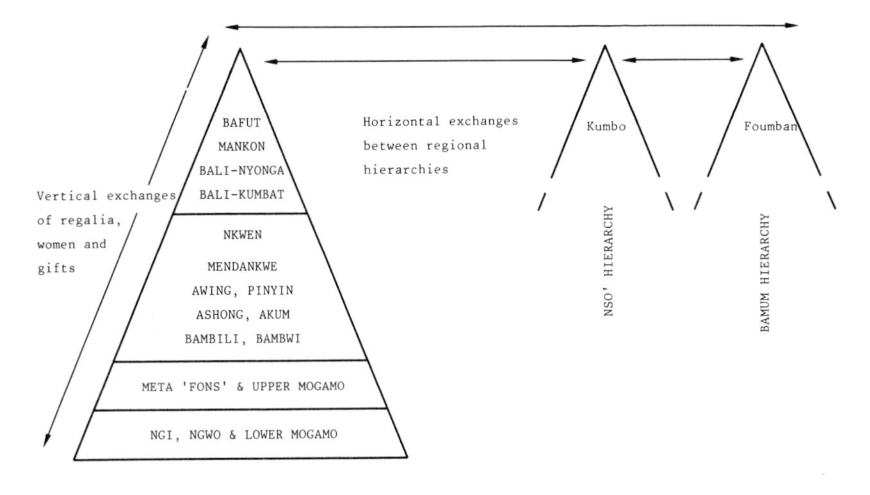

Figure 17.7 Hierarchy of Fons and Notables of the Bamenda Plateau and their relations with neighbouring hierarchies.

chiefdom in the western Grassfields, is suggested by the fact that informants were still able to take the author to named compound sites and shrines that were occupied by the ancestors of present elders early in the 19th century. A pattern of highly dispersed, low-density lineage-clan settlement attached to local shrines, oathing stones and places for sacrifices seems to have been transformed within a short period into a few centres of densely defended settlement around a palace-ritual complex during the early to middle 19th century. However, these centres were the product of a much longer period of intense rivalry and absorption of the populations of less fortunate neighbours. The distribution of four major chiefdoms on the Bamenda plateau at the end of the 19th century (Fig. 17.9) confirms that the centre of the plateau had emerged as the optimal position for political growth with dispersed, acephalous populations located in the hill ranges to the north and west.

The political, economic and ideological determinants of this process have been discussed elsewhere (Rowlands 1986), but there are several points that are of particular importance as far as understanding the kind of social reality that early German colonists were unwittingly involved in creating and then confronting as the burden of colonial administration. One was that the major regional markets and the centres of small-commodity production, such as the specialist iron-producing centres of the Ndop Plain, were all located at the interstices of the major political centres of the region or on the borders of the Bamenda regional economy (Fig. 17.10).

The absence of major markets and craft production in centres of densest population and political power was a source of considerable unease to European colonizers. Besides its irrational economic signification, it

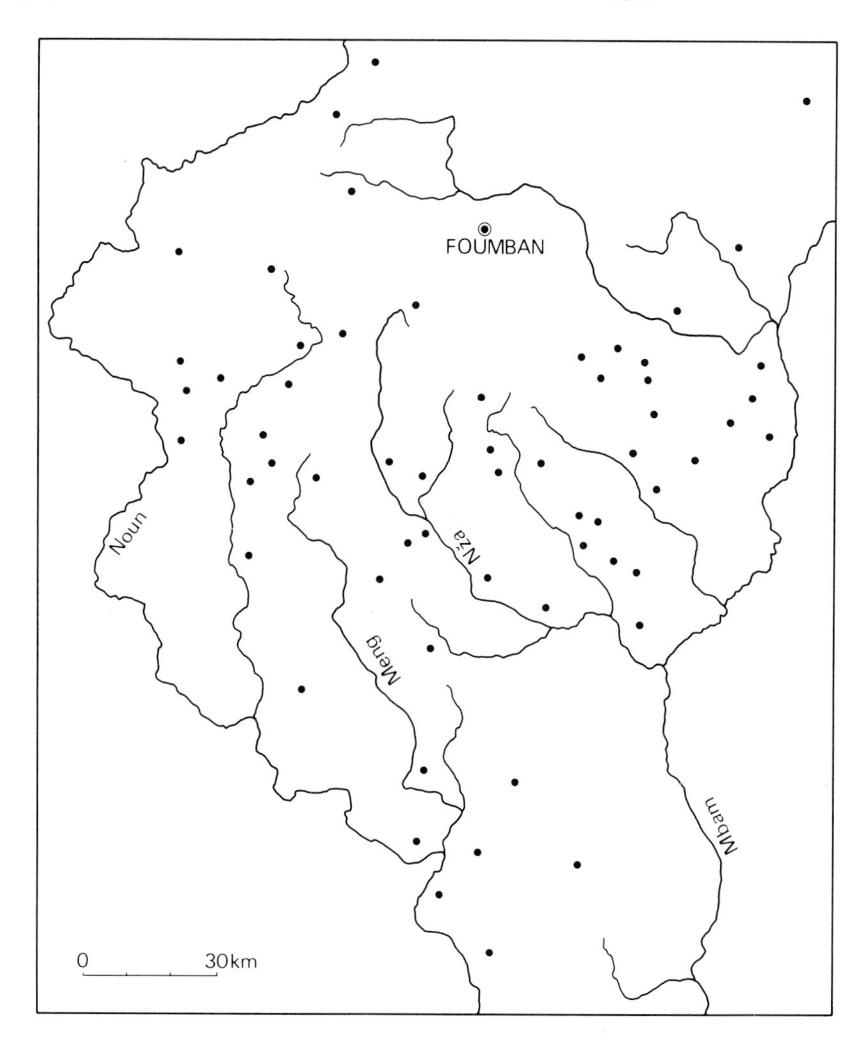

Figure 17.8 Distribution of surveyed sites abandoned by c. 1835. Populations either dispersed or incorporated by Foumban. (Sites identified by field surveys, eponyms and oral traditions, after Tardits 1980.)

meant, practically, the absence of food markets to supply soldiers and administrators at the military forts. Yet this unease was based on a misunderstanding of the reality of trade and economic specialization in the regional economy. The tendency for trade and production for trade to be controlled or marginalized in pre-modern states is quite well known (cf. Brumfiel 1983). The Grassfields shared a similar tendency to that described elsewhere, for acephalous polities exercise less control over trade. Hence, markets in these tended to attract both local and long-distance traders who specialized in the movement, often in large quantities, of local specialities

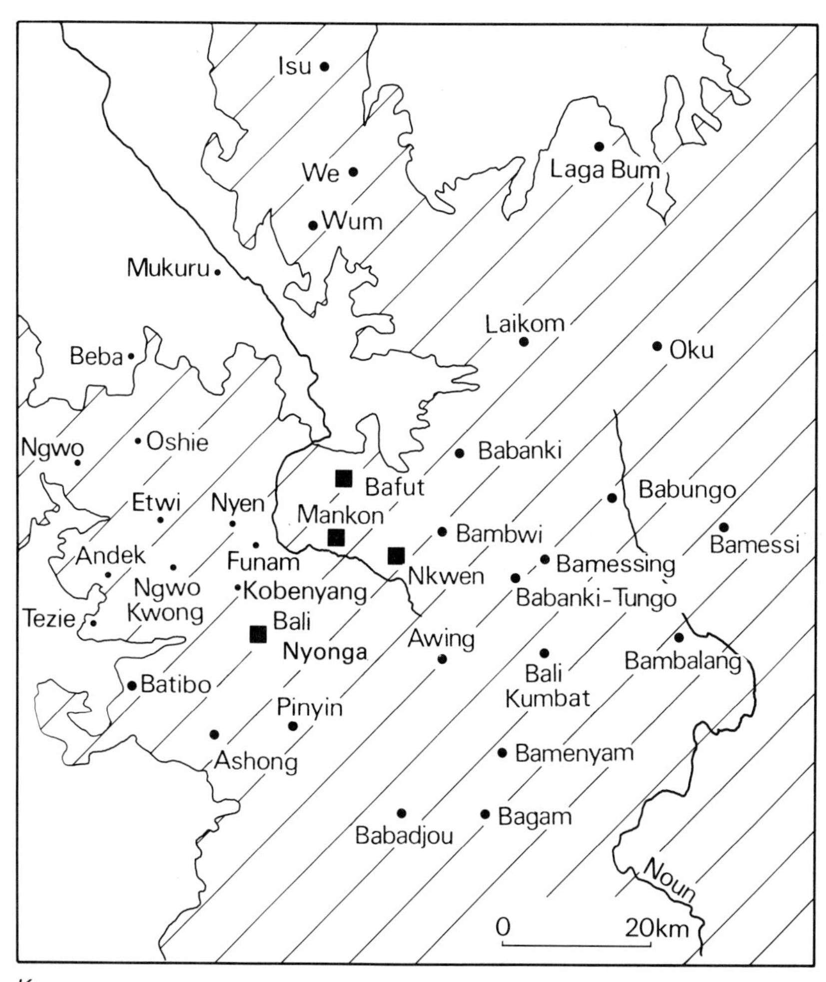

Key

- ■ 'chiefdoms of 8000+ inhabitants. Recognized as 'friends' by Nso + Bamum
- ● 'chiefdoms of 1000+ inhabitants and hereditary 'Fons'
- • settlement of less than 1000 inhabitants and without established 'Fons'

land over 1000 m shaded

Figure 17.9 Hierarchy of chiefdoms and Fons of the Bamenda Plateau in the late 19th century.

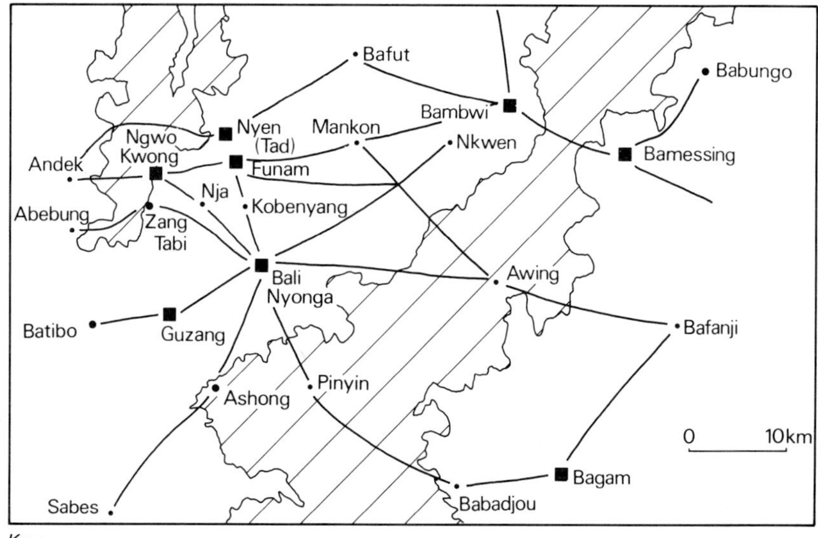

Figure 17.10 Principal markets on the Bamenda Plateau at the end of the 19th century.

and foodstuffs. It was rare that transactions involving prestige items, slaves or local products of high value would appear at these markets; instead their exchange was organized through 'merchant houses' in the larger chiefdoms, i.e. nobles or palace officials who had the title and wealth to organize trading expeditions in such items. Trading by poorer men in the centralized polities was effectively limited to local markets and the exchange of foodstuffs. The richer title holders–merchants would instead operate through trade partnerships, and formed marriage alliances with powerful traders in other chiefdoms – in some cases, apparently, extending to having partners in the European trading *entrepôts* at Calabar and Douala on the coast. Titled men, as heads of merchant houses, were able to restrict the trade in high-value commodities to their own households and networks of trade friends, and to limit free trading activity in the larger chiefdoms, except for the most localized of food markets.

Moreover, the production of iron hoes and weapons, woodwork and pottery was as costly in male labour time and, given that labour-accounting was differentiated by the value attached to the category of people involved rather than by valuation of the product, this meant that household heads would, if possible, avoid using household male labour for compound production, and use it for long-distance trading instead. The high costs of male labour in craft production would instead be passed on to smaller and less powerful chiefdoms, while the profits from trade could be converted into increased agricultural production by using wealth to acquire more wives to expand household production.

In the period before German annexation of the Grassfields it appears that the increasing importance of gaining access to European trade goods favoured the mercantile strategies of the central chiefdoms over that of producing for exchange. The value of European goods such as manufactured cloth, guns, gunpowder and personal ornaments was so great that only participation in the trade in slaves could provide the wealth needed to acquire them. The intensification of the spiral of political expansion and warfare to acquire war captives to sell; the need to belong to large and powerful households in large and powerful chiefdoms; the restructuring of regional economies into central trading polities dominating peripheral craft producers and border regional markets created a political economy that was expansionist and militaristic, and that relied increasingly on European support and, eventually, intervention.

With the change of colonial policy after 1906 towards a less-exploitative colonial regime, this trend appears to have been reversed for a while, at least until the beginning of the British mandate period. The post-1906 ethical policy reversed previous colonial policy for pragmatic as well as humanitarian reasons. German colonial interests required the free movement of wage labour to the coast and elsewhere, to work on plantations and government projects. A free trade in commodities had to be encouraged and new markets developed, cash crops to be promoted and the internal slave trade restricted. This resulted in a more open regional economy in which population movements, a cash crop economy, labour migration and new markets broke up the older mercantilist regimes. By the early 1900s significant alterations had occurred as far as the internal organization of the regional economy was concerned. Disaggregated from the original unity of the political economy of the old regimes, the autonomy of household enterprises, the apparent dominance of agriculture, the absence of markets, the limited nature of exchange and the strong control over the circulation of wealth through the indigenous title systems came to be viewed by European colonizers as the worst aspects of the 'primitive peoples' they had to govern and somehow bring into the modern world.

Conclusion

The strategy adopted in this chapter has been to understand the origins of European categories of thought about Africa, as well as to try to refute them empirically. In an important sense this means recognizing how such ideals have entered perceptions of, and consequently influenced policies and attitudes towards, reality in such a way that separating the two over time may no longer be possible.

Yet this can emphasize only further that certain priorities in African archaeology need to be re-thought. One of these is the need for an historical archaeology of Africa that would address itself more cogently to understanding the origins of the contemporary economic and political conditions that beset the continent. Many of these require a more long-term view of social change than 'colonial history' allows, yet African archaeology appears too preoccupied with demonstrating its value to an international audience concerned with the 'big questions' in human prehistory. The purpose of this chapter has been, instead, to show that a longer-term view of the development of West Cameroon is archaeologically possible. The limited insights of the social reality around which policy formulations were made in the early colonial period were themselves a product of contemporary European perceptions of what a precapitalist society should be like, as well as the limited experience of an empirical reality that itself had evolved as a response in part to precolonial contact with Europeans. Without the archaeology of the sequence that produced the conditions that facilitated this misrecognition, there would be no alternative but to accept the existence of an 'African peasantry' as a 'traditional' if recalcitrant category.

Acknowledgements

As usual, I am indebted to Mrs E. M. Chilver and Jean-Pierre Warnier for their comments and help with this text.

References

Ardener, E. 1968. Documentary and linguistic evidence for the rise of the trading polities between Rio del Rey and Calabar, 1500–1650. In *History and social anthropology* I. M. Lewis (ed.), 81–126. London: Tavistock.

Brumfiel, E. 1983. Aztec state making: ecology, structure and the origin of the state. *American Anthropologist* **85**, 261-84.

Chilver, E. M. 1961a. *Zintgraff's explorations in Bamenda, 1889–1892.* West Cameroon Ministry of Primary Education.

Chilver, E. M. 1961b. Nineteenth century trade in the Bamenda Grassfields. *Afrika und Ubersee* **45**, 223-58.

Chilver, E. M. 1967. Paramountcy and protection in the Cameroons: the Bali and the Germans 1889–1913. In *Britain and Germany in Africa.* P. Gifford & W. Roger Louis (eds). New Haven: Yale University Press.

Clark, J. G. D. 1971. *World prehistory: a new outline.* Cambridge: Cambridge University Press.

Connah, G. 1987. *African civilisations: precolonial cities and states in tropical Africa.* Cambridge: Cambridge University Press.

Diop, Cheik Anwa 1960. *L'Afrique noire précoloniale.* Paris.

Fage, J. D. 1981. The development of African historiography. In *General history of Africa* J. Ki-Zerbo (ed.), Vol. I, 25–42. London: UNESCO, Heinemann.

Garlake, P. 1982. Prehistory and ideology in Zimbabwe. *Africa* **52** (3), 1–9.

Guyer, J. 1984. Naturalism in models of African production. *Man* **19** (3), 371–88.

Hall, M. 1984. The burden of tribalism: the social context of Southern African Iron Age studies. *American Antiquity* **49** (3), 455–67.

Hirschman, A. 1977. *Passions and interests.* Princeton: Princeton University Press.

Hopkins, A. 1973. *An economic history of West African.* London: Longman.

Hussain, A. & K. Tribe 1983. *Marxism and the agrarian question.* London: Macmillan.

Jeffreys, M. D. W. 1952. Some notes on the Bikom blacksmiths. *Man* **75**, 49–51.

Kitching, G. 1984. *Development and underdevelopment in historical perspective.* London: Methuen.

Mauss, M. 1969. *Sociologie et Anthropologie.* Paris: Presses Universitaire de Paris.

Miller, D. J. 1986. *Blank darkness: Africanist discourse in French.* Chicago: Chicago University Press.

Mitrany, D. 1954. *Marx and the peasantry.* London: Heinemann.

Phillipson, D. 1985. *African archaeology.* Cambridge: Cambridge University Press.

Richards, P. 1985. *Indigenous agricultural revolution.* London: Longman.

Rowlands, M. 1979. Local and long distance trade and incipient state formation on the Bamenda Plateau in the 19th century. *Paideuma* **25**, 1–25.

Rowlands, M. 1984. Conceptualising the European Bronze and Iron Age. In *European Social Evolution.* J. Bintliff (ed.), Bradford: Bradford University Press.

Rowlands, M. 1986. Power and moral order in precolonial west-central Africa. In L. Brumfiel and T. Earle (eds). *Specialisation and exchange in complex societies* Cambridge: Cambridge University Press.

Sabel, C. & J. Zeitlin 1985. Historical alternatives to mass production: politics, markets and technology in nineteenth century industrialisation. *Past and Present* **108**, 133–76.

Said, E. 1979. *Orientalism* New York: Random House.

Skinner, E. 1964. West African economic systems. In *Peoples and cultures of Africa.* E. Skinner (ed.)

Snowden, F. 1970. *Blacks in antiquity: Ethiopians in the Greco-Roman experience.* Cambridge, Massachusetts: Harvard University Press.

Stoecker, H. 1986. *German imperialism in African: from the beginnings until the Second World War.* London: Hurst.

Tardits, C. 1980. *Le Royaume Bamoum.* Paris: Librairie Armand Colin.

Trevor-Roper, H. 1963. The rise of Christian Europe. *The Listener* (28 November), 871.

Warnier, J-P. 1985. *Échanges, développement et hiérarchies dans le Bamenda pré-colonial (Cameroun).* Wiesbaden: Franz Steiner Verlag.

18 *Resistance to Western domination: the case of Andean cultures*

PEDRO PORTUGAL

Bolivia is a country in South America, classified as amongst the most 'underdeveloped' in the world. In fact, the South American continent is classified as 'underdeveloped', although some of its states are more 'backward' (according to Western criteria) than others. The poorest and most backward are generally those in which the majority of the population are native Indians. I believe that there must be some explanation for this situation, and I propose the following postulate: the native populations do not feel themselves to be members of the present states, and there exists an antagonistic relation between them. On the one hand, the state mechanisms act as ethnogenocidic oppressors and, on the other hand, the native populations have developed self-defence mechanisms based upon withdrawing back into their own communities. In this 'retirement' the native population retains its culture as an armour for its identity (e.g. language, traditions and customs) while maintaining a relationship of non-identification with the present state. This explains the level of underdevelopment; in the case of Bolivia, for instance, where the native population is 80 per cent of the total, the majority does not identify itself with the present state and the myth of a Bolivian 'nation'.

Since cultural features are differentiated as a form of defence from the official order, the realization of a 'national culture' is rendered impossible. In fact, there exist two sets of cultural values in opposition: that of the dominant minority and that of the resistant majority. For example, to take the question of language, Spanish is the official language of Bolivia but, notwithstanding official reports, it is not the language of the majority, who speak the native languages of Quechua and Aymara. It is therefore understandable that the few efforts at 'education' in Spanish should have failed. Even today such education as is provided for Indian children, where there are schools, is in Spanish. It is a question of imposing a foreign language on children whose mental structures have been shaped by their own culture. As the system values Spanish and downgrades the native languages, not only is it difficult to learn this foreign language, but a lack of confidence and initiative results in both the native world and the ruling state.

The native opposition is not only 'cultural' in the strict sense of the term. It is important to point out that traditional economic methods also persist in the agricultural sphere. Native systems have prevented the imposition of modern systems of marketing which, where they do exist, suffer from being seen simultaneously as the 'dominant' system (which also conditions the national economy and foreign affairs), but also a minority system as against the subsistence economy whose methods and modes of production originated in the period before the Spanish invasion.

The clash between these two economies creates inefficiency in both. The capitalist element in the economy of Bolivia is not only 'underdeveloped' and 'dependent' because of the external conditions of dependence, but also because of internal restraints and impediments arising from the colonized native population. Conversely, the Western economic system creates the backwardness and 'underdevelopment' of the native economy, with the further difficulty that it is a denied economy, subject to continuous destructive experiments. This situation may be found at all levels of society.

It is important to analyse the basic causes of this native resistance. It would be wrong to think that it is a matter of a vigorous and dynamic native system resisting the destructive tendency of the invading system. It is rather the encounter of a people who are conscious of their strength, originality and authenticity with another human group seeking to hinder and dominate them. If it is true that the native culture, society and economy reject this influence, such resistance is also influenced by more than four centuries of domination by Western systems and culture. These resistance mechanisms are not conscious, but rather there exists a deep alienation from Western models. We believe that where a great proportion of the population does not feel part of a state or 'nation', even though it is dominated by its institutional and legal forms, we cannot speak of 'national unity'. If national unity and consciousness of unity is absent, then none of these dominating ideals can be assumed, except superficially, and the same goes for the economy. The Western system is accepted, as it is 'official', but it coexists with the native economy, even though when, due to imposed pressures, the latter suffers from a feeling of inferiority and native forms are the subject of contempt. The result is essentially incoherence and misery.

To understand the foregoing better, it is necessary to give a short historical précis. Before the arrival of the invading Spaniard, present-day Bolivia was part of 'Tawantinsuyu', known to the West as the 'Inca Empire'. This Tawantinsuyu, or Federation of the Four Regions, incorporated Kollasuyu, which extended over the greater part of what is now Bolivia, southern Peru, northern Argentina and northern Chile. In 1492, when Christopher Columbus 'discovered' the Americas, he precipitated the first colonization of modern history. This started in the Andean region of South America in the first decades of the 16th century. We must consider this fact not as a 'discovery', but as a real invasion and conquest of the existing peoples. For several complex reasons, too long to discuss here, Tawantinsuyu fell to the Spanish onslaught. However, after more than four centuries it is plain that these indigenous peoples have not vanished as cultures or forms of life. The point to stress now is that such colonization phenomena were to be repeated later in other continents. Europe colonized Africa, Asia and Oceania. However, in these areas colonization was followed by 'de-colonization': that is to say, the conquered people recovered their independence, if though a transformed political-economic system. In the American continent this type of de-colonization did not take place; what happened was something akin to what we can see at present in South Africa (of course, saving points of specific difference). On the whole the phenomena were the same: the descendants of the original colonizers came into conflict with the motherland and attained their independence, to the detriment of the rights of the native inhabitants. Colonialism did not end, but became an internal colonialism, an 'endocolonialism'.

'Underdevelopment' – that is, economic backwardness – according to Western standards is particularly acute where internal colonialism is encountered. The Western model cannot become consolidated in those countries, except through bringing about an extraordinary process of acculturation, resulting in the negation and destruction of different cultures, but also creating economic misery. Such internal colonialism must be understood not only in its most obvious form – that is, where a minority of foreign extraction oppresses a majority of native origin – but also in its more ample sense, as for example where the state may be governed by natives dependent on Western models. How can we explain this in the case of Bolivia? Perhaps it would be better to give an example directly related to the economy, from among many others which could be equally well applied. Through this example we may see how different concepts of economy can be encountered in Bolivia, and how they apply to actual practice.

Any foreigner, however poor an observer, is usually surprised to find special forms of 'fiestas' or festivities in Bolivia, which are held in villages, communities or different districts of the cities. Such festivities last several days, with an abundance of music, drink and food. All the expenses of these 'fiestas' are paid for by one couple, who – man and wife – are called 'pasantes'; they must also pay other expenses of different kinds: wages to the musicians and dancers, transportation for guests, rental for premises, rewards to the officiating priest, and so on. To be able to cover these expenses, the 'pasantes' spend all their savings and their profits made over the course of one year in special preparation for this end. Then 'prestes' are named, that is 'pasantes' for the next festivity a year later. If the 'pasantes' have not been able to accumulate enough money, they turn to borrowing and become indebted, often catastrophically.

Such cases are aberrations of economic and social conduct, according to Western criteria, for money should play its role for accrument and investment, and not be 'burnt' or 'dilapidated' on festivities and fireworks (in such festivity the 'pasantes' spend sometimes the equivalent of US $5000). However, such practices have a rational explanation according to the economic and ethical criteria of the Andean world. Andean economy is one of reciprocity, and its ethical values are qualified according to the services rendered to the community. In the Andean world people acquire prestige not for the amount of money or worldly goods they may have, for the tendency is towards the reduction of disparities. Prestige comes when one's possessions may be placed at the disposition of the rest; this is a way of levelling economic disparities which have arisen from the different capacities of individuals to accrue wealth, and such accrument is thereby redistributed.

The example described above shows a certain set of realities, and it is not far-fetched to say that at present, at least 70 per cent of agricultural production in Bolivia is achieved by autochthonous means and systems, which have nothing to do with their Western counterparts, and at many levels are even antipathetic. So, for instance, in the communities there are different institutionalized forms for agricultural work, called *mink'a, ayni*, and so on, which do away with the notion of the salary earner, the latter being a form applicable mainly in the towns.

The result of this clash of economic systems is underdevelopment, and should be taken more as the result of a clash of civilizations than a purely economic struggle. To this end, perhaps we should define what is understood by 'Western', a term used to indicate the oppressing civilization in the terminology used by the different Indian movements on the American continents. In this context 'West' means the set of values which were created by the European part of the world, and which occupied and deprived other cultures and civilizations of their autonomy. Strictly, it lacks geographical significance, for 'Westernized' people, wherever they may be, are part of that oppressing identity, nor does it have a precise political-economic meaning, i.e. capitalist or socialist, but rather alludes to the set of values shared by both systems; for example, their attitudes towards nature, the ideology of industrialization and their similar concepts of development. Therefore, it would be good to stop and consider the general relationship of the West with the rest of the world – this is to say, Westernization.

Westernization presents cultural imperialism as one of its most visible facets. De-culturization, which is the consequence of this process, is presented by the defenders of Westernization as a 'necessary' and 'transitory' evil on the way to industrialization, and thence to social realization *par excellence* (for some, communism; for others, a liberal society of consumption). However, we have found that Westernization invariably leads up a blind alley, an impasse. The liberal society of consumption is not attained, and Marxist socialism (as a step towards communism) comes, not as a logical consequence of the 'evolution' of the society in question, but as a great leap, as it foregoes previous periods. Then let us ask if that great leap is a continuation in the evolution of non-Western societies, or if it is the easiest road to attain the Westernization of societies which could not be converted by any other system.

We believe that cultural imperialism must be understood, not in the strictest sense, but in the ample sense which should also enclose economy, as one of the essential expressions of man and his societies. We do not believe cultural imperialism to be a 'reflection' of economic imperialism, nor do we try to state the contrary. We believe that it refers to a single movement, and to put it all together we should use the word 'culture'. This is easier to understand if the phenomena are considered from a non-

Western point of view. In fact, all non-Western societies see reality as a harmonic group of different forces, in which the notion of balance should prevail. To us the West seems to be, on the contrary, preoccupied essentially by the notion of cause. Thus, at a social level, it would rather find primordially the fundamental causes of social 'development', or economic 'evolution', while religion, economy, biology, etc., all dispute the privilege of any one causal domain.

Economic aspects are but symptoms of a vaster phenomenon: the phenomenon of civilization. This explains that different economic systems can only be imposed when the conceptions of which they form a part have previously been established. The forceful Christianization of the Indians was needed in order for the invading economy to be implanted in the Americas, which exploits them to this day. What is known as the 'Third World' is the result of the development project born of colonization; it does not define the intrinsic nature of these peoples, but their subjection, strongly and directly, to the different powers of the Western world. This 'third' world (whose denomination is itself valid only in relation to the other two, the socialist and the capitalist) may come to be a world in itself, subject to the provision of a real development project. Dependent development needs to be strengthened with its own development. This is what some authors call 'ethno-development'.

We believe that every civilization has its own standards of development, consequent to which it develops its activities at different levels of social life. For the Indian peoples of the Andean region, ethno-development should be, fundamentally, the development of that which refers to social life; this is the community. The community has a life in itself, it is the social universe of the Andean world, and this community in Aymara and Quechua is called *Ayllu*, which means 'we' which in turn is included in another concept: a universal 'we'. At this level, language is a very revealing element. In Aymara, there are two terms to indicate 'we': *nanaka* means 'we of the community' or of the restricted universe, and *jiwasanaka* means 'we with all others of the universe'.

Western development is an outward development; ethno-development is an inward development. At this level development should be of communities, and not state-nations. We believe that in parts of the world there still exist communities and, even though they have been nearly done away with, they can be re-established with greater ease than the efforts used to create the depersonalizing and nameless media of the Western world, i.e. great urban concentrations, and so forth. It is important to grasp the idea that man's life has meaning according to the references that define it. The natural reference is the group, and it is only through the group that the individual can relate to other groups, with nature, and the cosmos. Adequate development would be something that would favour this process. The Western type of development has brought about the contrary. The individual has been isolated and, when he exists collectively, he can only identify himself in abstract entities such as 'The Party', in ideas such as 'comfort', and so on. Western development has cut man off from nature, and has created isolated units. When there is a community, the attitude of the individual is regulated by the respect for the equilibrium of that community, which is a form of respect for 'human rights' by those individuals, which is different from 'human rights' as we know them at present. In the West the individual lives for himself, but in an illusory way, and therefore needs states, planners, state machineries and parties to think and decide in his stead. Western 'human rights', by insisting on individualism, in fact prepare the justification for the social invalidity of those individualities.

19 *The development of an urban working-class culture on the Rhodesian Copperbelt*

OWEN B. SICHONE

Introduction

Culture is not a biologically transmitted complex. (Benedict 1934.)

Culture is everything that is man-made, not natural and transmitted over the generations in a continuous, cumulative and modifying process of social change (Bromley 1977). From a spiritual point of view, 'what really binds men together is their culture – the ideas and the standards they have in common.' (Benedict 1934, p. 16) Even in homogeneous societies this will be based on a mixture if not a conflict of old and new ideas and standards.

In a colonial society in rapid flux, where modern and traditional, European and African cultures are in vigorous interaction, it is not always easy to know which culture is being transmitted to the next generation. In the past, the separation of the races in Southern Africa and the persistence of traditional ideas, institutions and structures has caused some social anthropologists and historians to think the old culture had either resisted the new or was at least effectively coexisting with it.

Southern Africa has been labelled the Africa of the labour reserves by Samir Amin and others (for example, Cliffe 1979, p. 149). These reserves are said to produce labour rather than commodities. In essence, what they produce and sell is labour power which, as a commodity, is the same as any other on the market. In other words, there is nothing traditional about labour reserves, even though their 'backwardness' tends to reinforce their traditional appearance. They are part of the capitalist economy. The labourer produced by the labour reserve only appears not to be a participant in the modern capitalist economy. Thus, he or she is a 'migrant worker', a 'peasant in town' even a 'target proletarian', but never completely part of the modern society because he or she is still seen as part of the traditional sector.

The first aim of this chapter is to argue that even in the labour reserves, the tendency of the colonial capitalist economy is to peasantize and then proletarianize subsistence cultivators, and that the colonial superstructure slows down this process by various non-economic mechanisms. The second aim is to show that a culture that is urban or working class, or both, did develop in the Rhodesian mining towns in spite of the various attempts to prevent the detribalization of the migrant workers.

Although certain old ideas and standards persist in the new society, this need not mean that traditional culture is prevalent amongst African miners. What this shows in my view is that the colonial order retains aspects of the old culture that are compatible with its needs. In other words, what we have is not two cultures coexisting, but the incorporation into, and the subordination of, one culture by another. The urban African culture is different from the European one, but it is not traditional.

Tribesmen, townsmen and peasants

> African migrants on the Copperbelt were men of two worlds: they were still tribesmen, with homes in distant villages, but they were also workers and townsmen. (Roberts 1976, p. 201.)

The tribe and the tribesman are to traditional culture what the nation and the townsman are to modernity. Thus, even when migrant labourers were participating in the capitalist economy, they were regarded by the colonial intellectual and political superstructure as tribesmen, insofar as they 'observe traditional law and custom in their relationships with each other' (Roberts 1976, p. 201).

The problem with this picture of the tribesmen is that it implied that becoming modern meant becoming Westernized and completely abandoning the traditional culture. What is more likely to happen in any historical situation is that those elements of the inherited culture that have ceased to be functional or are incompatible with the new order will be discarded or will be transformed in their meaning. In the colonial ideological system modernization did mean Westernization to the extent that the practice of ancient European religious rituals associated with Christian and pagan ceremonies such as Christmas and Easter were not considered traditional. Easter fertility symbols alone do not make Christians tribesmen.

It is not the paying of *lobola* alone that makes a miner or government clerk a tribesman. If traditional law is still meaningful, it will be incorporated into the modern culture. For example, in recent years there has been a revival of traditional ceremonies in Zambia in almost every chieftancy. The Ngoni have their *nchwala*, the Chewa their *kulamba* and the Ila their *Shimunenga*, to name but a few. What is significant is that the leading role played in the organization of these annual events is by wealthy, educated and Westernized Zambians normally resident in the towns. This cultural nationalism (once per year during which tourists, television cameras and bus loads of urbanites invade a village to witness the dancing and singing of praises to the ancestors and chiefs) cannot turn bank mangers into tribesmen.

Tribesmen are found in tribal society, which is a socio-historical community associated with communal property and the emergence of chiefs, warlords or politico-religious rulers. In a colonial setting the tribe as a whole participated in the modern political and economic system, and therefore ceased to be a separate community. When people stopped offering tribute to their chief and began instead to pay tax to the colonial government, a new community and culture emerged. I am questioning the existence of the tribe not just in the towns, but also in the villages. Of course, the socio-historical community can be replaced by an ethnic entity with the same language and customs but, insofar as it is not a political or economic community, the ethnos is not a tribe.

From an economic point of view the problem of defining the role of the migrant worker in the colonial system creates similar problems. Is he a peasant or a wage earner? It is obvious he is not a subsistence or primitive cultivator, because he has to pay his taxes and buy salt at least. Insofar as 'peasants are those whose ultimate security and subsistence lies in their having certain rights in land and in the labour of family members on the land, but who are involved through rights and obligations, in a wider economic system which includes the participation of non-peasants' (Saul & Woods 1974, p. 407), the migrant worker whose ultimate subsistence lies in food production and who works for wages only for short periods, is indeed a peasant. However,the moment the migrant worker and his family start to depend on wage employment for their subsistence, even if they reside in the village, they are no longer peasants, never mind tribesmen.

As a class, peasants can, of course, depend for their production:

(a) more on family production than on wages;
(b) entirely on family production for food as well as cash; or
(c) on family production and hired labour whenever money or food for paying the casual workers is available.

Apart from these, one must also include the two extremes that are not quite peasants:

(d) those whose means of production are so poor that they depend more on wages than on their own farming for subsistence; and
(e) those who are so rich that their family does not participate in production, using instead a permanent labour force of wage labourers.

All these peasantries were to be found historically in the setting of Northern Rhodesia and their differentiation developed with the colonial capitalist economy (Richards 1939). Yet all have been defined as tribesmen by social anthropologists. A more accurate definition of the incompletely proletarianized migrant worker, in my view, is that offered by recent research on Mozambican migrant workers which has shown that they are not tribesmen but worker-peasants because, whether they are in the mining towns or in the villages, their labour is shaped by the dominant capitalist mode of production. What is important for our argument is that 'As a miner the migrant worker has become part of a concentrated labour force, subject to industrial work discipline, exercising work skills, acquiring experience of labour unity and organisation' (First 1983, p. 184).

This is the key to the emergence of a working-class culture, one which has an impact even on the rural community.

In Northern Rhodesia/Zambia the circulatory labour migration system did not last as long as it has done in South Africa, so the new culture developed not only among the miners, but also among their wives and children. However, in the final analysis what is important is how one makes a living, rather than where one resides, and it is well known that the South African bantustans have failed to support 87 per cent of the population on 13 per cent of the land. Even when very low, wages are crucial for the reproduction and subsistence of the migrant workers and their families, which thereby places a questionmark on their peasanthood.

The process of urbanization

> The length of stay, which is the closest comparable index to detribalisation, seems to increase rapidly with the age of the mine. (Coulter 1933.)

An urbanized African was considered detribalized because he had been separated from the tribe physically or spiritually. Gluckman (1970, p. 83), for instance, says 'in a sense every African is detribalised as soon as he leaves his tribal area, even though he continues to be acted on by tribal influences. He lives in different kinds of groupings, earns his livelihood in a different way, comes under different authorities'.

Unlike Gluckman, I see detribalization in cultural and not geographical terms, and I do not consider it reversible. It is incorporation into the colonial system rather than migration that I see as the cause of detribalization. Encompassing this is the process of urbanization of hitherto rural dwellers. The incorporation of villages into the colonial system or the penetration of peasant systems by capitalism detribalized and urbanized African society and created a new culture in in the process. The 'new attitudes; a new range of felt needs – for shoes, bicycles, manufactured furniture and so on – gradually can cause the decline of uncompetitive cottage industries, or it can motivate a young peasant to move to the city to acquire these possessions' (McGee 1971, p. 29). The latter option characterized Northern Rhodesia's urbanization process.

At first the Africans were reluctant to leave their villages and had to be forced out by violent tax collectors but, as soon as the new needs became established, the journey to town became voluntary. However, the view that the town was a place of death, violence and corruption persisted for a long time, and miners tried to save their children from an urban upbringing by sending them to their relatives in the rural areas. The European missionaries, mine officials and district officers also wanted to keep Africans out of the towns, except as guest workers, because they considered the detribalized Africans as troublemakers.

The colonial superstructure was therefore against the urbanization of the Africans from both the African and the European point of view.

However, in the long term the bringing up of miners' children in the villages, the influx control regulations and the stories about violence in the city failed to check the urbanization of African peasants. Even those African farmers who were able to sell maize or cotton and did not migrate to town became urbanized in their life-style. The less successful peasants had to leave their villages in order to obtain money, and the longer their stay in town was, the more detribalized, urbanized and Westernized their tastes became. When the miners lengthened their stay in town it was not just because the mines had become older, safer and better serviced, but also because the miners' need for money had increased.

During times of economic recession the problem of unemployment was evident in the urban areas when the rural areas were supposed to have taken back all the jobless miners and their dependants. In the absence of any government or company unemployment benefit schemes, the urban unemployed became parasites on the fortunate few. This was via direct dependence on members of the extended family, or indirectly as petty traders, criminals or prostitutes. If we refer to the definition of Saul & Woods (1974) of peasants, these migrants were already removed from peasant farming and were in the process of transformation into another class.

Although economic forces favoured free migration for Africans seeking work, political authorities, especially after the 1935 Copperbelt riots, insisted on controlling the process by relying on labour recruiting agencies and tightening other influx control regulations so as to prevent the further depopulation and ruin of the rural areas and to save the unfit men an unfruitful trip to the Copperbelt (Heisler 1974, p. 53).

Although it was not in the interests of either the companies or the government to allow the ruin of the peasantry, it was the responsibility only of the government to cater for the rural areas. The political superstructure therefore imposed its will over the economic base and slowed down the ruin of the peasantry. In the final analysis the rationale for controlling the urbanization process was itself economic, since the labour reserves were a peculiar feature of the colonial capitalist mode of production.

The making of the urban culture

> It is the colonized who wants to go forward and it is the colonizer who keeps him back. (Aimé Césaire 1966.)

The persistence of tribesmen in towns is essentially a European creation, first through reinforcing tribal identity administratively and, secondly, by continuing to see tribesmen where and when they no longer exist. Let us take tribal dances, for instance. As far as some missionaries were concerned life was 'a series of rhythms' to the African: 'This powerful dynamo must be discovered, thoroughly understood and harnessed to the task of vitalising and making joyous the new order of society' (Davis

1967, p. 365). Knowing very well how traumatic the transition to the new order was for the Africans, it is not surprising that the Church would use tribal dances to support industry (van Onselen 1976, p. 82).

Tribal dances were indeed an opium if, as van Onselen (1976, p. 187) shows, apart from being performed for pleasure 'these dances also had the important implicit function of reasserting the worker's individual and group identity amidst an industrial setting which too often denied his humanity altogether'. The reasons for the colonial authorities' desire to control the 'pace and form of detribalization' were political as well as economic but, from a cultural point of view, the use of tribalism to defuse class consciousness is probably of greater importance.

The use of tribal elders as representatives of African interests was a deliberate attempt to prevent the emergence of trade unions, even when the 1935 troubles showed that the time was ripe for the unionization of the African miners, since they were coming to regard themselves as industrial workers as well as members of different tribes (Epstein 1958, p. 81). The argument that unions were inappropriate because the 'great bulk of labourers were primitive and uneducated men and would be an easy prey to dishonest schemers' (Berger 1974, p. 81) demonstrated the paternalism of the colonial authorities. In a protectorate, who protects the subjects from their colonial power? Similarly, who was to protect the uneducated miners from scheming mining companies? Clearly the colonial superstructure was holding back the development of the working-class culture.

Although anthropologists see tribes in towns, since 'In situations involving relations within the African field, tribalism remains a potent factor' (Epstein 1958, p. 40), I see an entirely new phenomenon. When Chitimukulu and other chiefs send messages to their tribesmen in town 'advising' them not to join in strikes or riots, they are acting neither as traditional nor tribal rulers, but as colonial government employees (Berger 1974, p. 83). The chief is part of the colonial capitalist superstructure – his authority rests on his role in the new system rather than in his traditional rights to tribute and respect, for it is the colonial government that makes or unmakes chiefs. Also, there cannot be tribal rulers or tribalism, if there is no tribe; my view is that the ethnos based on self-identity, language and custom is not a tribe. When a miner refers to a neighbour as *uwakumwesu* (the so called 'home-boy') this 'home' can be anything from a village to a province, and is not urban tribalism. Home-boy ties are 'a common feature of personal networks in mobile populations' (Harries-Jones 1971, p. 341).

Another aspect of the urbanization process is the rise in the standard of living. In Northern Rhodesia the stabilization of the labour force and the steady rise in wages between the end of World War II and independence in 1964 greatly enhanced the urbanization of the African population. Berger (1974) has noted that the role played by the African mine workers union in the raising of miners' wages above the Congolese and South African levels by 1960 was not insignificant. The stabilization of the labour force did not just improve the quality of life in the townships, it also accelerated the differentiation of the African population. Even this did not escape a tribalist analysis, since the uneven development of African education in the colonies reflected a regional pattern. Most clerical jobs were held by 'Nyasas' and Lozi men while the majority of the unskilled labourers were from the northern parts of the country. Inevitably, any disagreement between office workers and miners appeared to be a clash between 'Nyasas' and 'Bembas'.

African advancement was another issue on which the needs of the economy and the superstructure did not coincide. Using politics to prevent Africans from becoming skilled workers, as the colonial government did during the period of the Central African Federation, culminated in the establishment of nationalist parties by the more educated Africans. In order to advance, it was necessary for the political brakes to be removed, and the democratization of the capitalist economy, it became clear, was not possible without 'the creation of an independent state based on majority rule' (Roberts 1976, p. 218). Politically, therefore, the new urban culture had a working-class character manifested in trade-union activity, as well as a nationalist or anti-colonial aspect. Of course, the latter was national rather than urban, but the work of the nationalist parties spread form the towns to the villages.

The urban community was also known to attach a lot of importance to flashy clothes, and even European dances (Wilson & Wilson 1968, p. 9). These were not just new tastes or attitudes, but elements of the urban culture that were at the same time the cause and effect of continued participation in the money economy. The rural areas were also, to a lesser degree, or at a slower rate, undergoing the same process. Thus, clothes were greatly valued in the villages, chiefs used their allowances to hire labourers for their farms or to buy trucks for their businesses, thereby extending social differentiation to the 'traditional' village.

Those villages that happened to be close to the mining towns became urbanized in an even more dramatic fashion. For example, the village of Kazembe in the Luapula Valley developed into a town with hotels, dance halls and beer halls to the extent that locals felt that 'it is the Copperbelt here (*Kuno ni ku migote*)' (Cunnison 1959, p. 25). At the same time, the urbanized African still showed interest 'in the Kingship, tribes and lineages, in history, custom, ceremonial and ritual. These aspects of the old society are also contemporary; . . . not fossil but living forms' (Cunnison 1959, p. 29).

The African and European elements did not just coexist, but were combined in the new urban African culture. Its further development was quite independent of the traditional society whose independent existence had no material foundation. The impact of colonialism does not exclude anybody 'even those who have never left their peasant homes – have for long been geared into a large scale society of the "western" type' (Mayer 1971, p. 2). In the towns the establishment of African trade unions can only be satisfactorily explained within a much wider and more embracing politico-economic system (Epstein 1958, p. xiii). If social scientists in the colonial period have found it difficult to place African society in its proper historical context it is because their anthropology is part of the colonial superstructure. Not all of them fail to realize the meaning of colonialism, of course, but the dominant ideas compelled researchers to search for the tribe in the union and the political party – a trend which has not yet lost its appeal in African studies.

Conclusion

> In our civilization there is, in the anthropological sense, a uniform cosmopolitan culture that can be found in any part of the globe. (Benedict 1934.)

It is inevitable that during a period of transition society tends to have a dual structure, in the end the new usually replaces the old and that dualism ends. Thus, peasants and wage earners can coexist in a capitalist economy with the latter representing the new and tending to grow at the expense of the former. The colonial superstructure for various political and economic reasons slows down the proletarianization of African workers, but cannot prevent the emergence of a new culture.

Whereas certain elements of the old society survived the destructive impact of colonialism, they did not exist in their traditional form, and were incorporated into the colonial capitalist system in a distorted form. For example, whereas the tribe is destroyed by colonialism as an independent political and economic community, certain features persist in the form of an ethnos within the colonial society. The colonial society has an urban culture that is neither traditional nor European – it is an urban African culture.

References

Benedict, R. 1934. *Patterns of culture*, 7th edn. Boston: Houghton Mifflin.
Berger, E. L. 1974. *Labour, race and colonial rule.* Oxford: Clarendon Press.
Bromley, Y. V. 1977. The term 'Ethnos' and its definition. In *Races and peoples*, I. R. Grigulevich (ed.). Moscow: Progress Publishers.
Cliffe, L. 1979. Labour migration and peasant differentiation: Zambian experiences. In *Development in Zambia*, B. Turok (ed.). London: Zed Press.
Cunnison, I. 1959. *The Luapula peoples of Northern Rhodesia: custom and history in tribal politics.* Manchester: Manchester University Press.
Davis, J. M. 1967. *Modern industry and the African.* London: Frank Cass.
Epstein, A. L. 1958. *Politics in an urban African community.* Manchester: Manchester University Press.
First, R. 1983. *Black gold: the Mozambican miner, proletarian and peasant.* Brighton, New York: Harvester Press/St Martin's Press.
Gluckman, M. 1970. Tribalism in modern British Central Africa. In *African politics and society*, I. L. Markovitz (ed.). New York: Free Press.
Harries-Jones, P. 1971. Homeboy and political organisation in a Copperbelt township. In *Social networks in urban situations*, J. C. Mitchell (ed.). Manchester: Manchester University Press for the Institute of African Studies.
Heisler, H. 1974. *Urbanisation and the government of migration.* London: C. Hurst & Co.

Mayer, P. 1971. *Townsmen or tribesmen*. Cape Town: Oxford University Press.
McGee, T. G. 1971. *The urbanization process in the Third World*. London: Bell & Hyman.
Onselen, C. van 1976. *Chibaro*. London: Pluto Press.
Richards, A. I. 1939. *Land, labour and diet in Northern Rhodesia*. London: Oxford University Press.
Roberts, A. 1971. The political history of twentieth-century Zambia. In *Aspects of Central African History*, T. O. Ranger (ed.) 154–89. London: Heinemann.
Roberts, A. 1976. *A history of Zambia*. London: Heinemann.
Saul, J. S. & R. Woods 1974. African peasantries. In *Essays on the political economy of Africa*, G. Arrighi & J. S. Saul (eds). Nairobi: East African Publishing House.
Wilson, G. & M. Wilson. 1968. *The analysis of social change based on observation in Central Africa*. Cambridge: Cambridge University Press.

20 *Class formation in precolonial Nigeria: the case of Eastern and Western Nigeria and the Middle Belt*

GLORIA THOMAS-EMEAGWALI

This analysis focuses on the process of class formation in parts of Eastern and Western Nigeria, and the Middle Belt[1] in particular (Bingel 1985, Agboola 1985, Obayemi n.d.). We concentrate on the 18th and 19th centuries although there is occasional reference to earlier periods. In the first section we examine the theoretical issues related to the process of class formation. We then proceed to evaluate the extent of surplus production in the area in question, as well as the varied manifestations of the division of labour, which, it is argued, have particular linkage with class formation in the Nigerian region. Central to the discussion are the particular modes of appropriation of the surplus product at the varied levels of sociopolitical organization. We conclude with an overview of the area of focus, with particular reference to the extent of differentiation that emerged amongst groups by the eve of the imposition of colonial rule.[2]

Theoretical considerations on the question of class formation

In the collected writings of Marx and Engels there are several references to the phenomenon of class formation, particularly so in *The German ideology*, *The poverty of philosophy*, *Principles of communism*, *The communist manifesto*, *The Grundrisse* and the *Anti-Duhring* (Marx & Engels 1976a, pp. 32–45, 1976b, p. 211, 1976c, p. 343, 1976d, pp. 484–96, 1981, 1978, pp. 340–4). The issue has also been elaborated by several contemporary writers, some more successfully than others (Cohen 1977); and from these sources it is possible to identify some basic propositions with respect to the phenomenon in question.

Classes come into existence in the context of the division of labour and surplus production (Marx & Engels 1976c, p. 353, 1978, pp. 236, 341). In the early stages of development of society the division of labour is elementary, confined to its natural phase, and is determined primarily by biological and sexual considerations (Thomas-Emeagwali, 1984a, pp. 202–4). We may refer to this phase as 'the natural division of labour', and the question of gender differentiation is inescapably bound up with it. Some of the features of the 'natural division of labour' persist into later periods of historical development (Thomas-Emeagwali 1984a, pp. 355–62, see also Thomas-Emeagwali 1985). The division of labour as it develops over time involves not only specialization, technical change and market expansion in the Smithian sense, but also the emergence of contradictions which give rise to class formation (Smith 1981, Rattansi 1982).[3] For example, there is an increase in the extent of surplus available and differentiation in the distribution of such surplus, a phenomenon which is not indistinguishable from the varied forms of property ownership that come into being, since property itself is to be seen in terms of the distribution of instruments of production and the product of labour (Marx & Engels 1976b, pp. 195, 197).

Over a period there emerges 'a superstructure of distinct illusions, modes of thought, views of life', a superstructure of political, religious and legal forms created in the context of the existing social relations and material conditions of existence (Marx & Engels 1976e, p. 128). It is in this context that we view the emergence of the state and the varied forms of religion and law which can hardly be understood in isolation from the general process of class formation. In the literature on class in general, a distinction is made between 'class in itself' and 'class for itself' (Marx & Engels 1976b, p. 211, 1976e, p. 187, Nzimiro 1983). In this chapter class formation is viewed in the former context. There is a focus on the process of evolution of groups of individuals whose objective conditions of existence are identifiable by virtue of their relation to the means of production, their role in the social organization of labour and their actual share of what is produced. In terms of the last of these issues we are concerned with how the product resulting from the division of labour is actually distributed (Gouldner 1980, p. 183, Cohen 1978, p. 74, Thomas-Emeagwali 1984a, pp. 153–209, 1984b). The focus is therefore largely related to the question of surplus production and the varied modes of appropriation of this surplus labour over time, from one formation to another.

The understanding of this process of class formation, as it has evolved over a period in the Nigerian region, necessitates a careful reinterpretation of archival and secondary sources and a firm determination to de-mystify some of the illusions and unfounded claims that have been inherited from earlier researchers. It is hoped that the following discussion is a contribution to this exercise.

Surplus production

Most parts of the Nigerian region engaged in production for exchange value in the 18th and 19th centuries, a phenomenon which is to be viewed in the context of the network of markets that emerged and the vast extent of inter-regional and intra-regional trade which characterized the exchange sector and the circulation of commodities throughout the region. In precolonial Nigeria there was growth in the economy over time, and what was valid for Ibadan, Western Nigeria was characteristic of several other parts of the country, namely that 'the people produced far in excess of their immediate needs and there were avenues through the highly organized trading system to dispose of the surplus' (Falola 1984, p. 87). Additionally, the disposal of surplus has to be understood in the context of the varied mechanisms of appropriation which emerged with the evolving class system, an issue which will be highlighted in the course of the discussion. However, at this point it is important to focus on the complex market systems that evolved and the intra-regional and inter-regional network of trade that developed, so as to emphasize the degree of surplus production in the region.

Ibadan, Western Nigeria, provides a classic example of continuous market expansion (Falola 1984, p. 31). Old markets were extended and new ones constructed in the course of time. There were daily and periodic large-scale markets, in addition to itinerant hawking by children and women, house-to-house sales by pedlars, sales within family compounds and temporary shops set up for the purpose of commercial activity in one form or the other (Falola 1984, 32, 105, Akintoye 1980), a situation which is similar to the market systems that emerged in the Oyo empire during its heyday a century earlier (Akinjobkin 1980). The Ojaba market of Ibadan, famous for locally manufactured as well as imported goods, has its counterpart in the Jakin market of the Oyo empire, a century earlier, and they are both similar to some of the market structures that emerged in parts of Eastern and Central Nigeria (Laird & Oldfield 1971, Burdo 1880, Trotter *et al.* 1968).[4]

Nineteenth-century travel reports have provided us with some detailed information of the kinds of markets that emerged in the East and the confluence area. The Onitsha market of Western Igboland is the scene of hundreds of people and dozens of canoes, a major means of transport in the region, and so, too, are the markets referred to as the Ikiri or Oniah market and the Egarrah market further north (Ifemesia 1979). What was common to the latter, as well as to the market centres in the West, was the wide range of products available and the large extent of commercial activity, factors extensively discussed by contemporary observers.[5] Commodities in these centres ranged from agricultural produce such as yams, corn and palm oil, livestock such as goats and chickens, to manufactured items such as blue and white cotton, beads and a variety of pottery (Trotter *et al.* 1968, p. 219, Crowther & Taylor 1859, p. 254).

The markets in question reflected a wide range of products and a fair amount of regional and inter-regional specialization. This is a phenomenon which is not unrelated to the ecological diversity within and between regions, the degree of specialization in the production process from one area to another, the level of development of communication within the region and the scale of intra-regional and inter-regional exchange.

In the Western Region, beads from Ife, camwood from Ondo and Owo, shea butter and locust beans from Oyo, as well as palm oil from Ekitiland, constituted some of the major items of trade along with daggers, rings, knives, beads and hides from Nupeland; salt, groundnuts and horses from Borno; and copper, leather, onions and groundnuts from Hausaland in the north (Akinjobkin 1980, pp. 35–54, Falola 1984, p. 112, Akintoye 1980, pp. 55–65). In the middle Benue region, salt, iron and antimony constituted important items of trade from regions such as Akwana and Arufu in Wukari (Churcher 1913, Hamman 1983), whereas in the present Plateau State in the Middle Belt there evolved a network of trading relations whereby products such as acha and millet from the high Plateau were exchanged for rice, guinea corn and yams from the plains. Pottery was one of the areas of specialization of some Birom polities as well as with the Ngas, and constituted a major item of trade with the Yergam and Pankshin. Textile products were associated with the Mwahavul, the Goemai, the Jarawa and the Ngas. The last of these were also producers of calabash carvings (Foulkes 1910, Isichei 1982, pp. 1–57). In Igboland the pattern of technical change included specialist potters in Orlu, Agidi and Enugu; weavers in Nsukka and Aguleri; wood-carvers in Uga and Awka; and iron-workers in Nkwerri, Nsukka and Abakaliki (Onwuejeogwu 1972).

Manifestations of the natural and technical divisions of labour

In the Nigerian region varied forms of specialization emerged in the production process despite the persistence of the natural division of labour in some cases. The weaving of baskets, pottery and the brewing of beer, as well as weeding and harvesting, the collection of firewood and water, the sweeping of compounds, meal preparation and the processing of vegetable oil were some of the tasks which are largely allocated to women in the Tiv region, southern Zaria, as well as the Igbo-speaking area (Makar 1975, p. 53, Gbande 1982, Bonat 1981, Thomas-Emeagwali 1984a). There was a tendency for crops such as sweet potatoes, cocoyam and groundnuts to be grown by women, while crops such as yams and millet were confined largely to male cultivators (this observation is valid for the Jukun too; Gbande 1982, p. 78).

In the case of the Oyo empire women were the major traders in terms of food crops and other commodities, as well as in the dyeing of textile material (Akinjogbin 1980, pp. 49–50). They predominated in ceramic manufacture in Ojaba and Oranyan and other centres of 19th-century Ibadan (Falola 1984, p. 97). The salt works described by Unomah with respect to Awe and Azara in the River Benue lowlands were also largely worked by women (Unomah 1982, p. 160). Throughout most of Central, Eastern and Western Nigeria there was a tendency for tasks such as the making of ridges, ploughing, the construction of houses, hunting and blacksmithing to be done by men (Bonat 1981, Falola 1984, Hamman 1983).[6]

However, the emergence of guilds throughout the region testifies to the development of specialization beyond the confines of the natural division of labour, and this was also reflected in the degree of professionalism reflected in the items of trade. In the West, in the Yoruba-speaking area, there were guilds which encompassed varied aspects of the production process; for example, guilds of weavers, potters, blacksmiths and other craftsmen, as well as trader guilds specializing in particular commodities such as pepper, soap, dye, mats, and other items (Akinjogbin 1980, p. 49). In the case of Benin the guilds of goldsmiths and brass-workers were answerable to the Oba and his officials, given the degree of direct interventionism of the state in the production process (Aderibigbe 1965, Ryder 1980, pp. 109–20). The development of guilds was not, however, confined to only the Western region. In the plateau region in the Middle Belt there were guilds of blacksmiths and iron-smelters, and in some cases they consisted of particular lineages. Three lineages specialized in pottery in the case of Birom, a case parallel with the Jukuns of Wukari where the Ba-Nzimi specialized in the latter (Isichei 1982, Hamman 1983, p. 97).

As pointed out above, the division of labour is of importance in the production process, not only in terms of the possibilities which emerge with respect to the development of technical expertise, and the scope which develops for surplus production, but also in terms of the contradictions that emerge with respect to class formation. In the following discussion we examine the evidence available with respect to the latter phenomenon, specifically in terms of the modes of appropriation of surplus labour at the varied levels of societal organization.

The appropriation of surplus

The compound unit

There emerged in precolonial Nigeria specific trends and patterns with respect to the appropriation of the products of surplus labour and the overall relationship between producers and non-producers. The primary unit of organization was the compound or household unit, and this consisted of a group of people living together in the context of production and consumption activities and specific work and property relations, at the micro-level. The growth of dependent relations within socio-economic formations and the genesis of differentiation between one group and another in the Nigerian area can be traced to this domestic unit, insofar as the system of production relations that developed within it have significant implications for the latter. At the level of the compound it was the family head and the eldest members who determined access to the means of production. They decided on the distribution of land amongst the various members of the household, the fields to be cleared, the type of crops to be cultivated, and co-ordinated farming activities (Mangvwat 1984, pp. 1–62). What is important to note here, however, is that their role in the production process itself was minimal, insofar as dependants within the compound were the major source of labour. Whether in the case of Nupeland, the plateau, the Middle Benue region, Igboland or the Yoruba-speaking area, for example, heads of compounds had access to the labour of dependants who might be wives, sons and daughters, male and female relatives or simply those who voluntarily attached themselves to the compound, as in the case of Ibadan in the 19th century (Falola 1984, p. 45). In the case of the plateau region in the Middle Belt we are told that 'it was the remaining members of the households who engaged in either direct work or social production . . .' rather than the compound head himself (Mangvwat 1984, p. 23). A similar observation was made about Ibadan. Falola points out that the proceeds of labour are invariably under the control of the compound head and that dependants are compensated with food and clothing. Of course, the latter amounts to a *necessary labour*, and it is the differential between this and total output that constitutes *surplus labour*. It is therefore not surprising that most people were anxious to establish separate compounds in 19th-century Ibadan.[7] In the case of southern Zaria, the plateau and the Jukun-speaking area in the Middle Benue, for example, the head of the household had direct access to the central barn, and therefore had control of food rations. Women in the latter region were not allowed to enter the stores, and so had little choice but to cultivate small farms to supplement the supply given by the family head if it was exhausted during his absence (Bonat 1981, Mangvwat 1984, Gbande 1982).

It is true that relations within the compound were characterized by respect and obedience *vis-à-vis* the compound head, invariably the oldest male, and that his authority was consolidated by religious sanctions (Ajayi 1985, p. 12). The compound head had to be consulted for activities such as marriage and the erection of new buildings, could veto decisions taken in his absence, and played a central role in religious matters whether in the *agbo ile* (Yoruba), the *ohuoje* (Ebira) (Ibrahim 1968, pp. 40–58), the *Ya* (Tiv) or the *Idumu* (Igbo) (Makar 1975). However, power and authority should not be seen in isolation from the network of dependent relations which emerged within the units, and the aforementioned patterns of accumulation which evolved. The number of wives, children and dependants, as well as the size of farms, were not merely 'symbols', but constituted significant prerequisites for the accumulation of surplus within the existing structures (Ajayi 1985, p. 13). In some cases there would be the utilization of surplus in entertaining visitors to the compound, in burial ceremonies, in the payment of bridewealth, in festivals, as well as in the repair of broken equipment. A part of the proceeds may have had to be surrendered to other centres of power and authority such as the lineage heads or the head of the clan. It is not being suggested that there was no accountability with respect to the head of the compound. What is important to note is that there was significant accessibility to the accumulated surplus on the part of the latter and, as to be expected, some compound heads invariably abused this privilege more recklessly than others (Mangvwat 1984, pp. 10, 22, 23).

Other levels of socio-economic organization

There were varied levels of political organization beyond the compound unit in the case of precolonial Nigerian formations, and these varied in features from one area to another. However, what was particularly common to all was that from one centre of power to another there emerged more-complex arrangements for accumulation on the part of the officials and administrators who occupied positions of importance in these units, invariably titled or untitled elders.[8]

In the case of the Idoma in the Middle Benue, for example, the *Oche*, or administrative head of the chiefdom, was invariably the most senior elder as well as the religious head. He was entitled to a percentage of tolls, parts of animals killed, and might receive slaves as tribute, and some of these privileges were enjoyed by the members of the *Ojira*, or council of elders, who constituted the major centre of power at this level of organization (Brooke 1920, Frampton n.d.). His counterpart in Tivland was also entitled to a percentage of the booty gained in war, along with the councillors of the Tar, a structure parallel with the *Ojira* in the Idoma case (Bohannan 1968, Gbande 1982). The elders who constituted the council received gifts of varied dimensions, ranging from kola to live elephants, and were no different from their counterparts in other parts of the Nigerian area with respect to miscellaneous avenues for accumulation (Nadel 1961, pp. 56–62).

In the case of the Ebira the clan head was entitled to the hind leg of game killed within the territory, and all income from land held in trust was his own. Proceeds from oil palm or locust bean trees were his (Ibrahim 1968, p. 45). Similar practices are identifiable in Igboland, where there was automatic entitlement to parts of animals killed. The legs of any cow sacrificed went to the Onyeishi in the case of Imilike in northern Igboland,[9] and similarly the Eze Aro was entitled to the head of any animal given as fees to the council.[10] A percentage of hunting game was to be surrendered to the Obi in Aboh (Crowther & Taylor 1859). Nadel (1961, pp. 56–9) pointed out that in Nupeland there were, on the part of chiefs, special rights to game killed or to fish caught, and this was in addition to land tax collected from family heads (see also Jacobs & Kolo, pp. 114–30). Further north in Kufana, part of the rib of hunted animals was given to the head of the unit (Abbashiya 1964).

The existence of royal monopolies enhanced the avenue for accumulation in Benin (Ryder 1980) but, even so, there were few political units in precolonial Nigeria where there was non-involvement in trading activities by the clan head or chief administrator of the political unit. There was often direct involvement in the establishment of markets, which in some cases were located directly in front of the chief's compound (Falola 1984, p. 106). The Attah of Igala had a monopoly over ivory collected in the confluence area (Baikie 1856, p. 59), and Ibadan military chiefs, like the Amanyanabo in the Delta area (Alagoa 1985, Falola & Oguntomisin 1984, pp. 44–62), were entitled to tolls from traders. The Oches of the Idoma-speaking area in the Middle Belt were patrons of markets, and they received tolls like their Tiv counterparts (Erim 1981, Gbande 1982, Bohannan 1968, see also Gbande 1985).

It is not only the compound heads who were able to appropriate surplus labour directly. In Birom polities, Nupeland, Ibadan and other areas, corvée labour on the farm of the chief was an established practice (Mangvwat 1984, p. 19, Nadel 1961, Falola 1984). Of course, there were other forms of labour organization. There were co-operative work groups, where there was mutual exchange of services (Falola 1984, p. 75); labour that was exchanged for seedlings, grain or tools (Mangvwat 1984, p. 19), forms of debt slavery whereby labour dues are tantamount to the interest on loans,[11] labour in the context of *gaya* where an entire village unit got together for the purpose of work on a project in good faith, and during which time drink and food were provided (Webster 1921, see also Pam 1964); and there was slave labour, an issue which constitutes the focal point of the discussion that follows.

Slavery

There are a few important observations which have to be borne in mind in any discussion of slavery in the period in question. First of all, it is important to note that in most parts of Nigeria in the precolonial period what was crucial for accumulation was not access to land *per se*, but the accessibility to labour. Throughout the area there were various means through which a large percentage of the inhabitants of some formations had access to land.[12] It is not true that the land was as communally owned as is sometimes claimed. What is true for the Igbo is equally true for several parts of Nigeria – namely that there was a distinction between individual trees which might be privately owned and a belt of fertile land that was held in common, and there were individual plots around compounds (Thomas-Emeagwali 1984a, pp. 309–12). Even so, it is important to note the procedure for the distribution of the 'common land'. The proposed area for farming was marked out and central paths and cross-paths were cut. The plots were then selected according to seniority. Often the eldest took the end-plots and, in the end, clear differentiation emerged between some plots and others. There were various determinants of differentiation, such as the location of the plot, the accessibility to water, the capital available for the purchase of seedlings and, very important for our present discussion, the extent of labour at one's disposal (Thomas-Emeagwali 1984a). As pointed out by Falola in his reference to 19th-century Ibadan, there were those 'who had access to labour in form of slaves, pawns, dependants and a host of other followers. Through the use of the labour they had extensive farmlands and could engage in trade or any other occupation of their choice. The surplus produced by their labour was appropriated by the master' (Falola 1984, p. 75).[13] Ibadan in the 19th century was basically a class society.[14]

The second issue that must be borne in mind in terms of the slave question and precolonial Nigeria is that it is a contradiction in terms for slaves to exist in a classless society. Egalitarianism and slavery are incompatible situations. The observation is important for our discussion, given that several Nigerian socio-economic formations had slaves by the 19th century, and what differentiated one part of the region from the other in terms of this issue was simply the degree of consolidation of the institution and the extent to which there was transformation to feudal and other forms of labour appropriation in certain areas. We shall focus briefly on Igboland, and shall then proceed to comment on other parts where there is evidence of the existence of the institution.

As mentioned elsewhere, there is no shortage of material with respect to slavery in Igboland despite the fact that many researchers have tended to ignore the phenomenon or to pretend that it did not exist. Not only do we have the 19th-century travel reports, conference reports and court cases, which examine the issue in varied ways, there are elderly informants who, in some cases, can be persuaded to provide information about this issue (Thomas-Emeagwali 1984a, pp. 280–8, Ohadike forthcoming). The fact remains that the stigma of a slave background in earlier periods persisted even into the 1930s. About this issue the District Officer of Awgu had this to say:

> Although the status of an ex-slave is better than before the advent of government in that he is emancipated from rendering his services and from rendering his children to his master he and his descendants do not appear to be free from the stigma which still attaches to them nor is he free from the custom which enforces intermarriage between slaves. (International Slavery Convention 1936.)

Captain Leeming, the District Officer of the Nkanu area, commented that, in Enugu in particular, the people were either *amadi* (freeborn) or *awbia* (descendents of slaves captured in war or purchased) (International Slavery Convention 1936). The point to note is that, although the slave-dealing ordinance was passed in 1874, cases of slave-dealing repeatedly come before the courts for adjudication and, at the start of the present century, there continued to be a regular flow of inmates for the home for liberated slaves at Unwana, Afikpo, established in 1903.[15]

Slaves in the Igbo case were involved in the clearing of land, the digging of yam heaps, wood cutting, the tapping of palm wine, palm oil production and other such activities which were sometimes performed by the *amadi* as well (Thomas-Emeagwali 1984a, pp. 280–8). The difference between the freeborn and the slave, though, was that in the case of the slave there was no access to the means of production and to the surplus generated in the course of labour.[16] Additionally, there was the actual exclusion of the latter from specific ceremonies and some of the privileges enjoyed by the *amadi*. Slaves ate separately from the freeborn, were not allowed to wear ornaments of ivory, or bracelets made from copper rods, and in several areas they were debarred from intermarriage with the free-born (Equiano 1789, pp. 27, 53, Talbot 1926, pp. 704–7). For example, a slave woman could not be taken as a wife by a freeborn male in Asaba, a practice which persisted well into the present century in other areas as well. To do so constituted an offence in terms of customary law even as late as 1928. We have the evidence of three court cases brought before the Ihila Native Court, Onitsha Division, where a fine was imposed on a 'freeborn' male for attempting to marry a slaveborn woman.[17] The Obi of Onitsha provides a clear testimony of the persistence of the tradition, in his own communication with the District Officer of Onitsha on the question, stating clearly that there were certain privileges such as Ozo title-taking and intermarriage with the freeborn which were denied to slaves.[18]

In the case of Calabar, also in the eastern part of the country, by the middle of the 19th century there were several slave villages and plantations (Isichei 1973, p. 62). Slaves provided the labour force, and also constituted a naval force for protection of the trade routes. It is the antagonism generated between slave and freeman, exploited and exploiter, which generated the upheavals in the 1850s whereby the slaves of Duke Town agitated for improved conditions in the Order of Bloodmen (Alagoa 1985, p. 82, Ifemesia 1979).

Ibadan is said to have had the largest concentration of slaves in 19th-century Yorubaland (Falola 1984, p. 144). Slaves were used as soldiers in private armies, as porters, traders and craftsmen, and in agricultural production. Before the 1850s they supplemented the labour provided by the *iwofa* or pawns but, according to Falola, between the 1850s and 1890s they became the most important source of labour for the military chiefs (Falola 1985a, p. 113, 1985b). Akintoye (1980) points to the case of a prominent madame with as many as 2000 in her farm, and prominent Ibadan citizens had 'large compounds as big as palaces, several wives and numerous children, slaves and followers' (Falola & Oguntomisin 1984, p. 101).

As we move further north into the Middle Belt, a few common features become apparent in terms of socio-economic organization. In some cases the use of slaves in production is not as generalized as in the regions cited earlier, but there is evidence for the existence of slaves. For example, in the case of Tivland they constituted part of the labour force of the household and were a clear necessity in the case of aspiring members of the community who saught to acquire the title of *Tor Ruam* (chief of food) (Gbande 1982, p. 121). There is the case of Aburr Benga, who was said to have kept as many as 1000 slaves (Kpur-kpur 1976). Slaves were often bought with the *Tugudu* cloth but, as in the case of the above formations, the existing judicial system played a central role in creating a regular supply of slaves.[19]

In the case of Kororofa, Wukari and Kona, which emerged as important political centres between the 18th and 19th centuries, there was the coexistence of slave labour and semi-hired labour, according to Hamman (1983, 1985) and, though it would seem that the working of the mines of salt, and of antimony (tozali) were largely done in the context of share cropping, whereby a percentage of the ores mined was received in payment, slaves were also involved in the exercise. Hamman (1983, p. 45) informs us that in the Muri emirate slaves constituted a large percentage of the population, and that the emirate ruling aristocracy 'attached more importance to the appropriation of surplus in labour and produce than on the actual control of land for purpose of regulating the processes of production'. We have a detailed account on the Middle Benue lowlands, in terms of the input of labour in the salt industry – from the salt impregnation of the soil to the washing of the salt from the briny soil and the production of salt from salt crystals (Unomah 1982, p. 162). Women constituted a major part of the labour force, and we cannot rule out the possibility that some of them were slaves.[20]

In the Plateau region in the Middle Belt 'criminals' could be condemned to slavery, and so too could prisoners of war, but it would seem that there were no cases of generalized slave labour, as in some other parts of the Nigerian area. Slavery was not common with the Rukuba, and in the case of the Birom and Mwahavul the institution was very much in its embryonic stage according to existing secondary writings on the issue (Mangvwat 1984, Isichei 1973, Mathews 1934). In the case of the Jarawa, the Sura and the Fyam, land was distributed to 'slaves' and, insofar as they had access to means of production and the fruits of surplus labour, they were not slaves in the true sense of the word (Pam 1964, pp. 74–96). A similar observation is valid for those of the dependent population in the West who became traders and absentee landlords and were themselves able to accumulate surplus.[21] These privileged 'slaves' were clearly distinct from the generality of dependants who did not have access to the means of production and the products of surplus labour. Their deprived status was reinforced by ideology, but it may be that they constitute evidence of the evolution of feudal relations. It is not unusual historically for feudalism to emerge from the wombs of slavery, and similar changes seem to have taken place in 19th-century Nupeland with the rise to prominence of the Ena Wuzi and the distinguished 'slave' élite of bodyguards, police, tax collectors and overseers (Nadel 1961, p. 106, Abubakar 1985).

It is the onus of the researcher-historian to have some conceptual clarity in terms of those who are slaves and those who are not, and to differentiate between those who have access to the means of production and those who are themselves means of production and have no possibilities of accumulation. In Eastern and Western Nigeria, as well as parts of the Middle Belt, the latter constituted a large percentage of the population in the 19th century, and formed an important faction of the productive elements in the population. They were excluded from the centres of power and domination, existed in the context of dependent relations and were, in fact, an important force in the accumulation process. Their contribution to the total gross product was significant and outstanding, but their share in the distribution of surplus was marginal and restricted. They constituted a class.

Aspects of accumulation

The various processes of surplus appropriation brought into being various forms of property ownership and diverse patterns of accumulation. There was co-existence of communal and individual possession and ownership of land, and some had more access to labour than others. The means of production were accessible to identifiable groups of individuals, most of whom were councillors and state officials who emerged throughout the region in various levels of administration and with various roles in the political, legal and religious superstructure. Insofar as they were in most cases not directly involved in production, they constituted part of the ruling class of non-producers with distinct modes of identification, reflecting various forms of class solidarity. In the case of Tivland, in the Middle Benue region in Central Nigeria, members of this dominant group wore colourful and expensive cloth such as the locally made *angor* cloth (Makar 1975). The wealthy man (*shagbaor*) engaged in lavish feasting of visitors, used salt rather that the potash used by the poor, and engaged in community dances which reflected his status (Makar 1975, p. 190, Gbande 1985). With the *tor agbande* institution, which emerged in the 19th century, there was indulgence in the music of praise singers, and the display of iron tongs, ceremonial spears and fly whisks.[22] The privileged had a retinue of dependants, including many wives and slaves, a phenomenon which is to be seen not only as symbolic, but also as a central factor in their accumulation. As in several other socio-economic formations in the Nigerian region in the 18th and 19th centuries, there was a close association between prominent elders and the phenomenon of Tsav (aspects of the supernatural), a clear case of the manipulative use of religion (Gbande 1985).

In other formations in the Middle Belt there evolved varied forms of distinction. With the Idoma there were titles such as the *ai-aigabo* title, which was a mark of distinction and at the same time opened up other avenues for further accumulation (Erim 1981, Heath n.d.). Title holders were very often located in the corridors of power, and had access to a wide range of fees. With the Igbirra Tao, the largest of the four major groups of the Ebira-speaking people, the men of prominence, the *ozukata*, very often acquired titles such as Idu, Attah, Ananyuwa and others, and here, as in other parts of Nigeria, title-taking was accompanied by the slaughter of cows and elaborate feasting (Ibrahim 1968, pp. 48–9).[23] It may be noted that in Igboland, Eastern Nigeria, senior title holders were exempt from special manual duties. Title holders in Ake-Eze, Afikpo, were not to go to the bush to cut palm nuts, were not to carry strips of cane for basketry, and nor were they to take yams to the market or fish.[24]

Crowns of cowries, fly whisks, sceptres and staffs decorated with beads were some of the symbols of distinction identifiable within the western part of the region in the Yoruba-speaking area.[25] The Oni of Ife and his Iwarefa palace officials;[26] the Alaafin of Oyo, subordinate rulers and residents (Akinjogbin & Ajandele 1980, Atanda 1985); and the Ologun of the Awori Kingdom of Lagos and supporting council members, were all distinguished in one way or another as members of the dominant and ruling group (Falola & Oguntomisin 1984). However, although the palace of the Oba of Benin or the abode of the military factions of the ruling class at Ibadan, Ijaye, Abeokuta and Oke-Odan (Ryder 1980, Anene 1970, Obayemi 1985) in the 19th century may actually have differed in form, structure and scale from that of the Gwolong (*Ngas*), the Miskaham (*Mwahavul*) or the Gwom (*Birom*),[27] the fact remains that it was in various degrees distinct from the humble abode of the dependent peasant or slave in any of the socio-economic formations which emerged in these areas.

Conclusion

We have argued that there is a clear case of class formation in the area in question, and we have focused specifically on the differentiation taking place in terms of the division of labour and the various forms of surplus appropriation that emerge. The phenomenon of slavery constituted one of the focal points of the discussion and it has been seen that slavery varied in parts of the region, differing mainly in terms of the degree of exploitation. Various forms of class differentiation have been identified, ranging from the type of dress worn, titles, food and housing, to more peripheral areas of distinction. It is hoped that we have succeeded in clarifying some of the prevailing myths with respect to the nature of socio-economic organization in the region.

Notes

1 The Middle Belt includes parts of present Niger, Kaduna, Bauchi, Kwara, Gongola and Benue States.
2 The protectorate of Southern Nigeria would be established from 1 January 1900, and in 1914. Northern and Southern Nigeria would be merged into a single government of Nigeria.
3 Reference here is specifically to the pre-Marxian perspective on the question of the division of labour.
4 These references are specific to the Niger–Benue confluence area as well as Eastern Nigeria.
5 See the travel reports cited above for details of the wide range of products on display.
6 In addition, we may confirm the same for Idoma. Glasson contends that women in the Ebira-speaking area do no farmwork except the cutting of corn. See *National Archives Kaduna – LOKOPROF 296*, Notes on Igbirra history.
7 Here we may challenge Falola's concept of 'the family mode of production' (Falola 1984, p. 60). Even if the system of land tenure in Ibadan 'did not allow a few people to own, control and exclude others from the land', as Falola suggests, the critical issue here *vis-à-vis* the production process is not access to land, but control of labour power. The existence of several dependents and hangers-on 'with no fixed compounds' (Falola 1984, pp. 45, 53, 75) suggests that 'the family' as an analytical principle should be used with considerable caution.

8 The phenomenon of titles is common to most areas in the region of focus.
9 The information on Imilike, Northern Igboland, was collected during fieldwork in September 1984.
10 See *National Archives Enugu – NAI/C SO 26/29017*, Intelligence report on Aro Clan, Shankland, 1933.
11 *National Archives Kaduna – JOSPROF 3407A*, Slavery and pawning, kidnapping. The information here may be relevant to earlier periods. See also *National Archives Enugu – EP 5279 1936*. Debt slavery.
12 The point is stressed in most of the sources available.
13 Of course, this situation seems incompatible with the 'family mode' concept cited earlier. See note 7.
14 It is important to recognize the class basis of the military in 19th-century Yorubaland. Falola classifies the various formations into 'military republics' as in Ibadan, 'military federations' as in Abeokuta, and 'military dictatorships' as in Ijaye, etc. (Falola 1985a, p. 105, Falola & Oguntomisin 1984, p. 44–98). However, in the final analysis it is important to recognize that systems of surplus appropriation become central to all these various forms of military government. The material basis of the military superstructure consists of surplus labour appropriated from numerous dependants who work the extensive farmlands. The military are also engaged in some form of primary (primitive) accumulation through plunder and booty acquisition.
15 *National Archives Enugu – EP 581/06 CALPROF 16/B1/B222*, Slave home, Unwona, 1903.
16 The appropriation of surplus is, of course, central to class society. What differentiates one kind of socio-economic formation from another is the way in which this surplus is appropriated.
17 See *National Archives Enugu – OP 289*.
18 *National Archives Enugu – ONDIST 12/I/1987*, District Officer Onitsha Division to Senior Resident, Onitsha, 1928.
19 *National Archives Kaduna – MAKPROF 3/17 AR/INT/T/I*.
20 For insight into the salt works in the region, see Lovejoy (1985).
21 Falola (1985b) cites cases where 'slaves' become considerably wealthy. We suggest that these are no longer *slaves*.
22 *National Archives Kaduna – LOKOPROF File 296*, Comments by Captain R. C. Abraham on the prestige associated with iron. For an account of the emergence of the *tor agbande* institution, see Makar (1975).
23 See also *National Archives Kaduna – LOKOPROF 16A/1926*, Customs and beliefs of the Igbirra tribe; *Lokoprof 296*, Notes on Igbirra history.
24 See *National Archives Enugu – NAE/EP 7656A*, Intelligence report on Ake-Eze, 1930.
25 The various dominant classes become central to the process of state formation in the region. They play significant roles in the religious and legal superstructure and control the apparatus of power and the forces of coercion. Symbols of various kinds are used to indicate hegemony.
26 For information on political organization and the accompanying symbols of power in the region, see Adeniran (1984).
27 In terms of political organization and symbols of power in the Plateau Region, see Isichei (1982, pp. 1–57). The whisk of a cow's tail is symbolic in the case of the Angas, and the Gwolong may have a complex of up to 400 huts (see Foulkes 1910).

References

Abbashiya, C. S. 1964. Report on parts of Zaria Province. In *Traditional land tenure surveys*. Zaria: Institute of Administration.

Abubakar, S. 1985. Political evolution or revolution: the case of Kin Nupe before the advent of colonial rule. In *Evolution of political culture*, A. Ajayi & Ikara (eds) 67–77. Ibadan: Ibadan University Press.

Adeniran, B. 1984. Ife–Western Yoruba dynastic links re-examined. *Afrika Zamani*, **14** & **15**.

Aderibigbe, A. A. 1965. Peoples of Southern Nigeria. In *A thousand years of West African history*, J. F. A. Ajayi & I. Espie (eds). Ibadan: Ibadan University Press.

Agboola, S. A. 1961. The concept of the Middle Belt of Nigeria – the basis of its unity. *Nigerian Geographical Journal* **4** (1), 41–6.

Ajayi, A. 1985. Factors in the evolution of political culture in Nigeria. In *Evolution of political culture*, A. Ajayi & Ikara (eds). Ibadan: Ibadan University Press.

Akinjogbin, I. A. 1980. The economic foundations of the Oyo Empire in the 18th century. In *Topics on Nigerian economic and social history*, I. A. Akinjogbin & S. Osoba (eds), 35–54. Ile-Ife: Ife University Press.

Akinjogbin, I. A. & E. A. Ayandele 1980. Yorubaland up to 1800. In *The groundwork of Nigerian history*, O. Ikime (ed.), Ibadan: Heinemann.

Akintoye, S. A. 1980. The economic foundation of Ibadan in the 19th century. In *Topics on Nigerian economic and social history*, I. A. Akinjogbin & Osoba (eds). Ile-Ife: Ife University Press.

Alagoa, E. J. 1985. In *Evolution of political culture*, A. Ajayi & Ikara (eds), 77–83. Ibadan: Ibadan University Press.

Anene, J. C. 1970. In *Africa in the 19th and 20th centuries*, J. C. Anene & G. N. Brown (eds), 270–90. Ibadan: Ibadan University Press.

Atanda, J. A. 1985. Collision and coalition in the politics and society of Western Nigeria. In *Evolution of political culture*, A. Ajaji & Ikara (eds), 85–103. Ibadan: Ibadan University Press.

Baikie, W. B. 1856. *Narative of an exploring voyage up the Rivers Kwora and Binue in 1854*. London.

Bingel, B. T. 1985. Historical demography of the Nigerian Middle Belt Department Seminar, History Department, ABU, Zaria.

Bohannan, P. 1968. *Tiv economy*. London: Longman.

Bonat, Z. 1981. The political economy of the Atyab people in historical perspective. Paper presented at the Katab History Seminar, Samaru-Katab, Nigeria, December.

Brooke, J. 1920. *National Archives Kaduna – MAKRES/I/AR/ASS/I/12*, Assessment report Okwoga Division.

Burdo, 1880. *Niger et Benue voyage dans l'Afrique centrale*. Paris: Plon.

Churcher, R. E. 1913. *National Archives Kaduna – MAKPROF 3/II AR/ASS/W/I*, Assessment report Wakuri District.

Cohen, G. 1978. *Karl Marx's theory of history*. Oxford: Clarendon Press.

Crowther, S. A. & J. S. Taylor 1859. *The gaspel on the banks of the Niger*. London.

Equiano, O. 1789. *The interesting narrative of the life of Olaudah Equiano*. London.

Erim, E. 1981. *The Idoma nationality 1600–1900*. Enugu: Fourth Dimension.

Falola, T. 1984. *The political economy of a pre-colonial African state, Ibadan 1830–1900*. Ile-Ife: Ife University Press.

Falola, T. 1985a. The political system of Ibadan in the 19th century. In *Evolution of political culture*, A. Ajayi & Ikara (eds), Ibadan: Ibadan University Press.

Falola, T. 1985b. Power relations and social interactions amongst Ibadan slaves

1850–1900. Paper presented at the Department of Sociology Seminar, Ife University, May.
Falola, T. & D. Oguntomisin 1984. *The military in 19th century Yoruba politics*. Ile-Ife: Ife University.
Foulkes, H. D. 1910. *National Archives Kaduna – JOSPROF 379/1910*, Angas customs.
Frampton, A. *MAKRES/AR/ASS/I/I*, Assessment report Egedde District.
Gbande, D. 1982. Trade and settlement in the Middle Benue 1850–1960. M.A. thesis, ABU, Zaria.
Gbande, D. 1985. The chiefs and the Europeans. Paper presented at the 30th Annual Congress of the Historical Society, Nsukka, May.
Gouldner, A. 1980. *The two Marxisms*. London: Macmillan.
HAumman, M. 1983. The rise and fall of the emirate of Muri 1812–1903. Ph.D. thesis, ABU, Zaria.
Hamman, M. 1985. The political economy of the Middle Benue Basin. Paper presented at Department Seminar, ABU, Zaria, April.
Heath, D. F. *National Archives Kaduna – AR INT/I/I*, Report on Oturkpo District.
Ibrahim, U. 1968. The search for leadership in a Nigerian community: the Igbirra Tau. M.A. thesis, ABU, Zaria.
Ifemesia, C. 1979. *South-East Nigeria in the 19th century*. Nok Publishers.
International Slavery Convention 1936. *National Archives Enugu – EP 5279*, Vol. II.
Isichei, E. 1973. *The Ibo people and the Europeans*. London: Faber & Faber.
Isichei, E. 1982. *Studies in the history of Plateau State, Nigeria*. London: Macmillan.
Jacobs, A. T. & J. Kolo 1964. Report on Nupe areas of Niger and Ilorin provinces. In *Traditional Land Tenure Survey*. 114–30, Institute of Administration, Ahmadu Bello University, Zaria.
Kpur-kpur, A. I. 1976. Slavery and slave trade in Tivland in the advent of colonization. B.A. thesis, ABU, Zaria.
Laird, M. & R. Oldfield 1971. *Narrative of an expedition into the interior of Africa*, Vol. 1. London: Frank Cass (1st edn 1837).
Lovejoy, P. 1985. The proprietorship of salt works in Borno in the 19th century. Paper presented at Department Seminar, History Department, ABU, Zaria, June.
Maddocks, K. P. 1936. *National Archives Kaduna – MAKPROF 3/17 AR/INT/T/I*, Intelligence report Utange District.
Makar, T. 1975. A history of political change among the Tiv in the 19th and 20th centuries. Ph.D. thesis, ABU, Zaria.
Mangvwat, M. 1984. A history of class formation in the Plateau Province 1902–1960: the genesis of a ruling class. Ph.D. thesis, ABU, Zaria.
Marx. K & F. Engels 1976a. *Marx and Engels collected works*, Vol. 5: *The German ideology*. Moscow: Progress Publishers.
Marx, K. & F. Engels 1976b. *Marx and Engels collected works*, Vol. 6: *The poverty of philosophy*. Moscow: Progress Publishers.
Marx, K. & F. Engels 1976c. *Marx and Engels collected works*, Vol. 6: *Principles of communism*. Moscow: Progress Publishers.
Marx, K. & F. Engels 1976d. *Marx and Engels collected works*, Vol. 6: *The communist manifesto*. Moscow: Progress Publishers.
Marx, K. & F. Engels 1976e. *Marx and Engels collected works*, Vol. 2: *The 18th Brumaire of Louis Bonaparte*. Moscow: Progress Publishers.
Marx, K. & F. Engels 1978. *Anti-Duhring*. Moscow: Progress Publishers (reprint).
Marx, F. & F. Engels 1981. *The Grundrisse*. Harmondsworth: Penguin (reprint).

Mathews, A. 1934. *National Archives Kaduna – JOSPROF 231*, Administration of Montol tribe; *JOSPROF 2952*, Hill Angas.
Nadel, 1961. *A Black Byzantium: the kingdom of Nupe in Nigeria*, London: Oxford University Press.
Nzirimo, I. 1983. Against the mystification of class, *Journal of African Marxists*, **4**, 1–12.
Obayemi, A. n.d. Some observations on the history of Nigerian Middle Belt. Department of History, ABU, Zaria (mimeo).
Obayemi, A. 1985. State and peoples in the Niger–Benue confluence area. In *The groundwork of Nigerian history*, O. Ikime (ed.), 144–64. Ibadan: Heinemann.
Ohadike, D. (forthcoming). The decline of slavery among the Igbo people. In *The suppression of slavery*, S. Miers & I. Kopytoff (eds). Madison: University of Wisconsin Press.
Onwuejeogwu, A. 1972. An outline account of the dawn of Igbo civilization. *Odinani* **1** (1).
Pam, J. 1964. Report on Jos Division of Plateau Province. Land Tenure Survey 1964.
Rattansi, A. 1982. *Marx and the division of Labour*. London: Macmillan.
Ryder, A. 1980. The Benin Kingdom. In *The groundwork of Nigerian history*, O. Ikime (ed.), 109–20. Ibadan: Heinemann.
Smith, A. 1961. *The wealth of nations*, E. Cannan (ed.), Vols I & II. London: Methuen.
Talbot, P. 1926. *The peoples of Southern Nigeria*, Vol. III. London.
Thomas-Emeagwali, G. 1984a. Model-building explanation and history: the Marxian pre-capitalist model and pre-capitalist socio-economic formations in Eastern Nigeria. Ph.D. thesis, ABU. Zaria.
Thomas-Emeagwali, G. 1984b. Political institutions in pre-19th century Nigeria. *Odu* No. 2
Thomas-Emeagwali, G. 1985. The Woman Question in the context of pre-capitalist socio-economic formations in Nigeria: some comments. In *Women in Nigeria Today*, Bappa *et al.* (eds). Zed Press.
Trotter, H., W. Allen & T. Thomson 1968. *A narrative of the expedition by Her Majesty's Government to the River Niger in 1841*. London: Frank Cass.
Unomah, C. 1982. The Lowlands salt industry. In *Studies in the history of Plateau State, Nigeria*, E. Isichei (ed.), London: Macmillan.
Webster, G. 1921. *National Archives Kaduna – JOSPROF 277/1921*, Gaya in Northern Provinces, Minute by the Resident Sokoto.

21 *Violence and consent in a peasant society*

B. K. JAHANGIR

Introduction

The aim of this chapter is to explore the class situation in rural Bangladesh, to situate hegemonic relations imposed on the civil society by the military society within the state structure and to examine the correspondence between the two. It also focuses on violence generated by the corresponding relation enforced within the two positions: class and hegemonic relations. Hence, the relational moment is composed of two elements: class violence and hegemonic violence. The specificity of the link between class and hegemony is the specificity of the hegemonic link (Laclau & Monffe 1985).

Class situation

The class position of the rural mass of Bangladesh is immobilized (Jahangir 1982). This immobilization is achieved through coercion, both political and economic. There is ample evidence which points to the fact that the peasants are aware of these happenings: misdeeds of the influential, corruptive practices and exploitation. This awareness is internalized by the peasants, since they are afraid of repression. The rural rich, through their control of land and related local institutions, impose coercion while the state, through its developmental policies, precipitates repression. Therefore, community-based relations in the rural areas, though operative, become less real, and class relations reinforced by authoritarian capitalist development emerge strengthened.

This produces immobilization. The process of appropriation of surplus labour and the part the political instance plays in the process shapes immobilization and points to the subordination of a capitalist mode of production in an authoritarian social formation. This is the defined social space of the peasantry, the point I want to explore here in detail. In the village structure the principles of residence (*ghor*) and of descent are equally basic. The principles of residence derive from private property, which institutes the precise economic relations between the head of the family and its members, between the members of *bari* (homestead) and *para* (neighbourhood) where, with personal property acquisition, each head of the family acquires increasing influence and power. First, over a period an internal hierarchy emerges within the lineage system; secondly, within the lineage system there exist relations of hierarchy and unequal status. Thus, differences of status exist between individuals, between *ghor* and *bari*, and the corresponding socio-economic relations are reinforced by the lineage system, based on the principle of stratification of unequal status-generating relations of dependence. Therefore, it is imperative to distinguish between lineage and property-based relations. Within the first, i.e. lineage, it is between relations of personal and lineage dependence, between *murubbi* (elder) and *nabalog* (junior), and within the second, i.e. property, it is relations between *matabbor* (headman) and *somajilok* (member of the community). At the lineage level the relation of personal dependence stratifies the village society; at the economic level it reveals the development of processes of differentiation. Thus, at the village level, various types of relations cut across each other, and this makes possible the diverse and alternative roles of the same institution or a single social category. In this manner both kinds of relations, the private and the public, are intertwined while constituting the totality of social relations. The private relations generated by *ghor* and *bari* become public, and are based on the autonomy of the household to disassociate and to join a *somaj* (community) of a different *para*, or perform *namaj* (prayer), with kin, friends and like-minded people: freedom to join a group, to leave or to abstain. Again, at the lineage level, public relations become private, when lineage segments, without breaking the original ties, join the richer segments of the lineage of a different *para* on a *somaj* plane, even with other villages. Instances of this nature make explicit the private character of lineage relations and point to the formation of factional groupings, revealing the private choice and socio-economic-political roles of the units of descent.

This interpenetration of the public and the private fields occurs at the *bari* and *para* village level. Since the institutional base of power (the *somaj*) within a village is weak, the overall balance of power tends to be uneven from village to village. Since power is not institutionalized, it appears in personalized forms when linked to private property. Thus, a *murubbi* becomes a *matabbor*, where his power is personalized, based on private property, and this personalization of power is important in the village schema. This produces dependence, and contains the relations of dominance and subordination, but at the same time it is given a dyadic form. This personalized character of authority (*murubbiana*) and of power (*matabbori*) creates a delicate balance of forces in the village, a system of compensation which masks coercion and dominance. At the same time, this is also a system of labour control. Thus, the interpenetration of the various systems (lineage authority, class authority and labour control), through the medium of an individual agent, locates power in a form that is strongly personalized, instead of being institutionalized.

On the other hand, the social and economic bases of the political subordination of the peasantry fit in with the authoritarian development of capitalism. Within a differentiated peasantry, capital penetrates, and this precipitates increased polarization. This penetration is distanced from commercial capital yet does not reach the stage of monopoly capital, and therefore we find the destruction of the self-sufficient base of the peasantry, with attendant simultaneous 'package' development of new agricultural technology, and changing intersectoral terms of trade. The destruction of peasant self-sufficiency largely affects the middle tier of peasants; the penetration of monopoly capital thus precipitates within the differentiation process a different kind of polarization between capitalist and proletariat, between landless peasants and landless labourers. At the level of the state this produces a crisis of hegemony and the state becomes authoritarian and more centralized, and proceeds to install at various levels the institution of control which it needs at this phase of reproduction.

The ideological level of class position and class practice constitutes an interesting point of analysis. In the rural areas there are diverse ideologies (apart from religious ideology, there is kinship ideology), and although this diversity does not indicate heterogeneity, it does assume a degree of coherence as well as a rupture in a lineage society penetrated by capital (depending on location in terms of geographical region and on selection in terms of produce, soil and technology). This pattern of coherence and rupture within the ideology (Althusser & Balibar 1979) is symptomatic of the crisis with the interpretative function of the ideology being disrupted. As it does not associate individual order with social order, the individual's history is not explained by reference to the social order (genealogy, heredity and alliance) and in relation to that with which it is placed, either positive or negative (respecting or ignoring the rules of *somaj*, the institutionalized forms of behaviour in the presence of a *murubbi* or a *matabbor*).

The reproduction of the individual, at present, is within the framework of class, which is emerging, confronting him with his self-definition inherited from the community structure. He defines himself in terms of high or low (*choto* or *boro*), abstracts it from the lineage connotation, places it within the framework of the relations of production, and implicitly discusses the beneficiaries and victims of the production process (the rich peasants' *matabbor* and local-level officials as the beneficiaries, and the poor peasants and landless labourers as victims with attendant bribery, corruption and repression). This double dependence on the rich peasant and *matabbor* and the state officials ruptures his ideological coherence: the individual order and social order are confronted with sarcasm, with more social knowledge and cunning (he learns the habits of the powerful in order to deal with them more effectively), as well as with defiance in certain circumstances (peasant protest, revolt or uprising).

At this stage of my analysis I wish to stress that the village is still a tentative class battleground. Subordination still defines the social space of the peasantry and, because of this, they are continually exploited. Within subordination, various elements are intertwined: political, economic, social and ideological. The intermingling and interconnectedness of the various elements of class positions limits the class practice and contributes to their tentative militancy and relative immobilization.

The unfolding level of polarization in the rural areas has taken a specifically twisted turn because of the nature of the state, which since 1975 in Bangladesh has been under military hegemony in different forms.

Imposition of military society

Since 1975 militarism propounded by military ideologues prevented 'non-capitalist' forms of development and carved out the area of political autonomy for the armed forces. The strategies are based on the usual military discourse (Tapia-Valdes 1985):

(a) to secure the unity and survival of the military institutions;
(b) to secure the autonomy of the military institutions with regard to any particular social section, class or political body;
(c) attribution of an exclusive, authentic but non-accountable national representativeness;
(d) millennarian and revolutionary approach, marking the end of a period of turmoil and decadence and the beginning of a new era;
(e) conception of a 'missionary role' regarding the protection of the state and definition of national values and goals;
(f) permanent supervisory role in the governmental process and the political arena;
(g) adoption of economic policies that secure the continuation of surpluses to pay for the needs of security;
(h) aggrandizement of the international identity and presence of the nation-state.

Table 21.1 The relationship between class structure, political structure, and process of class formation within military organizations.

	Military organizaton	Nation-state	International system
Technology	improvements in technology of force (weapons and technological software.	modernization via imports of technology of force	technological dependence upon the technology of force of the advanced industrial powers
Economy	transformation of economic surpluses into armaments	relationship between accumulation of means of force and national economy	economic dependence, depletion of scarce foreign exchange through the international arms economy
Political structure	maintenance of military hierarchy and increase in its capacity to coerce	use of military force to uphold (or challenge) power of politically dominant groups and classes	political clientage, vulnerability to great power intervention and influence
Class structure	positions in military hierarchy as basis of class alignment	role of military in formation and reproduction of social classes and uneven development	transnationalization of class structure via military professionalism

Source: Luckham (1977).

The military initiated a political project to guarantee stability by means of controlling and shaping social change consistent with the permanence of the military as direct or indirect rulers. How did the military establish their hegemony?

From Table 21.1 it becomes clear that there is a correspondence between the class structure and the political structure, and a process of class formation generates within military organizations themselves. The Bangladesh army was part of Pakistan's military force and inherited the political structure of Pakistan's armed forces in terms of military hierarchy and class alignment.

Militarism: national and international class structures

Huntington (1968) made an attempt to synthesize the social origins of the officer corps and the different process of modernization in order to explain military radicalism *vis-à-vis* military conservatism. His explanation is silent about the connections between the position of the military in the class structure and its international dimensions. Luckham (1977a, b) placed the military both within national and international class structures, and established connections between the two. The merit of Luckham's explanation is that it reveals the interrelatedness of the ideology of the military, on the one hand, and a military's position in the structures on the other, and that it shows the degree to which the two are analytically related. This suggests to me, and I think that the Bangladesh evidence also supports this, that the project at this stage should be to explore further the complex dynamic of the connection between military ideology and class. Professionalism is the international ideology of the military, and there are close similarities between military élites as well as the various inter-relations created by training at home and abroad. Military academies and training schools in Bangladesh are modelled on those in Pakistan, which again have been built at second remove from British and American professional military values and modes of military organization (50 per cent of the troops and 70 per cent of the officers of the Bangladesh army were trained by Pakistan's military academies).

Britain and the USA are the usual training centres for Bangladesh military personnel and Bangladesh receives military assistance from both. The implications of military training and assistance programmes generated from the core capitalist countries are threefold: (a) Bangladesh's soldiers are trained in the technologies of the donor countries; (b) a common social relation of force binds the professional armies of both the metropole and periphery; and (c) this creates professional networks involving metropolitan military academies and their periphery.

Generally, military professionalism creates, on the one hand, military nationalism directed towards the creation of an internationally effective nation-state supported by a well-developed conventional army, increasingly linked through its arms purchases to the international economy. On the other hand, international pressure for political 'stability' at the periphery requires an internally powerful state machinery and the enlisting of military commitment to doctrines of 'national security'; thus legitimizing its role in internal repression. This position of the Bangladesh army in the international class structure has a certain correspondence to the national class structure in the shape of the 'officer and gentleman' ethic. This distinctive military value articulates the officer corps in the national class structure, which corresponds to the military's interstitial position both in relation to the dominant class(es) and as part of the state ideology committed to national security.

National security: hegemony crisis

From Ziaur Rahman onwards, military institutions have enforced their principle of organization and their system of values in the overall network of social relations and political processes in Bangladesh. A strategy is devised by the ideology of the military to impose military society on civil society and, once the capacity of the civil society to organize mass movements is blocked, there remains no decisive group, class or sector to influence the decision making processes against the will of the military rulers. The imposition of a military regime has unveiled the class reality of this allegedly class-neutral institution, the army, while intervention by the armed forces in favour of 'stability' has thus temporarily resolved tensions in the class structures of the civil and the military societies.

At this point it is pertinent to explore the nature of the military's political project. A new kind of political system has emerged, different from not only democracy, but also from simple authoritarianism. The specificity of the model is developed at the national and international level to make the military play a permanent political role within civil society by creating insecurity in response to the crisis of security, and to institute a new pattern of civil–military relationships where civil political power is subordinated to military power. The objective is to instill a value system of repressive disposition that forces members of the society to exercise self-discipline and contain opposition.

The doctrine of national security is built on the relationship between power and security, with security defined as the maintenance of influence, participation, sharing, belongingness and group identification. For the common people security means, if need be, the capacity to resist pressures from those exercising power. The point is to preserve an element of autonomy. The doctrine of national security negates individual autonomy and maximizes individual insecurity. The political project initiated by Ziaur Rahman rejected civil authority in the ultimate analysis and related security to development in order to ensure the political autonomy of the armed forces.

Class project and political project

It is proposed to establish a correspondence between the class project and the political project of the military by exploring the style of economy formulated by Ziaur Rahman and the successive military regime. A strong nation-state is the desired objective of the military, because this gives control over the surpluses generated in the national economy. This class project of the military is achieved in two ways: first, through linkages between the Bangladesh state and international capital, areas where the military has its own institutional and material interests; secondly, through the role of organized forces in repressing crises of dependent capitalist development.

Case study of violence by the military establishment

On 14 February 1983 the students confronted the state security police, and a number of people were killed. The people took between five and 15 bodies. On 15 February the students assembled in the Dhaka University campus to protest against the killing (Bangladesh International Action Group 1983). The students recovered only one body from Dhaka Medical College, Joinal Abedin, an honours student of Dhaka University. Although he was properly registered at the University, the government constantly (so much so that people decided it was probably 'false information') broadcast that he was a poor boy working in an electrician's shop. At that time, about 1 pm there were already about 200 severely injured students in the hospital. They took the body to the University at noon to hold Namaz-i-Janaza at the University campus, in front of the Arts Building. Thousands of students, professors, political leaders and other passers-by were present. Suddenly, 21 trucks with hundreds of policemen and soldiers, armed with sticks and machine guns, entered the campus. They attacked the crowd, beating them indiscriminately, including children and women. The police and army had surrounded the campus so that there was no escape. Hundreds of people were seriously wounded, some covered with blood, trying to escape, and beaten again – hundreds of broken arms, legs and skulls. Some people tried to escape and took shelter in the building. About 200 took refuge in the Dean's office, 145 were arrested there and the others escaped again. No single room was left intact. Police and soldiers entered all of them, smashing the doors and taking people out to beat them. About 50 girls were raped and ill-treated.

For hours there were shouts, cries of the wounded, and moaning. People were even beaten when taken away inside the ambulances and again in the hospital. It was not possible to count the number of people killed, because of the panic and because of the large number of police officers and soldiers who took away all bodies, dead or wounded. Several reports mention three dead bodies waiting to be taken away in front of the building.

Trucks took hundreds of people to the police room, and it was rumoured that hundreds of the severely wounded had been taken to Rajarbagh Police Hospital. Some of the victims were interviewed: 'Both my hands were broken by stick beatings. Dozens of people fell on me. I was left unconscious for some time. When I came to my senses, I understood I was being dragged away by several infuriated policemen. They were still beating me. In front of the Dean's office I saw three dead bodies, with smashed heads, lying in a pool of blood. I saw several girls being beaten too, they were desperate, with their clothes torn in shreds and crying violently. Along with other wounded students I was thrown into a police truck. Seriously wounded students were just thrown and piled into the trucks. Human bodies were dumped one on top of the other like debris. A large number of people were there, scattered on the truck floor. When we reached the Rama police station there were hundreds of young men waiting, in horrible shape'.

Conclusion

Our exploration of the Bangladesh situation points to the fact that social relations contain relations of force. We need to know the ways by which relations of force are transformed into symbolic power, capable of producing effects, but at the same time neutralizing the challenging power of the dominated classes and demobilizing them. This brings us to social relations: they exist within our thought and outside it, as generators of social division they link individuals irrespective of classes. In this way they create both antagonisms and the conditions for acceptance. Social relations thus involve both force and ideology. They generate power expressed in the imposition of politico-economic systems and in the displacement of social relations through ideological systems. This means that power is a determinate relationship between those who exercise it and those who accept it. In this structured relationship domination is produced and reproduced, and acceptance is produced and reproduced.

Thus power is domination, and domination is composed of two elements: violence and consent. Of the two, consent is the strongest. Without making any distinction between enforced consent and passive acceptance, cautious support and shared conviction, it can be said that a major force for the reproduction or transformation of rural Bangladesh is, *sharing* – the way everyone, irrespective of status or class affiliation, shares in the force of ideas, of ideologies. Thus, relations of domination and exploitation, in order to reproduce themselves in a 'lasting' fashion, present themselves as an exchange, as an exchange of services (Godelier 1978). This gains acceptance and appears as the active or passive consent of the ruled. Based on these observations an hypothesis can be constructed that within a structure of internal differentiation of social status, and the formation of new hierarchies founded on classes, an important role is played by the military society of the dominant class related to productive forces and monopoly (or near-monopoly) of the means of force and ideological reproduction. This constitutes the structure of power, and takes the form of an unequal exchange between the landlord and the tenant, between the patron and the client, between the *murubbi* and the *somajilok*. It also constitutes a different structure of power imposed on the civil society by the military society through the hegemonic link between class structure and military structure.

References

Althusser, L. & E. Balibar 1979. *Reading Capital*. London: New Left Books.

Bangladesh International Action Group 1983. *Report*. Dhaka: Bangladesh.

Godelier, M. 1978. Infrastructures, society and history. *New Left Review* **112**, 84–96.

Huntington, S. P. 1968. *Political order in changing societies*. New Haven: Yale University Press.

Jahangir, B. K. 1982. *Rural society, power structure and class practice*. Dhaka: Centre for Social Studies.

Laclau, E. & C. Monffe 1985. *Hegemony and socialist strategy*. London: New Left Books.

Luckham, R. 1977a. Militarism: arms and internationalization of capital. *IDS Bulletin* **8** (39) March.

Luckham, R. 1977b. Militarism: force, class and international conflict. *IDS Bulletin* **9** (28) August.

Tapia-Valdes, A. J. 1985. Security crisis and institutionalized militarism. *Praxis International* **4**.

Index